THE
ASIAN AMERICAN
ENCYCLOPEDIA

THE
ASIAN AMERICAN
ENCYCLOPEDIA

Volume 5

Philippines, Republic of the – U.S.-China relations

Editor

FRANKLIN NG

Managing Editor

JOHN D. WILSON

Marshall Cavendish
New York • London • Toronto

Published By
Marshall Cavendish Corporation
2415 Jerusalem Avenue
P.O. Box 587
North Bellmore, New York 11710
United States of America

∞ The paper in these volumes conforms to the American National Standard for Permanence of Paper for Printed Library Materials, Z39.48-1984.

Library of Congress Cataloging-in-Publication Data

The Asian American encyclopedia / editor, Franklin Ng.
    p. cm.
    Includes bibliographical references and index.
    Contents: v. 5. Philippines, Republic of the—U.S.-China relations.
    1. Asian Americans—Encyclopedias. I. Ng, Franklin, 1947-   .
E184.O6A827 1995
973′ .0495′003—dc20
ISBN 1-85435-677-1 (set).
ISBN 1-85435-684-4 (vol. 5).

94-33003
CIP

First Printing

PRINTED IN THE UNITED STATES OF AMERICA

Contents

THE
ASIAN AMERICAN
ENCYCLOPEDIA

Philippines, Republic of the: Archipelago consisting of about 7,100 islands and islets situated about 500 miles off the southeast coast of Asia. Some 2,000 of these islands are inhabited. The country is surrounded on the east by the Philippine Sea, on the south by the Celebes Sea, and on the west and north by the South China Sea. Its total land area of about 115,800 square miles contained a 1992 population of 63.6 million people.

The distinctive character of the Philippines among the nations of Southeast Asia reflects its complex history of conquest and occupation by colonial powers—first Spain, and then the United States. The majority of its people are Catholic, reflecting centuries of Spanish influence, and at the same time it is the most "Americanized" country in Southeast Asia. The islands are named after PHILIP II of Spain, who ruled during the Spanish colonization of the country in the sixteenth century. The capital and largest city is MANILA.

Years of Foreign Rule. Portuguese navigator Ferdinand Magellan "discovered" the Philippines in 1521 and Spain officially declared domination of the nation in 1573. Spain ruled the country until 1898, when U.S. naval forces defeated the Spanish fleet in Manila Bay. U.S. forces would occupy the Philippines from that date until 1946.

Filipino nationalists protested and fought both colonial powers, Spanish and American. The Filipinos believed that when the American troops defeated the Spanish forces, the Philippines would be granted independence. The United States, however, decided to occupy the Philippines in order "to prepare it for self government." For several years Filipino soldiers fiercely fought American troops during the PHILIPPINE-AMERICAN WAR (1899-1902), but U.S. forces prevailed.

From 1941 to 1945, during World War II, Japan occupied the Philippines. Again there was bitter fighting and Manila was nearly destroyed. On July 4, 1946, the American government granted the Philippines independence. Over time, aspects of American culture such as clothes, music, films, television, advertising,

World War II memorial site in Corregidor, Philippines. (Philippine National Tourist Office)

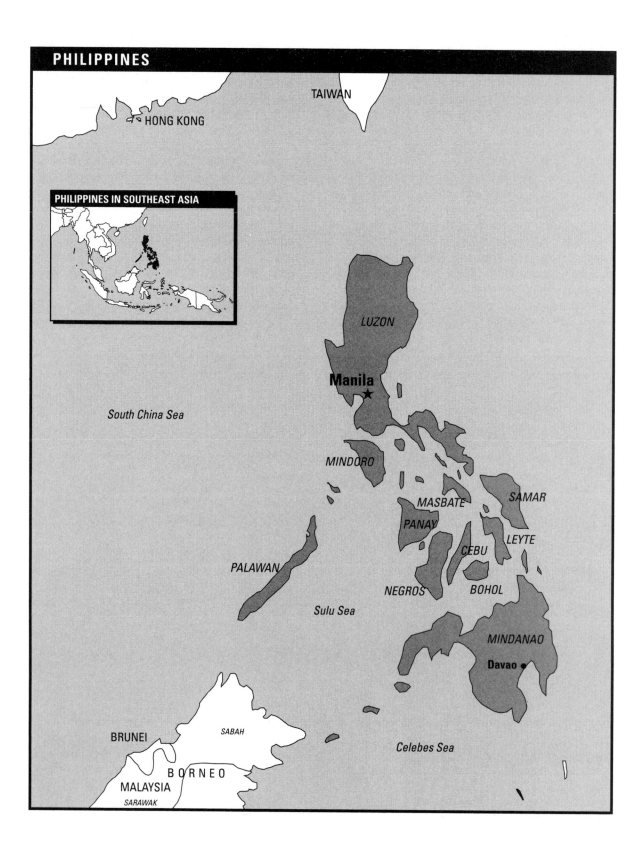

Steeple of a Roman Catholic church in the Philippines, which remains the most Catholic nation in Asia. (Philippine National Tourist Office)

and newspapers were brought to the Philippines. Eventually the Philippines became a market for American products.

National Profile. Anthropologically, Filipinos belong to the Malay race. Early settlers migrated from Malaysia and Indonesia, and as far away as southern China. Early traders also came from India and other Muslim nations bringing that religion to the southern part of the Philippines. In the early 1990's, Muslims are only about 4 percent of the population. At 85 percent, Roman Catholicism remains the dominant religion.

Because of nearly four hundred years of foreign domination, there have been many intermarriages between Filipinos and Spaniards, Chinese, Americans, and others. There are an estimated 2.1 million Chinese, or 4 percent of the population, in the Philippines.

PILIPINO, a version of TAGALOG, is the national language of the Philippines, although most official transactions are carried out in English. There are as many as 70 to 150 different languages and dialects and several language groups such as Cebuano, Ilocano, and Pan-

gasinan. The country's educational system is patterned after the U.S. model. Most courses are taught in English. There are a number of colleges and universities in Manila, with the University of the Philippines being among the leading institutions. The University of Santo Tomas was started by the Spaniards in 1611.

The national government in Manila is modeled after the U.S. system, with a president, a vice president, a senate, and a house of representatives. The islands are divided into provinces and administrative regions. At the local level there are units called *barangays*, or villages.

The major industries of the Philippines are fishing, agriculture, and forestry. The nation's primary exports include rice, copra, abaca, sugar, bananas, pineapples, tobacco, and timber. About two-thirds of the nation's population live in the provinces, or rural areas, making a living on farming, fishing, or timber. It is common for rural families to have many children. Hence there is more poverty in the rural areas.

After Marcos. Land reform, widespread poverty, religious fervor, and foreign influence, especially the presence of American military bases on Philippine soil, historically have been the sources of discontent among certain factions and political parties in the Philippines. The need for land reform continues to be particularly acute, according to observers. About 20 percent of the population receives 50 percent of the national income. Historically during the Spanish occupation, large tracts of land were taken over and given to Spanish subjects, the Catholic church, and other supporters of the Spanish occupation. This pattern was intensified when former president Ferdinand MARCOS was in power from 1965 to 1986, especially after he declared martial law in 1972. After he was deposed, he fled to Hawaii, where he died in 1989.

The issues posed by two American military bases, Clark Air Base and Subic Bay Naval Station, were resolved in 1991. That year Clark was abandoned by the U.S. government after the installation had been buried by volcanic ash from the eruption of Mount Pinatubo. The Americans chose to withdraw from Subic Bay after failing to reach an agreement with the Philippine government over a new base lease.

Another domestic problem is the nation's rapidly growing population, 50 percent of which is under the age of twenty. This young demographic group has educational and occupational needs that are vital to the future of the Philippines.

The Philippines of the early 1990's is still recovering from the years of neglect when Marcos was in power. Its economy is improving, the U.S. military bases have been dealt with, the government has been in communication with insurgent rebel groups such as the New People's Army, and there is a growing sense of national pride and stability. Meanwhile, the government continues its effort to upgrade its infrastructure, including establishing pollution controls and increasing energy/electricity supplies. It also hopes to attract more foreign investment to provide additional jobs and to help reduce foreign debt.—*Donald Guimary*

SUGGESTED READINGS: • Agoncillo, Teodoro A. *Introduction to Filipino History*. Manila: Radiant Star Publishing, 1974. • Bresnan, John, ed. *Crisis in the Philippines*. Princeton, N.J.: Princeton University Press, 1986. • Doronila, Amando. *The State, Eco-*

Tribespeople of the Ifugao, found in the northern mountains of the Philippine Islands. (Philippine National Tourist Office)

In the years since Marcos left office, the Philippine economy has managed to improve. This Robinson's department store forms part of a modern shopping center complex in Manila. (Philippine National Tourist Office)

nomic Transformation, and Political Change in the Philippines, 1946-1972. New York: Oxford University Press, 1992. • Karnow, Stanley. *In Our Image.* New York: Random House, 1989. • Kikuchi, Yasuchi. *Uncrystallized Philippine Society: A Social Anthropological Analysis.* Detroit: Cellar Book Shop, 1992. • Ludszuweit, Daniel. *The Philippines: Cockatoo's Handbook.* Manila: Cockatoo Press, 1988. • Pomeroy, William. *The Philippines: Colonialism, Collaboration, and Resistance.* New York: International Publishers, 1993.

Philippines, U.S. military bases in the: From the late nineteenth century, the varying strategic interests of the United States in Asia were influenced by the Philippine Islands. Many American naval strategists favored the establishment of bases in the archipelago, but Army planners pronounced them indefensible. Filipino nationalists resented the installations' violations of Philippine sovereignty, and American legislators and presidents repeatedly revised base agreements until the United States military withdrew from the islands in 1992.

Early Arguments and Debate. Since 1898, the United States' military interests in Asia have played an important role in U.S.-Philippine relations. The islands' acquisition by the United States prevented their seizure by a hostile power and helped to uphold the Open Door policy. Naval strategist Alfred Thayer Mahan wanted titles to coaling and repair bases in the archipelago that would be used as way stations to the China trade. Soon American naval admirals advocated the deployment of ships from Manila in the Philippines to Chinese waters and urged the construction of a dockyard in the islands.

Japan's victory over Russia in 1905, however, made apparent the strategic vulnerability of the Philippines, or what President Theodore Roosevelt called "our Achilles' heel." Nevertheless, and despite several war scares, the U.S. Navy strove to anchor a large fleet in the islands and considered various locations. Most attention targeted Olongapo village on Subic Bay, situated along Luzon's western coast and sixty miles northwest of Manila. The U.S. Joint Army and Navy Board, however, judged Subic to be indefensible because the site was open to landward attack.

For three decades, the American navy longed for a Philippine base. Still, the Naval War College concluded that no fleet anchorage could be defended, and, in 1938, the chief of naval operations excluded any consideration of a major Philippine installation. The

U.S. Army was likewise opposed. In 1907, General Leonard Wood, commander of the Philippine Department, said Subic Bay was impossible to protect. Army opposition continued into the 1930's, and, consequently, only a small naval station was constructed a short distance southwest of Manila at Cavite.

Legislative and Executive Actions. President William Howard Taft's decision against a Subic fleet base in 1909 was written into the Naval Limitation Treaty of Washington in 1922. The United States hoped to reassure Japan that it had no hostile intentions by keeping the Philippines vulnerable. Filipino nationalism also had an effect. When the U.S. Congress passed the HARE-HAWES-CUTTING ACT OF 1933, providing for Philippine independence, Filipino legislators rejected the act because its grant of military lands to the United States would violate the islands' sovereignty. The next year, Filipinos found the TYDINGS-MCDUFFIE ACT acceptable since it made provisions for talks about bases after independence.

President Manuel QUEZON of the Philippine Commonwealth, fearful of Japan, proposed perpetual American control on any of the archipelago's harbors outside the island of Luzon. Naval strategists wanted an inconquerable base that could support the American fleet once it entered Philippine waters. Against the Army's resistance, Washington policymakers approved a small seaplane installation while Congress appropriated money for workshops to service the Asiatic Fleet.

When World War II ended in 1945, Americans and Filipinos wished to maintain their mutually beneficial wartime tie after the date of Philippine independence, scheduled for 1946. The year before, Congress had adopted a joint resolution canceling the Tydings-McDuffie provision about military bases. President Quezon supported the congressional decision, making it possible for the United States and the Philippines to discuss military leaseholds.

In 1945, Secretary of the Navy James Forrestal mentioned fourteen locations as promising base sites, and Secretary of War Henry Stimson set forth his proposal to erect air installations on Luzon and Mindanao, complemented by bases for fighter aircraft and assembly areas for ground troops. Stimson likewise pressed President Harry S Truman to prohibit the Filipinos from allowing another country the right to build bases in the islands unless the United States agreed.

Philippine president Sergio Osmeña supported American requests for liberal basing privileges. He agreed to permit installations desired by the American navy and requested by the army. The arrangement would also forbid a third country from owning military bases in the archipelago.

By 1947, Philippine president Manuel Roxas, expecting American military assistance, offered generous terms. If the United States would withdraw its forces from Manila as a concession to Philippine nationalism, Roxas would give the Americans a ninety-nine-year lease on a large tract at Clark Field on Luzon, on a location close to Olongapo at Subic Bay, and on several minor sites throughout the islands. The Truman Administration consented, and an executive agreement, later to be amended, was endorsed in Manila on March 14.

Issues and Agreements. Because of the Cold War and the Department of Defense's insistence, the United States opposed Filipino attempts to change the 1947 accord. The Filipino leadership wanted extended jurisdiction on American installations, hoping to ease the appearance of colonialism. Such issues as American authority over Filipinos on the bases, Philippine control over Americans off the installations, the flag to be flown, funding by the American government, the right of Filipinos to revise the pact, as well as the misbehavior and racism of American personnel led to negotiations in 1959. The resulting agreement reduced the amount of territory held by the United States, shortened the lease period to twenty-five years, assigned jurisdiction of Olongapo to Filipinos, and allowed more Philippine military influence concerning base operations.

Subsequent negotiations produced more concessions in 1979 that reduced the Clark and Subic base areas, named the installations "Philippine," and compelled their flying of the Philippine flag. The accord also required both parties to reexamine the accord's provisions at five-year intervals up to 1991, whereupon the twenty-five-year term would end. The American president was to make every attempt, over the following half decade, to effect a congressional grant of assistance.

American Withdrawal. Philippine president Corazon AQUINO, unlike her predecessors, responded to popular demands urging the removal of the American bases. An interim agreement in 1988 permitted the United States to stay up to September of 1991 in exchange for military and economic aid until the treaty expired. Three years after that agreement, the Americans promised the gradual termination of operations at Clark and Subic into the ensuing decade even though American aid would continue to flow into the Philippines.

Under President Corazon Aquino, the Philippine government expelled the U.S. military from its bases in the islands. (AP/Wide World Photos)

Two events, however, reversed the deal. Once Mount Pinatubo's volcanic eruption had ruined Clark and the Philippine Senate had vetoed the new arrangement, President Aquino told the United States to leave Subic by the last day of 1992, an order the Americans obeyed.—*Rodney J. Ross*

SUGGESTED READINGS: • Brands, H. W. *Bound to Empire: The United States and the Philippines.* New York: Oxford University Press, 1992. • Colbert, Evelyn. *The United States and the Philippine Bases.* Washington, D.C.: Foreign Policy Institute, The Johns Hopkins University Press, 1987. • Friend, Theodore. *Between Two Empires: The Ordeal of the Philippines, 1929-1946.* New Haven, Conn.: Yale University Press, 1965. • Greene, Fred, ed. *The Philippine Bases: Negotiating for the Future: American and Philippine Perspectives.* New York: Council on Foreign Relations, 1988. • Miller, Edward S. *War Plan Orange: The U.S. Strategy to Defeat Japan, 1897-1945.* Annapolis, Md.: Naval Institute Press, 1991.

Philippines Mail: One of the oldest continuous Filipino American newspapers in the United States. Published first in 1921 in Salinas, California, as the *Philippine Independent News*, it assumed its present name in 1930. Its reporting includes news items primarily from the Philippines, Hawaii, and other regions of the United States.

Guerrilla troops of ousted Cambodian premier Pol Pot cross the border into neighboring Thailand after sustaining heavy attacks from pro-Vietnamese forces in Cambodia in April, 1979. (AP/Wide World Photos)

Phnom Penh: Capital of Cambodia. Phnom Penh, founded in 1434, is located at the confluence of the Tonle Sap and Mekong rivers. After Angkor Thom was abandoned in the fifteenth century, Phnom Penh was established as capital of the Khmer nation. Because of Cambodia's repeated conflicts with her neighbors, Siam and Annam, the city was deserted several times until 1866, when King Norodom moved his court from Oudong to Phnom Penh. The French assumed control of Cambodia in 1884, and it was not until 1953 that the country regained its independence. Along with its French colonial architecture and Buddhist temples, Phnom Penh boasted universities and cultural attractions such as a ballet, a theater, and museums.

Refugees fleeing from fighting in the 1960's and 1970's brought a tremendous increase to the population of Phnom Penh. In 1975, however, the KHMER ROUGE, led by POL POT, seized control of the government, and a reign of terror began throughout the country. Most of Phnom Penh's population was forcefully evacuated to the countryside in a radical effort by leaders to transform Cambodia into an entirely agrarian state that would match the grandeur of the ancient Angkor civilization. Although intellectuals were especially targeted by the Khmer Rouge, more than a million people in Cambodia either died from the wretched working conditions in the fields or were murdered. Phnom Penh was also ransacked by the Khmer Rouge, who destroyed numerous buildings and defaced Buddhist images. In 1979, the Pol Pot regime was overthrown by Vietnamese forces, who created in its place the puppet government headed by Heng Samrin. Vietnam has since withdrawn its troops from Cambodia creating a power vacuum in the region with different factions—the Khmer Rouge included—contending for power.

Phnom Penh has been recovering slightly ever since the overthrow of the Khmer Rouge. Its population was estimated at eight hundred thousand in 1989, and foreign goods can be found in abundance. The city, however, is still desperately poor and lacking, among many things, hospitals and sanitation. Furthermore, the political instability of the country raises uncertainty over the future of Phnom Penh.

Picture brides: Japanese and Korean women who, under a marriage arrangement that flourished from about 1908 until 1924, arrived in the United States and the Territory of Hawaii as the wives of Japanese and Korean immigrant men living there. Altogether almost 67,000 Japanese and more than 1,000 Korean women landed there during that time. This practice enabled many migrants to establish families overseas.

Large-scale Japanese migration to the United States began not long after the passage of the CHINESE EXCLUSION ACT OF 1882. In 1907 the U.S. and Japanese governments signed the GENTLEMEN'S AGREEMENT, under which Japan promised to stop sending immi-

Courtship photograph of Henry Shinn, submitted to Kang Aie Park for her consideration. At the heart of the picture-bride process was the mutual exchange of photographs among the men and women, the end of which might lead to an arranged marriage—between two people who were essentially strangers. (The Korea Society/ Los Angeles)

Kang Aie Park—picture-bride candidate of Henry Shinn. (The Korea Society/Los Angeles)

grant contract laborers to the United States. The treaty did not, however, prohibit Japanese aliens living in the United States and Hawaii from bringing over their relatives and, based largely on photographs, numerous women from Japan (hence the phrase "picture brides"). For the many Japanese men desiring to settle permanently overseas, therefore, the picture-bride arrangement was a useful means of marrying and starting a family.

Any Japanese American male who wanted to import a wife from Japan first had to apply for a certificate of endorsement from the Japanese consulate in the United States. Upon obtaining it, the prospective bride and groom, who in the great majority of cases had never met, exchanged photographs and other biographical information by mail with the help of matchmakers in Japan. The matchmakers were instructed to pair the men with sturdy, young females who could bear them children and work alongside them as well. Upon a decision to marry, their union was legalized under Japanese law, which required neither a formal wedding ceremony nor the actual presence of either participant if a ceremony was performed. After obtaining a passport and other travel documents, the bride sailed for her new home, where, generally for the first time, she would meet her new husband. Once there, the conditions under which these women were forced to live and work were often bleak and harsh. Moreover, many of the men had lied about their ages and circumstances; marital desertions by their wives were not uncommon.

By 1910 there were 8,000 Japanese American women in the United States, 5,600 of them married, compared with only 850 Japanese American women (400 married) in 1900. By 1920, the number had risen to 38,000 (22,000 married). In Hawaii there were 48,000 Japanese American women. The number of Japanese American children, too, jumped dramatically. A total of 30,000 Japanese American children were living on the U.S. mainland in 1920, compared with only 4,500 ten years earlier; by 1930 that figure reached 68,000 for the mainland and 91,000 for Hawaii.

It was not until 1917 that the U.S. State Department finally recognized picture-bride marriages as legal. Prior to that, the men and their new wives had been forced to marry a second time to satisfy all American legal requirements. By 1919 the picture-bride system had come under fire by anti-Japanese agitators, who contended that the Gentlemen's Agreement had been violated. In 1920 California enacted a law that brought the practice to a halt, and the government of Japan,

under pressure and with the endorsement of the influential Japanese Association of America, agreed to stop issuing passports to picture brides bound for the United States. Many continued to enter Hawaii. The IMMIGRATION ACT OF 1924 finally put a stop to the practice with its severe restrictions on immigration from Asia to the United States and Hawaii.

More than 1,000 Korean women came as picture brides during roughly the same time period. Most of them—about 950—immigrated to Hawaii; slightly more than one hundred immigrated to the mainland. In the years leading up to Japan's annexation of Korea in 1910, the Japanese colonial government suspended all immigration to America. As anti-Japanese hostility intensified, both within Korea and overseas, Japanese officials sought to defuse the political situation by allowing small numbers of Korean women to leave the country as picture brides.

Pidgin: Simplified version of a language used as a means of rudimentary communication by two or more groups who do not share a common tongue. "Pidgins," especially, have significantly reduced grammars and vocabularies and are often used only in economic contact situations, such as to conduct trade or communicate with workers. There have been hundred of pidgins and what are called "creoles" throughout human history, and dozens are still in use today. Though the two words are often used interchangeably in everyday speech, pidgins and creoles are technically quite different phenomena, both linguistically and culturally.

The Process of Pidginization. When two groups who speak different languages first meet, not much can be communicated besides simple pointing and gesturing. If more sophisticated communication is desired, genuine effort must be made by both parties to devise some kind of code to be used among themselves. What often happens is that one of the two languages becomes simplified and adapted for the specifics of the situation. It is not the case that one language has broken down or degenerated, nor is it that one group of people has only half-learned the language of some other. Though much simpler than native languages, pidgins are highly structured and follow their own strict rules of syntax and vocabulary formation.

In pidgins, grammatical categories such as tense, mood, number, or person are dropped; however, most communicative tasks can still be accomplished. When referring to things in the future, for example, a pidgin may use a phrase such as "by and by," as in, "By and by me come look 'em you" (I'll be coming to see you).

Some Famous Pidgin and Creole Examples

Common Name	Base Language	Location	Main Time Frame	Number of Speakers (in thousands)
Bamboo English	English	Japan	1945-1960	1,000?
Bazaar Malay	Malay	Indonesia	16th-20th centuries	9,000?
Bislama	English	Vanuatu, Fiji	19th century-present	200
Camaroon Pidgin English	English	West Africa	?-present	2,000
Chinook Jargon	Chinook	northwest coast, North America	18th-19th centuries	100?
French Creole	French	Louisiana	17th century-present	40
French Creole	French	Haiti	18th century-present	5,000
Gullah	English	seacoast, southwest U.S.	19th century-present	100?
Hawaiian Pidgin/Creole	English and others	Hawaii	1880-present	500
Krio	English	West Africa, Sierra Leon	?-present	1,000
Police Motu	Motu	Papua New Guinea	19th century-present	150
Tay Boy	French	Vietnam	1850-1950	1,000?
Tok Pisin	English	Papua New Guinea	19th century-present	2,000
Yokohama Dialect	Japanese	Japan	1860-1920	500?

Notes: (1) If "present" is cited in "Main Time Frame" column, the number of speakers is a 1990 estimate. (2) Other time frames are estimates of greatest historical number of speakers.

The vocabulary of pidgins is also greatly restricted, usually being only between one and two thousand words (compared to the ten to twenty thousand words used by most speakers of native languages in everyday conversation). Thus words and word-compounds may often end up doing double duty and become extended in meaning or else become used in different ways. Some examples of this can be seen in Tok Pisin (talk pidgin), a pidgin derived from English and used in Papua New Guinea. The word "eye" can mean not merely the human sight organ but also the headlight of a car, a tip, a point, or a lid. The English word for "us" is rendered "yumi" (you-me). The word "belong" becomes a simple way of indicating possession (for example, "eye belong you," or "your eye[s]"). Context, then, becomes critical in determining the ultimate meaning of a sentence.

Pidgins can develop when any two groups come into contact, regardless of economic dominance or dependence. Pidgins became well known in the West during the period of European colonization, expansion, and slave trading. By the nineteenth century, pidgin languages based on English, French, Portuguese, Spanish, and Dutch had developed all over Asia, Africa, the Pacific, and the New World. Thus terms such as "Pidgin English" or "French Creole" often still carry pejorative connotations. Many times throughout history, however, non-Western peoples have developed and used pidgins among themselves regardless of European contact.

The Process of Creolization. A creole is a pidgin that has developed into a native (first) language. In many places in the world, large numbers of different languages are spoken in relatively small areas. Papua New Guinea, for example, contains upwards of seven hundred languages though it is only a little larger than California. People from different villages, then, may trade—and even intermarry—with one another while communicating in a local pidgin. Children, however, being naturally exposed to this language, will learn it as one of their native tongues. Likewise, children of slaves or colonial indentured laborers may find their parents communicating with masters, supervisors, and other workers in pidgin. Again, they will likely grow up speaking this pidgin as a first language. Within one or two generations, there will usually be a critical mass of native pidgin speakers who will speak this tongue more than any other language in the community. The result of this—in effect, a new language—is called a "creole."

It is important to note that while pidgins are auxiliary languages used to supplement communication with outsiders, creoles are indeed full-fledged vernaculars in their own right, used for everyday conversation within a group. It is not enough, then, to use a creole to "just get by"; creoles need to be able to convey the full range of linguistic, expressive, and emotional needs of the members of their speech communities. Thus creolization involves a complex process of expanding vocabulary, as well as reinventing many of the grammatical features that were dropped in the pidgin. For example Hawaiian Pidgin English spoken before World War II dropped auxiliary verbs and the "-ed" tense markers found in standard English (for example, "We had walked to the store," became, "Us two walk store"). In Hawaiian Creole English, however, a sort of past-perfect tense has developed using the marker "bin" (been), as in "Us two bin walk da store." Yet there is little intentional effort by speakers to make creole languages more sophisticated; all this comes about naturally.

Pidgins and Creoles in Hawaii. By the late nineteenth century Hawaiian sugarcane plantations had greatly increased their productivity, and an expanded work force was needed to tend the fields. By the 1920's thousands of Japanese, Philippine, Chinese, and Korean workers had immigrated to the islands, now outnumbering the local population two to one. This mixture of speakers of different languages, together with an already polyglot Hawaiian society, led to the development of several English-based pidgins, such as Japanese Pidgin English or Korean Pidgin English. Eventually the children of these different immigrant groups, together with the local Hawaiian population, developed a version of Creole English particular to Hawaii. Varieties of this are still spoken in the islands today.

"Da Kine talk" (or "talking the thing," a local name for this register of speech) includes many borrowings from Hawaiian (*pau hana*, or "finished working"), Japanese (*daikon*, or "radish-shaped legs"), Tagalog (*tubo*, or "sugar cane"), Samoan (*ufamea*, a term of insult), Korean (*yobo-ji*, a Korean person), Chinese (*sai-min* or "noodle soup"), and Portuguese (*pakalaio*, or "codfish"). English words abound but are often used in different ways or for different grammatical functions. For example the English "da" (the) can be used as an intensifier ("Oh, da hot!" or "It's so hot!") or modifier ("Oh, da cute!" or "How cute!").

Pidgins, Creoles, and Dialects. It is often difficult to say exactly when a pidgin becomes a creole, or when (or if) a creole becomes another variety or dialect of a standard language. For example the pidgin Bislama is the official language of Vanuatu and the pidgin Tok Pisin is the quasi-official language of Papua New Guinea; both, however, are the most widely used languages in their respective countries and have many native speakers. Likewise the Jamaican or Hawaiian varieties of English may be "creoles" to one person but "dialects" to another. Also, many times speakers of these varieties are bidialectal, using the standard version of speech in school or at work and a local variant at home.

Implications of Pidgins and Creoles for Theories of Language. Since the 1980's linguists have been studying pidgins and creoles to gain insight into language history and development and to see how children acquire language. There are remarkable similarities in the way all pidgins and creoles are structured. It is not yet clear, however, whether this is attributable to all pidgins possibly deriving from a single source (such as fifteenth century Mediterranean Pidgin Portuguese) and spreading to the rest of the world through European exploration; the external similarities of all language-contact situations (trade, colonization, and so forth); or some special property of the human mind in the way it processes words and grammatical rules or categories. It is likely that these languages reflect both linguistic and social universals; whenever there is a need for pidgins and creoles to develop, they will undoubtedly arise.—*James Stanlaw*

SUGGESTED READINGS: • Berreby, David. "Kids, Creoles, and Coconuts." *Discover* 13, no. 4 (April, 1992): 44-53. • Bickerton, Derek. "Pidgin and Creole Languages." *Scientific American* 249, no. 1 (July, 1983): 116-122. • Bickerton, Derek. *Roots of Language*. Ann Arbor: Karoma Publishers, 1981. • Carr, Elizabeth Ball. *Da Kine Talk: From Pidgin to Standard English in Hawaii*. Honolulu: University of Hawaii Press, 1972. • Hymes, Dell, ed. *Pidginization and Creolization of Languages*. Cambridge, England: Cambridge University Press, 1971. • Nagara, Susumu. *Japanese Pidgin English in Hawaii: A Bilingual Description*. Honolulu: University of Hawaii Press, 1972.

Pilipino: The adopted national language of the Philippines. Since its selection for nationalistic reasons, Pilipino has expanded quickly throughout the islands despite a persistent use of local vernaculars. Taught in all the grades and on the university level, Pilipino became the official language of instruction in the 1970's once the proportion of Filipinos conversing in the national language surpassed that speaking English.

The United States' acquisition of the Philippines aggravated the archipelago's linguistic fragmentation. English was added to the abundant variety of spoken tongues, though only nine languages—TAGALOG, Cebuano, Ilocano, and Pampango among them—predominated. In the early twentieth century English turned into the primary means of teaching and exchange because Tagalog was confined to areas of Luzon, and only a small percentage of the population spoke Spanish. English was declared the language of the schools with the goal of making Filipinos more cosmopolitan.

The prolonged endeavor to gain political separation from the United States assisted the forging of a Filipino national consciousness. One expression of the developing sense of oneness was a determination to create a national tongue since the American colonial administration had made such an effort to expand the use of English. On the advice of commonwealth president Manuel QUEZON in 1936, the Institute of National Language was established and given responsibility for producing a standard tongue derived from an indigenous language.

The institute's delegates represented the Philippines' most important linguistic categories; these individuals deliberated for twelve months before suggesting the utilization of Tagalog as a source for a common tongue. Despite Cebuano's plurality of Filipino speakers, Tagalog was preferred because of its broad usage, rich literary heritage, nationalistic connotation, and, supposedly most influential, its prevalence in Manila and central Luzon. Tagalog's capital city concentration enabled the language to attain a higher standing than others in the islands.

Once Tagalog was endorsed by the institute, a wordbook and phrases were written and made public in 1940. That year legislation approved Tagalog's choice as the national language following the establishment of Philippine independence in 1946. By 1959 the chief educational administrator had commanded that Tagalog be renamed Pilipino, apparently hoping to encourage national cohesion because of the provincial and behavioral implications of the former term.

Pilipino American Network and Advocacy (PANA): California-based volunteer organization dedicated to the increased understanding of Filipino American culture. PANA members lobby for legislation designed to improve living conditions for Filipino Americans and other Asian Pacific Americans.

Pilipino-English: Phrase used to describe the various ways the English language is used in a Philippine context. The term can have two meanings. In the first, "Pilipino-English" often refers to the English spoken by educated Filipinos and commonly acceptable to them in their writings and conversations. In this sense, Pilipino-English could be considered as simply another recognized non-European dialect—or variety—of the English language, such as Jamaican English or Indian English. The term "Pilipino-English," however, is also used to denote the language combination that results from the mixing of English words and phrases in everyday TAGALOG/PILIPINO speech (or occasionally some other Philippine language). This variety of English is not so standardized and can be spoken by both highly educated and less-educated Filipinos, both at home and abroad. It is sometimes pejoratively referred to as "Engalog" or "Taglish."

The Philippines is a vast archipelago consisting of more than seven thousand islands covering one hundred thousand square miles. Cultural and linguistic diversity, then, is extensive. Most Filipinos are at least trilingual: A dominant local vernacular such as Cebuano or Ilocano is learned growing up as a child. From the schools, radio, and television, children learn Pilipino, the standardized version of Tagalog that is the accepted national language of the Philippines. In schools, most children also study English, the second official language. Thus, most Filipinos have at least some English vocabulary and syntax in their linguistic repertoire.

When people who speak several languages in common meet, what often happens is a phenomenon that linguists call "code mixing" or "code switching." Words and phrases from one language become mixed into sentences originally started in another language. For example, in vernacular Pilipino-English, a person may tease a friend by saying "I'll kurot you!" ("I pinch you!") the Tagalog *kurot* meaning to "pinch" or "take a piece." One might also ask a person to stay "dito sa little place namin" ("here at our little place.") In this variety of speech, there are also many specific Anglicized words that have special meanings in a Philippine context, such as *jeepney* (a chrome-glittered U.S. Army jeep from World War II now used as a taxi) or *standby* (some idle person simply standing around). Sometimes one language may influence sentence constructions using vocabulary items from another language, as in, "Go here!" ("Come here!"—from Tagalog *punta*, meaning either "go" or "come") or "Open the radio" ("Turn on the radio"—from Tagalog *bukas*, which means "to open something up").

More than thirteen million Filipinos speak English as either a first language or a fluent second language. Standard Pilipino-English probably finds its greatest manifestations in works of famous twentieth century Filipino writers, such as N. V. M. GONZALEZ, Nick Joaquin, Stevan Javellana, and Jose Garcia VILLA. Though English was the language of the American colonizers, these authors used this language as a vehicle to explore the problems of attempting to unify an island nation while still acknowledging ethnic diversity. Several contemporary Filipino authors, such as Jessica HAGEDORN, have a substantial following in Europe and America and have used their Pilipino version of English as a stylistic device to convey a wide range of emotions and a variety of narrative voices.

Pinay: Slang for Filipina, or female Filipino. Considered by some Filipinos to be derogatory, the term was used in the early twentieth century by Filipino immigrants who came to the United States primarily in search of work. The majority of these immigrants were *PINOYS,* or Filipino males.

Ping-Pong diplomacy: Unofficial name for U.S. president Richard M. Nixon's foreign policy attempt to normalize relations with the People's Republic of China. His historic visit to China in February, 1972, during the Vietnam War, opened doors that had been shut between the two countries since the 1949 Communist takeover of China. Both countries subsequently agreed to develop and expand trade. The phrase was coined as a result of China's invitation for a U.S. ping-pong team to play against a Chinese team prior to Nixon's visit.

Pinkham, Lucius Eugene (Sept. 19, 1850, Chicopee Falls, Mass.—Nov. 2, 1922, San Francisco, Calif.): Business leader and political appointee. Son of a prosperous New England mill owner and manufacturer, Pinkham was educated in Connecticut and had plans to attend Yale University until a serious accident cut short his academic career. With his father's encouragement, Pinkham began developing extensive business contacts through his travels in Europe and in Asia, including the Philippines and China. He lived in Hawaii between 1891 and 1894 and settled there in 1898. Pinkham was hired by Benjamin Dillingham to work

as a bookkeeper for the Oahu Railroad and Land Company while simultaneously employed as manager of the Pacific Hardware Company.

In 1904, Governor George Roger Carter appointed Pinkham to serve as president of the Territorial Board of Health, a cabinet-level position. During his four-year term, Pinkham earned a reputation as a diligent worker under trying conditions, was praised for his effective handling of outbreaks of cholera and bubonic plague, and was recognized for his efforts to improve living conditions at the leper colony on the island of Molokai. In 1908, Pinkham joined businessman Oswald A. Stevens in promoting recruitment of laborers from Hong Kong and the Philippines to work in Hawaii. Using his extensive contacts, Pinkham hired agents to recruit workers and arrange their transportation to Hawaii to work on plantations owned by members of the HAWAIIAN SUGAR PLANTERS' ASSOCIATION (HSPA).

Pinkham's recruiting efforts took him away from the Hawaiian Islands for five years, but his influence with the HSPA led to his political advancement. President Woodrow Wilson appointed Pinkham to serve as governor of Hawaii in 1913. Although Pinkham was considered to be tainted with Republican leanings and alienated members of Hawaii's Democratic Party by failing to appoint a sufficient number of loyal members to political office, Pinkham won praise from Native Hawaiians for his administration's efforts to provide them with homesteads. His administration also worked to pass laws favoring workers' compensation, providing pensions to teachers, and funding the reclamation of swampland in Waikiki through the construction of a canal that was completed between 1922 and 1924. After leaving office, Pinkham moved to San Francisco in 1918 and lived there until his death in 1922.

Pinoy: Slang for a Filipino male. Considered by some Filipinos to be derogatory, the term was used in the 1920's by Filipino immigrants who came to the United States primarily in search of work. The majority of these men settled in Hawaii or on the Pacific Coast, particularly California, both states being among the leading sources of American agricultural products. In time many *pinoys* left for the U.S. mainland in search of new opportunities after Hawaii's need for Filipino laborers decreased.

Pinyin: System for Chinese romanization based on the MANDARIN dialect and officially adopted by the government of the People's Republic of China. It has become the method of transliteration preferred over the Wade-Giles system.

Pioneer Centers: Japanese American community associations established in the United States during the late 1960's. The centers were designed to offer programs and public services suited to the needs of Japanese senior citizens, particularly the ISSEI. Pioneer Centers sprang up in different parts of the country. In Los Angeles' Little Tokyo, the Japanese Community Pioneer Center (JCPC) began operations in October, 1969. The creation primarily of young Asian American activists, the centers were founded in the early years of the ASIAN AMERICAN MOVEMENT.

Plessy v. Ferguson (1896): U.S. Supreme Court case that established the famous "separate but equal" principle of legalized segregation. The decision came to affect Asian Americans as well as African Americans.

During and immediately after Reconstruction, most public facilities in the North and many in the South were not segregated. The racial idealism of the Civil War rapidly ebbed, however, partly eroded by cries for protectionism against Asian immigration from California politicians, the ideological impact of dispossessing and destroying the culture of the Plains Indians, and the rising tide of American imperialism overseas. By 1890, Southern states and white citizens had closed off most parks and restaurants to African Americans. In that year, Louisiana passed a law requiring separate

Schoolhouse for black children, circa 1939. The rule of legalized segregation established in Plessy *was written primarily for use against African Americans, but it was used to penalize Asian Americans as well.* (Library of Congress)

cars for black passengers on railroads. Other states did likewise.

Homer Plessy, a light-skinned African American, fought the new restriction. In 1892 he deliberately rode in a "white" railroad car, refused to move, and was arrested. Convicted of violating the Louisiana law, he appealed to the Supreme Court. In a seven-to-one decision, the court held that because the law provided for separate cars for blacks, it did not violate Plessy's rights under the Fourteenth Amendment. The decision legitimized segregation of African Americans throughout the Southern and border states. Often "Orientals" or "Mongolians" were also proscribed; some states passed laws making it a felony for a "Mongolian or Negro" to marry a white person, for example.

Many Northern jurisdictions followed suit informally. By 1920 African Americans could not travel even in the North without careful planning to learn where they might eat, sleep, and use rest rooms. Research by Richard LaPiere in 1930-1932 confirmed that Asian Americans in California also faced discrimination in public accommodations. His research did show, however, that white hoteliers and restaurateurs were more likely to say they would discriminate against Asian Americans than to do so in practice.

The 1927 *Gong Lum v. Rice* decision applied *Plessy v. Ferguson* directly to Chinese Americans, barring them from white public schools. *Plessy* was finally overruled in 1954 by *Brown v. Board of Education*, which stated that segregated schools were inherently discriminatory because they stigmatized the excluded group.—*James W. Loewen*

Poindexter, Joseph B. (Apr. 14, 1869, Canyon City, Oreg.—Dec. 3, 1951, Honolulu, Territory of Hawaii): Governor of Hawaii. A lawyer from Montana who had lived in the islands since 1917, he was governor from 1934 until 1942, when martial law was imposed throughout the Territory after the Japanese surprise attack on PEARL HARBOR. On December 7, the day of the bombing, Major General Walter C. Short told Poindexter that martial law was necessary to prevent a Japanese invasion of the islands. Following President Franklin D. Roosevelt's express approval, Short became military governor of Hawaii.

Pol Pot (Saloth Sar; b. May 19, 1928, Kompong Thom, Cambodia): Despot. After going to Paris on a Cambodian government scholarship in 1949, Saloth Sar joined the Communist Party of France. In 1953, when agricultural collectivization, defiance of the Soviet Union, and mass mobilization for public works were motifs of Yugoslavian Communism, he spent a summer constructing housing at the University of Zagreb. In 1953, with no evidence of passing examinations, his scholarship was terminated, and he returned to Phnom Penh to work as a schoolteacher. With the underground Communist Party dominated by Vietnamese living in Phnom Penh, he was consigned to kitchen duties by the Vietnamese leaders. In 1963, when his membership in the Party was exposed, he left town to join the VIET MINH in Cambodia, and in 1965 he visited China, North Korea, and North Vietnam. In 1966, when the party formed an army, he assumed the nom de guerre Pol Pot. After the American bombing of Cambodia in 1969 and the coup against Prince Norodom Sihanouk in 1970, Pol Pot's forces mobilized support in the countryside to topple the new pro-American government, the Khmer Republic, by 1975.

Party factions vied for control, but when Pol Pot emerged as the clear leader in 1977, he presided over a regrouping of society into self-sufficient communes, while ordering a "killing fields" purge of capitalists (shopkeepers and traders), feudalists (Buddhists, intellectuals, and the royal family), and imperialists (Cambodians who collaborated with Americans, Russians, or Vietnamese). As a result, approximately one million persons died, mostly from disease and starvation. (See KHMER ROUGE.)

Responding to repeated attacks from the Cambodian army inside Vietnam, Hanoi sent troops in 1978 to drive Pol Pot's army out of Cambodia. Thereafter, his forces received support from China, and his regime remained seated in the United Nations until 1990.

After officially retiring from the army to head a military institute in 1985, Pol Pot continued working as a political leader from a base in Thailand, seeking to prevent Vietnam from achieving total victory in Cambodia. Although his party's leaders signed a peace treaty in Paris in 1991, he refused to implement the agreement.

Police Tax. *See* **Capitation taxes**

Polynesian Cultural Center: Major tourist attraction that seeks to entertain and educate people in regard to Polynesians, founded in 1963. It conducts walking tours, canoe tours, lectures, and demonstrations throughout seven villages that replicate aspects of the island cultures of Hawaii, Samoa, Tonga, Tahiti, New Zealand, Fiji, and the Marquesas. The center has hosted more than twenty-three million guests since opening.

Samoan village chief on display at the Polynesian Cultural Center. (Brigham Young University, Hawaii)

The center covers forty-two acres and is located approximately forty miles from Honolulu on the north shore of Oahu. It is a nonprofit enterprise owned and operated by the Mormon church. The center was developed to perpetuate Polynesian culture and provide jobs for students at Brigham Young University, Hawaii, which is adjacent to the cultural center. In addition the center donates significant amounts of money annually to the university for various student scholarships.

There has been a long-standing close relationship between the center and the university, which used to be Church College of Hawaii. In fact, the forerunner to the cultural center was the Polynesian Institute, developed by Church College faculty members to help Polynesian students finance their education. In the 1950's the institute encouraged Church College students to perform Polynesian songs and dances at the International Market Place, a famous tourist attraction in Waikiki, as a means of making money to pay for school and living expenses.

In the early 1960's the institute sponsored performances of "Polynesian Panorama," a polished production of songs and dances performed at various sites in Honolulu. The presentation was such a success that in 1962 the Mormon church authorized the construction of the Polynesian Cultural Center.

The construction of the cultural center utilized the labor of about a hundred Mormon volunteers serving two-year "labor missions." The volunteers worked with skilled Polynesian artists and craftspersons who were brought to Hawaii to ensure authenticity of the village buildings. The Polynesian Cultural Center officially opened on October 12, 1963.

Poon, Wei Chi (b. Canton, China): Librarian. Head of the Asian American Studies Library at the University of California, Berkeley, she was the first to establish an Asian American library and Chinese American research collection at a U.S. university. Author of *The Directory of Asian American Collections in the United States* (1982) and *A Guide for Establishing Asian American Core Collections* (1989), she established Asian American subject headings that were recognized by the Library of Congress as national alternatives to standard subject headings.

Porterfield v. Webb (1923): U.S. Supreme Court ruling that affirmed the constitutionality of California's ALIEN LAND LAW OF 1920, under which aliens ineligible for American citizenship (such as the Issei) were barred from buying, owning, or leasing agricultural land. California resident W. L. Porterfield wanted to lease land in Los Angeles County to Y. Mizuno, an Issei farmer. Since state law prohibited this, however, Porterfield filed suit in federal court to challenge the statute.

The case went all the way to the Supreme Court, which issued an opinion that found the statute to be constitutional. Before the Court, Porterfield's lawyers argued that treaty provisions binding the United States and Japan and giving Japanese citizens rights to "own and lease and occupy homes" or to "lease land for residential and commercial purposes" conflicted with the California statute and therefore mandated its annulment. The justices rejected that reasoning, however, stating that these terms did not encompass the right to lease agricultural land. That same day, in the case of TERRACE V. THOMPSON (1923), concerning an alien land law in the state of Washington, the justices handed down another ruling to much the same effect.

Portsmouth Square: An intersection in the city of San Francisco so near Chinatown that the words are sometimes used synonymously. In 1850 Portsmouth Square was the center of San Francisco. While it is no longer the center of modern San Francisco, the character of Portsmouth Square's early development colored the place now known as Chinatown.

In 1846 San Francisco had a population of about a thousand and could be considered no more than a small frontier outpost. With the discovery of gold in the nearby Sierra Nevada mountain foothills in 1848, San Francisco became the major port nearest the gold fields, and its population soared. By the 1880's San Francisco was a thriving city with a population easily rivaling that of some of the older, larger Eastern cities.

In 1848 Portsmouth Square was a stockyard with only mud-brick huts or tents in the neighborhood, but a decade later, it became the city center with hotels, offices, restaurants, shops, and even gambling joints, all clustered about this major intersection. Originally the center had a polyglot character with a wide variety of immigrant groups, and the Chinese were only one among many ethnic groups. Portsmouth Square offered the Chinese many special advantages. Its proximity to the docks allowed them to meet non-English-speaking relatives, friends, and compatriots as they arrived. As a center of hotel and restaurant trade, it became attractive for the Chinese to live in the lower-cost hotel units and to open restaurants and laundries to service their customers nearby. Houses for opium use, gambling, and prostitution also developed (for the use of Chinese and others), and the area took on a disreputable character.

As other ethnic groups prospered, their members tended to move to more spacious parts of San Francisco, but the Chinese remained. In addition to the factors that led to their moving to Portsmouth Square in the first place, the Chinese apparently were more tolerant of the hustle and bustle of such a crowded area but probably had little choice in the matter. Economic discrimination kept Chinese income low. As white intolerance of the Chinese grew, the Chinese were denied access to housing in other areas.

The gold rush San Francisco of the 1850's was a raucous, violent place with seven or eight murders a week on average. So serious was the violence and so inadequate were public authorities that vigilante committees formed at various times (in 1851 and 1856, particularly) to cope with the situation by meting out "justice" on their own terms. Initially such vigilante efforts were directed only at obvious criminal activities; in the following years, Chinese immigrants would become the target of these efforts. Increasingly the Chinese were forced to remain in areas they already occupied.

Although Portsmouth Square and the original Chinatown were destroyed in the earthquake of 1906, the Chinese continued to live in essentially the same location of the city, which became the well-known Chinatown in San Francisco.

Poston: One of ten U.S. government camps under the administration of the WAR RELOCATION AUTHORITY (WRA) used to house Japanese American evacuees during World War II. Officially the camps were designated as "RELOCATION CENTERS." The camp at Poston, located in Arizona on 72,000 acres of American Indian reservation land near the California border, was operational from May 8, 1942, until November 28, 1945.

The barracks-style buildings constructed by the Army at Poston offered each family approximately four hundred square feet of living space. By the summer of 1942, the center housed close to eighteen thousand internees. With a total capacity of twenty thousand, Poston was the largest of the ten WRA relocation centers.

Poston camp authorities planned agricultural and industrial projects at the camp, but for various reasons, these projects were never fully implemented. Still, the internees were responsible for all the labor associated with maintaining life in the camp. The able-bodied ones were expected to work forty-eight hours per week and were paid between sixteen dollars and nineteen dollars per month. Eventually, schools, social programs, and recreational activities were conducted to alleviate boredom and frustration.

Upon arrival, the evacuees had a sense of being pioneers and of "roughing it," and their initial adjustment to camp life was favorable. Through gardens and cover crops to combat the dust storms, the camp became more attractive and colorful. As the camp filled and the pressures of imprisonment continued, however, intergroup antagonisms developed, morale declined, and the internees' faith in the camp administrators diminished considerably.

Eventually, the Western Defense Command announced that as of January 2, 1945, the mass exclusion orders that had led to relocation would be revoked. By the fall of 1945, the WRA had closed the Poston camp.

Poston strike (1942): Protest staged by internees at the POSTON relocation center in Arizona over the arrests of two popular inmates. Given the conditions of camp life, much of which was regulated by camp administrators, tensions between the internees and the administrators and among the inmates themselves soon began to mount. The buildup of hostility and resentment found expression as angry internees physically assaulted suspected *INU* in the camps. After one such incident on November 14, camp authorities rounded up fifty internees for questioning; of these, two were further detained and then scheduled for trial in an Arizona state court. An initial protest over the arrest then ensued, followed by a general internal strike shortly thereafter when officials refused to release the two men. As the strike ran its course, all camp services stopped, save for a few. By November 23 administrators had agreed to release one of the prisoners. Days later the strike began to wane.

Powderly, Terence V. [Vincent] (Jan. 22, 1849, Carbondale, Pa.—June 24, 1924, Washington, D.C.): Labor leader and immigration official. In staunch opposition to the immigration of foreign laborers to America, Powderly supported legislation barring immigrants from Europe and Asia, especially the immigration of Chinese laborers.

Powderly was the eleventh of twelve children born to Irish immigrants Terence and Margery Walsh Powderly. Son Terence attended school until he was age thirteen, when he went to work for the Delaware and Hudson Railroad as a switch operator. Powderly was married twice, first in 1872 to Hannah Dover, who died in 1901, and then in 1919 to Emma Fickenscher, his former secretary. He served as mayor of Scranton, Pennsylvania, from 1878 to 1884. Powderly was also a self-educated lawyer.

Powderly joined the Machinists' and Blacksmiths' Union of Carbondale in 1871, serving as local chapter president in 1872. In 1874 he was initiated into the Order of the KNIGHTS OF LABOR and served as general master workman from 1879 to 1893. He thus became the head of what was then the most powerful labor union in the United States. In 1894 he resigned from the order under fire and was expelled until 1900.

Powderly campaigned for William McKinley in 1897 and was rewarded with an appointment as U.S. commissioner-general of immigration (1897-1902), heading the newly created Bureau of Immigration. As commissioner, Powderly's anti-Chinese sentiment came forward. He opposed any foreign labor immigration but took special interest in preventing Chinese immigration. He vigorously supported the CHINESE EXCLUSION ACT OF 1882 and its extensions. He used his labor influence to help U.S. president Grover Cleveland push the Alien Contract Labor Act of 1885 through Congress. During his tenure Powderly feverishly sought out illegal Chinese immigrants already in the country. He appointed immigration officials who supported American labor and were anti-Chinese, and he established harsher rules and regulations to control the Chinese.

U.S. president Theodore Roosevelt dismissed Powderly in 1902. He was later reinstated and appointed chief of the Division of Information of the Bureau of Immigration from 1907 to 1921. There he gathered information useful for the employment of immigrants.

Prasad, Rajendra (Dec. 3, 1884, Zeradei, Bihar, India—Feb. 28, 1963, Patna, Republic of India): First president of India. Prasad was persuaded by nationalist leader Mahatma GANDHI to join the noncooperation movement for independence against the British colonial rule. Prasad served as president of the Indian National Congress before being elected national president, an office he held from 1950 until 1962.

Prasad was born into a landowning family of modest means. At age eleven he was married to a seven-year-old girl. After graduating from law school, he began his practice and, in 1916, established the *Bihar Law Weekly*. By 1920 he was an active player in the Indian resistance movement. In order to serve the cause more effectively, he left law to become a jour-

nalist; he started a Hindi weekly, *Desh* (country), lobbied for the establishment of HINDI as the national language, and played an active and influential role as a member of the Indian National Congress. As national president, he set a precedent by limiting his role to that of nominal and ceremonial head of state.

PRC. *See* **China, People's Republic of**

Prefectures: In Japan, administrative districts under the authority of the national government. They are similar to states in the United States, counties in Great Britain, and provinces in other countries. The prefectural system was installed in 1871, during the MEIJI RESTORATION, which did away with the feudal domains ruled by *DAIMYO* as part of an overall plan to adopt Western-style nationwide reforms and restore centralized power to the emperor. Originally, there were more than three hundred prefectures, each corresponding to what had formerly been a feudal domain. This system was inefficient, however, and many prefectures were consolidated into larger units. In Japan today there are forty-seven prefectures. Of these, forty-three are prefectures proper (*ken*); the other four are the cities of Tokyo, Kyoto, and Osaka and the territory of Hokkaido. Each prefecture has a governor and a legislative assembly.

Proposition 13 (1956): California state initiative that repealed the ALIEN LAND LAW OF 1913. The recall was initiated by the JAPANESE AMERICAN CITIZENS LEAGUE (JACL), which lobbied the state legislature and campaigned to support its passage on the November, 1956, general election ballot. The proposition won approval with two-thirds of the vote, thus abolishing the state law that made it illegal for persons ineligible to become citizens to own land in California.

Proposition 15 (1945): California state ballot measure that proposed voter approval of amendments by the state legislature to the ALIEN LAND LAW OF 1920, amendments that would strengthen existing anti-Japanese restrictions. The JAPANESE AMERICAN CITIZENS LEAGUE (JACL) helped coordinate the campaign that eventually defeated the measure.

Protect Kahoolawe Ohana: Organization founded in 1976 to stop the bombing of the island of Kahoolawe, which had been used for target practice by the U.S. Navy since World War II. The organization formed shortly after Native Hawaiians occupied the island to protest its misuse. It thus created a lasting network of Native Hawaiian activists and brought an end to the military's bombardment of Kahoolawe in 1990.

Protect the Emperor Society. *See* **Baohuanghui**

Protecting Diaoyutai movement. *See* **China politics in the Chinese American community**

Protectorate Treaty (1905): Treaty between Korea and Japan signed on November 17. It secured Japan's control over Korea's foreign relations, thus forcing the Korean government to secure the Japanese government's approval for any international agreements. It also provided for the stationing of a Japanese resident-general in Seoul. Coupled with the TREATY OF PORTSMOUTH (September, 1905), which approved Japan's gradual domination of Korea, it mobilized Korean Americans to unify their organizations in the struggle for independence.

Public Law 405. *See* **Denationalization Act of 1944**

Public Proclamation No. 1 (1942): World War II Japanese American internment order issued by General John L. DeWitt in compliance with EXECUTIVE ORDER 9066 (1942). It was the first step taken by the U.S. military in establishing military zones from which the government could exclude civilians. Issued on March 2, it designated the western halves of California, Oregon, and Washington and the southern part of Arizona as Military Area No. 1, in which section most of the exclusion zones would eventually be situated. Under the proclamation all persons of Japanese ancestry were to be excluded from this area. These individuals were further advised to move to the interior of the United States. Three weeks later, however, PUBLIC PROCLAMATION NO. 4 prohibited further movement out of Military Area No. 1. (See also PUBLIC PROCLAMATION NO. 2; PUBLIC PROCLAMATION NO. 3.)

Public Proclamation No. 2 (1942): World War II Japanese American internment order issued by General John L. DeWitt in compliance with EXECUTIVE ORDER 9066 (1942). Issued on March 16, it was part of the U.S. military's continuing attempt at "voluntary" resettlement, requiring enemy aliens and all Japanese Americans (citizens and noncitizens) on the West Coast to execute change of residence notices required by Public Proclamation No. 1. (See also PUBLIC PROCLAMATION NO. 3; PUBLIC PROCLAMATION NO. 4.)

Public Proclamation No. 3 (1942): World War II Japanese American internment order issued by General John L. DeWitt in compliance with EXECUTIVE ORDER 9066 (1942). Issued on March 24, it established curfew and travel regulations for enemy aliens and all Japanese Americans. Within Military Area No. 1, the curfew was to be in effect from 8:00 P.M. to 6:00 A.M. (See also PUBLIC PROCLAMATION NO. 1; PUBLIC PROCLAMATION NO. 2; PUBLIC PROCLAMATION NO. 4.)

Public Proclamation No. 4 (1942): World War II Japanese American internment order issued by General John L. DeWitt in compliance with EXECUTIVE ORDER 9066 (1942). Issued on March 27, it marked the government's departure from its original plan of "voluntary" resettlement by prohibiting all persons of Japanese ancestry residing in Military Area No. 1 from leaving that area without military approval. This laid the groundwork for the subsequent forced relocation and mass internment of Japanese Americans. (See also PUBLIC PROCLAMATION NO. 1; PUBLIC PROCLAMATION NO. 2; PUBLIC PROCLAMATION NO. 3.)

Puja: Hindu religious ceremony by which the worshiper pays tribute to various deities. It ranges from brief daily rites performed in the home to more elaborate rituals conducted in temples on a weekly basis. The ceremony includes singing, chanting, burning of incense, and offerings of food, clothing, and flowers. While the different elements involved may vary from sect to sect, the general purpose of a *puja* is to honor the deity as a royal guest in the home, with special services that extend from morning until evening.

Pukui, Mary Abigail Kawena (1895, Hawaii—May 21, 1986, Hawaii): Linguist, composer, and author. Born the daughter of Henry Nathaniel Wiggin, a New Englander, and his wife Paahana, a Native Hawaiian, Pukui was reared first by her maternal grandmother, who provided Pukui with a thorough foundation in Hawaiian culture and folklore. Fascinated from an early age by the cultural resources and work done at Honolulu's BISHOP MUSEUM, Pukui decided to pursue her education at the Hawaiian Missionary Academy. By the time she was in her twenties, Pukui had been graduated from the academy and was married. At first, she was unable to get employment at the museum because of the anti-Hawaiian prejudice of its director, but eventually she worked with Dr. Edward Handy, who paid her wages for her linguistic work. When a new museum director took over, she was hired full time. Pukui eventually prepared several dictionaries, ethnographies, and lexicons of the Hawaiian language, many of which were published in collaboration with Samuel H. Elbert. Her work helped preserve and extend the knowledge of the Hawaiian language. Pukui possessed a vast knowledge of native plants and of traditional crafts and dances; in addition, she was a talented composer of traditional Hawaiian songs. During her lifetime, she worked closely with her natural daughter, Pele Sugunuma, and her adopted *hanai* daughter of Japanese descent, Pat. During her career, Pukui received many honorary degrees and awards, was named Hawaiian of the Year, and was honored as a Living Treasure.

Punjab: State in northwest India. With an area of more than 19,400 square miles, Punjab is bordered by the Indian states of Jammu and Kashmir to the north, the state of Himachal Pradesh to the east, the states of Haryana and Rajasthan to the south, and Pakistan to the west. Its population in 1991 was almost 20.2 million people, and its capital city is Chandigarh. The area historically known as the Punjab was larger, encompassing part of present-day Pakistan.

The name "Punjab" is a combination of two words: *punj*, which means "five," and *ab*, which means "water." The name refers to the five rivers: Jhleum, Chenab, Ravi, Beas, and Sutlej, which flow out of the Himalayas and merge into the Indus River. During the colonial period, the Punjab was bounded on the east by the river Jumna (a tributary of the river Ganges), on the north and west by a chain of rugged mountains, the Hindu Kuksh and the Sulaiman, and on the south by the Thar Desert; it was also pierced by several passes such as the Bolan and the Khyber.

The Land and Its People. The Punjab, as one of the main gateways to the Indian subcontinent, has in its long and eventful history undergone many important territorial changes. A significant change occurred in 1947, when the Punjab was divided into four different provinces in two different nations: INDIA and PAKISTAN. Settled agriculture evolved in the Indus Valley in the third millennium B.C.E. and provided the agricultural surplus for the development of the urbanized Harappan civilization, which came to an end sometime before 1500 B.C.E. with the invasion of the Aryans. The Aryans were followed by many other invaders such as the Persians, Greeks, and Arabs. The caste system known as *JATI* in the Punjab is frequently divided along occupations, and the number of castes is estimated to be three thousand or more. The dominant agricultural

jati is the Jat, who were often praised by British ethnographers as excellent farmers. Over the centuries these *jatis* were divided into Hindus and Muslims. Though everywhere the population was mixed, Muslims were more numerous in the northwest and Hindus in the southeast. The first attempt to create religious unity in the Punjab was a result of the *bhakti* movement, which was born in south India and reached the Punjab by the end of the fourteenth century. The *bhakti* movement propagated a syncretic path of simple love of God. In the Punjab, NANAK preached an ecstatic monotheism based on the love for "one God, the Creator," whose name was Truth. Thus, Nanak became the first guru (divine teacher) of the Sikh faith. Nine other gurus followed until 1708. The followers acquired a headquarters at the Golden Temple in AMRITSAR. During the seventeenth century the Sikhs evolved into a separate community. The religious movement that had started as a unifying force for Muslims and Hindus turned into a third major religion in the Punjab. In 1820, Ranjit Singh welded the disparate elements of the Punjab into a powerful state. This Sikh kingdom lasted until 1849; the last few years of this rule were characterized by constant strife and near political anarchy. The British brought stability to the Punjab when they annexed it in 1849.

Though divided along religious and caste lines, the Punjab was united by the PUNJABI language, with a well-developed literary heritage and folklore. Though the spoken language is the same, Muslim Punjabis write it with Persian script, and the Sikhs write in Gurmuki.

The Raj. The Punjab became an important province during the British colonial hold on the Indian subcontinent. The Punjabis contributed manpower to the various British expeditions within the subcontinent and helped the British police the overseas territories. The military became an important source of employment for the Punjab; about half of the British Indian army were recruited from the Punjab. The British named the people of the Punjab "the martial races of India."

Under the British rule the Punjab was also transformed into one of the most important areas of commercial farming in Asia. One of the important changes introduced by the British related to property rights. The British organized a standard revenue assessment and collection system that encouraged individual property rights. Moreover, development of land and rail transport aided the marketing of agricultural produce, which resulted in increased monetary value of the land. As the farmers entered more into the money economy, their debt burden increased, which led many of them to mortgage their lands to moneylending and commercial castes. After 1880 there was a substantial increase in forced land sales in the Punjab as a result of unredeemed mortgages. The British colonial government was alarmed by this trend, which it viewed as weakening the position of agricultural castes on whom it relied for political support, revenue, and military recruitment. In 1900 the government passed an unprecedented law, the Punjab Alienation of Land Act, which forbade the passing of land from agricultural to nonagricultural castes.

Another significant development under the British colonial rule was the extension of cultivation into the land known as *doab* (tract of land between two rivers). Until the 1880's the existing irrigation system in the Punjab was limited to land contiguous to rivers, but evidence of former habitations and earthworks in the area indicated the existence of irrigation networks in the past. The process of building canal colonies into western Punjab started in 1885 and continued into the final years of British rule. A network of canals was constructed that fed off the rivers, with branches and distributaries spread over the flat, alluvial plains of the western Punjab. The canals were constructed primarily in uncultivated land that had been sparsely inhabited by seminomadic populations of cattle grazers and camel owners. Between 1885 and the end of British rule in 1947, the canal-irrigated area in the Punjab increased from less than three million to around fourteen million acres. This made possible the migration into western Punjab of people from other parts of the Punjab. The British government's policies in the Punjab earned for them the loyalty of the rural elites, who remained pro-British until the partition in 1947.

Partition. During the partition of British India in August, 1947, western Punjab became part of Pakistan, and eastern Punjab became a province of India. The Indian Punjab received roughly 34 percent of the land and 47 percent of the population. Most of the Hindu and the Sikh population of western Punjab, about four and a half million, migrated to eastern Punjab, and roughly the same number of Muslims moved from eastern Punjab to Pakistan. There was a further partition of Indian Punjab in 1966, when the province was divided into the states of Punjab and Haryana. The former consisted of Punjabi-speaking Sikhs, and the latter had the majority of Hindi-speaking Hindus. The two states continue to share Chandigarh as a state capital.

In the 1960's and 1970's, both the Indian and the Pakistani Punjab experienced a "green revolution": a substantial increase in agricultural output through the use of high-yielding varieties of grain crops sustained by fertilizers and an assured water supply. The people of the Punjab continued to be more mobile than many other communities of South Asia. There has been a long tradition of migration to other parts of South Asia as well as emigration abroad to find work. A sizable number of Punjabis have settled in the United States, Canada, the United Kingdom, and countries of East Africa and Southeast Asia.—*Farhat Haq*

SUGGESTED READINGS: • Fox, Richard. *Lions of the Punjab: Culture in the Making.* Berkeley: University of California Press, 1985. • Gilmartin, David. *Empire and Islam: Punjab and the Making of Pakistan.* Berkeley: University of California Press, 1988. • Grewal, J. S. *The Sikhs of the Punjab.* New York: Cambridge University Press, 1990. • Jeffrey, Robin. *What's Happening to India? Punjab, Ethnic Conflict, Mrs. Gandhi's Death, and the Test of Federalism.* New York: Holmes & Meier, 1986. • Singh, Mohinder, ed. *History and Culture of Punjab.* New Delhi, India: Atlantic Publishers and Distributors, 1988.

Punjabi: Indo-Aryan language. It is spoken by most inhabitants of the Punjab, an area divided between India and Pakistan.

Punjabi is derived from SANSKRIT, the language of the Aryans. Because Sanskrit, however, retained its purity by refusing to admit words of local languages, it soon became restricted to a small group of Brahmins (members of the highest social class). The common people therefore began to borrow from the indigenous non-Aryan languages and developed local accents.

In the Punjab, the Sanskrit of the Aryans mingled with the languages of the Jat tribes, which had moved northward from Rajasthan into the Punjab. This mixture produced a variety of regional dialects from which, around the eleventh century, evolved the Punjabi language.

The arrival of Muslims in the Punjab further subjected Punjabi to other linguistic influences, such as Arabic, Persian, and Turkish. Punjabi is written in two different scripts: Gurmukhi and Arabic. Gurmukhi is used in the Sikhs' sacred scriptures, known as the *Granth Sahib.* There is a dispute among scholars regarding the origin of the Gurmukhi script. One generally held opinion is that Gurmukhi, like many other scripts used in northern India, was derived from Brahmi letters that were used at the time of Emperor Asoka (third century B.C.E.), but no precise dates can be fixed about its evolution. Punjabi Muslims have used the Arabic script to write Punjabi.

Punjabi boasts rich folk literature developed mostly by Muslim Sufis and Sikh gurus. The first great name in Punjabi literature is that of the famous Sufi Farid Shakarganj (twelfth century), who made his home in Pak Pattan in the western part of the Punjab. Continuing the tradition of the Sufis and the bhaktas, Shakarganj used the language of romantic love between men and women as a metaphor of human beings' search for God. The tradition was continued by the Sikh gurus. This style of love poetry as a mystical search for the sacred continues to be a dominant motif of Punjabi poetry and can be discerned even in what might at first appear as simple love stories such as the three great epics of Punjabi literature: *Heer Ranjha, Sassi Punnun,* and *Sohni Mahinval.* In all three of these epics, after a lifetime of separation and longing, lovers meet in death. Bullhe Shah and Varis Shah produced some of the best romantic and mystic Punjabi poetry, which has become a central part of the folk culture of the Punjab.

Punti: Cantonese pronunciation of *bendi,* meaning natives or indigenous people denoting, in the context of modern China, the Cantonese people of GUANGDONG and Guangxi. Although the areas inhabited by the Punti people were already incorporated into the Chinese Empire by the Han Dynasty (206 B.C.E.-220 C.E.), it was only with continuous immigration from the North lasting several centuries that the local population took on a distinctive Chinese character. Thus the Punti people came into existence. On the basis of linguistic and genealogical evidence, their formation can be dated to the end of the Song Dynasty (960-1279), at the latest.

Armed with a superior agricultural technology and supported by the imperial government, they staked out claims to the entire Canton River Delta and pushed west along the West River as far as Nanning. In possession of the best alluvial lands of the region and benefiting from the superb communication network furnished by the Canton River system, they forged ahead in material wealth and in cultural achievements. During the QING DYNASTY (1644-1911), for example, their settlements tended to be large and had a prosperous look; their scholars tended to be successful, usually garnering the lion's share of the honors at the triennial civil service examination held at the provincial capital of Guangdong. With no shortage of gentrymen, Punti communities set the standard in implementing gentry values such as making provisions for education and promoting lineage solidarity.

Punti identity evolved into sharper focus with the intrusion of an alien element, the HAKKA, who migrated south from their north China homeland in successive waves. The Hakka were first brought into Punti territory as tenant farmers but before long had acquired their own land and started their own communities. Differing in speech, customs, and economic interests, Punti and Hakka evolved into competing communal groups. In Guangxi the Hakka adherents of Hong Xiuquan clashed with Punti militias, precipitating the TAIPING REBELLION (1850-1864). In Guangdong communal tension flared up into open warfare in the 1860's when the provincial government was knocked out of commission by the allied troops of the Second Opium War (1856-1860), resulting in tens of thousands of casualties on both sides.

Purdah: Persian term meaning "veil" or "screen," referring to a Muslim practice of shielding women from public view, or, more particularly, from the presence of men and strangers. The custom mandates that the entire body, including the head and face, must be enveloped in clothing so as to be hidden from view. Such items as curtains may also be employed in the home to cover the windows.

Pure Land: In BUDDHISM, a land also known as the Western Paradise, created by the Buddha Amitabha (Sanskrit; in Japanese, Amida). Those who believe in Amitabha and chant his name with true faith will be reborn in the Pure Land (in Sanskrit, Sukhavati; in Japanese, Jodo), where they will remain in bliss until they reach complete enlightenment. On the level of popular practice, the Pure Land is held to be an actual place; on another level of practice, however, it is held to represent a state of consciousness.

Pure Land sects: School of BUDDHISM based on the practice of devotion to the Buddha Amitabha (Sanskrit; in Japanese, Amida; in Chinese, Omito), the buddha of infinite light. In the Buddhist literature, Amitabha is described as a king who renounced his throne when he heard the Buddhist teachings. He vowed to become a buddha and to create a paradise in which beings who supplicated him with true faith and with the desire to become enlightened would live in bliss until they reached final enlightenment. Consequently, adherents of the Pure Land (in Sanskrit, Sukhavati; in Japanese, Jodo) schools believe that if they chant the name of Amitbaha with absolutely pure faith and de-

Adherents of the Pure Land school of Buddhism worship the Buddha Amitabha. (Diane C. Lyell)

votion, they will be reborn in his PURE LAND, or Western Paradise, where they will remain until they become fully enlightened.

The Pure Land schools are significant in Buddhism because they represent an approach to enlightenment different from that taken by the meditative schools. The meditative schools hold that one becomes enlightened by means of one's own effort (in Japanese, *jiriki*), by working diligently at one's meditative practice, whereas the Pure Land schools hold that one must reach enlightenment through the effort of another (in Japanese, *tariki*), namely, Amitabha.

The first patriarch of Pure Land Buddhism was the Chinese scholar Hui-yuan, who stated that the degeneracy of the age made it impossible to become enlightened by dint of one's own effort; instead, one should chant the name of Amitabha with pure devotion. In 1175, Pure Land Buddhism was introduced to Japan by HONEN, and the practice of chanting the *nembutsu* ("Namu Amida Butsu," or "Adoration to the Buddha Amitbaha") became popular throughout the country. In 1224, SHINRAN, a disciple of Honen, founded the JODO SHINSHU ("True Pure Land Sect"), which became one of the most important sects of Pure Land Buddhism. Japanese immigrants brought Pure Land Buddhism to the United States, and most contemporary Japanese American Buddhists are Pure Land adherents.

Purple Heart Battalion: Nickname for the U.S. Army's 100TH INFANTRY BATTALION during World War II. Composed of 1,400 Hawaiian second-generation Japanese Americans, the unit was sent to northern Africa and then to Italy in September, 1943. With 350 soldiers killed and 650 wounded, the remainder of the unit joined the 442ND REGIMENTAL COMBAT TEAM in June, 1944. The combined 442nd earned a total of 18,143 individual decorations, including more than 3,600 Purple Hearts, the most in U.S. military history.

Pyongyang: Capital of the Democratic People's Republic of Korea, more commonly known as North Korea. Pyongyang, one of the country's oldest cities, was also the capital of the ancient Koguryo Dynasty (c. 37 B.C.E.-688 C.E.). The city was destroyed during the Korean War (1950-1953) but has since been rebuilt. Its 1987 population was more than 2.4 million people.

Qigong: An ancient Chinese method of promoting and regulating the vital energy of the human body. The practice of *qigong* was known in the Warring States period (481-221 B.C.E.) and described in the oldest Chinese medical treatise, *Huang Ti nei Ching* (third century C.E.; the Yellow Emperor's classic of internal medicine). In this treatise there is discussion concerning the origin, application, classification, and therapeutic value of *qigong*.

The general theory of *qigong* suggests that a vital component for good health is contained in the breath (*qi*), which cannot be allowed to stagnate in the body. If this happens, illness will follow, as the *qi* is the carrier of the vital energy (*zhen qi*) throughout the body. Therefore a method of stimulating the flow of *qi* to strengthen immunity from disease or to help reverse the effects of illness is viewed as necessary for health.

The *qigong* exercises involve the practitioner's attention upon posture, respiration, and the mind. Generally the exercises can be performed lying down, sitting, or standing, with little or no movement of the body. Upon assuming a posture, the practitioner will calm the mind and relax as much as possible. Next, the attention is directed to the breathing, which is performed in a slow, deep, and controlled manner. While breathing the practitioner will mentally direct the breath to various parts of the body. According to *qigong* theory, the breath will follow channels or pathways inside the body that join together the vital organs. Thus the organs of the body themselves receive the benefit of the practice as they are nourished and replenished with vital energy.

Although *qigong* has been practiced in China for at least two thousand years, it was not until 1979 that the Beijing Qigong Institute was established. It was the first such institute to research the effects of the practice. Its findings seem to suggest that *qigong* techniques are beneficial in certain chronic disorders affecting blood pressure and the nervous system.

Today *qigong* exercises are widely practiced in China by millions of people concerned with improving their health and preventing disease. *Qigong* exercises and techniques are also practiced by a small yet increasing number of people in the United States.

Qing Dynasty (1644-1912): Last dynasty in China. The Qing imperial family originated in northeast China, from outside the confines of the Great Wall. They were the Manchu, a militaristic ethnic group. In 1636, the Manchu adopted the name "Qing," which literally means "clear like water," as their state's title. In 1644, the Manchu army marched through the Great Wall and occupied Beijing, the capital of the earlier Ming Dynasty (1368-1644).

Upon conquering the remaining regions, the Manchus forced the Han people, the major ethnic group, to accept Manchu clothing and hairstyles; in turn, the Manchus adapted themselves to Han language, literature, and administrative institutions. Confucianism retained its power as the dominant ideology. Qing emperors supported the compilation of the most definitive dictionary and book collection in premodern Chinese history. Handicraft industry and commerce reached an unparalleled level of development. Further, Chinese population increased to four hundred million. A succession of eleven emperors ruled. Of these, the reign under the fourth emperor Qianlong saw the greatest prosperity.

Challenges from the West marked the nineteenth century, as Qing rulers gradually came to realize that they could not keep China isolated. Defeats in the First Opium War (1839-1842) and the Second Opium War (1856-1860) caused the Self-strengthening movement, a dedication to the promotion of Western technology. Emperors sent students overseas and purchased machines from the West. A new navy along with new engineering schools were established based upon Western models. The Qing, however, experienced yet another military defeat in the Sino-Japanese War (1894-1895). As a result, a group of intellectuals began advocating political reform in favor of a constitutional monarchy. These efforts were crushed in 1898 by a conservative faction of the royal family. In 1908, the Qing court finally relented, issuing its reform plan, but this initiative arrived too late. Calls for the overthrow of the Manchu government were gaining an ever greater amount of adherents. A republican revolution broke out on October 10, 1911. On February 12, 1912, the Qing court declared that the last emperor, who was six years old, had abdicated power. With the fall of the Qing Dynasty, the monarchical system was abolished in China.

Qing Ming: Chinese phrase meaning "clear brightness," also called the "tomb-sweeping festival." Qing

Confucius Church in Salinas, California. As Confucianism became more prominent in China, so did popular concern with ritual and filial piety to parents and ancestors.

Ming is one of twenty-four observances based on the solar calendar used in China from the Zhou Dynasty (c. 1122-221 B.C.E.). It is commemorated on April 5, about fifteen days after the spring equinox.

This spring festival is observed by a visit to the graves of ancestors and close relatives. After tidying the graves, family members light incense, burn paper money folded to resemble gold and silver ingots, and offer dishes of food, cooked rice, and wine for the well-being and enjoyment of the spirits. The family might partake of the foods in picnic fashion there. The ritual expresses reverence for the departed and reinforces family ties by linking participants and their ancestors, whose happiness or distress is believed to affect their descendants positively or negatively.

The origin of conducting this graveside ritual is uncertain. Late Zhou texts described elaborate rites honoring the dead and specified details for sacrifices at ancestral shrines or halls and temples. Concern with ritual and filial piety to parents and ancestors became

more pronounced during the Han Dynasty (206 B.C.E.-220 C.E.), when Confucianism became the dominant value system promoted by the state. By the Song Dynasty (960-1279 C.E.) sacrifices offered in family or clan ancestral halls to individual spirits, which are represented by wooden tablets inscribed with names and titles, had already been performed for centuries, as had ceremonies at grave sites.

Qing Ming rituals follow a common pattern, although regional and family practices may differ in such details as whether to venerate two, three, or more generations of ancestors. Ritual aspects of Qing Ming have generally ceased in the People's Republic of China. Overseas Chinese communities valued ancestral ties and observed traditional practices as conditions in their adoptive lands permitted.

Chinese immigrants in Hawaii formed associations by district or dialect grouping to provide burial rites for those without families. The first association, established in 1854, acquired and managed a cemetery for its members. At Qing Ming, Chinese families and those burial societies still in existence continue the tradition of conducting rites to ancestors.

Qing policy on emigration: When invaders from Manchuria established China's Qing Dynasty in 1644, they feared rebellion from those still loyal to the former leadership. Therefore in an attempt to prevent sympathizers from joining a revolutionary movement in exile, they made emigration from the Chinese mainland a capital crime. Such laws affected the ability of Chinese emigrants to leave home and pursue opportunities overseas. This penalty was only sporadically enforced but remained official policy until the nineteenth century, when it was replaced by governmental disownership of anyone who chose to "desert" China.

Qing treatment of emigrants as noncitizens enabled the American anti-Chinese movement to develop without the hindrance of diplomatic protests. Reports of mob violence overseas undoubtedly discouraged villagers from leaving home, but events such as the OPIUM WARS and the TAIPING REBELLION increased peasant suffering. Hunger and conscription into the military drove thousands from southern China to brave hostility in the United States. These emigrants usually went first to Hong Kong, where British rule would enable them to avoid openly challenging governmental prohibitions.

Despite its official position on emigration, Qing leadership did attempt to negotiate with foreign governments for the protection of overseas Chinese, through such media as the 1868 BURLINGAME TREATY. In the mid-1870's, however, Congress began to enact anti-Chinese legislation that moved mistreatment of Chinese beyond the local and state levels. In order to counter such growing disregard for its treaty rights, China finally decided to establish a permanent diplomatic mission in Washington, D.C.

When the Chinese diplomats arrived in 1878, they found American leadership irreversibly committed to exclusion and, therefore, focused only on securing promises of protection for resident Chinese. Thus the imperial government decided to recognize emigration as legitimate after losing the capability to assist its citizens in coming to the United States. From 1882 through the Chinese Revolution of 1911, China protested each new exclusionary law enacted by Congress, but the crumbling dynasty could not muster sufficient diplomatic leverage to influence the actions of a more powerful foreign nation. Such repeated failures demonstrated Qing weakness and helped make Chinese emigrants enthusiastic supporters of the revolutionary movement.

Qinghua University: One of China's first national universities as well as its most Americanized one. It had a leading role in introducing Western learning to China.

The school was founded in 1908 when the United States forgave the Qing Dynasty's government of $12 million of America's share of the BOXER REBELLION indemnity. In so doing, the United States hoped that the new school would train future Chinese leaders in Western values.

Qinghua University began as a foreign-staffed school that prepared students for study toward advanced degrees in the United States. It had an American liberal-arts curriculum that emphasized Western learning over Chinese subjects. Teachers and students spoke and read English.

In 1926, the prep school became Qinghua College, with a four-year baccalaureate program. In 1928, it was renamed National Qinghua University by the Nationalist (Guomindang) government, with Luo Jialun its first president. Under Luo, the curriculum was expanded to include engineering and graduate studies, as well as advanced research. Luo was succeeded by Y. C. Mei (Mei Yiqi), who was president from 1931 to 1948. Under Mei, the university developed a strong library, created specialized research institutes, and published academic journals, while continuing its traditional emphasis on the liberal arts. Under both presidents, Qinghua became one of China's best universities, particularly in science and engineering.

In July, 1937, the Japanese invasion of China forced Qinghua to withdraw first to Changsha, then to Kunming. In 1938 in Kunming, Qinghua joined Nankai University and Beijing University to form Southwest Associated University. Qinghua returned to Beijing when the war ended.

After 1949, the Communist government converted Qinghua into a polytechnical institution stripped of its liberal-arts program. The university was closed during the Cultural Revolution, becoming a battleground of the Red Guards. Despite repeated traumas from the Cultural Revolution and other political campaigns, Qinghua retained its academic excellence, with a reputation surpassed only by Beijing University. After 1976, it even managed to resuscitate its old ties with the United States.

Quakers: Common name for the members of the religious group officially known as the "Friends." They were among the few who spoke out against the World War II internment of Japanese Americans, and became instrumental in resettling interned Nisei so that the latter could attend college during the war.

Question 27: One of two "loyalty" and "allegiance" questions found on the registration questionnaires that the U.S. government distributed to relocation center evacuees during World War II. There were actually two sets of questionnaires, one formulated by the War Department as a Nisei male draft-fitness determinant, the other by the WAR RELOCATION AUTHORITY (WRA) as part of its resettlement program.

Question 27 on the War Department's "Statement of United States Citizens of Japanese Ancestry" (Selective Service Form 304A) asked: "Are you willing to serve in the armed forces of the United States on combat duty, wherever ordered?" The same question on the WRA's "Application for Leave Clearance" read: "If the opportunity presents itself and you are found qualified, would you be willing to volunteer for the Army Nurse Corps or the WAAC [Women's Army Auxiliary Corps]?"

Many internees, however, vexed especially by the content of questions 27 and 28, soon began to resent the registration program and questionnaire. On the War Department form, for example, all (male Nisei) respondents were expected to answer yes to question 27. In all ten relocation camps, however, the question received many negative replies. Both inquiries constituted a litmus test of loyalty and allegiance for Army recruiters, who in early 1943 had decided to create the voluntary, all-Nisei 442ND REGIMENTAL COMBAT TEAM as a way of allowing the evacuees to prove their devotion to the United States. Those who answered no to questions 27 and 28 became known as "NO-NO BOYS."

Some men answered question 27 in the negative because of reluctance to take arms against their own people, such as the Kibei (American-born Japanese receiving an education in Japan) or against Japanese relatives. The vast majority answered in the negative because as internees they had been deprived of full citizenship rights. They used their refusal to protest the abuse of their civil liberties.

Question 28: One of two controversial "loyalty" and "allegiance" questions found on the registration questionnaires that the U.S. government distributed to relocation center evacuees during World War II. There were actually two sets of questionnaires, one formulated by the War Department as a Nisei male draft-fitness deter-

minant, the other by the WAR RELOCATION AUTHORITY (WRA) as part of its resettlement program.

Question 28 on the War Department's "Statement of United States Citizens of Japanese Ancestry" (Selective Service Form 304A) asked: "Will you swear unqualified allegiance to the United States of America and faithfully defend the United States from any or all attack by foreign or domestic forces, and forswear any form of allegiance or obedience to the Japanese emperor, or any other foreign government, power or organization?" The same question on the WRA's "Application for Leave Clearance" read: "Will you swear unqualified allegiance to the United States of America and forswear any form of allegiance or obedience to the Japanese emperor, or any other foreign government, power or organization?" In deference to the Issei, and for Issei respondents only, number 28 was later amended to read: "Will you swear to abide by the laws of the United States and to take no action which would in any way interfere with the war effort of the United States?"

For many internees, however, the registration program in general, and questions 27 and 28 in particular, were perplexing and the source of deep resentment.

For Japanese nationals question 28 asked them to forswear allegiance to Japan and, in so doing, to renounce allegiance to any country whatsoever, since the United States categorically denied them citizenship rights. For the Kibei (Japanese Americans who received part or all of their education in Japan), there was fear that an affirmative answer might be taken to imply that they had previously harbored allegiance to Japan or to the emperor. Yet to answer in the negative could be equally as damaging. In short, they would be branded as disloyal regardless of their response.

The older members of the Nisei similarly found question 28 humiliating. Their allegiance to the United States had been demonstrated by the willingness and orderliness with which they had complied with evacuation orders. Many younger Nisei, most of whom were minors, ended up being identified as "disloyals." Those (male Nisei) respondents who volunteered for draft-registration by completing the War Department's form and who subsequently answered no to questions 27 and 28 became known as "NO-NO BOYS."

Queue Ordinance (1876): San Francisco law that directed the sheriff to cut the hair of all male Chinese prisoners within one inch of their scalps. The effect was to put the men in violation of a Chinese law whose prescribed punishment was execution. The purpose of

San Francisco Chinese children wearing braided queues. Photograph by Arnold Genthe, "Pigtail Parade," circa 1900. (Library of Congress)

the Queue Ordinance was to discourage Chinese from living in or passing through San Francisco and perhaps keep them out of the United States entirely.

Between 1644 and 1911 the law in China required Chinese men to wear their hair in a certain fashion (shaving part of their head and letting the unshaved part grow long, which then had to be put in a braid, or queue). This requirement served to show that Chinese accepted the authority of the ruling Manchu Dynasty; violation of the law was a capital crime. Almost all Chinese immigrants to the United States in the nineteenth century planned eventually to return to China (because of their ties to their motherland and their poor reception in the United States), so American laws that involved the immigrants' physical appearance had potentially far-reaching effects. Since San Francisco was the chief port through which Chinese entered the United States (with its Chinatown being the largest in the United States), ordinances passed in that city often had a significant effect on Chinese immigration.

Although they were not exactly clear as to why, anti-Chinese forces in San Francisco noticed that Chinese men were very protective of their queues. In an attempt to drive the Chinese out of San Francisco (and even out of the United States), in 1873 the Board of Supervisors passed an ordinance requiring the sheriff to cut the queue of all Chinese prisoners. The mayor vetoed this ordinance as cruel and unusual punishment and also as contrary to treaty provisions with China concerning the treatment to be accorded to Chinese in the United States.

In 1876, however, the board passed a similar ordinance and the mayor (a different man) signed it into law. This is the actual Queue Ordinance. The ordinance nowhere said that it was directed against the Chinese, but contemporary statements show that that was its specific aim. This intent was recognized when the matter was challenged in the federal courts by a Chinese immigrant, Ho Ah-Kow. In this famous 1879 case (*Ho Ah-Kow v. Nunan*), Justice Stephen Field found that since the rule's intent was to operate only against Chinese, it violated the Fourteenth Amendment and was therefore unconstitutional.

The Queue Ordinance should also be viewed in light of other ordinances then in effect in San Francisco. These laws put almost all Chinese in danger of spending time in jail (and so being subject to the Queue Ordinance) for living in crowded conditions, for carrying laundry in a certain fashion, for attending theatrical performances after midnight, and so forth. After the ordinance was overturned in the courts, however, San Francisco supervisors did not try to pass any further legislation related to how Chinese wore their hair.

Quezon [y Molina], Manuel [Luis] (Aug. 19, 1878, Baler, Philippines—Aug. 1, 1944, Saranac Lake, N.Y.): First president of the Philippine Commonwealth and leader of the push for independence. Quezon was the son of a schoolteacher and small landholder on the island of Luzon. In 1899, while studying law at the University of Santo Tomas in Manila, he chose to join the Philippine independence movement against the United States, spearheaded by freedom fighter Emilio Aguinaldo. Upon the latter's surrender in 1901, Quezon returned to the university, received his law degree, opened his practice, and won election to political office.

Quezon moved to Washington, D.C., in 1909 to serve as resident commissioner for the Philippines. While in office he continued to press the issue of independence. He left his post in 1916 following congressional passage of the Jones Act, which promised independence but declined to enumerate specific details. Returning to the Philippines, Quezon won a seat in the senate, eventually becoming senate president.

In 1934 Quezon again traveled to the United States to persuade lawmakers to repeal the HARE-HAWES-CUTTING ACT OF 1933, which had been rejected by Philippine legislators because it preserved the right of the U.S. government to maintain military bases in the islands. In its place U.S. lawmakers introduced another bill, the TYDINGS-MCDUFFIE ACT OF 1934, that guaranteed Philippine independence on July 4, 1946, and authorized the presence of American naval bases only as permitted by the Philippines.

The new act also approved the creation of a Philippine Commonwealth government to serve as the predecessor of an independent republic. Quezon was elected commonwealth president in 1935. In his new post he labored to strengthen the nation's military capability, sought to improve the conditions of landless tenant laborers, and battled graft and corruption in government. To honor him, newly built Quezon City became the national capital.

Quezon fled to the United States following the full invasion of the Philippines by Japan in 1942, during World War II. He died of tuberculosis. His autobiography, *The Good Fight*, was published posthumously, in 1946.

Quezon City: Second-largest city of the Philippines and the country's former capital (1948-1976). The city's 1990 population of almost 1.6 million people is exceeded only by that of Manila, the capital, with almost 1.9 million. Quezon City, a northeast suburb of Manila, is named after Manuel Quezon, the first president of the Philippine Commonwealth.

R

Racial formula: Term associated with antimiscegenation movements of the late eighteenth and early nineteenth centuries to determine mathematically an individual's racial makeup.

Radio Korea (KBLA): Korean-language radio station, 1580 AM, founded in Los Angeles in 1989. The number-one station in Los Angeles' KOREATOWN, an influential and sometimes controversial voice in the Korean American community, Radio Korea offers round-the-clock talk and music programming.

Rafu Shimpo: Japanese-language daily newspaper founded in Los Angeles, California, in April of 1903. At its inception, the paper struggled to establish a niche in a market dominated by San Francisco-based papers such as the *Nichibei Shimbun* and *Shin Sekai*, both of which had expanded to provide coverage of stories in Los Angeles by opening up branch offices in the south. By 1910, Los Angeles had the second-largest Japanese population in the United States, after San Francisco; in addition to attracting new immigrants, the city attracted many refugees who headed south in the wake of the devastating San Francisco earthquake of 1906. *Rafu Shimpo* took an active role in local affairs, and nearly folded after it was boycotted for its stand concerning the expansion of the Ninth Street Produce Market. After the paper was placed under new management in 1914, Henry Toyosaku Komai took over as manager; his family continued to be affiliated with the paper into the 1980's. The paper began to include an English-language section as a weekly feature in 1926 and later expanded the section as a daily feature in 1932. A number of talented editors helped keep the paper abreast of the times until 1942, when the paper was shut down as a result of the forced removal of Japanese Americans from Los Angeles and the entire West Coast.

In 1946, the paper resumed publication and grew in circulation from a postwar low of 500 to some 22,000 by 1990, making it the oldest and largest of the three Japanese-language dailies serving Los Angeles. Redevelopment of Little Tokyo during the 1950's and the 1970's prompted the paper to relocate its headquarters twice. Nevertheless, it retained its roots in the community, where it helped local Japanese Americans advertise their businesses and stay informed about local news and news in Japan. During the 1980's and 1990's, the paper enjoyed greater circulation as a result of the influx of Japanese employees who were temporarily relocated in Los Angeles to work for the American subsidiaries of Japanese multinational corporations.

Rai, Lala Lajpat (Sher-i-Punjab; 1865, Ludhiana, India—Nov. 17, 1928, Lahore, Pakistan): Martyr. Rai was a prominent freedom fighter during India's independence movement. He spent three years in New York, where in 1915 he founded *YOUNG INDIA*, a journal billed as an insider's view of the movement. He published the journal until 1919, when nationalist leader Mahatma GANDHI assumed the role of editor and publisher. Rai died from injuries received while participating in a freedom march in Lahore.

Raj: Term often used in reference to the British rule in India. The word itself is derived from the SANSKRIT *raja* (king). The English first came to India shortly after 1600 as traders with the BRITISH EAST INDIA COMPANY. Their first settlements were "factories" or warehouses located in some of India's coastal cities. As the Mughal Empire began to disintegrate, however, the English sought to strengthen their position in India to counter the designs of their European rival, France, by actively intervening in India's domestic political battles. The Battle of Plassey (1757), for the throne of Bengal, won by Robert Clive, who was supported by the British East India Company, marked a decisive phase in England's control of all India. Through conquest and political intimidation of local rulers, a trading company eventually became an empire builder.

After a century of territorial expansion, during which one Indian ruler after another lost out to England's superior force and organization, the local rulers, both Hindu and Muslim, finally made a last-ditch stand in 1857 in the famous Sepoy Mutiny. Marked by bloodshed on both sides, the British succeeded in suppressing the rebellion and decided to bring India directly under the control of the government in London. The Government of India Act of August 2, 1858, as enacted by the British Parliament, transferred the company's rights to the British crown. Queen Victoria was

British officer attends social function in India during the era after the dissolution of the British Raj in 1947. (Library of Congress)

crowned as the "Queen of India," and one of the secretaries in the British cabinet became responsible for the British administration in India.

Over a period spanning almost two centuries, English rule over India unified the country politically and transformed the Indian economy into a global one. The British also introduced modern railroads, telegraphs, and telephones. Reluctantly, starting in the early twentieth century, they also began introducing some representative institutions. Through English education, the Indians also came into contact with Western liberal ideas.

Despite the benefits of modern technological civilization, the English rule in India, "the brightest jewel" in the English crown, remained an alien administration. England took India into World Wars I and II without the consent of the natives, so the vast Indian army could fight England's wars for the security and interests of England.

Inevitably, a nationalist movement sought freedom from the British Raj. Initially led by a group of moderates through the Indian National Congress founded in 1885, the movement was gradually radicalized as it became clear that the British had no intention of leaving India. After World War I (1914-1918), the movement was led by Mahatma GANDHI through his mass campaigns based on nonviolent civil disobedience.

After World War II (1939-1945), the British found that they could no longer sustain their rule. The last British viceroy, Lord Louis Mountbatten, presided over the dissolution of the Raj in 1947, when British India was partitioned in the two independent countries of India and Pakistan.

Ram, Kanshi (Pandit Kanshi Ram; Maruli Kalan, Ambala district, Punjab Province, India—Punjab Province): Businessperson, activist, and community leader. He was one of the founding officers of the Ghadr Party. Arriving in the United States during the first decade of the twentieth century, Ram became a storekeeper in Seattle, Washington. He later moved to Portland, Oregon, where he was a successful labor contractor. He contributed to organizations such as the Indian Independence League, the Hindustani Association of the Pacific Coast, and the Ghadr Party. He returned to India in 1914 to participate in the Ghadr-inspired uprising against the British. (See GHADR MOVEMENT.)

Ram joined his fellow Asian Indians in a series of meetings held in California, Oregon, Washington, and British Columbia during 1912-1913 to discuss incidents of discrimination and problems with increasingly stringent immigration laws. In 1912, Ram helped form the Hindustani Association of the Pacific Coast, which opened an office in Portland, Oregon. In 1913, the association was transformed into the Ghadr Party, and its headquarters were moved to San Francisco. Ram, who had been elected treasurer of the association, held the same office in the new organization.

In 1914, Ram returned to India along with other members of the Ghadr Party to launch a revolution against the British colonial government. He reached Punjab Province by November, 1914, and assisted in planning a revolt of Indian troops against their British officers. On November 27, Ram was arrested following a police encounter near Ferozeshah, Punjab. One police officer and two revolutionaries were killed in the incident.

Ram and his associates were tried in a local Sessions Court (district court) and were convicted on sedition charges. The judge sentenced him and eight other revolutionaries to death by hanging.

Ramabai Sarasvati, Pandita (1858—1922): Social worker. An Asian Indian woman who labored to improve conditions for women, she founded the Arya Mahila Samaj, an organization to assist young widows, in the early 1900's. At Cheltenham College in England she was a professor of Sanskrit and Marathi from 1884 to 1886.

Ramadan: Month of fasting (*sawm*) in Islam. It is observed by the growing Muslim community in North America, where many Islamic mosques and centers have been established. Muslims residing in the United States and Canada, including those from Asian coun-

Evening prayers are an important part of Ramadan, the Islamic month of fasting. (Frances M. Roberts)

tries such as Indonesia, whose population is approximately 87 percent Muslim, gather in the mosques during Ramadan to break their fast and worship collectively. Ramadan is the ninth month of the Muslim year and lasts either twenty-nine or thirty days.

As one of the Five Pillars of ISLAM, the fast of Ramadan has a special significance in Muslim religious life. All Muslims who have attained puberty and who are in full possession of their senses are required to fast. Pregnant or nursing women, however, and persons who are sick or traveling, are exempted from fasting during this month. Eating, drinking, smoking, and having sexual intercourse is prohibited from dawn until dusk for those who are fasting. Generally, those who fast take a meal before dawn and break their fast right after sunset.

Muslim theologians emphasize that the main purpose of fasting during the month of Ramadan is to cultivate spiritual and ethical values among Muslims. Ramadan is also considered auspicious because this is the month during which the Quran, the Islamic scripture, first came down upon Muhammad, the founder of Islam. Ramadan, therefore, is a month of worship and charity. Muslims are urged to perform in the evening special prayers called *tarawih*. These consist of twenty prayer sequences (*rakahs*), which are generally performed in congregation.

The *laylat al-qadr* (night of power), during which the first revelation of the Quran took place, is one of the last odd-numbered nights, generally the twenty-seventh, of Ramadan. In its honor, many devout Muslims spend the better part of these nights praying and reciting the Quran. The end of Ramadan, signaled by the sighting of the new moon, is celebrated in the festival of Idul-Fitr, which marks the end of fasting.

Ramakrishna (Gadadhar Chatterji, Gadadhar Chattopadhyaya; Feb. 18, 1836, Hooghly, Bengal, India—Aug. 16, 1886, Calcutta, India): Hindu ascetic and mystic. Ramakrishna formulated a philosophical ethos built upon the idea of the "oneness" of all world religions, all of which, he taught, led ultimately to the same goal: the realization of God. His ideas were embraced by thousands; as a Hindu saint, he is considered an avatar of the god Siva.

Born into a poor Brahmin family, Ramakrishna received little formal education. At age twenty-three he was married to a five-year-old girl; his vow of celibacy, however, prevented the marriage from ever being consummated. He thus began a lifelong devotion to the realization of God through a life of austerity and of service to humanity, particularly the poor and the suffering. To this end, he sought to avoid the evils posed by sexual passion and money, which he believed blocked the path to true spirituality. He also rigidly opposed the CASTE system and instead sought to identify with all humankind.

Ramakrishna's study of various major world religions such as Christianity and Islam persuaded him of their essential unity. Seeing God in everyone and everything, he taught that all paths to spiritual enlightenment lead ultimately to God. His ideas became enormously popular worldwide, and he found himself in great demand as a teacher and speaker. His disciple and personally appointed successor, Swami VIVEKANANDA, became the foremost disseminator of his work across the globe. Vivekananda founded the Ramakrishna Mission in Calcutta in 1897 to spread these teachings and to upgrade social conditions in India. The Ramakrishna *math* (monastery) was established along the Ganges River near Calcutta in 1898. Also incorporated that year was the Vedanta Society of the City of New York, the oldest branch of the mission in the United States.

Ramnavami: Asian Indian festival celebrating the birth of Rama. This festival, one of the five major religious festivals of India, occurs in the month of *Chaitra* (mid-March to mid-April), on the ninth day of the ascending moon. Rama is one of the ten incarnations of Lord Visnu and is an extremely popular Hindu deity. His temples are found in every Indian state as well as throughout Asia, Africa, and Western countries such as England, France, and the United States, where large communities of Indians live.

The festival, which is celebrated with fervor throughout India as well as by Indian communities outside the country, can last up to nine days. (The San Francisco Bay Area, for example, has several temples where the festival is celebrated by Indians as well as non-Indian Hindus). During the festival, devotees fast and bathe in the holy rivers, especially the Narmada and Sarayu, close to which Rama lived. They visit Rama temples and offer gifts of food, clothing, and money to Brahmins (members of the priest caste), sannyasis (monks), and the poor. Religious songs celebrating the life of Rama are sung, sometimes all night, along with the Rama Charit Manas, composed by the legendary blind singer, Tulsidas. The epic *Ramayana*, the story of the life of Rama, purportedly composed by the divinely inspired sage Valmiki, is recited and many motion-picture theaters show *Ramayana* films, which are extremely popular at this time of year.

Rama was a prince of the celebrated Ikshwaku race, whose members were considered direct descendants of the sun. He was born in the city of Ayodhya in northern India (modern Uttar Pradesh). The son of King Dasaratha and Queen Kausalya, he gave up his kingdom to his younger brother Bharat to fulfill a promise made by his father. He then traveled through India for fourteen years, ridding the land of demons, especially the ten-headed Ravana, demon-king of Lanka (modern Sri Lanka), who abducted his wife Sita. He returned to rule Ayodhya and establish a reign of perfect justice and mercy. Rama is revered as the ideal son, husband, and king.

Rangaku: Study of Western medical sciences by reading Dutch medical texts, a practice common during the TOKUGAWA ERA (1600-1867).

Reciprocity Treaty (1875): Pact between the United States and the Kingdom of Hawaii providing for duty-free exportation from one country into the other and vice versa. Under the seven-year agreement, Hawaii was given free trade on such major goods as sugar, rice, fruits, and vegetables, while the United States was allowed the same on such goods as iron, steel, wool, and textiles.

The treaty did not actually become operable until September, 1876. Once it did, however, it immediately began to resuscitate the floundering Hawaiian economy. Sugar production, for example, experienced a sevenfold rise between 1875 and 1883. This in turn triggered a great need for more plantation laborers, the importation of which introduced significant changes. By about 1900, the population of Hawaii had almost tripled. Asians and Caucasians far outnumbered Native Hawaiians. The majority of Asians were Japanese.

Red Guard party: Radical political group founded in San Francisco's Chinatown in 1969. The group took its name from the Red Guards, the students used by MAO ZEDONG as shock troops in the Cultural Revolution (1966-1976). Like other radical factions of the ASIAN AMERICAN MOVEMENT, the Red Guards were also inspired in part by the Black Panthers, the African American revolutionary party then at the peak of its influence. The Red Guards organized community aid programs, including free distribution of food to senior citizens in PORTSMOUTH SQUARE, and challenged the CHINESE CONSOLIDATED BENEVOLENT ASSOCIATIONS and other elements of the traditional Chi-

natown power structure. In 1971, the Red Guard party merged with another radical Chinese American group, I WOR KUEN.

Red Turbans: Triad, or Chinese secret society, whose members wore red turbans and that staged a massive rebellion in the Canton River Delta area in 1854. Coming into prominence in the eighteenth and nineteenth centuries, Triad societies actively resisted MANCHU rule by violent and other means. They also existed to protect the lives of their members, who, on account of their lowly status in general Chinese society, could not depend on the government for help or personal protection.

Among the many Triad-inspired armed rebellions, that of the Red Turbans was probably the most devastating. Canton opera actors, the majority of whom belonged to Triad societies, provided much of the leadership behind the insurrection. As staunch believers in the Triad anti-Manchu ideology, they were effective recruiters for the cause; those who specialized in military roles served as martial-arts instructors for other Triad members. During the uprising, Li Wenmo, a celebrated military-role specialist, commanded the most potent of the rebel bands.

GUANGDONG in the mid-nineteenth century was seething with unrest. The First Opium War (1839-1842) disrupted the established trade patterns, throwing many Triads out of work. The war also destroyed the myth of the invincibility of the Manchu forces. Triad morale was further buoyed by the spectacular successes of the TAIPING REBELLION (1850-1864). The Red Turban rebellion erupted in June, 1854. In rapid succession, the rebels captured Tungkun, Fatsan, and other walled cities. Then, marshaling an enormous force, the insurgents besieged Canton from many directions but failed to take it. Before long, the tide turned. The rebels were defeated not by government troops but by militia armies raised from among the local gentry. The abortive rebellion took a heavy toll in human lives. For example, while pulling out of Fatsan, the rebels set fire to the city, killing an estimated 200,000 people. In Canton alone, 80,000 people implicated in the rebellion were executed. Fleeing the expected vengeance, the defeated rebels emigrated in droves, many found refuge in California, Australia, and the countries of Southeast Asia.

Redress movement: Grass-roots campaign conducted by Japanese Americans during the 1970's and 1980's to force the U.S. government to offer an apology and

During WWII approximately 110,000 Japanese Americans were evacuated to internment camps such as Manzanar, shown here. (National Archives)

compensation for imprisoning them during World War II. The road to attaining redress took several courses. The Japanese American Citizens League (JACL) and the National Coalition for Redress/ Reparations (NCRR) fought for redress through the legislature while the National Council for Japanese American Redress (NCJAR) filed a class-action lawsuit against the government. In the meantime a team of young Japanese American lawyers headed by law historian Peter Irons sought to vacate the wartime convictions of Fred Korematsu, Gordon K. Hirabayashi, and Minoru Yasui, who years earlier had challenged the curfew and exclusion orders that applied to Japanese Americans. The redress movement came to a close when President Ronald Reagan signed the Civil Liberties Act of 1988.

Background. The modern redress movement can be traced back to the 1970 JACL national convention. There, Edison Uno, who is often credited as the "father" of the redress movement, introduced a resolution for the organization to seek compensation and an apology from the U.S. government for interning Japanese Americans in concentration camps. The resolution passed, but the lack of enthusiasm within the organization obstructed any concrete action. Similar resolutions were introduced by Uno at the 1972 and 1974 conventions, but again, the group took no action.

In 1976 the JACL took its first serious action toward redress when it established the National Committee for Redress (NCR) at its biannual convention. The group was charged with researching the issue and adopting legislation to be considered at the next convention in 1978, where it adopted a proposal for $25,000 for each person interned and excluded under the Western Defense Command. The plan was short-lived and was attacked by S. I. Hayakawa, the conservative U.S. senator from California who was of Japanese descent. The NCR retreated from its demands and instead opted for the creation of a government commission to study the matter.

Dillon Myer directed the War Relocation Authority, which organized the internment of Japanese Americans during World War II. (AP/Wide World Photos)

Separate Paths. Not satisfied with the NCR, the NCJAR was formed in Seattle in May of 1979. It consisted of William Hohri of Chicago and members of the JACL. The first action by the NCJAR was to recruit Representative Mike Lowry from Seattle to sponsor redress legislation. Not surprisingly, the proposed legislation was almost a duplicate of the "Seattle Plan" written years earlier. The bill, which received no support from the NIKKEI members of Congress, died in committee. The NCJAR, however, was not discouraged. In 1983 it filed a $24 billion class-action lawsuit against the government that eventually reached the Supreme Court later in the decade.

In the meantime, in July, 1980, the COMMISSION ON WARTIME RELOCATION AND INTERNMENT OF CIVILIANS (CWRIC) was created by an act of Congress. Formed mainly to investigate matters surrounding the camps and to recommend appropriate remedies, the CWRIC had no power to correct grievances and was seen by some as a "cop-out" by the JACL. Still, hearings were set to be conducted in twenty cities across the nation beginning the next year.

One group that was upset with the formation of the CWRIC was the NCRR, which had been organized on July 12, 1980, primarily from the Los Angeles Community Coalition for Redress/Reparations (LACCRR) and other progressive community groups in San Jose, New York, and San Francisco. Like the NCJAR, the NCRR saw no need for a commission to investigate the camps and viewed the formation of the CWRIC with suspicion. Because the JACL had retreated from its demands for monetary compensation, the NCRR, by organizing around the CWRIC hearings, ensured that the Japanese American community's demand for reparations was heard. The NCRR added the necessary grass-roots angle in what was to become a long struggle for redress.

In 1981, while the CWRIC conducted its hearings, another important wing of the redress movement began. While Irons was conducting research on the wartime convictions of Korematsu, Hirabayashi, and Yasui for a book he was writing, he came across evidence that the government purposely suppressed evidence in presenting its cases against the three resisters.

(Left to right) George Togasaki, Saburo Kido, Dr. T. T. Yatabe, and George Inagaki—four JACL pioneers who contributed to the redress movement. (Pacific Citizen)

After his discovery he and a group of SANSEI lawyers worked to get the convictions overturned and in the process proved that there had been a government conspiracy to convict the three defendants in order to legitimize the exclusion of Japanese Americans. The research uncovered in the next round of court cases was instrumental to the advancement of the redress movement.

The commission hearings were the turning point of the redress movement. In 1983 the CWRIC issued its report, *Personal Justice Denied*, which documented the testimonies heard at the hearings and presented research conducted by a team led by Aiko Yoshinaga-Herzig. No recommendations were issued at that time, but it was clear that the commission was sympathetic toward the issue of redress. By the middle of the next year the CWRIC had recommended, among other things, $20,000 individual compensation for those interned and a formal apology.

Victory. In September, 1987, the two-hundredth anniversary of the U.S. Constitution, H.R. 442 passed by a margin of 243 to 141. The Senate passed its own version of the bill on April 20, 1988, and sent it to President Ronald Reagan for his signature. At first the president threatened to veto the bill because of so-called fiscal restraints in the federal budget. Several events, however, may have changed his mind in favor of the bill. One was the stunning defeat of fellow conservative Daniel Lungren in an election for California state treasurer. Lungren, who was a leader against the movement for redress, had been nominated for the office by the California governor and was rejected largely because of the vocal protests led by the Japanese American community. Another possible factor was the still-pending NCJAR class-action lawsuit, which if successful could have forced the government to pay up to $24 billion in damages. There were many reasons why the president eventually signed the re-

In 1988 previously interned Japanese Americans were compensated monetarily for their internment. Here Ronald Reagan signs the reparations bill into law. (Ronald Reagan Library)

dress bill; they will be debated by historians for years to come.—*Glen Kitayama*

SUGGESTED READINGS: • Hohri, William Minoru. *Repairing America*. Pullman: Washington State University Press, 1988. • Irons, Peter. *Justice at War*. New York: Oxford University Press, 1983. • Scott, Esther, and Calvin Naito. *Against All Odds: The Japanese Americans' Campaign for Redress*. Cambridge, Mass.: Case Program, Harvard Kennedy School of Government, 1990. • U.S. Commission on Wartime Relocation and Internment of Civilians. *Personal Justice Denied*. Washington, D.C.: Government Printing Office, 1982.

Reform Society: Originally founded in Hawaii in 1903 as the Central Japanese League, a Japanese labor organization. League members believed that they had been victimized by unfair practices perpetuated by the immigration companies responsible for bringing them to Hawaii. Under a law passed in 1894, all Japanese immigrant laborers had to have at least $50 in their possession or a valid employment contract on arrival in the islands. Steamship companies transporting these workers accepted the money from the latter in exchange for a certificate of deposit, which the workers would later redeem for cash at a Hawaii bank. Eventually, however, the laborers were unable to collect their money from the steamship companies because of a restriction imposed by the Japanese government. The league arose specifically to resolve this dispute.

Ultimately unable to help, the league was replaced by the Reform Society in 1905. The latter succeeded in persuading Japanese officials to halt the practice and so was dissolved in 1916.

Reformist Hindu sects: Even though mainstream HINDUISM remained unchanged through the millennia—indeed it is called *sanatana* (perennial)—it sought to respond to periodic challenges by developing reformist sects. Its two most formidable challenges came from ISLAM and Christianity, though it reacted creatively also against its own doctrinal rigidity.

Thus the eleventh century Vaishnavism movement of Ramanuja articulating a modified nondualist position in theology was a reaction against Shankara's absolute monism. In the fifteenth century, Ramanuja's Vaishnavism became an egalitarian movement cutting across traditional Hindu casteism under the influence of Chaitanya, whose eclectic and ecstatic devotionalism was a response to the dominant Turko-Afghan Islamic culture of fifteenth century Bengal. The

Sikhism is an example of a reformist Hindu sect. (Ben Klaffke)

Mughal period (1560-1707) was characterized by the widespread influence of Islam throughout India and a sharp decline of Hindu religion. On the one hand, the Rajputs and Marathas of western India attempted to reassert Hindu devotionalism vis-à-vis the political hegemony of Islam, and reformers such as Ramananda, Kabir, and NANAK assimilated the best aspects of Hindu and Muslim piety on the other. It was only when Nanak's followers encountered escalating persecution of the Mughals that they turned defensive and created the militant religion of SIKHISM.

The consolidation of British power in India and the subsequent rise of orientalism following the founding of the Asiatic Society of Bengal and Fort William College in Calcutta evoked scholarly interest in Indian culture primarily to help the BRITISH EAST INDIA COMPANY administrators to govern effectively. This development, along with the evangelical efforts of the Christian missionaries at Serampore in Bengal, stimulated the so-called Bengal Renaissance, leading, in the 1820's, first to the monotheistic Brahmo Samaj movement of Rammohan Ray in Bengal and the devotional Radha Soami movement in northern India, then to the rationalistic and monotheistic Arya Samaj movement of Dayananda Sarasvati in western and northern India in the 1870's, and finally to the Ramakrishna-Vivekananda Vedantic movement, first in Calcutta and subsequently in the Western world in the 1890's.

In the early decades of the twentieth century, the Hindu reformist movement became politicized, leading to the formation of two political organizations—the Hindu Mahasabha of M. M. Malavy and Jagatguru Shankaracharya in the 1920's, and the Bharatiya Janata Party of Morarji Desai in the 1970's. Hindu reformism hardened into Hindu fundamentalism under the aegis of Shiva Sena of Maharashtra in the 1960's and the Vishwa Hindu Parisad of Uttar Pradesh in the 1980's.

Refugee Act of 1980: U.S. legislation signed by President Jimmy Carter on March 17, 1980. This law was considered a long-term and long-overdue humanitarian response to the needs of refugees around the world. It established systematic admission and assistance procedures for all refugees experiencing or having a "well-founded fear" of persecution because of "race, religion, nationality, membership in a particular social group, or political opinion," provided that the refugees were medically eligible for entry and had not themselves engaged in acts of persecution. Spouses and children of refugees were also allowed entry. This law also eliminated the seventh preference category created by the IMMIGRATION AND NATIONALITY ACT OF 1965, that of conditional entrant (for refugees).

The number of refugees to be admitted into the United States under the 1980 act was set at 50,000 per year through 1982; those figures were later raised considerably, to 230,000 in 1980, 217,000 in 1981, and 140,000 in 1982. For the years after 1982, the president, in consultation with Congress, was authorized to set additional quotas (with overall numbers remaining a point of political contention).

The major changes instituted by this law were the elimination of country, area, and ethnic quotas and the fact that the law could be extended indefinitely. The law also brought the United States into nearly complete accordance with the 1967 protocol addition to the International Refugee Convention of 1951 (although economic refugees were still excluded to some extent).

Under the Refugee Act of 1980 large numbers of Southeast Asians, many of whom were persecuted during the years following the 1975 withdrawal of American military forces from South Vietnam, were admitted into the United States. Even before passage of the 1980 act, refugees from Southeast Asia had begun to enter the United States in significant numbers. Between 1975 and 1990, more than one million Southeast Asian refugees came to the United States.

Various amendments to the Refugee Act of 1980 were passed in the ten years that followed its adoption, generally with the intent to adjust refugee numbers, to expand definitions of eligible refugees, and to improve the care given to new refugee arrivals.

Refugee camps in Southeast Asia: The major refugee camps existing in Southeast Asia are those for the thousands of Indochinese refugees who have fled their Communist-controlled lands since 1975. These camps are widespread, from Hong Kong in the northeast to Indonesia on the southwest, from Thailand on the west to the Philippines on the east. They are of two types: those for first-asylum refugees and those for refugees to be resettled elsewhere.

Refugees in Southeast Asia. In recent decades, refugees have come to exist wherever there has been political turmoil in the region. Conflict in Myanmar (formerly Burma) has led to groups taking refuge in Bangladesh and Thailand. Muslims in the southern Philippines have fled to Sabah in Malaysia. Many of these refugees blended into the countryside, and there was no need for camps as such to house them.

Camps have been needed in the region to accommodate the huge outpouring of people from the countries of Indochina since 1975. That year saw lowland Lao and highlanders such as the HMONG and the Mien cross the Mekong River into Thailand to join similar ethnic groups. The Thai government, however, enclosed them in camps scattered about the northeast. At that time, the Vietnamese refugees went straight to the United States, and few left the Cambodia of the KHMER ROUGE. The year 1978 then saw conflict

President Jimmy Carter signed the Refugee Act of 1980. (White House Historical Association)

Cambodian family with fish ration, Khao-I-Dang refugee camp, 1982. (Eric Crystal)

Viet boat people receive counseling at Pulau Bidong refugee camp in Malaysia, 1988. (A. Hollmann/UNHCR)

among the People's Republic of China, Vietnam, and Cambodia together with a Vietnamese attempt at urban economic reform. Chinese within Vietnam came under pressure politically and economically and began to take boats across the South China Sea. Vietnam subsequently attacked Cambodia, and thousands of the KHMER took refuge along the Thai border. Eventually Vietnamese followed the Chinese out of Vietnam and onto the seas.

Since 1978, the tide of refugees, particularly the "BOAT PEOPLE," has ebbed and flowed from Indochina onto neighboring shores. More than a million have sought asylum, and the countries of first destination have had to provide places for them. These are the refugee camps of Southeast Asia.

First-Asylum Camps. In earlier centuries, Southeast Asian countries had taken in foreign populations for their labor value. More recently, however, the nations adjacent to Indochina have found themselves in no position to absorb the refugees, particularly as the numbers grew. The response of these nations has been to put the new arrivals immediately into camps, preferably isolated ones, until the fate of the refugees can be determined. Since very few are allowed to stay, the

choice has been either to resettle them elsewhere or to repatriate them.

The first-asylum camps, particularly at the beginning, tended to be makeshift affairs. As the BOAT PEOPLE crossed the South China Sea and the Gulf of Siam, many reached the Malaysian coast. Here, off Trengganu, the deserted volcanic island of Pulau Bidong became a camp that would hold as many as 54,000. Only a kilometer square, its steep hillsides were at one time crammed with rickety shacks and initially possessed no sanitation system. Basically left alone, with minimal supplies, the Vietnamese and Chinese organized themselves and kept the camp going. They built a hospital and organized schools. A marketplace system of free enterprise existed. Five other first-asylum camps also existed in Malaysia, the larger ones being in Pahang (Cherating), Johore (Pualu Tengah), and Kelantan (Kota Bharu) in west Malaysia. Two smaller camps were in east Malaysia, one in Sarawak (Kuching) and the other in Sabah (Labuan).

Further south, in northeast Indonesia, refugee boats scattered along the island coasts were gathered into two main camps on Jamaja in the Anambas Islands (Air Raya and Kuku). Others were held on Bintan and

Galang islands in the Riau Archipelago. Then, in late 1980, Galang became the major camp and the refugees were shifted there. The first-asylum camp was run by the UNITED NATIONS HIGH COMMISSIONER FOR REFUGEES (UNHCR), which began to provide language and cultural orientation. Indonesian organizations began to play a positive role in the camps. The Philippines, with far fewer refugees, put the latter initially on Lubang Island and then moved them to Tara Island on northeast Palawan. This island, like Pulau Bidong, was deserted, bleak, and isolated. Here too the refugees at first had to fend for themselves. Yet improvement came and the camp was expanded. Another camp existed in Manila, it did not differ much from nearby slums.

To the northeast of Vietnam, refugees hit Macao and particularly Hong Kong. Macao had the policy of moving them along as much as possible. It did, however, have three camps run locally with little to occupy the refugees. Hong Kong at first ran a very different operation. Until July, 1982, camps such as Sham Shui Po were open, and the refugees could work in and mingle with the local community. Nevertheless, the heavily overcrowded conditions led to much friction

and riots within the camps of Kai Tak and Kaitak North in Kowloon. From 1982 new arrivals entered closed camps located on outlying islands and under armed guard, camps such as Chi Ma Wan, Hei Ling Chan, and Tuen Mum. There the refugees generally live in large warehouse-like structures, divided into tiny living spaces marked only by straw mats. Tedium is prevalent. Almost eight years would go by before they were all opened (May, 1990). At the beginning of 1990, there were fourteen detention centers, two open centers, and four liberalized closed centers scattered on outlying islands, in the New Territories, in Kowloon, and on Hong Kong Island itself. They held 56,000 refugees.

In Thailand, the question has been one not of space but of sheer numbers. As late as 1988, there were still about 100,000—Khmer, Lao, Hmong, Vietnamese—remaining refugees. The UNHCR stepped in to help run the camps (more than thirty in 1981), aided by voluntary agencies. The Hmong and Lao had five camps (Chiang Kong, Nong Khai, Ban Nam Yao, Ban Vinai, and Sob Tuang) in the northeast. Life was easier for the Lao, who were related to the northeast Thai, than for the minority Hmong. The huge Khmer camps

These Vietnamese refugees participated in the Orderly Departure Program. Suan Phlu, Bangkok. (A. Hollmann/UNHCR)

further south tended to be stark and raw by comparison. These camps included Nong Chan, Sa Kaeo, Khao I Dang, and a variety of others with names such as Camp 511. In the south, on the Malay Peninsula, were two camps, Song Khla and Laem Sing, for the Vietnamese boat people. By 1987 six UNHCR camps remained—Ban Na Pho (Lao), Ban Nam Yao (Hmong), Ban Vinai (Hmong), and Chieng Kham (Lao and Hmong) in the northeast, and Kab Cherng and Khao I Dang (both Khmer) to the east. In addition, the United States Border Relief Operation helped run thirteen camps along the Thai-Cambodian border. Technically, these camps were for the quarter million "displaced persons" (who could be repatriated) rather than refugees per se, mainly Khmer but with a few Vietnamese.

Refugee Processing Centers. These camps are for those refugees accepted for resettlement abroad. Where the emphasis in the first-asylum camps is on physical survival, with much autonomy generally allowed the refugees, these processing centers are structured to prepare the refugees to live in their new lands. The camps are thus more organized, disciplined, and purposeful.

The major centers are Galang Island in Indonesia and Bataan on Luzon in the Philippines, both with direct links to the United States' refugee program. The Galang center is more comfortable than its associate first-asylum camp and draws refugees from Singapore and Malaysia as well. Bataan, by contrast, is the major processing center for those refugees going to the United States from Hong Kong, Thailand, and Malaysia as well as from Vietnam itself via the United States' ORDERLY DEPARTURE PROGRAM. On Bataan they follow a tight schedule of four to six months of language instruction and orientation. When Bataan was established, another processing center, near Puerto Princesa on northwest Palawan, was phased out.

The other countries providing refuge have their own processing centers, sending refugees to the above camps or directly to other third countries. In Malaysia, four camps existed around the capital of Kuala Lumpur (the Convent, the Friary, Belfield, and Sungai Besi). Singapore had, first, St. John's Island, then Hawkin's Road Refugee Camps for those picked up by passing ships and guaranteed resettlement. In Hong Kong, there were Sham Shui Po, Jubilee, the Red Cross Centre, and more recently Kai Tak, as well as one for those rescued at sea. Thailand has three centers for handling resettlement through which the refugees move in succession: first the processing center, then the transit center of Thanat Nikhom, and finally Bangkok.

The one lasting impression of these refugee camps is the overwhelming lassitude. Months and years have passed in these camps, giving rise to chronic boredom and uncertainty as to the future.—*John K. Whitmore*

SUGGESTED READINGS: • Bui, Diana D. *Hong Kong: The Other Story*. Washington, D.C.: Indochina Resource Action Center, 1990. • Chantavanich, Supang, and E. Bruce Reynolds, eds. *Indochinese Refugees: Asylum and Resettlement*. Bangkok: Institute of Asian Studies, Chulalongkorn University, 1988. • Davis, Leonard. *Hong Kong and the Asylum-Seekers from Vietnam*. Basingstoke: Macmillan, 1991. • Rogge, John R., ed. *Refugees: A Third World Dilemma*. Totowa, N.J.: Rowman & Littlefield, 1987. • St. Cartmail, Robert Keith. *Exodus Indochina*. Auckland: Heinemann, 1983.

Refugee Relief Act of 1953: U.S. legislation signed by President Dwight D. Eisenhower on August 7, 1953, largely to replace the recently expired DISPLACED PERSONS ACT OF 1948. The Refugee Relief Act of 1953 expired on December 31, 1956.

This law permitted the granting of up to 205,000 special immigrant visas (in addition to quotas imposed under general immigration statutes) to essentially two types of refugees: those in noncommunist countries or rendered homeless and in need of assistance, and those who had escaped from communist countries and, because of actual or anticipated government persecution for race, religion, or political opinion, were unable to return to their home countries. The law also permitted entry of refugees' spouses and children.

Refugee visas were to be apportioned among specific countries or areas, including 3,000 to Eastern Asia (the Far East), 2,000 to Palestinian refugees of Southwestern Asia (the Near East), and 2,000 to the Chinese Nationalist government (Taiwan).

In addition to the foregoing 205,000 visa totals, two other immigration categories were created under this law, for a total limit of 214,000 new immigrants. One category allowed for a change to permanent resident status for up to 5,000 nonimmigrants who had legally entered the United States before July 1, 1953. Another category allowed for the adoption, by married American citizens, of up to 4,000 orphaned or abandoned children under the age of ten (orphans of all countries considered).

Every immigrant of working age was required to have employment and housing assured by U.S. citizens, with the additional condition that neither employment nor housing would be taken from anyone

President Dwight Eisenhower signed the Refugee Relief Act in 1953. (White House Historical Association)

already living in the United States.

Initial overseas administrative problems and problems finding enough U.S. citizens willing to assure employment and housing were eventually surmounted, with the total number of refugees ultimately admitted under this act reaching approximately 189,000. This law, with its ethnic inclusivity and reduced emphasis on ideology, was the first American law to address the international refugee situation in a broadly humanitarian manner.

Refugees, Asian nations' responses to: Political turmoil throughout Asia has led to thousands of refugees. The countries of first asylum for these refugees have had to decide how to handle them—turn them back, let them live locally, or process them for resettlement elsewhere. India took in Tibetans in the 1950's and Tamils from Sri Lanka in the 1980's, while Muslims from Burma and Cambodians were repatriated by Bangladesh and Thailand respectively. Hong Kong turns back all Chinese. East and Southeast Asian nations have mainly resettled the largest group of refugees, the multiethnic Indochinese, in Western countries.

Asian Refugees. Since the 1940's, decolonization,

Communist revolution, and local troubles have caused Asians to seek refuge in neighboring countries. Southeast Asia has been the scene of the most recent large refugee movements. In the 1970's, Muslims in Burma and the Philippines sought refuge, in Bangladesh and Sabah (Malaysia), respectively. Bangladesh repatriated its refugees back to Burma, while Sabah absorbed its refugees for political and economic reasons (more Muslims and the need for labor).

During those same years, the Indochina scene exploded, sending hundreds of thousands of refugees—Chinese, Vietnamese, Lao, KHMER, Hmong, and so forth—into neighboring countries. Initially, the fall of Phnom Penh, Saigon, and eventually Vientiane to the Communists during 1975 led to 130,000 Vietnamese coming to the United States via the Philippines and Guam and many HMONG and Lao crossing the Mekong River into northeast Thailand. Few were leaving the Cambodia of the KHMER ROUGE. Yet only from 1978 on did the flow of refugees put pressure on the adjacent states. Vietnamese conflict with China and Cambodia together with internal economic reforms led resident Chinese to take to the seas, followed by anti-regime Vietnamese. These were the "BOAT PEOPLE," whose craft crossed the South China Sea and the Gulf of Siam, washing up on the East and Southeast Asian shores. Then the Vietnamese attack on POL POT led to hundreds of thousands of Cambodians taking refuge in eastern Thailand. Within a decade, more than a million Indochinese left their homelands.

The Indochinese in East Asia. The countries of East Asia received refugees mainly from northern Vietnam. In 1978, 100,000 Chinese crossed the border from Vietnam into Quangxi in China and were resettled there. Ultimately, another 200,000 went to other provinces in China. Yet many of the overseas Chinese were not interested in such resettlement, and China, perhaps reflecting the ambivalence of earlier regimes toward overseas Chinese, seemed uninterested in receiving them. The movement of refugees out of the north, at first Chinese, then increasingly Vietnamese, came by small boat along the Chinese coast. In addition, some larger ships arrived from Saigon. Macao did not want to take them in, showing a "determined hostility," and encouraged the refugees to keep moving on toward Hong Kong.

Hong Kong became the major focus for this northern route. The first boatload of 3,700 refugees had arrived in May, 1975. Now many thousands more were coming. The problem was room. The British colonial enclave is much too small to accommodate many more

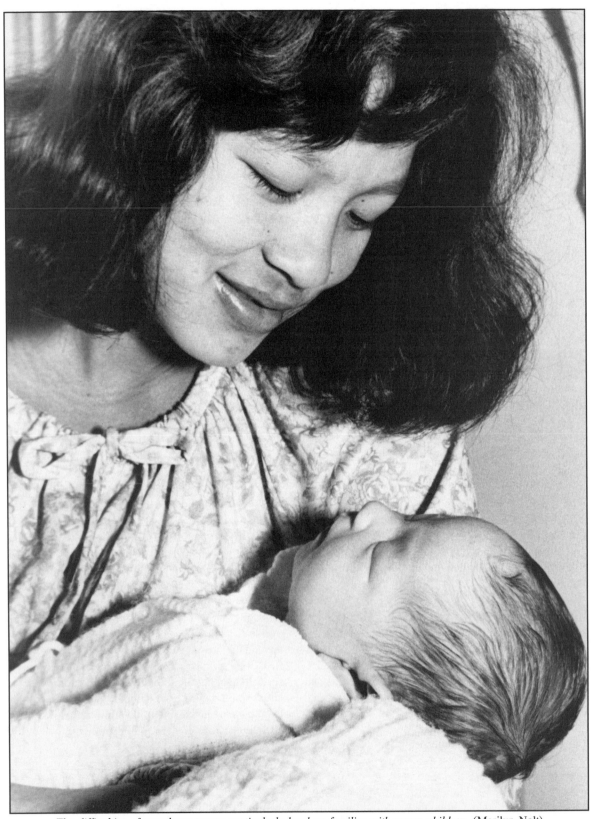

The difficulties of resettlement were particularly hard on families with young children. (Marilyn Nolt)

people. All seeking refuge from China were immediately returned. Those from Vietnam were, however, taken in. Until July, 1982, these refugees, both Chinese and Vietnamese, were encouraged to seek work and mingle in the community while awaiting resettlement. Then, for the next eight years, to May, 1990, the arriving refugees, mainly Vietnamese, were placed in closed and guarded camps located on islands away from the community. This was meant to deter further refugees. Finally, in June, 1988, the British began a policy of actively attempting to persuade refugees in the camps to return home. From then until mid-1993, this policy has gone forward in fits and starts, depending on international reaction. It is meant to both clear the camps and further discourage future arrivals.

The final East Asian country involved is Japan. It has received few refugees and is inclined to resettle even less. It has preferred to contribute money to help operations elsewhere than to become directly involved in the resettlement process itself.

The Indochinese in Southeast Asia. The southern and western movement of refugees has been larger and more diverse, particularly for Thailand. Whereas before the twentieth century such people were desired for labor and absorbed into local society, now there was no question of the wish to keep them in the periphery until they could either go elsewhere or return to Indochina. None of the Southeast Asian countries was a signatory of the 1951 Geneva Convention and Protocol Concerning the Status of Refugees. They thus have the option of receiving, rejecting, or returning any who seek refuge in their territory. Such refuge depends on the pleasure of the receiving country.

For Thailand, this has meant providing first asylum, while actively discouraging local resettlement. Indeed, with the rush of Cambodians following the Vietnamese invasion, the Thai government denied them refugee status, claiming them to be "displaced persons" who would eventually return home. In certain instances, Cambodians were forced back across the border. Only the United States' intervention (negotiations and resettling Hmong, Lao, and eventually Cambodians) calmed the situation.

Malaysia too showed a distinct lack of interest in receiving and resettling the refugees who came to its shores. In this case, the fact that initially many were Chinese aggravated the sheer problem of numbers. Refugee boats were towed back to sea, and the refugees themselves were segregated from the local population (as on Pulau Bidong). Only with international involvement were they taken into camps on the Malay

Many Asian nations rejected Southeast Asian refugees. Here a successfully resettled Laotian refugee woman leads a productive life in New York City. (H. Gloaguen/UNHCR)

Peninsula. Singapore too followed such a policy, despite being heavily Chinese.

Indonesia was also sensitive to the Chinese issue but was under much less pressure because of both its large size and the fact that the refugee contacts were distant from the population. These contacts occurred on islands slightly south of Singapore, as Indonesia received boats rejected by Thailand and Malyaysia. In mid-1979 the Indonesian government announced that it would join Malaysia in blocking the refugee boats. American intervention then led to the establishment of a Regional Processing Center on the island of Galang as a transit camp for the refugees. From its opening in late 1980, the handling of the refugees by the Indonesians has aimed at resettlement elsewhere, mainly the United States. The other major center was established by the American and Philippine governments at Bataan on Luzon. This transit camp was to serve both the first-asylum refugees arriving in the Philippines and those coming from other first asylum countries of the region. It was meant mainly for those accepted by the United States.

The responses of the countries of East and Southeast Asia to the flood of Indochinese refugees were almost entirely to keep the refugees moving—either on to new lives in Western countries or back to their old lives in their countries of origin.—*John K. Whitmore*

SUGGESTED READINGS: • Chantavanich, Supang, and E. Bruce Reynolds, eds. *Indochinese Refugees: Asylum and Resettlement.* Bangkok: Institute of Asian Studies, Chulalongkorn University, 1988. • Grant, Bruce. *The Boat People: An "AGE" Investigation.* Harmondsworth, Middlesex, England: Penguin Books, 1979. • Hawthorne, Lesleyanne, ed. *Refugee: The Vietnamese Experience.* New York: Oxford University Press, 1982. • Rogge, John R., ed. *Refugees: A Third World Dilemma.* Totowa, N.J.: Rowman & Littlefield, 1987. • St. Cartmail, Robert Keith. *Exodus Indochina.* Auckland, New Zealand: Heinemann, 1983.

Reinecke, John E. (July 2, 1904, near Devon, Kans.—June 11, 1982, Honolulu, Hawaii), and **Aiko Reinecke** (Aiko Tokimasa; b. Jan. 9, 1907, Kahuku, Territory of Hawaii): Teachers. The two were charged on November 25, 1947, with violating the law that made it illegal for a public school teacher to be a member of the Communist Party. The charge, leveled at them by the superintendent of the public schools of Hawaii, caused their suspension without pay the following month. John had arrived in Hawaii in October, 1926, and had married Aiko, daughter of a Japanese immigrant couple, on March 21, 1932.

The Reineckes' hearing before the six-member Territorial Commission on Public Instruction began in August 1948, eight months after their suspension began, and lasted thirty-three days, the case being front-page news. The commission found the Reineckes "not possessed of the ideals of democracy," discharged them without pay for the period of their suspension, rescinded their 1947-1948 teacher contracts, and revoked John's teaching certificate.

On August 28, 1951, John, who had a Ph.D. degree from Yale University and was a gifted researcher and writer, was among seven persons arrested in Honolulu on the charge of violating the Smith Act (1940), which makes it a criminal offense to advocate the overthrow of any government in the United States by force or violence. (See HAWAII SEVEN.) The seven were found guilty, and the six male defendants were sentenced to five years in prison and fined five thousand dollars. The only female, Eileen Fujimoto, was sentenced to three years and fined two thousand dollars.

On January 20, 1958, the U.S. Ninth Circuit Court of Appeals reversed the Honolulu Federal District Court conviction and acquitted the seven. John and five of the others had served a week in jail; the seventh, Jack HALL, the regional director of the INTERNATIONAL LONGSHOREMEN'S AND WAREHOUSEMEN'S UNION (ILWU) in Hawaii, had been free on bail from the day of conviction.

In October, 1976, the State Board of Education, which had replaced the Territorial Commission on Public Instruction, expressed deep regret at the action of its predecessor against the Reineckes, reversed the decision discharging them, and recommended that they be compensated for lost pay and other damage related to their dismissal. The state legislature followed this decision by awarding them compensation of $250,000.

Reischauer, Edwin O. (Oct. 15, 1910, Tokyo, Japan—Sept. 1, 1990, La Jolla, Calif.): Diplomat, scholar, and author. As an expert on matters pertaining to East Asia, he served as the American ambassador to Japan (1961-1966) during the Kennedy and Johnson administrations.

Reischauer was born to Christian missionary parents and was graduated from the American School in Tokyo in 1927. He received his undergraduate degree from Oberlin College (Ohio) in 1931 and an M.A. degree in history from Harvard University in 1932. As a Traveling Fellow sponsored by the Harvard-Yenching Institute, he spent three years studying in France, China, and Japan, returning to obtain his Ph.D. degree in 1938.

During World War II (1939-1945), Reischauer served in various intelligence positions within the State Department, the War Department, and the U.S. Army. In 1946, he returned to a joint appointment in the Department of Far Eastern Languages and the Department of History at Harvard University, where he remained (primarily as a historian of modern Japan, rising to the status of Distinguished University Professor) until his retirement in 1982.

In an article appearing in *Foreign Affairs* in 1960, Reischauer wrote of the "broken dialogue" between the United States and Japan resulting from conflicts over the implementation of a security treaty. The article was brought to the attention of President John F. Kennedy, who subsequently appointed Reischauer ambassador to Japan with the hope that the breach might be healed. As ambassador, he staffed his embassy with experts, worked closely with Japanese politicians and bureaucrats, and sought to use his influential position to encourage Japanese toward greater self-assurance. While always careful to report American policies, Reischauer also sought to convey accurate impressions

Edwin Reischauer served as American ambassador to Japan during the Kennedy and Johnson administrations. (AP/Wide World Photos)

of Japanese positions to Washington. In the end, his tenure served to reestablish a "fruitful partnership."

In 1938, with George M. McKune, Reischauer devised a system for Korean romanization. While at Harvard University, he authored or coauthored twelve books, including several basic texts, and for nearly fifty years cotaught an extremely well-received course on East Asian civilizations. A coterie of graduate students studied under his direction, eventually spreading Japanese Studies programs throughout the American university system. The Reischauer Institute at Harvard University memorializes his contributions to Japanese scholarship, Japanese American relations, and the establishment of Japanese Studies programs in the United States.

Relocation centers: Official term for the ten U.S. government camps under the administration of the WAR RELOCATION AUTHORITY used to house Japanese American evacuees during World War II. Many Japanese Americans (and others) prefer the term "CONCEN-TRATION CAMPS," contending that "relocation centers" is a euphemism that masks the actual nature of the camps. There is no overwhelming consensus in popular or scholarly usage, though in the 1980's and 1990's the term "CONCENTRATION CAMPS" has appeared with increasing frequency. Some sources refer to the relocation centers as "internment camps," a term which officially designated several camps administered by the Immigration and Naturalization Service (INS) under the U.S. Department of Justice. (See INTERNMENT CAMPS.)

The ten WRA camps were located at GILA RIVER in southern Arizona, GRANADA (also known as Amache) in southeastern Colorado, HEART MOUNTAIN in northwestern Wyoming, JEROME in southeastern Arkansas, MANZANAR in central California, MINIDOKA in southern Idaho, POSTON in western Arizona, ROHWER in southeastern Arkansas (not far from Jerome), TOPAZ in central Utah, and TULE LAKE in northern California. (In addition to entries on individual camps, see JAPANESE AMERICAN INTERNMENT.)

Reluctant Thirty-nine: Thirty-nine people who refused to testify before the House Select Committee to Investigate Un-American Activities during hearings in Hawaii in April, 1950. The committee was in the islands to investigate charges of Communist Party infiltration within the INTERNATIONAL LONGSHOREMEN'S AND WAREHOUSEMEN'S UNION (ILWU), with which the thirty-nine were affiliated. A crippling dockworkers strike the year before had exacerbated hostilities between plantation unionists and owners, who in an effort to supplant public support for the former began calling them Communist sympathizers. A group of sixty-six Hawaii residents, including ILWU leader Jack HALL, were called by the committee. Thirty-nine of them, however, claimed protection under the U.S. Constitution's Fifth Amendment and refused to answer any questions. The committee held them in contempt of Congress, but a federal judge later cleared them of the charge. Some of the thirty-nine later became known as the HAWAII SEVEN, a group of alleged Communist leaders who were prosecuted for violating the Alien Registration Act of 1940 (Smith Act).

Republic Day (Jan. 26): Anniversary of the proclamation of the Republic of INDIA on that day in 1950. It is observed as a national holiday in India and is celebrated by Asian Americans of Indian origin. Festivities on this day occur all over India, with the main celebration taking place in New Delhi, the national capital,

Jawaharlal Nehru served as a prominent member of the Indian Congress when India gained dominion status in the British Commonwealth. (AP/Wide World Photos)

and at India Gate. Military parades, folk dances, and pageantries accompany the celebrations.

After India became independent on August 15, 1947, it had a dominion status until the new constitution was adopted in 1950. As a dominion in the British Commonwealth of Nations, India was subject to the legal and constitutional authority of the Crown. For example, the head of state—Louis Mountbatten, the first governor general of independent India, and his successor Chakravarti Rajagopalachari—was appointed by the British Crown upon the recommendation of the prime minister of India.

The Congress Party which dominated the constituent assembly that wrote the constitution under the chairmanship of B. R. Ambedkar over a period of two-and-a-half years, had committed itself on January 26, 1929, to work toward the establishment of a sovereign republic. Four prominent congress leaders—Jawaharlal NEHRU, Vallabhbhai Jhaverbhai Patel, Mavlana Azad, and Rajendra PRASAD—played the most important role, through their domination of the party and eight committees of the assembly, in framing the constitution. Provisions of the constitution of India

therefore reflect the aspirations of the nationalist movement and commitment of the Congress Party.

The preamble of the constitution, which summarizes the aims and objectives of the constitution, declares India to be a democratic, federal, republican, and secular state. It also states that the people of India will be the source of all authority under the constitution, which means that India will not be subordinate to external authority and that it will be free and independent of the British Crown. India decided, however, under the leadership of Prime Minister Jawaharlal Nehru, to remain a member of the Commonwealth without acknowledging allegiance to the British Crown; this transformed the "British Commonwealth" into the "British Commonwealth of Nations"—a free association of independent states. India's example was followed by other former colonies of Great Britain in Asia and Africa that gained independence in the 1950's and 1960's.

Though the constitution was signed by the president on November 26, 1949, and some of its provisions, especially those related to elections, citizenship, and provisional parliament, became effective immediately, it was formally adopted on January 26, 1950—the twenty-first anniversary of the Congress Party's declaration to establish a sovereign republic.

Restoration Association (Kwangbokhoe): Korean independence organization founded in 1913 that advocated freedom from Japanese colonial rule (1910-1945) by means of military aggression. It was organized by political activist Chae Ki-jung and later strengthened by fellow activist Pak Sang-jin and others.

Revive China Society. *See* **Xingzhonghui**

Rhee, Syngman (Yi Seung-man; Mar. 26, 1875, Pyongsan, Korea—July 19, 1965, Honolulu, Hawaii): First president of South Korea. Elected by the parliament in 1948, Rhee had remained as president during the KOREAN WAR (1950-1953), successfully mobilizing the nation's war efforts. Until his return to the liberated Korea in 1945, he had spent four decades in the United States waging a personal crusade against Japan's colonial rule of Korea.

Political Activism. Born in northern Korea as a distant royal clan member, Rhee was active in politics from the 1890's, establishing a prominent identity in popular independence movements against the disoriented CHOSON court. He was instrumental in organizing the People's Assembly, demanding that the court

Prior to the Korean War, Syngman Rhee spent four decades in the United States crusading against Japan's colonial rule of Korea. (AP/Wide World Photos)

During his tenure as president of South Korea, Syngman Rhee thanks major Dean Hess for the efforts of his fighter air squadron in slowing down the advance of North Korean forces. (AP/Wide World Photos)

resist the undue political influence of China, Japan, and Russia. He was imprisoned for his Independence Association activities and released in 1904, when Japan's systematic takeover of Korea was under way. He left the country for the United States the same year.

Rhee spent the next forty-one years in the United States as a student and later as the self-appointed Korean delegate to Washington, D.C. He earned his doctoral degree in political science from Princeton University and served as the leader of the Korean community in the United States. In 1919 he was elected as president of Korea's provisional government, newly formed in Shanghai, China. Throughout the dark period of the independence struggle, Rhee remained in Washington, convinced that the United States would play a crucial role in the eventual resolution of the Korean question. He returned to Korea in 1945 after the conclusion of World War II.

Rhee's long struggle in Washington was a personal campaign against Japan's colonial rule of Korea. The fact that the Allies decided to grant Korea independence in "due course" seems to suggest that his efforts bore fruit. Yet his effectiveness was questionable, as illustrated by his inability to persuade the United States to accept him as the head of the exiled Korean government. He collected considerable sympathies and friendships but no diplomatic recognition. Yet, as a result, he became a keen observer of American politics.

Leader for a New Nation. Upon returning to Korea Rhee promptly became the leader of the nation's anticommunist political movement. His credentials made him an ideal candidate for a new government that would need extensive American support. Yet he rejected the United Nations (UN) trusteeship, a temporary arrangement that the United States and its war allies had devised to prepare Korea for its new democratic system. Rhee was sure that the country, led by himself, would not benefit from such a humiliating experience. The public generally agreed with him. He became president of South Korea in 1948 following a general election, which had been held only in the territory under the United States' control.

The Rhee government remained beset by numerous postliberation difficulties when North Korea invaded South Korea in June, 1950. Rhee's lightly equipped defense force was no match for the highly mechanized invaders. Within three days the capital was taken by the Communists. Rhee appealed to the United States for military intervention. U.S. Army General Douglas MacArthur hastily assembled the forces to counter the invasion, Rhee promptly surrendered his sovereign right to command the national military in favor of the commander of the UN forces. Rhee remained as president during the entire period of the war, demonstrating his considerable political savvy in mobilizing the nation for the conflict.

Rhee's Political Color. Rhee's tenure was most prominent in terms of three characteristics: a steadfast unification drive that was based on anti-Communist zeal, provocative anti-Japanese policies that were detrimental in mending the past, and excessive authoritarianism that gradually tarnished the image of his government. His early political activism against the Choson court, his long American exile, the nation's nonexistent political tradition, and his advanced age all contributed to Rhee's highly controversial politics.

Rhee objected to the division of the country by the United States and the Soviet Union. Yet he was unwilling to negotiate with the Korean Communists for a unified government. Like his counterpart in the North, KIM IL SUNG, he insisted that unification occur under his leadership. From the beginning he showed neither inclination nor tolerance to political compromise. When the United States, under the auspices of the United Nations, prepared the truce along the current Demilitarized Zone (DMZ) in 1953, he objected vehemently. Only Washington's extensive security and reconstruction promises persuaded him to support the negotiation, although most reluctantly. Throughout his regime northward unification remained the sacred national goal.

Rhee's anti-Japanese sentiment was deep and lasted throughout his life. He not only witnessed imperial Japan's systematic annexation of his country but also experienced imprisonment under the Japanese. He dedicated more than forty years of his life to fighting the Japanese. Even after the new regime was established, Rhee was unwilling to normalize relations with now-defeated Japan. On the contrary he adopted in 1952 the Rhee Line, which extended Korea's territorial waters to sixty miles at the painful expense of Japanese fishermen. The Rhee Line was Rhee's public statement of his unbending anti-Japanese policy.

For a man who long observed the American political landscape, Rhee's authoritarian rule was beyond logical explanation. His followers worshiped him as the George Washington of Korea, but his opponents despised him as a ruthless and manipulative politician. He often let his Liberal Party undertake dubious parliamentary maneuvers only to ensure another term for himself. In his late years he was unable to comprehend the political oppression and economic difficulties that the public endured. Yet the public never questioned his good intention and lifelong dedication to the nation.

Syngman Rhee embarks on his journey back to Korea for the election in which he became president of South Korea in 1948. (AP/Wide World Photos)

Rhee's regime lost popular support throughout the 1950's because of his authoritarian rule and his party's mishandling of the nation's rebuilding programs. In 1960 election fraud committed by the ruling Liberal Party, but without Rhee's personal sanction, sparked nationwide student protests. Rhee stepped down voluntarily from the presidency when he learned that the public had chosen to side with the students. Shortly thereafter, he left the country for Hawaii, the place where he had launched his anti-Japanese campaign in 1904, and died there in 1965.—*Byung I. Jung*

SUGGESTED READINGS: • Allen, Richard C. *Korea's Syngman Rhee: An Unauthorized Portrait*. Rutland, Vt.: Charles E. Tuttle, 1960. • Oliver, Robert T. *Syngman Rhee: The Man Behind the Myth*. New York: Dodd, Mead, 1954. • Oliver, Robert T. *Syngman Rhee and American Involvement in Korea, 1942-1960*. Seoul: Panmun Book Co., 1978. • Sunoo, Harold H. *America's Dilemma in Asia: The Case of South Korea*. Chicago: Nelson-Hall, 1979.

Rizal Day (Dec. 30): Celebrated by Filipinos all around the world to honor José Protasio RIZAL, hero-martyr of the Philippines. It is commemorated on December 30, the date when in 1896 Rizal was executed by the Spanish colonial government in the Philippines for treason.

Celebration of Rizal Day may take many forms. Filipino communities or organizations may plan festivities that include school holidays, fiestas, queen contests, picnics, banquets, pageants, and oratorical contests. In the Philippines, most towns have a statue of Rizal in the town square. On Rizal Day, a parade led by local officials and prominent citizens wends its way from the town's school to the Rizal statue, onto which a wreath is placed. Programs in schools typically include plays reenacting Rizal's life, from the beginnings of his role as an intellectual leader in the fight for Filipino rights from Spain, to his execution in Manila.

In the first half of the twentieth century, for Filipinos in the United States, commemorating Rizal Day and later Philippine Independence Day were two of the most significant community activities. Filipinos on Hawaii sugar plantations got a work holiday on Rizal Day. They held outdoor parties, complete with music, food, speeches, gambling, and fund-raising beauty

The Filipina Society of America and the Filipino United Organization join to celebrate Rizal Day in 1937. (Filipino American National Historical Society)

1929 Rizal Day Queen, San Francisco. (Filipinos: Forgotten Asian Americans by Fred Cordova)

queen contests. Rizal Day remembrances also gave Filipinos in the United States an opportunity to discuss issues about the Philippines. A Rizal Day program from an American city in the 1930's listed events such as an invocation, welcoming and closing remarks, a recitation of Rizal's "Last Farewell," a eulogy of Rizal, and a pageant. The pageant focused on U.S.-Philippines relations. Characters included "Uncle Sam," "Miss Philippines," "Miss Luzon," "a businessman," and "a politician."

Contemporary Rizal Day celebrations in the United States seem to be less elaborate and less well attended by second- and later-generation Filipinos, many of whom know little about the life of Rizal. Nevertheless, for the early Filipino immigrants to the United States, celebration of Rizal Day was often a focal point for the community and the most significant annual event for some of the Filipino organizations. Remembering it helped Filipinos away from home maintain their ethnic identity and cultural traditions.

Rizal y Mercado, Jose Protasio (also, Jose Protasio Rizal y Alonso; June 19, 1861, Calamba, Philippines—Dec. 30, 1896, Manila, Philippines): Writer, physician, and patriot. Rizal was a Philippine national hero whose life and writings helped inspire the country's nationalist reform movement against the Spanish occupation.

Early Years. Rizal was born in the province of Laguna. At the time of his birth, the Philippines was a colony of Spain. Other surrounding countries had also been colonized by European power. Thus, European imperialism was felt in almost all Asian countries.

Rizal was the seventh of the eleven children of Francisco Mercado and Teodora Alonso Realonda. Altogether the family included two sons and nine daughters.

When he was a little boy, Rizal loved to hear the stories told by his mother. What fascinated him most and deeply affected his character was the story of a young moth that "had died a martyr to its illusions." The Rizal family owned the best private library in Calamba, which contained more than a thousand books. When he was only six years old, Rizal began to spend much time in the family library.

Troubled by the cruelties and injustices inflicted by the Spaniards on the people of the Philippines, Rizal was further aroused by news of the martyrdom of fathers Mariano Gomez, Jose Brugos, and Jacinto Zamora in February, 1872. The three priests had been executed by the Spanish after having defended the right of Filipino clergy to occupy the parishes and other church offices of the Philippines. Subsequently, the eleven-year-old Rizal decided to dedicate his life to securing his country's national welfare and avenging the deaths of the three priests and other victims of the Spanish tyranny.

Student Life. Rizal attended the Ateneo de Manila in 1872 and was graduated with highest honors on March 14, 1877. His literary victories were impressive. His poem "A La Juventud Filipino" (to the Filipino youth) won first prize in 1879, and his allegorical drama "El Consejo de los Dioses" (the council of the gods) won first prize in 1880. In 1882 he finished the fifth year of the medical course at the University of Santo Tomás. His brother, Paciano, helped finance Jose's studies in Europe. He obtained his license in medicine in June, 1884, and his license in philosophy and letters in June, 1885. Aside from these courses, Rizal studied painting and sculpture at the Academia de Bellas Artes de San Fenando located in Madrid. In his spare hours, he took lessons in foreign languages (French, German, and

English) under private tutors. He also took lessons in fencing and shooting. To further enrich his mind, he attended operas and concerts; visited art galleries and museums, particularly the world famous Museo del Prado; and read voraciously books on all subjects from engineering and agriculture to arts and magic.

From October, 1885, to January, 1886, Rizal worked as an assistant to Louis de Wecker, the most famous ophthalmologist in Europe. He acquired further knowledge of ophthalmology under the direction of Otto Becker at the Eye Clinic of the University of Heidelberg, in Germany. On his return to the Philippines in August, 1887, he practiced medicine in Calamba. During his spare moments, Rizal devoted time to community welfare. He opened a gymnasium, where he introduced European sports, such as fencing, shooting, gymnastics, and Roman-style wrestling. He also promoted native sports, such as *sipa* (Filipino football using a small rattan ball) and *arnis* (native fencing).

Harriet Beecher Stowe's *Uncle Tom's Cabin* (1852) inspired Rizal to write *Noli me tangere* (*The Social Cancer*, 1912) in 1886. The novel portrayed the miseries and sufferings of the Filipino people under the tyrannical rule of Spain. His aim was to awaken the conscience of the American people. In March, 1891, while in Biarritz, the famous tourist resort at the French Riviera, Rizal finished his second novel, titled *El Filibusterismo* (1891; *The Reign of Greed*, 1912). This book denounced Spanish rule in the Philippines; his later execution by the Spaniards on charges of instigating insurrection would lead to full-scale rebellion.

Years of Exile. Despite the opposition of Governor-General Despujol to his plan to colonize North Borneo, Rizal decided in May, 1892, to return to the Philippines. While in Manila, he founded the *Liga Filipina* (Philippine League) in July, 1892, at the home of Doroteo Ongjunco, a patriotic Filipino-Chinese *mestizo.* The society's motto was "One Like All." In July, 1892, Rizal was arrested by order of Despujol and was jailed at Fort Santiago. Without any trial, he was exiled in Dapitan (1892-1896). Rizal built his own house by the sea in Talisay, near Dapitan. Near his home, he opened a school for young boys and a clinic for his patients. Aside from practicing medicine, Rizal engaged in farming and business. He built a lighting system as well as a water system for the town of Dapitan. Also, he invented a wooden machine that could make about six thousand bricks daily.

Exile. While in Dapitan, Rizal fell in love with a

Jose Rizal's execution for instigating insurrection against the Spanish domination of the Philippines led to full-scale rebellion. (*Filipinos: Forgotten Asian Americans* by Fred Cordova)

pretty Irish young woman from Hong Kong, Josephine Bracken. She arrived in Dapitan in March, 1894, accompanying her adopted father, George Taufer, a blind American. The latter desperately sought Rizal's medical treatment. No Catholic priest wanted to marry Rizal and Josephine because of Rizal's membership in the Freemasons. Nevertheless, they lived happily as man and wife. Their only child—a son—was prematurely born and lived only for a few hours. Rizal named him "Francisco" after Rizal's own father and buried him in Dapitan.

As a scientist, Rizal conducted scientific investigations during his exile in Dapitan. He built up a personal collection of 346 shells representing 203 specimens. He discovered some rare specimens of fauna that foreign scientists later named in his honor. Among them were *Draco rizali*, a flying dragon; *Apogonia rizal*, a small beetle; and *Rhacophorous rizal*, a rare frog.

Rizal was tried in December, 1896, by a military tribunal on charges of inciting a rebellion, founding illicit societies, and writing books with seditious ideas. Luis Taviel de Andrade, bodyguard of Rizal in Calamba in 1887-1888, served as his defense attorney. He was condemned to death by seven Spanish army officers, without any substantial evidence of guilt. On December 28, 1896, Governor-General Camilo G. de Polavieja approved the decision of the military court and ordered Rizal to be shot to death the morning of December 30 at Bagumbayan Field (now Rizal Park), Manila.—*Ceferina Gayo Hess*

SUGGESTED READINGS: • Hessel, Eugene A. *The Religious Thought of Jose Rizal.* Rev. ed. Quezon City: New Day Publishers, 1983. • Russell, Charles Edward, and E. B. Rodriguez. *The Hero of the Filipinos: The Story of Jose Rizal—Poet, Patriot and Martyr.* New York: Century, 1923. • Sanchez-Arcilla Bernal, Jose. *Rizal and the Emergence of the Philippine Nation.* Quezon City: Office of Research and Publications, Ateneo de Manila University, 1991. • Terranel, Quintin C. *Jose Rizal: Lover of Truth and Justice.* Metro Manila: National Book Store, 1984. • Zaide, Gregorio F. *Rizal: His Martyrdom.* Santa Cruz, Manila: Saint Mary's Publishing, 1976. • Zaide, Gregorio F., and Sonia M. Zaide. *Jose Rizal: Life, Works and Writings of a Genius, Writer, Scientist, and National Hero.* Metro Manila: National Book Store, 1984. • Zaide, Gregorio F., and Sonia M. Zaide. *Rizal and Other Great Filipinos.* Metro Manila: National Book Store, 1988.

Roberts Commission Report (1942): U.S. government report prepared by a committee charged with investigating Japan's surprise air assault on PEARL HARBOR. The committee was headed by Associate U.S. Supreme Court Justice Owen J. Roberts. The report concluded that the bombing had been assisted by Japanese spies in Hawaii and stated or inferred that some of the Japanese resident population there had conducted espionage activities against U.S. military installations. With regard to the U.S. mainland, the report warned that preventive action there might be well-advised for the sake of national security. Shortly thereafter, President Franklin D. Roosevelt issued EXECUTIVE ORDER 9066 (1942), authorizing the forced relocation of Japanese living on the Pacific Coast away from designated militarily sensitive zones.

Rock Springs riot (1885): In Rock Springs, Wyoming, a major race riot in which white miners drove their Chinese competition out of town, burned down the entire local Chinatown, and killed close to thirty Chinese. The Rock Springs riot was followed by anti-Chinese mob action throughout the state. From there it spread into New Mexico, Utah, Alaska, Idaho, and California.

Wyoming was coal-mining territory in the late nineteenth century, and Rock Springs (also called Bitter Creek) was a coal town founded in 1867. The UNION PACIFIC RAILROAD constructed a railroad through Wyoming, extending a railway to Rock Springs in 1869. It acquired most of the coal-rich land near the town (as elsewhere in the state) and drove out independent competitors. The railroad contracted out the operation of its Wyoming mines to Thomas Wardell. Under Wardell's direction, by the early 1870's the Rock Springs mines had become the most productive in Wyoming, possibly in the entire Western United States.

In 1874 the famous financier Jay Gould took control of Union Pacific. He decided that the railroad would operate the mines directly. Shortly after Wardell's removal, however, coal prices began to decline, and Gould ordered the coal miners' wages cut. The miners, mostly immigrants from England and Scandinavia, began to unionize in the face of this threat, and late in 1875 they went on strike in Rock Springs.

To break the Rock Springs strike, Union Pacific brought in Chinese miners and fired more than half the white laborers. Martial law was declared for a time. The strike ended, and the union disappeared. Prosperity returned, and over the next decade mining operations expanded. By the mid-1880's there were nearly six hundred miners in Rock Springs, about two-thirds Chinese and one-third Caucasian. Chinese and Caucasian lived in separate parts of town.

In the early 1880's a new wave of union organizing hit the Western mining towns. The effort was spearheaded by Terence V. POWDERLY's KNIGHTS OF LABOR. The union may at first have been color-blind, but it soon took a strong stand favoring white miners over Chinese. In 1884 Union Pacific again cut wages, and strikes broke out in several of the Wyoming coal towns. These were stopped, and the union failed to secure its demand that the railroad fire the Chinese miners. Claiming that Union Pacific had long given preferential treatment to Chinese, Caucasians (especially miners) engaged in sporadic violence against Chinese.

In September of 1885 an argument between a white and a Chinese miner in Rock Springs over a seam of coal exploded into a full-fledged attack against the Chinese. Over a period of hours an angry mob stormed

White miners killed thirty Chinese and drove all remaining Chinese competitors out of town in the Rock Springs riot, Wyoming, 1885. (Bancroft Library, University of California at Berkeley)

the Chinatown, torched the houses and chased the fleeing residents into the desert. Twenty-eight Chinese were killed, and fifteen were wounded. Within days, similar outbreaks took place in Wyoming's other mining towns; the violence then spread to other Western states. As a result, thousands of Chinese returned to China, and thousands more took refuge in San Francisco's better-protected Chinatown. In the century since the Rock Springs riot, Wyoming has not had a significant Chinese population.

Roh Tae Woo (b. Dec. 4, 1932, near Taegu, Korea): President of South Korea. He held a variety of public offices before becoming president in 1987, among which were national security minister, home minister, and head of the country's 1988 Summer Olympics organizing committee. A four-star general, he retired from the army in 1981. He became chairman of the ruling Democratic Justice Party (DJP) in 1985. In June of 1987 Roh was personally selected by outgoing South Korean president Doo Hwan CHUN as ruling party presidential candidate: Roh then won the direct presidential election that December. Earlier in the year he had devised a reform program that reinstituted direct presidential elections in South Korea.

Rohmer, Sax (Arthur Sarsfield Wade or Arthur Sarsfield Ward; February 15, 1883, Birmingham, England— June 1, 1959, London, England): Adventure novelist. Rohmer achieved international popular acclaim by creating the sinister Chinese criminal FU MANCHU. Rohmer was a London reporter when the series' first volume, *Dr. Fu Manchu*, was published in 1913. Besides appearing in Rohmer's books, the character was featured in films, television programs, and radio plays, from which Rohmer made a fortune.

Rohwer: One of ten U.S. government camps under the administration of the WAR RELOCATION AUTHORITY (WRA) used to house Japanese American evacuees during World War II. Officially the camps were designated as "RELOCATION CENTERS." Rohwer was located in southeastern Arkansas.

The Rohwer camp was built by the Army in early 1942 on land owned by the Resettlement Administration, previously intended for distribution to farmers dispossessed by New Deal programs. The camp had a capacity of ten thousand internees, but its maximum population during its operation was slightly less than eighty-five hundred.

Rohwer opened on September 18, 1942, and closed three years later on November 30, 1945. Among the ten camps operated by the WRA, the Rohwer camp, the Topaz camp in central Utah, and the Jerome camp in Arkansas were the last three camps to be occupied; the last, Jerome, opened on October 6, 1942.

By mid-1943, a system of community organization began to operate in the Rohwer camp. While other camps, such as Poston in Arizona, Tule Lake in California, and Gila River in Arizona, elected Issei advisory boards that worked with various councils, the organization at Rohwer was brought about without a formal agreement among the groups involved. The management arrangements at Rohwer, however, were similar to those at other camps: Nisei councils, along with mostly Issei managers of camp blocks, represented their community and served as liaison officers with the camp's staff.

Despite the fact that the Rohwer internees worked productively in the camp and managed all the services necessary to maintain themselves there, including operating a school system, printing a camp newspaper, and organizing social events and recreational activities to occupy the evacuees, they never forgot the fact that they were incarcerated against their will and through no fault of their own.

In early 1945, the original military order for the evacuation of the Japanese American population on the West Coast was rescinded. Thereafter, the WRA gradually dismantled all of its camps, including Rohwer.

Romulo, Carlos Pena (b. Jan. 14, 1901, Camiling, Luzon, Philippines): General, diplomat, and journalist. He became known for his assistance to the Allied forces during World War II, his service to the Philippine government and the United Nations (UN), and his reportorial analyses of current world events.

After attending the University of the Philippines, Romulo entered Columbia University in New York to pursue graduate studies, receiving an M.A. degree in English there in 1921. He then went home to become an English professor at the University of the Philippines, eventually serving as department chair from 1923 until 1928.

Prior to the outbreak of the war, Romulo was a newspaper publisher and editor. After Japan's full invasion of the Philippines in 1941, he assisted the U.S. military effort in the islands by producing a series of anti-Japanese broadcasts that came to be called the "Voice of Freedom." He subsequently became secretary of information in the Philippine government-in-exile of President Manuel Quezon in Washington, D.C.

As a journalist, Romulo became the only Filipino ever to be awarded the Pulitzer Prize, which he earned in 1941 for his prewar analyses of the Pacific region's political and military situation. When American military forces under General Douglas MacArthur returned to the Philippines in 1945, Romulo accompanied them. He also became the first Asian to serve as president of the UN General Assembly; he served from 1949 until 1950, when he became Philippine foreign affairs secretary. In 1952 he was named ambassador to the United States. Election to several more government posts followed through the 1960's.

Romulo also published a number of books. *I Walked with Heroes*, his autobiography, was released in 1961.

Roney, Frank (Aug. 13, 1841, Belfast, Ireland—Jan. 24, 1925, Long Beach, Calif.): Labor union leader and advocate of Chinese exclusion. Roney was an Irish immigrant who arrived in the United States after being expelled by the goverment for conspiring to overthrow the British rule in Ireland. In Omaha, Nebraska, he found a job in an ironworks and joined the local ironworkers union, eventually becoming its president and secretary. Roney also took an active interest in the National Labor Reform Party, the political arm of the National Labor Union, and became president of the party's Nebraska chapter.

In 1875 Roney came to California, became a naturalized American citizen, and began employment with San Francisco's Pacific Iron Works. Subsequently, he joined Denis Kearney's Workingmen's Party of California and ardently supported its anti-Chinese politics. Around 1878, following Kearney's return to power and a related internal dispute, Roney left the party to pursue a more radical and socialistic brand of trade unionism.

Roney's next stop was as chairman of the Seaman's Protective Association, a labor union composed of firemen and sailors and established in 1880. At a convention of trade and labor unions held the next year, Roney drafted a bill mandating that two out of every three crew members working aboard American ships be U.S. citizens. Stepping up the effort to expel the Chinese from America, convention delegates launched plans for a joint meeting of various related organizations to be held in San Francisco in 1882. The result was the birth of the League of Deliverance—again, with Roney as chairman. Formed for the purpose of resisting the Chinese presence with the goal of eventual exclusion, the league organized a boycott in San Francisco of all Chinese-made goods, printed and distributed handbills proclaiming the superior quality of American-made goods, and pressured employers to fire their Chinese workers. Shortly thereafter, the U.S. Congress passed the CHINESE EXCLUSION ACT OF 1882, putting a stop to the further immigration of all Chinese laborers to the United States.

Root, Elihu (Feb. 15, 1845, Clinton, N.Y.—Feb. 7, 1937, New York, N.Y.): Lawyer and statesman. He was instrumental in negotiating with Japan over the issue of school segregation in San Francisco and won concessions from all sides in agreements that eventually developed into the GENTLEMEN'S AGREEMENT (1907-1908) with Japan. (See SAN FRANCISCO SCHOOL BOARD CRISIS.) He played a pivotal role in maintaining friendly relations with Japan. As U.S. secretary of state from 1905 to 1909, he negotiated the Root-Takahira

Diplomat Elihu Root played a pivotal role in maintaining friendly relations with Japan. (AP/Wide World Photos)

Agreement (November 30, 1908) with Japan, which eased the mounting tensions between the United States and Japan by mutually recognizing their policies and influence in the Pacific. He also established governing policies for the Philippines in 1900. Root won the Nobel Peace Prize in 1912.

Roque Espiritu de la Ysla v. United States (1935): State and U.S. federal court ruling that denied naturalization rights to a native-born citizen of the Philippines. Roque Espiritu de la Ysla applied for U.S. citizenship but was turned away by a California state court. After the U.S. Ninth Circuit Court of Appeals upheld the California decision to deny citizenshsip, he appealed to the U.S. Supreme Court. Before the bench, he argued that he was not an alien, but that as a citizen of a country owing allegiance to the United States he was therefore entitled to the same constitutional protections (such as citizenship rights) as native-born Americans. The Court, however, declined to review the case, and the petitioner was refused naturalization.

Rosca, Ninotchka (b. 1946): Writer and journalist. Rosca, a Filipina writer now living in the United States, is the author of two collections of stories, *Bitter Country and Other Stories* (1970) and *The Monsoon Collection* (1983), two novels, *State of War* (1988) and *Twice Blessed* (1992), and a work of nonfiction, *Endgame: The Fall of Marcos* (1987). In addition, she is a widely published journalist whose credits include a regular column in *FILIPINAS* magazine.

Ross, Edward Alsworth (Dec. 12, 1866, Virden, Ill.—July 22, 1951, Madison, Wis.): Scholar. One of the founders of sociology as an academic discipline in the United States, he advocated social engineering and scientific racism. Arguing against Asian immigration to the United States, he helped provide the rationale for the exclusion of Chinese. He taught sociology at Stanford University (1893-1900), the University of Nebraska (1901-1906), and the University of Wisconsin (1906-1937); he also taught at Cornell and Indiana universities. Among his seminal books are *Social Control* (1901), *Foundations of Sociology* (1905), and *The Changing Chinese* (1911).

Rotating credit associations (RCAs): Voluntary loan associations whose members are allowed to borrow money contributed into a common pool by all the members. All funds are pooled at regular intervals, and each member receives the entire sum collected at each

The Joy Luck Club *motion picture features the informal rotating credit clubs enjoyed by Chinese Americans and their Asian American counterparts.* (Museum of Modern Art/Stills Archive)

interval on a rotating basis until everyone has had a crack at the money.

RCAs are still widely found in Asia, Africa, and Central America. The name of the RCA naturally varies from culture to culture, as do the specific rules, but the principle of fund rotation is universal. Asian Americans brought the RCAs with them to the United States. They used and continue to use them for business, home purchase, higher education, and purchase of consumer goods. Some evidence suggests that the RCAs encourage saving and entrepreneurship in the Asian American communities. RCAs are sociable activities as well as financial institutions. They can lend money to people whose credit history is missing, who are unemployed, and who have no collateral so long as those people have good reputations in the community. The RCAs pay high interest. The chief disadvantage is the risk involved: If a member defaults on his or her payment, the other members suffer a financial loss.

Description. RCAs collect a sum of money from the members at each meeting. This sum is the pool. The pool is awarded to a different member at each meeting until each member has taken the whole sum of money once. At the last meeting, the club is disbanded, but new

clubs form quickly with different participants. RCAs range in size from about eight to eighty people with an average size of thirty. They meet weekly, biweekly, or monthly. The money pool may be quite small, but sums in excess of one million dollars also change hands this way. RCA participants assign ownership of the rotating pool to a specific member by prior agreement of the members, by lottery, or by bidding. When a bidding system is used, the successful bidder pays interest to the other contributors. Mechanisms of interest collection vary, but the bidder normally prepays interest by relieving the other contributors of some share of what she or he would otherwise be owed.

Prevalence. Rules and names vary. Koreans call their RCA *kye.* Chinese call their RCA *hui* or *biao hui.* Japanese call it *ko* or *tanomoshi-ko.* In Vietnam people call their RCA *ho.* RCAs are about four hundred years old in Asia. Although evidence is fragmentary, they remain quite popular with urban people as well as with rural people. Business owners and well-educated people are the most frequent participants in RCAs in Asia. A 1991 survey of Taiwan found that more than 60 percent of households acknowledged that some member had participated in a *hui* within the preceding year.

RCAs are, however, illegal in Singapore. Experts once thought that RCAs would disappear in the course of modernization. Yet research finds that RCA use is declining very slowly in Asia—if at all.

Asian Americans. Asian Americans have always made much use of RCAs. True rates of RCA participation are difficult to obtain because participants are reluctant to discuss the subject with poll-takers. A 1988 survey of immigrant Korean business owners in Los Angeles found that 77 percent of households had participated in *kye*s in the United States and that participation was actually higher in Los Angeles than in Korea, where it had been only 55 percent. Historical research shows that Asian Americans used RCAs in the nineteenth and early twentieth centuries; ethnographic studies of RCA participation report that the practice remains common. As in East Asia, where the management of household finance is a woman's responsibility, most Asian American RCA participants are women. RCAs meet in restaurants and private homes. Participants usually share a meal before they turn to business. Some RCAs are largely social. Their members stress the conviviality that the group affords. These groups typically assign the fund by agreement or lottery. Other RCAs are oriented to business; these clubs utilize bidding systems in which early takers pay interest to late takers.

Advantages. RCAs can lend money to people who cannot borrow money from banks because they have either no collateral, no credit rating, or no steady employment. Since these credit problems commonly bedevil immigrants, RCAs have enabled Asian Americans to borrow and save despite lack of access to banks. RCAs lend money, without paperwork or delay, against a person's good reputation and community standing. Money saved in RCAs is accessible to community members for local uses, whereas money saved in banks is frequently invested in Wall Street securities, U.S. Treasury bonds, building projects, and so forth. RCAs are also convenient and pleasant ways to save money—some participants save a higher proportion of their income than they otherwise would, thus permitting them to move up more rapidly in economic status. Interest rates run as high as 30 percent per year, and savers can and do unlawfully evade taxation of their interest income.

Disadvantages. The chief disadvantage is the risk of default. If a participant does not repay a loan, the other participants suffer a financial loss unless the association organizer makes good on the debt. Organizers are commonly expected to assume this obligation in ex-change for interest-free access to the first loan. The true extent of default is unknown, but a common opinion maintains that the rate of default is higher in the United States than in Asia because social cohesion is weaker in the former. RCAs are completely legal under American law so long as investors do not collect more than the maximum interest allowed under federal law and pay tax on the interest they receive. Both restrictions are commonly violated. Asian countries have laws that define the rights and obligations of RCA participants, but American case law is only beginning to cover RCA transactions. Therefore laws governing the exact rights and obligations of organizers and participants remain unclear.—*Ivan Light and Zhong Deng*

SUGGESTED READINGS: • Ardener, Shirley. "The Comparative Study of Rotating Credit Associations." *Journal of the Royal Anthropological Institute* 94, pt. 2 (1964): 201-229. • Geertz, Clifford. "The Rotating Credit Association: A Middle Rung in Development." *Economic Development and Cultural Change* 10 (1962): 241-263. • Hsiao, Michael, and Chung-Chen Lin. "Investment and Saving Pattern of Taiwanese." In *Survey Report of General Social Survey in Taiwan.* Taiwan: Academica Sinica, Institute for Social Science, 1992. • Light, Ivan. *Ethnic Enterprise in America.* Berkeley: University of California Press, 1972. • Light, Ivan, and Edna Bonacich. *Immigrant Entrepreneurs: Koreans in Los Angeles, 1965-1982.* Berkeley: University of California Press, 1988. • Light, Ivan, Jung-Kwuon Im, and Zhong Deng. "Korean Rotating Credit Associations in Los Angeles." *Amerasia* 16 (1990): 35-54.

Roy, M. N. [Manabendra Nath] (Narendranath Bhattacharya; Mar. 21, 1887, Arbelia, West Bengal, India—Jan. 25, 1954, Dehra Dun, Uttar Pradesh, Republic of India): Marxist revolutionary, writer, and founder of Radical Humanism. It was while he was studying in a school in a village near Calcutta that Roy came into contact with a revolutionary underground organization. The partition of Bengal by the British in 1905 provoked a nationwide protest. This also proved a turning point in Roy's life, and he now joined the underground nationalist movement in Bengal. He was arrested by the British government more than once but had to be released each time because of lack of sufficient evidence. Hoping to obtain money and arms from the Germans after the outbreak of World War I, he traveled twice to Southeast Asia. The arms promised by the Germans never made it to India. While he was on his second visit, the British learned of the plot and almost crushed the movement by imprisoning its prominent leaders.

Rather than returning to India, Roy decided to proceed to the United States. He reached San Francisco in 1916 and immediately established contacts with Indian revolutionaries operating from U.S. soil. The United States, however, joined the war in 1917 as a British ally and, at London's behest, decided to suppress the activities of Indian revolutionaries in the country. Roy then moved to Mexico.

Roy's sojourn of two and a half years in Mexico proved to be the most important period in his life in shaping his ideology. From a militant nationalist, he first became a socialist and then a Marxist. His conversion to Marxism was primarily the result of his contact and friendship with Michael Borodin, an emissary of the Comintern, founded in Moscow in 1919. With Roy playing an active role, the majority in the Mexican Socialist Party decided to rename itself as the Communist Party of Mexico. Roy was now invited by Soviet leader Vladimir Lenin to the Comintern congress in Moscow.

Traveling on a Mexican passport with an assumed Mexican name, Roy reached Moscow in May, 1920, and attended the Comintern's Second Congress in July and August. Openly disagreeing with Lenin's "Theses on the National and Colonial Questions," he presented his own "Supplementary Theses." While Lenin had pointed to the necessity of Communist parties in the backward countries rendering assistance to the bourgeois-democratic liberation movement, Roy asserted that rather than supporting "the nationalist aspirations . . . of the native bourgeoisie," the main task of the Communist parties must be to organize the peasants and workers in order to establish Soviet republics. With some modifications, the congress adopted both views.

As one of the leading lights of the Comintern, Roy published *India in Transition* (1922), the first major Marxist analysis of conditions in India; established contacts with revolutionaries in India in order to establish an Indian Communist party; was elected a full member of the international organization's Executive Committee at its Fifth Congress in 1924; and wrote a remarkable number of pamphlets, articles, and books. In 1927 he went to China as the Comintern's representative during the Guomindong's Northern Expedition but got caught up in the internal struggle between the left and right factions of the party and the developing split and hostility between the GUOMINDANG and

the Chinese Communists. His China mission ended in a total disaster. Upon his return, he became disenchanted with the Comintern, which had now come under Joseph Stalin's authoritarian control. Roy was expelled from the organization in 1929.

After completing *Revolution and Counter-Revolution in China (1946), one of his most important works, Roy returned to India in 1930. He attended the Indian National Congress' session at Karachi but was soon arrested for his past activities and jailed for six years. On his release he joined the socialist wing of the congress but found he could not support the policies of both Jawaharlal* NEHRU *and Mohandas K.* GANDHI, the two most important leaders of the party. He left it during World War II when the congress decided not to support the British war effort, which Roy fully backed. In December, 1940, he founded his own Radical Democratic Party. Despite an all-India following of committed revolutionaries, the party failed to win any significant popular support. Now fully disillusioned with both Communism and developments in India, he founded Radical Humanism, a movement of ideas that rejected all forms of dictatorship and authoritarianism and brought together a number of prominent intellectuals from different parts of India. The Radical Humanists were not to become members of a political party seeking political power; instead they were to devote their energies toward the establishment of grassroots democracy and a philosophical revolution that was necessary to sustain and nurture a genuine democratic order.

Roy died still engaged in popularizing and propagating the ideas of Radical Humanism. Although the Communist phase of his life had little impact on India, the Radical Humanist movement, which still survives, remains his most important legacy to his country.

Roy, Ram Mohun (May 22, 1772, Radhanagar, now in West Bengal, Republic of India—Sept. 27, 1833, Bristol, England): Scholar, philanthropist, and social and religious reformer. Considered the "father of modern India," Roy was born into a Brahman family and finished his early education in a Bengali school. He became an ardent student of languages, learning not only Sanskrit, India's classical language, but also Arabic, Persian, and Hebrew. Although reared in an Orthodox Hindu family, he came under the influence of Sufi and VEDANTA philosophies. He worked for some years for the BRITISH EAST INDIA COMPANY, which enabled him to gain mastery of the English language.

Roy settled in Calcutta in 1815 and earnestly began

his crusade to reform Hindu society. One of the inhuman practices in a small section of Hindu society at the time was *sati*, the self-immolation by widows. Roy challenged the custom on the basis of its inhumanity and also pointed out that it had no sanction in the ancient Hindu scriptures. He made use of his mastery of SANSKRIT and his deep study of Hindu texts and produced a tract in 1818 that created a commotion in Orthodox Hindu circles. Although *sati* was made illegal in 1829 as a result of an official order issued by Governor General Lord William Bentinck, it is doubtful whether the British government would have interfered in Hindu religious matters without the support given by Roy's crusade.

Roy also undertook campaigns against such practices as polygamy and the CASTE system. In the debate that raged in Bengal at this time between the merits of traditional education and English education, he came out strongly in favor of the latter, believing that India's salvation eventually lay in combining its traditional heritage with Western liberal ideas. He also stood for freedom of the press and worked assiduously for the promotion of English and Bengali journalism.

Roy's criticism of some Hindu social practices attracted to Calcutta some Christian missionaries, who thought they could convert him to save his soul, but Roy held true to his reformist HINDUISM. As far as Christianity was concerned, he interpreted the Gospels in a universalistic and liberal way, coming close to the position of the Unitarians. Like the Hindu Orthodox groups, he also faced angry reactions from Orthodox Christians.

Symbolizing his reformist zeal was his founding in 1828 of the Brahmo Samaj movement, or "Society for the Cosmic Soul," which stood for a monotheistic Hinduism dedicated to the ideals of social justice and spread of reason. It later attracted a band of young reformers, who, despite their small number, became influential in the nineteenth century Hindu Renaissance.

Roy died as an emissary of Delhi's Mughal emperor. As one who sought to instill pride among the Hindus for their heritage, fought Hindu religious Orthodoxy through the weapon of scriptural authority, and yet welcomed Western liberal ideals of reason and social justice, he led a movement that was to have a decisive influence in shaping the social and political ideals of modern India.

Ruef, Abraham (Sept. 2, 1864, San Francisco, Calif.— Feb. 29, 1936, San Francisco, Calif.): Politician. The only son of French Jews who came to San Francisco in 1862, he was graduated from the University of California at age eighteen, became a lawyer, and later led the Union Labor Party of San Francisco. He became mayor in 1906 but shortly thereafter was brought down by a corruption scandal. Extremely anti-Japanese, he used the anti-Asian movement to further his political career and as mayor called for segregation of Japanese immigrant students in public schools. (See SAN FRANCISCO SCHOOL BOARD CRISIS.)

Rushdie, Salman [Ahmed] (b. June 19, 1947, Bombay, India): Novelist. Rushdie studied at King's College, Cambridge (M.A.), and was a freelance advertising copywriter from 1970 to 1980 before turning to writing full-time. His first important novel, *Midnight's Children* (1981), won for him the Booker McConnell Prize, England's most prestigious fiction award. An allegory that chronicles the history of India since the country's independence, it is narrated by Saleem Sinai, who was born at the moment of independence and thus is gifted with supernatural powers along with a thousand other children born at the same hour. The novel traces Saleem's adventures across India and Pakistan, pitting him against his archrival, Shiva, another of midnight's magical children, switched at birth with Saleem. The novel has been compared to works by Gabriel García Márquez, Günter Grass, and V. S. NAIPAUL.

Rushdie's next novel, *Shame* (1983), blends myth, history, politics, and fantasy in a tale that is set in a country that resembles Pakistan. It recounts the history and struggles of two men, Raza Hyder (based on Zia ul-Haq) and Iskander Harappa (based on Zulfikar Ali Bhutto). The novel explores the concepts of *sharam* (shame, modesty) and honor through the character of Sufiya, daughter of Hyder, who absorbs the unfelt shame of others and finally turns into a monster. The book was nominated for the Booker Prize.

Rushdie's best known and most controversial novel is *The Satanic Verses* (1988), winner of the Whitbread Award. It explores the themes of good and evil and the plight of Indians living in England, and it attacks religious fundamentalism. Written in a typically irreverent, fragmented style, it begins with a hijacked plane exploding over London, causing the two main characters, Gibreel Farishta and Saladin Chamcha, to begin a magical journey through history and fantasy.

Fundamentalist Islamic groups rioted in protest soon after the book was published, bookstores were bombed, and several countries, including India, banned the novel. In February, 1989, Ayatollah

Winner of several British book awards, Salman Rushdie created a great deal of controversy with his novel The Satanic Verses. (AP/Wide World Photos)

Iran's Ayatollah Khomeini claimed that Rushdie's novel defamed the prophet Muhammad and the Quran and decreed that Rushdie should be executed. (AP/Wide World Photos)

Ruholla Khomeini of Iran claimed that the book defamed the prophet Muhammad and the Quran and decreed that Rushdie should be executed. A bounty of $5 million was offered as payment, and Rushdie went into hiding. Several countries broke off diplomatic ties with Iran in an incident of unprecedented international tension over a book.

Following Khomeini's death in June, 1989, his successor explicitly proclaimed that the *fatwa* or decree sentencing Rushdie to death was still in force. Attacks on translators of *The Satanic Verses*—two of them fatal—and bookstore bombings underscored the seriousness of the threat. Rushdie remained in hiding, with security provided by the British government, surfacing infrequently for unscheduled appearances. In September, 1993, *Midnight's Children* was chosen as the best book among the twenty-five novels that had been awarded the Booker Prize since it was first given in 1969. Rushdie appeared in person at Waterstone's Bookstore in Kensington, West London, to receive this "Booker of Bookers."

Other works by Rushdie include *Grimus* (1975), a fantasy quest tale; *The Jaguar Smile: A Nicaraguan Journey* (1987), a critique of Nicaraguan politics based on his stay in that country; *Haroun and the Sea of Stories* (1990), a children's book; and *Imaginary Homelands: Essays and Criticism, 1981-1991* (1991).

Russo-Japanese War (1904-1905): War between Japan and Russia over dominance in Manchuria and Korea. Japan had gained hegemony over Korea with the SINO-JAPANESE WAR OF 1894-1895 and regarded control of Korea as vital to Japanese strategic and economic interests. The completion of the Trans-Siberian Railroad, the Russian-operated Chinese Eastern Railway shortcut through Manchuria in 1896, and the Russian lease on the Liaodong Peninsula in 1898 alarmed the Japanese, who considered the growing

Russian influence in Asia as a threat to Japanese supremacy in Korea. Russian troops occupied Manchuria during the Boxer Rebellion (1900), and when the Czarist government refused to remove these forces, Tokyo began intensive, but ultimately disappointing, negotiations with Russia. After serious deliberations Japan's leaders decided on war as the only means of removing the Russian threat.

Japanese diplomats had negotiated the ANGLO-JAPANESE ALLIANCE in 1902 (the treaty was to extend from 1902 to 1923). It stated that any other power that might side with Russia would have to fight the British. Thus the war that began in 1904 would be fought solely between Russia and Japan.

Hostilities began two days before a declaration of war as Japanese ships attacked the Russian naval base at Port Arthur on February 8, 1904. The land war in Manchuria was characterized by costly Japanese victories at Port Arthur and Mukden. In May, 1905, in the Tsushima Straits, the Japanese navy destroyed the Russian Baltic Fleet, which had sailed around the world

President Theodore Roosevelt mediated treaty negotiations that ended the Russo-Japanese War. (Library of Congress)

to engage the Japanese. The naval disaster prompted the Russians to agree to U.S. president Theodore Roosevelt's proposals to arrange a peace settlement. Although Japan had won a series of tactical victories, she was exhausted by the demands of the war; the Japanese government was therefore eager to negotiate a peace. Negotiations were held in Portsmouth, New Hampshire, under the guidance of Roosevelt.

Terms of the TREATY OF PORTSMOUTH (1905), gave the Japanese control of the former Russian lease of the Liaodong Peninsula, turned the South Manchurian Railway over to Japan, and ceded the southern half of Sakhalin Island to Japan. Thus Russian influence in Manchuria dissipated, and Japan's hold on Korea tightened. The Japanese public, criticizing the lack of an indemnity to be paid to Japan, rioted in Tokyo.

Japan's victory solidified her position as a major Asian and world power and encouraged anti-imperialist movements in other Asian nations.

Ryukyu Islands: Archipelago between Taiwan and Kyushu, Japan, constituting Okinawa Prefecture. The Ryukyus' total land area of about 871 square miles contained a 1991 population exceeding 1.2 million people. "Ryukyu" and "Okinawa" are often used interchangeably, but the first designation is generally used in reference to the early history of OKINAWA.

The people of Ryukyu and Japan are of the same ethnic and racial stock. The Ryukyu language is a dialect of Japanese—although this dialect has become unintelligible to speakers of standard Japanese because a separation between the two occurred between fifteen hundred and two thousand years ago. The Ryukyuan indigenous religion is very similar to early SHINTO of Japan: Natural objects, natural phenomenon, and people that are awe-inspiring are held in reverence.

In general, Ryukyuan development lagged about a thousand years behind that of Japan. The first historical ruler emerged in the late twelfth century. Writing was introduced sometime in the twelfth or thirteenth century. A centralized bureaucratic state was established in the late fifteenth century.

For a large part of its history, from 1372 until 1871, Ryukyu was a tributary state of China. For most of this period, until 1609, Ryukyu was an independent kingdom. In 1609, however, it was conquered by the Satsuma *han*, the southernmost *han* of TOKUGAWA Japan. In 1879 it was made an integral part of Japan when the MEIJI government established it as a prefecture.

As a tributary state of China, Ryukyu gained the privilege of educating its elite in China and of exchanging tribute and trade goods. At the beginning of the relationship China sent educated and skilled Chinese, including shipbuilders and navigators, to Okinawa. During the fourteenth and fifteenth centuries, the exchange of trade goods enabled the Ryukyuans to prosper in maritime trade, not only with China but also with Southeast Asia and Japan. Spices and other products from Southeast Asia and swords and copper from Japan were exchanged in China for silk and chinaware, which, in turn, were sold to the other trade partners for profit. In this period the Ryukyuans were significant middlemen who united much of Asia in trade.

S

Sacramento labor camp (Sacramento, Calif.): One of sixteen temporary assembly centers set up for the mass relocation of Japanese Americans during World War II. Under EXECUTIVE ORDER 9066 (1942), more than 120,000 Americans of Japanese ancestry were first evacuated to temporary centers and later incarcerated in camps administered by the WAR RELOCATION AUTHORITY (WRA). Other temporary centers were in Mayer, Arizona; Portland, Oregon; Puyallup, Washington; and California locations at Fresno, Manzanar, Marysville, Merced, Pinedale, Pomona, Salinas, Santa Anita, Stockton, Tanforan, Tulare, and Turlock.

Saibara, Seito (1861, Izuma, Shikoku, Japan—Apr., 1939, Tex.): Politician and rice farmer. A member of the Japanese parliament as well as university president, Saibara abruptly left his homeland for the United States. Settling in southeast Texas, he organized one of the first successful Japanese rice-farm colonies in the country.

Saibara was born into the Tosa clan, which was allied to other powerful clans supporting the MEIJI RESTORATION (1868-1912). As a young man, however, he was drawn to the views of Taisuke Itagaki, a Tosa official who attempted to bring reform to the new government and who founded the Risshisha (Society of Free Thinkers) for that purpose. As a sixteen-year-old, Saibara attended the Risshisha English School in Kochi Prefecture, briefly studying English and western philosophy. A short time later, however, his studies were interrupted by an uprising staged by samurai disenchanted with the changes implemented by the Meiji government. Soon, Saibara himself was publicly opposing the emperor and advocating greater openness toward the much more progressive West. Some time later, he enrolled in Shigematsu Law School, was married, and after passing the bar in 1886 went back to Kochi to set up his practice.

There Saibara's involvement in national political affairs intensified. He was arrested and accused of

The Saibara residence in Webster, circa 1904. (Institute of Texan Cultures, San Antonio, Texas)

plotting to assassinate the governor, an appointee of the Meiji regime, but was cleared following a lengthy appeal. During Japan's first-ever parliamentary elections, in 1890, he successfully campaigned for the four local candidates of the Liberal Party, which had been founded by Itagaki. Japan was transformed into a constitutional monarchy as a result of the elections.

During the years 1891 through 1898, Saibara moved to Osaka, practiced law, and continued his active involvement in Liberal Party politics. He also won a seat in the Japanese House of Representatives. After converting to Christianity, he became a member of the Tamon Congregational Church of Kobe. In 1899 he was named president of Doshisha University, a Christian college in Kyoto. From his seat in government, he strongly argued for the rights of Christians in Japan.

To the surprise of many, Saibara resigned his posts and sailed for Connecticut in 1902 to attend Hartford Theological Seminary. He met Sadatsuchi Uchida, the Japanese consul-general, while passing through New York. Uchida, while on a tour of the South that same year, had noted with great interest the vast untapped potential for rice farming, particularly across the expansive prairies of Texas. Much of his interest had to do with Japan's growing need to develop new sources of imported rice. After talking with Uchida, Saibara decided to go to Texas and establish a rice-farm colony there.

To fill his new colony with settlers, Saibara wrote to relatives and friends back home in Japan, urging them to join him as soon as possible. Those coming as salaried laborers were promised $250 a year; wives accompanying their husbands, $90 a year. In the fall of 1903, he bought his first parcel of land—a 304-acre tract in Webster, a small town near Houston. As additional migrants arrived from Japan, the colony began to increase in size. Saibara himself built a six-hundred-foot well on his property to store water for irrigation.

The small cluster of rice farms operated by Saibara and the other migrants prospered the first year. The flat, relatively uncluttered landscape made for considerably easier and faster cultivation. The Shinriki rice

Seito Saibara (center) standing beside the well on his Webster farm, circa 1904. (Institute of Texan Cultures, San Antonio, Texas)

Seito Saibara (top row, center), Webster, Texas, 1932. (Institute of Texan Cultures, San Antonio, Texas)

brought over from Japan and planted by the colonists on their new farms provided abundant crops at harvesting time. By 1909, the Saibara colony encompassed more than nine hundred acres. Nearby, thousands of additional acres were under cultivation by Japanese farmers. Also in 1909 it was the Webster area that boasted the largest concentration of Japanese immigrants—seventy-six men, women, and children. Saibara also found time to publish pieces in Japanese emigration company magazines describing the new opportunities available to emigrants; pieces written about him and his rice-farm venture also boosted Japanese immigration to the area. Domestically the demand for rice remained fairly stable, and, until after World War I, rice prices rose.

Sometime before the close of 1924 the government of Japan asked Saibara to return as its minister of education, but he rejected the offer, preferring the life of a farmer. Under U.S. law, however, he was never able to acquire naturalized American citizenship. Finally forced to leave the United States because of steadily declining rice prices and the ban erected by the IMMIGRATION ACT OF 1924 against Japanese labor immigration (which cut his labor pool), Saibara and his wife moved to Brazil in 1924. They returned to Webster in 1937; Saibara lived there until his death.

SUGGESTED READING: • Walls, Thomas K. *The Japanese Texans.* San Antonio: University of Texas Institute of Texan Cultures at San Antonio, 1987.

Saiki, Patricia Hatsue Fukuda (b. May 28, 1930, Hilo, Territory of Hawaii): U.S. representative and educator. A second-generation Japanese American, Saiki attended public schools before enrolling at the University of Hawaii. After receiving her B.A. degree in 1952, Saiki began a career as a teacher and was employed at various high schools in her native state. In 1954, she was married to Stanley Mitsuo Saiki. Secretary of the Hawaiian Republican Party in 1964, Patricia Saiki later served as the party's vice chair from 1966 to 1968. In 1968, she was elected to a seat in the Hawaii state legislature, where she served until 1974. In that year, Saiki campaigned for and won a seat in the Hawaii state senate.

Reelected for an additional four-year term in 1978, Saiki continued to work on behalf of education and women's rights, fighting for the establishment of a teacher's union, serving on the Western Interstate Commission on Higher Education, and accepting an appointment to serve on the President's Advisory

Patricia Saiki. (Asian Week)

Council on the Status of Women. She also served as trustee for Hawaii Pacific College and for the University of Hawaii Foundation. Saiki was nominated as the Republican candidate for lieutenant governor of Hawaii in 1982 but was defeated in the election and chose to leave her state senate seat to chair the Hawaiian Republican Party.

In 1983, Saiki was elected to the U.S. House of Representatives from Hawaii's First Congressional District. During her two-year term, Saiki was the sole Asian American woman in Congress. She served on a variety of committees, including the House Select Committee on Aging, the Merchant Marine Committee, and the Banking, Finance, and Urban Affairs Committee. Appointed by President George Bush to serve as head of the Small Business Administration (SBA), Saiki held this position through 1992. In 1994 she ran as the Republican candidate for governor of Hawaii.

Sa-i-ku pok-dong: Korean phrase meaning "the April 29 riots," referring to the LOS ANGELES RIOTS OF 1992.

Sakadas: Term used to refer to Filipino laborers who were recruited and transported to Hawaii to work on sugar plantations. In Hawaii, the term is used specifically to distinguish those Filipino workers who came between 1906 and 1946 from other Filipinos who followed. The term "sakada" also refers to the process of recruiting contract laborers.

Sakamoto, James Y. (1903, Seattle, Wash.—1955, Seattle, Wash.): Publisher. A star athlete in high school, he made a career out of boxing in the 1920's, but he returned to Seattle bruised, battered, and nearly blind. He became founder and publisher of the newspaper the *Japanese American Courier*, through which he exhorted Japanese readers to be loyal Americans. An influential member of the JAPANESE AMERICAN CITIZENS LEAGUE (JACL) serving as the organization's president in 1938, he epitomized the group's stance of cooperation with the U.S. government and acceptance of Japanese American internment.

Sakata, Harold T. (Hawaii—July, 1982, Honolulu, Hawaii): Actor, weight lifter, and wrestler. A star athlete, Sakata also won fame as an actor, becoming familiar to many as the ruthless bodyguard Oddjob in the James Bond thriller *Goldfinger* (1964). The eldest of ten children growing up on the Big Island, Sakata worked as a plantation laborer and stevedore, never finishing high school. He built himself into a cham-

pion weight lifter, capturing a silver medal in the 82.5-kilogram class at the London Olympics of 1948 and several U.S. championships as well. Sakata then wrestled professionally as "Tosh Togo." In the early 1960's he was discovered by Harry Saltzman, producer of the James Bond series, and British film director Guy Hamilton. The pair cast Sakata in what became his most famous role. In addition to motion pictures, he filmed commercials and such television shows as *Gilligan's Island* (1964-1967) and *Hawaii Five-O* (1968-1980).

Sake Bill of 1896: Legislation imposing a sizable tax on *sake* (Japanese rice wine), enacted by the Republic of Hawaii chiefly to discourage further emigration from Japan. The new law—which taxed *sake* at a dollar a gallon—was another attempt in the ongoing effort by the Hawaiian government to cut off the flow of Japanese arriving in the islands. The bill was, in addition, backed by numerous California winemakers, whose own market share in Hawaii was smaller because of *sake* imports from Japan. Hawaiian president Sanford Dole vetoed the bill because of its clear discriminatory intent, but lawmakers approved it anyway.

Sake being served as part of the New Year's celebration in Los Angeles. (Diane C. Lyell)

Sakoku: Japanese term ("closed country") for the 1639-1854 national seclusion policy of Japan. After taking control of Japan at the beginning of the seventeenth century, the Tokugawa family began restricting the activities of foreigners in Japan in an effort to secure a better hold on power. Responding to the influx of Western missionaries and traders during the late 1500's, Tokugawa rule initially focused on crushing Christianity and banishing priests, then all Christians, in a series of edicts and anti-Christian crusades between 1612 and 1639. By the end of that period, the Western faith had been largely eradicated.

Similarly, the new government attempted to control trade and thus prevent southwestern lords from enriching themselves and becoming potential rivals. To this end, Tokugawa officials enacted a series of increasingly tight restrictions that finally isolated Japan almost completely from the rest of the world. Beginning with a licensing system, the Tokugawas gradually restricted the movements of traders from individual countries, then banned some traders completely, until, by 1639, only the Chinese, Koreans, and Dutch were allowed even minimal trade privileges.

The *sakoku* policy was perfected in a series of five edicts between 1633 and 1639, which proscribed Christianity, prevented Japanese from leaving Japan— or from returning if they left—and spelled out the trade restrictions. As a result, for the next two centuries, the only trade allowed in Japan itself was with a few Chinese, who were restricted to Nagasaki, and the Dutch, who were allowed to bring only two ships per year to Deshima, a small manmade island in Nagasaki harbor. Off the coast, Chinese trade was permitted with the Ryukyu Islands, as was Korean trade on the island of Tsushima.

Across the next two centuries, the government kept abreast of international developments through annual reports required of the Dutch at Nagasaki and a small, covert group of students of the West, developed largely through the medium of interpreters for the Dutch. For all other Japanese, the outside world was sealed off, with even Western books proscribed.

The term *sakoku* itself came into use early in the 1800's, not long before Commodore Matthew Perry persuaded the Tokugawa government to sign the 1854 Treaty of Kanagawa, opening two ports to American ships and thus bringing national seclusion to an end.

Salii, Lazarus Eitaro (Nov. 17, 1936, Anaguar, Palau, now the Republic of Belau—Aug. 20, 1988, Koror, Belau): President of Belau. After earning a degree in

Lazarus Salii. (AP/Wide World Photos)

government from the University of Hawaii in 1961, Salii began a career in public service to his home country, a United Nations trust territory administered by the United States. He was chosen to represent Palau in the newly formed Congress of Micronesia in 1964, winning election to the Micronesia Senate, Palau District, in 1968. Anxious to improve all prospects for the future of the islands, in 1967 Salii agreed to head the Congressional Committee on the Future Status of Micronesia and began voicing his concerns in talks with the U.S. government. From 1969 until 1979 he chaired the Future Political Status Commission in its negotiations with the United States.

Eventually, Salii managed to blend the separate interests of both governments into a mutually acceptable and workable policy known as "free association." This formula established Micronesian self-rule in domestic matters and continued U.S. control of military and foreign affairs. In exchange for the right to establish military bases in the islands, the U.S. government was to subsidize Micronesia financially. Palau became the Republic of Belau in 1981. Salii was elected president of the tiny island state in 1985.

During the last years of his administration, Salii was forced to deal with reports of political corruption in office. In 1987 he was accused of—and subsequently admitted—accepting a sizable bribe in connection with the building of a power plant in Belau. In August of the following year, the U.S. government notified him that it was renewing its investigation of corruption associated with his government. On August 20, at his home in the capital city of Koror, Salii was found dead from a gunshot wound to the head. The discovery of his death, which was eventually ruled a suicide, occurred the day before he was scheduled to announce his candidacy for reelection.

Salinas lettuce strike (1934): Walkout by Filipino lettuce workers in Salinas, California, that began on August 27. That day, the Vegetable Packers Association, an American Federation of Labor (AFL) affiliate, asked the Filipino Labor Union (FLU) to join the strike in order to present a united worker front. FLU leaders agreed, and for a week the lettuce fields were shut down.

During the summer of 1934, Filipino labor leaders negotiated with local growers for improved wages and adequate working conditions. These uneasy labor discussions prompted the growers to organize the Filipino Labor Supply Association to hamper the growth of the FLU. By using labor contractors who would hire "safe Filipino workers," the growers hoped to avert a strike.

This move, however, proved an impossibility, and the strike began in late August. After four days of picketing, the strike was successful, but the AFL believed that Filipino workers were making unreasonable demands. Therefore, on September 1, Joseph Carey, an American AFL official, was sent to Salinas to urge Filipinos to accept union leadership and end the strike. In a threatening tone, Carey suggested that if Filipinos did not agree, they faced the possibility of striking without outside support.

Many Filipino labor leaders were experienced union organizers in the Hawaiian sugarcane fields. When they arrived in California, they displayed a sophistication about labor tactics that surprised local growers. This sign of Filipino labor militancy frightened the large growers in the Salinas Valley. During the strike, Mrs. D. L. Marcuelo, wife of the president of the FLU, and James Sells, an official of the Vegetable Packers Association, were arrested for unlawful assembly, but Filipinos continued the strike.

Finally, the growers agreed to an arbitration proceeding. When Thomas A. Reardon, director of the California Department of Industrial Relations, suggested a fact-finding committee and the acceptance of binding arbitration, the growers readily agreed. Over the next few weeks, these proceedings were difficult ones.

A rift developed between the Vegetable Packers Association and the FLU, and the growers attempted to buy off the white union. On September 1, 1934, the FLU held a boisterous meeting, and Carey urged Filipinos to end their strike. They voted overwhelmingly to continue the strike with or without the Vegetable Packers Association.

After this meeting, there was a noticeable increase in violence toward Filipino workers. The Vegetable Packers Association severed its ties with the FLU, and a new wave of anti-Filipino violence descended upon the Salinas area. After three separate shootings, there were pressures to end the strike.

On September 3, 1934, the Monterey County Industrial Relations Board announced that the Salinas lettuce strike had ended. This agreement, however, was reached without the consent of the FLU. Filipino farm workers subsequently held a meeting and voted 785 to 58 to continue the strike.

This action set off a series of riots throughout the San Joaquin Valley. The September 10-11 riots were followed by a highly organized propaganda program from the Associated Farmers of California, which charged that the FLU was a communist group. The Salinas Grower-Shipper Association distributed sophisticated literature citing the dangers of Filipino labor activity. This program was calculated to induce California legal authorities to invoke against Filipino labor organizers the Criminal Syndicalism Law of 1919.

Filipinos were indiscriminately arrested, and Rufo Canete was reappointed the FLU president. Canete, a respected labor leader, organized a unity day. On September 24, 1934, the FLU announced that Mexican and Filipino workers would begin a new strike. This demonstrated an unusually high degree of ethnic labor solidarity.

Many of the striking Filipino farm workers lived at Canete's labor camp. Thus local vigilantes marched on the camp and firebombed it. In the aftermath of the attack, the local sheriff charged Canete with intimidating other Filipino labor contractors. It was to Canete's credit that he recognized the danger to Filipino workers and settled the strike.

On Monday, September 24, 1934, the Salinas lettuce strike ended. Wages were increased, and the FLU was recognized as a legitimate farm workers' union. Once it was established in the Salinas lettuce fields, the FLU became an important force in the California agribusiness. Two years later, the FLU carried out another successful strike in Salinas, and in 1937 the organization was granted an AFL charter.

The Salinas lettuce strike of 1934 was one of the first successful victories for an ethnic labor union in the California fields, and it was an early example of Filipino labor unity. The need for ethnic agricultural organization made Filipino unionists an important role model for other ethnic unions from the 1930's to the 1960's.

Salinas rodeo grounds: One of sixteen temporary assembly centers set up for the mass relocation of Japanese Americans during World War II. Under EXECUTIVE ORDER 9066 (1942), 110,000 Americans of Japanese ancestry on the West Coast were first evacuated to temporary centers and later incarcerated in camps administered by the WAR RELOCATION AUTHORITY (WRA). Other temporary centers were in Mayer, Arizona; Portland, Oregon; Puyallup, Washington; and California locations at Fresno, Manzanar, Marysville, Merced, Pinedale, Pomona, Sacramento, Santa Anita, Stockton, Tanforan, Tulare, and Turlock.

Salvador Roldan v. Los Angeles County (1931): One of the most significant court cases challenging the application of California's antimiscegenation laws to Filipinos. *Roldan* forced the California court system to give a definitive ruling on the racial classification of Filipinos.

In the early twentieth century the legal status of Filipino interracial marriages in California was not firmly established. Since 1880 Section 60 of the *California Civil Code* had stated that "all marriages of white persons with Negroes, Mongolians, or Mulattoes are illegal and void." Section 69 of the *Code* prohibited the issuance of marriage licenses to couples in which one member fell under the racial categories named in Section 60. County clerks who issued the marriage licenses were left with the decision of whether or not Filipinos were considered to be "Mongolians." This led to confusing inconsistencies between counties within the state with regard to the issuance of marriage licenses. Filipino-Caucasian couples denied a marriage license in one county could travel to the next county and apply for a license. Leaving California to marry in a state without antimiscegenation laws was another solution. A third solution for Filipino-Caucasian couples was to take court action.

In 1931 Salvador Roldan, a Filipino, and Marjorie

Rogers, his Caucasian fiancé, were denied a marriage license by the office of the Los Angeles County clerk. Roldan then petitioned for a writ of mandate requiring the clerk to issue them a marriage license. Roldan won his case in the county superior court, only to have the decision appealed by the county. On January 27, 1933, the court of appeals affirmed the lower-court ruling that Filipinos were "Malay," not "Mongolian," and as such could legally marry Caucasians.

The reaction by the California legislature to the Roldan decision was swift. Less than three months after the decision, Governor James Ralph signed two bills that had passed the State Assembly. The bills amended sections 60 and 69 of the California Civil Code to include "Malay" as another race prohibited from marrying Caucasians. The bills also retroactively invalidated any existing Filipino-Caucasian marriages. The laws took effect in August of 1933. They remained in effect until 1948, when they were ruled unconstitutional by the California Supreme Court.

Salwar kameez: Punjabi phrase meaning "pant shirt," a knee-length, long-sleeve top worn over loose, drawstring pants. This full outfit is worn most commonly by women in north India and in Pakistan. Having originated in Punjab, it is also called a "Punjabi suit."

Sam Fow: Cantonese name for Stockton, California. It literally means "third city" (after San Francisco and Sacramento, the largest centers of the early Chinese American community in California). A large Chinese population resided in Stockton in the late nineteenth century, with most of the Chinese drawn to the city because of its rural setting and low cost of living.

Sam Wo Restaurant: Small Chinese restaurant in San Francisco Chinatown, California. It was built shortly after the 1906 earthquake, when laws of inspection were overlooked. The restaurant is noted for its peculiar architectural structure: Built without its own side walls, it instead relies on the walls of the buildings on either side of it. The restaurant is also noted for its rice conjee, known in Cantonese as *jook*.

Sam Yup (Sanyi): Collective term meaning "three counties" or "three districts," referring to Nanhai (Namhoi), Panyu (Punyu), and Shunde (Shuntak) counties located west, south, and southwest respectively of Canton, China. The subdialects spoken in this region are closely related to the Cantonese spoken in Canton, which is considered standard pronunciation and is taught in Chinatown Chinese schools.

During the Qing Dynasty (1644-1911), the eastern half of Canton was part of Panyu and the western part of Nanhai. This changed in 1925, when the city became a separate administrative unit. Another major change took place after the founding of the People's Republic of China (1949), when Panyu north of the Pearl River became part of Canton. In 1949 Foshan (Fatshan) also became administratively separate from Nanhai.

There were about 350,000 people of Nanhai ancestry outside China in the 1980's. Immigrants to America before 1965 came mostly from one of three areas: Jiujiang (Kowkong), Xiqiao (Saichew), and Shishan (Szeshan). Panyu people abroad numbered about 480,000. Pre-1965 immigrants to America came mostly from Yahu (Ah Woo) and Panghu (Pong Woo) in what is now Canton's Baiyun District. Shunde immigrants abroad number around 400,000. Those in America before 1965 came mostly from Gean, Pingbu, and Luzhou. Of the three groups Nanhai people are the most numerous in America and Shunde the smallest. They are concentrated mostly in San Francisco, Los Angeles, and New York. There are also a number of people of Sam Yup descent in towns in the San Joaquin Valley.

During the nineteenth century Sam Yup had highly developed handicraft industries and commerce. In San Francisco, Sam Yup merchants monopolized the import-export business until it was broken by a Sze Yup boycott in the 1890's. There were also many Sam Yup people in skilled work such as shoemaking and garment making as well as the crafts, clerical work, and the performing arts. During the twentieth century, however, many of the younger American-born generation have become professionals.

Sam Yup people have always been a minority among the Chinese in America. Even at its height during the 1870's the population did not number more than 12,000. During the exclusion era the population steadily dropped, but it has risen again after the 1970's because of immigration from China, Hong Kong, and Vietnam. There has been, however, no accurate count of the population during the twentieth century.

Sam Yup Company (Canton Company; also, Sam Yup Benevolent Association, Sanyi Huiguan): District association, or *huiguan*, founded in 1850 or 1851 in San Francisco for people from Nanhai (Namhoi), Panyu (Punyu), and Shunde (Shuntak) counties in China. The organization also established California branches in Stockton (1851), Sacramento (1854), Folsom (1850's), Angel's Camp (1857), Sebastopol (1880), Merced (1880), Bakersfield (1880), Hanford (1886), Fresno (1888), and San Jose (1889) and in Portland, Oregon (1864). As the Sam Yup population dwindled during the twentieth century, however, many of these branches ceased operation.

During the nineteenth century the association also provided services to immigrants from neighboring counties. These included people from Hua Xian (Fa Yuen), Sanshui (Samshui), Qingyuan (Tsingyuen), Sihui (Szewui), Gaoyao (Koyiu), and Gaoming (Koming). All but Hua Xian withdrew in 1901 after the group failed to obtain equal rights in the association (these immigrants could not become *huiguan* officers). Hua Xian people later also seceded when the Fah Yuen Association was established in 1955.

The Sam Yup Association once played an important role in community affairs. When California Governor John Bigler made an anti-Chinese speech in 1852, the association's interpreter, Chun Aching, and Tong K. Achik of the Yeong Wo Company wrote the Chinese letter of rebuttal. In 1893 association president Chan Ta Chiu rallied all the *huiguan* to challenge the registration requirements of the Geary Act (1892). He also promoted the establishment of the Wai Leong Kung Sur to protect law-abiding Chinese against the *tongs*. The Sam Yup Association's influence, however, diminished during the exclusion era.

Other organizations have been established under the Sam Yup Association. The Nam Hoy Fook Yum Benevolent Society (Nanhai Fuyintang), the Pon Yup Chong How Benevolent Association (Panyu Changhoutang), and the Hang On Association (Shunde Xingantang) were founded to provide charitable services. The first group also supports the Nam Kue Chinese School (founded in 1920) and a senior center (founded in 1990), while the Hang On Association sponsors a youth group (founded in 1960). The Chong How Association was formerly connected with the Yee Shan (Yushan Xinju), which provided a mail service for Panyu and Hua Xian people. The Chew Yee Association is now a social club but during the days of the *tong* wars was a group devoted to self-defense. There is a Som [sic] Yup Association in Philadelphia and a Nom Hoy Shun Tuck Association and a Yee Shan Benevolent Society in New York.

In 1975 the Sam Yup Association published the first scholarly book-length work on an American *huiguan*, *A History of the Sam Yup Benevolent Association in the United States, 1850-1974*, edited by Yuk Ow.

Samoa: Three-hundred-mile-long archipelago located in the southwest Pacific Ocean. Of relatively recent geological origin (late Pliocene to mid-Pleistocene), the islands have low coastal areas with fringe reefs and sand beaches (where the majority of the villages are found) and verdant slopes rising to highland ridges, the highest peaks reaching 6,095 feet on the island of Savaii and 3,170 feet on the island of Tau. This is a tropical environment with temperatures averaging 83 degrees Fahrenheit year-round and an annual rainfall of approximately 125 inches.

The archipelago consists of sixteen islands (ten in-habited), politically divided into Western Samoa (an independent nation since 1962) and American Samoa (an unincorporated territory of the United States since 1900). In Western Samoa the island of Savaii is the second largest (659 square miles) Polynesian island in the Pacific. Moving east one finds the tiny islets of Apolima and Manono followed by Upolu (432 square miles), which is the site of the principal harbor, commercial center, and capital (Apia). Forty miles further east is American Samoa, with tiny Aunuu and Tutuila, the largest (53 square miles) of this group, with the deepest, best protected harbor in the South Pacific at

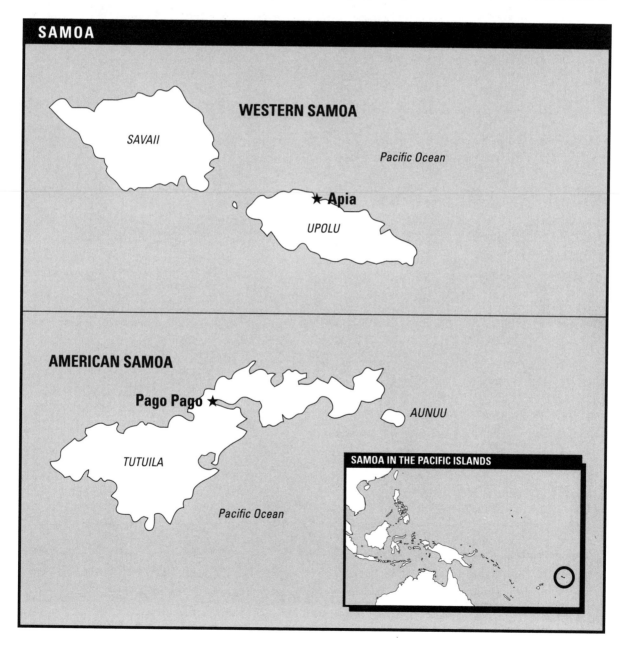

SAMOA

WESTERN SAMOA

SAVAII

Pacific Ocean

★ Apia

UPOLU

AMERICAN SAMOA

Pago Pago ★

AUNUU

TUTUILA

Pacific Ocean

SAMOA IN THE PACIFIC ISLANDS

Samoan man in traditional native clothing, circa 1890. (Brigham Young University, Hawaii)

Pago Pago Bay, Tutuila Island, American Samoa. (John Penisten, Pacific Pictures)

Pago Pago. Still further east are the islands of Ofu, Olosega and Tau, collectively known as the Manua Islands, and there are two outlying atolls, Swains and Rose islands.

The total population of the archipelago in 1990 was approximately 206,000, the vast majority being full-blooded Polynesians noted for their conservative lifestyle, referred to as *FaaSamoa* (the Samoan way). The economy of Western Samoa is based primarily on agriculture plus light manufacturing, while in American Samoa the majority of the people work in government jobs or in the tuna industry, there being little soil cultivation.

The Samoan archipelago was settled by immigrants from Southeast Asia about three thousand years ago. The first European discovery of the islands was made in 1722 by Dutch navigator Jacob Roggeveen. In 1768 Louis de Bougainville named the archipelago the "Navigators Islands" because of his perceptions of the people's ability as sailors and boat builders.

Samoan Civic Association: Social organization formed in 1960 by Samoans living in the United States. A substantial number of Samoans have emigrated to the United States, settling chiefly in states along the Pacific Coast (as many as twenty thousand Samoans were living there in 1970). Several hundred Samoans created the association for the purpose of organizing projects to serve their communities.

Samoan special events: Independence Day in Western Samoa, Flag Day in American Samoa, White Sunday, church dedications, and *palolo* night are celebrations of special importance in the Samoan Islands.

Western Samoa's Independence Day and American Samoa's Flag Day commemorate two different political events but are celebrated in a similar way. Western Samoa became independent from New Zealand in June, 1962; the American flag was first raised over American Samoa on April 17, 1900. Each year these events occasion visiting between the two countries, with feasting and competition in dancing and singing. The greatest rivalry involves races in *fautasi* (long, streamlined rowing boats), each with forty-six oarsmen. This latter event draws competitors from the Kingdom of Tonga, also.

White Sunday is observed on the second Sunday in October. On this day all the children wear new white clothing made or purchased for this event. A church service features children reciting Bible verses and singing, with the adults of the village looking on in admiration. Afterward, children of each household are seated in the front of the house (a place of honor) and served a special meal. The adults must wait until later to eat. These customs are a reversal of the usual procedures in this adult-dominated society.

Few occasions rival a church dedication in importance in Samoa. Every village has at least one church, and the building of a new one precipitates elaborate preparation for the dedication ceremonies. This gala event lasts several days and brings visiting delegations from churches throughout the islands and from Samoan migrant communities in the United States. They bring monetary contributions to help defray the cost of the church. Events include congratulatory speeches by the pastors of the delegations represented, performance of special songs by the choirs, dance performances, and a great deal of feasting. The climax is a procession to the new church to unlock the doors.

Every fall when lunar and tide conditions are right, *palolo* (reef worms) rise to the surface to mate. A carnival-like atmosphere prevails as whole villages go to the reef at night, scooping up *palolo* and eating them raw.

Samoans: Western Polynesians who inhabit the Samoan archipelago. There are sixteen islands (ten inhabited) divided politically into Western Samoa (nine islands), an independent nation since 1962, and American Samoa (seven islands), an unincorporated territory

Village children, Western Samoa. (John Penisten, Pacific Pictures)

Banana market, Apia, Western Samoa. (John Penisten, Pacific Pictures)

Samoan American Statistical Profile, 1990

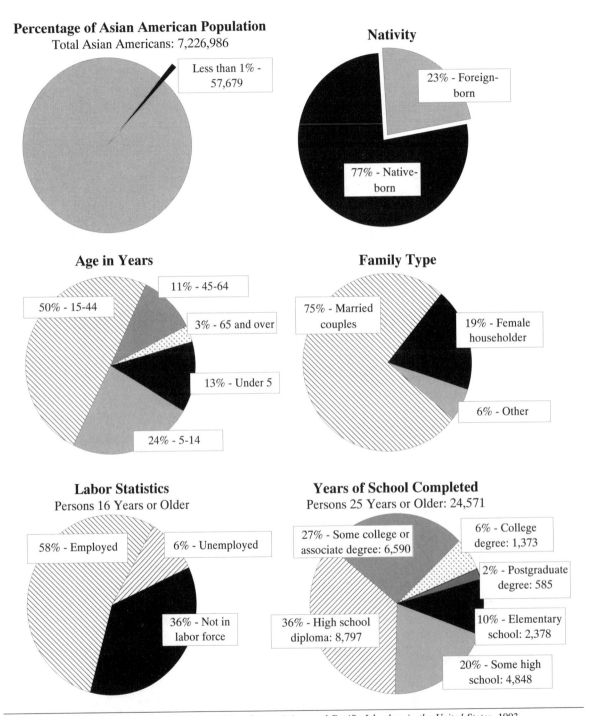

Percentage of Asian American Population
Total Asian Americans: 7,226,986

Less than 1% - 57,679

Nativity

23% - Foreign-born

77% - Native-born

Age in Years

11% - 45-64

3% - 65 and over

50% - 15-44

13% - Under 5

24% - 5-14

Family Type

75% - Married couples

19% - Female householder

6% - Other

Labor Statistics
Persons 16 Years or Older

58% - Employed

6% - Unemployed

36% - Not in labor force

Years of School Completed
Persons 25 Years or Older: 24,571

27% - Some college or associate degree: 6,590

6% - College degree: 1,373

2% - Postgraduate degree: 585

36% - High school diploma: 8,797

10% - Elementary school: 2,378

20% - Some high school: 4,848

Source: U.S. Bureau of the Census, *1990 Census of Population: Asians and Pacific Islanders in the United States,* 1993.

of the United States since 1900. The Samoa Islands were originally populated as early as 1,000 B.C.E. by migrants from Southeast Asia, who were carriers of a culture that has been associated archaeologically with a form of pottery known as Lapita.

These original migrants were a seafaring people with outstanding boat-building and sailing skills. They were agriculturalists, having brought a variety of plants such as coconut, taro, breadfruit, and bananas, as well as such domesticated animals as chickens and pigs, with them from the West. Over the years they have maintained contact with the people of Tonga and Fiji, who share their cultural designation as Western Polynesians, if not their racial or linguistic type.

Physical Type. Samoans are a racially hybrid group exhibiting a blend of Caucasoid, Negroid, and Mon-

Occupation

Employed Persons 16 Years or Older	Percentage
Managerial and professional specialty	13.5%
Technical, sales, and administrative support	32.3%
Service	20.0%
Farming, forestry, and fishing	1.4%
Precision production, craft, and repair	11.1%
Operators, fabricators, and laborers	21.7%

Income, 1989

Median household income	$27,511
Per capita	$7,690
Percent of families in poverty	25%

Household Size

Number of People	Percentage
1	6.5%
2	13.6%
3	16.1%
4	17.2%
5	15.4%
6	12.0%
7 or more	19.2%

Source: U.S. Bureau of the Census, *1990 Census of Population: Asians and Pacific Islanders in the United States*, 1993.

goloid physical characteristics, reflecting their migration history from their homeland to Samoa. They are average to tall in height and robust in body build with a medium yellow-brown skin color. Faces are broad with straight noses of medium breadth and with full lips. Hair is black or dark brown and wavy to straight in form; eyes are brown. Approximately 90 percent of Samoan islanders are full-blooded Polynesians.

Language. Samoan is a dialect of the language family known as "Austronesian," which spread throughout the Pacific between five thousand and six thousand years ago. It is a pleasant-sounding language with abundant use of vowels and is often referred to as the "Italian of the Pacific." It is one of the earlier established languages of Polynesia, although more recent than Tongan or Fijian.

Social Organization. Samoans are highly family-oriented, and the dominant feature of social organization is the *matai* system. A *matai* (chief) is elected by the extended family (*aiga*) to hold a hereditary title and serve as head of the family. The title might be that of *alii* (chief) or *tulafale* (talking chief); the *matai* holds the position for life. Since the *aiga* is usually a very large group of kinspeople, the *matai* has a formidable responsibility, including administration of the family's communally owned property, coordinating economic and social activities, mediating family squabbles, and representing the family in the village council (*fono*).

The *fono* is made up of the *matai* from each family in the village, who meet regularly to deliberate over problems in the village. Each chief has an opportunity to speak, and the goal is to reach unanimity on decisions, which may come after long periods of discussion and compromise.

The *matai* also heads his own household, which is typically made up of at least three generations and averages seven or more people. All but the very youngest have responsibilities within the household.

Traditionally Samoan men engaged in subsistence agriculture, cultivating small plots of land on the slopes above the villages. Women often tended pandanus plants used in mat making and paper mulberry bushes used in making barkcloth. They scavenged the reef for shellfish and octopuses and sometimes assisted in village fishing drives on the reef flat. Men fished from outrigger canoes or bonito boats. Most of the cooking for the family or for ceremonies was done by men.

Samoan villages tend to have populations of a few hundred people except in the port town areas. Houses

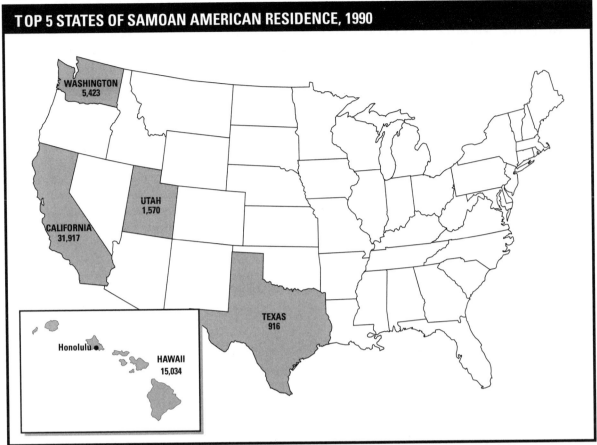

TOP 5 STATES OF SAMOAN AMERICAN RESIDENCE, 1990

WASHINGTON 5,423

UTAH 1,570

CALIFORNIA 31,917

TEXAS 916

Honolulu

HAWAII 15,034

Source: Susan B. Gall and Timothy L. Gall, eds., *Statistical Record of Asian Americans.* Detroit: Gale Research, 1993.

are on the low-lying land near the beach. The traditional Samoan house (*fale*) was an oval-shaped structure, open all-around, with a coral stone floor and numerous houseposts supporting a beehive-type roof covered with thatch. Families often had a sleeping house, a guest house for entertaining, and a cookhouse behind the others. Furnishings were minimal as people slept and sat on mats on the floor.

Religion. The indigenous religion of Samoans included worship of a high god, Tagaloa, who appeared in various forms. There were many lesser gods (*atua*), spirits (*ata*), and ghosts (*aitu*). Unlike the people of eastern Polynesia, samoans had neither *marae* (ceremonial centers), temples, altars, nor an elaborate polytheistic pantheon of high gods.

The first mission contact in Samoa was in 1828, but it was not until 1830, when John Williams of the London Missionary Society arrived, that missionary efforts became effective. The Samoan language was written for the first time and the Bible translated, which had great influence on literacy. Samoans were Christianized. The church established by the London

Missionary Society, now called the Congregational Christian Church of Samoa, remains the dominant denomination. Methodists, Catholics, and Mormons are also well represented in the population.

Religion is a dominant force in Samoa. Every village has a church of some denomination, and dedication of a new church is one of the more important events in Samoan life. There is also no more respected person in any village than the *faifeau* (pastor).

Art. Art forms in which Samoans excel include oratory, group dancing (*siva*) and singing, barkcloth (*siapo*) manufacture, and the weaving of finemats. The latter are important articles for gift exchanges at weddings, funerals, and title ceremonies. Old finemats are extremely valuable and have the quality of heirlooms. Samoans do very little wood carving other than bowls, but tattooing is a very important art form. Traditionally young Samoan men would be tattooed from a little above the waist to the knees as a mark of bravery and manhood.

Cultural Change. Although Samoans have long been considered culturally conservative, Western Sa-

Samoan villager attempts to start a fire by rubbing sticks together. (Brigham Young University, Hawaii)

moans have been able to retain somewhat more of their traditional way of life than has been the case in American Samoa. The forces of modernization are apparent in both countries, but in the early 1960's, the American government embarked on a program of deliberate change in American Samoa. Electricity, television, automobiles, telephones, jumbo jets, and pizza are known to most Samoans, but in American Samoa these things are considered essential.—*Ellen Rhoads Holmes*

SUGGESTED READINGS: • Grattan, F. J. H. *An Introduction to Samoan Custom.* Apia: Samoan Printing and Publishing Company, 1948. • Gray, J. A. C. *Amerika Samoa.* Annapolis, Md.: U.S. Naval Institute, 1960. • Holmes, Lowell D., and Ellen Rhoads Holmes. *Samoan Village: Then and Now.* 2d ed. Fort Worth: Harcourt Brace Jovanovich, 1992. • Keesing, Felix, and Marie M. Keesing. Elite Communication in Samoa. Stanford, Calif.: Stanford University Press, 1956. • Mead, Margaret. *Coming of Age in Samoa.* New York: William Morrow, 1928.

Samse: Korean term for third-generation persons of Korean ancestry residing outside Korea.

San Francisco earthquake and fire of 1906: The shaker that struck a few minutes after 5:00 A.M. on April 18 devastated San Francisco, a city of about 400,000 people at the time, including about 30,000 Chinese. Great fires then erupted, raging out of control and burning until April 21. When it was over, about four square miles of the center of the city had been demolished. Twenty-eight thousand buildings had been destroyed. Total property losses amounted to about $500 million. As many as 700 people may have died; many more (250,000) were rendered homeless by the quake and were forced to take up temporary shelter in Golden Gate Park.

Much of San Francisco's Chinatown was affected by the disaster. The fires destroyed countless documents, including those of many Chinese immigration applicants. Moreover, aware that the city's birth records had also been lost, many Chinese claimed that they had been born in San Francisco and therefore were American citizens. After establishing their own citizenship, they next claimed to have sons back in China who, under the rule of derivative citizenship, were eligible for admission to the United States. (This provision allowed the minor children and grandchildren of American-born Chinese to gain entry as U.S. citizens.) The majority of these "PAPER SONS" bore no

Chinatown residents watch helplessly as great fires ravage the city in the wake of the San Francisco earthquake of 1906. From an Arnold Genthe photograph, "San Francisco, April 18, 1906." (Library of Congress)

relation whatsoever to their so-called fathers but still managed to enter the country.

U.S. immigration authorities did their best to expose and outwit the would-be immigrants. Many of these new arrivals would experience lengthy delays or grueling interrogation sessions while being detained at San Francisco's ANGEL ISLAND IMMIGRATION STATION.

San Francisco Journal: Bilingual Chinese-English weekly newspaper. The *San Francisco Journal* began publication in February, 1972, the week of the historic visit of President Richard M. Nixon to the People's Republic of China (PRC). The newspaper's peak circulation numbered more than ten thousand with subscribers in all fifty U.S. states.

The *San Francisco Journal* relied on a volunteer staff for the first eight years of its existence. As many as forty writers, typesetters, graphic artists, contributors, and layout and circulation personnel devoted their time and effort. Its coverage included international and national as well as local news.

A distinctive feature of the *San Francisco Journal*

was its extensive coverage of news about the PRC. The paper was founded in part to promote American-Chinese relations and the development of friendship between the people of the two countries. During the period between the Communist victory in China in 1949 and the early 1970's, prior to Nixon's historic visit, the mainstream media offered skimpy coverage of China. Moreover, in Chinese American communities, many of the established newspapers were funded or subsidized by the Nationalist government in Taiwan (see CHINESE AMERICAN PRESS; also, CHINA POLITICS IN THE CHINESE AMERICAN COMMUNITY). This created a virtual vacuum of news regarding developments in the PRC. The *San Francisco Journal* played a significant role in filling this gap.

The paper also sought to increase Chinese Americans' pride in their culture and history through the dissemination of news from their ancestral homeland and to encourage constructive activism within the Chinese American community. Its local and national coverage highlighted struggles for civil rights and equal opportunities for Chinese Americans. As a result, cultural relations between Chinese living in the United States and those living in China were improved.

The Chinese edition of the *San Francisco Journal* subsequently became a semiweekly and later a daily. It ceased publication in December, 1986.

San Francisco school board crisis (1906): Controversy initiated on October 11 of that year when, following the San Francisco earthquake, the board declared that henceforth all Chinese, Japanese, and Korean children would attend a single school. At that time, a total of ninety-three students of Japanese descent (twenty-five American-born) were enrolled in twenty-three different local schools. Although the board was eventually forced to rescind its action following the intervention of President Theodore Roosevelt, the crisis attracted national attention, increased anti-Japanese sentiment throughout the United States, and led directly to a significant limitation being placed on subsequent Japanese immigration into the country.

California law, under provisions established by *Plessy v. Ferguson* (1896), permitted local school districts to establish separate schools "for children of Chinese or Mongolian descent." The board's decision to include Japanese students came in the midst of a well-publicized series of racial incidents resulting from the transfer of earlier anti-Chinese intolerance to the resident Japanese population. Japanese immi-

grants, following Japan's recent victory in the Russo-Japanese War, had by 1906 come to public attention because of that nation's expanding power in the Pacific. Many "nativists" also feared that unfettered immigration rights granted to the Japanese would result in a significant loss of job opportunities at home. Local concerns also arose from the possibility that older Japanese males, some into their twenties, placed in lower elementary grade classrooms because of their lack of English-language skills might assault female classmates.

This attempt to segregate the local Japanese school-age population provoked an immediate diplomatic outcry from the Japanese government, ever sensitive to the treatment accorded its emigrant population. Roosevelt, in turn, sent Victor H. Metcalf (secretary of commerce and labor) on a fact-finding mission to San Francisco; later the president prevailed upon the membership of the school board to meet directly with him in Washington, D.C.

Ultimately, the school board backed down, and Japanese immigrant schoolchildren were allowed to continue attending neighborhood schools. Within eighteen months, however, in reaction to the rising tide of anti-Japanese intolerance fostered by the crisis, the United States and Japan had negotiated an informal end to the immigration of laborers from Japan to the United States or to the adjacent territories of Canada, Mexico, and Hawaii. Though not formalized by treaty, the GENTLEMEN'S AGREEMENT (1907-1908) remained in force until replaced by the exclusion provisions of the IMMIGRATION ACT OF 1924.

San Francisco State College strike (1968-1969): Student strike that forced campus administrators to initiate the first School of Ethnic Studies established by any American college or university. The movement's principal organizer was the Third World Liberation Front (TLWF), a coalition consisting of student associations from various ethnic groups within the school. The strike, begun in the fall of 1968, broke out in the latter stages of a turbulent decade characterized by some of the most prolonged and intensified civil rights and antiwar activism in American history. During the strike, and because of it, Asian Americans and other ethnic minorities achieved new levels of political awareness and identity.

The TWLF launched the longest student-led demonstrations in U.S. history to voice demands centered essentially on three distinct but related issues. First, the coalition pressed for changes in the college's admissions criteria to ensure ethnic applicants greater access to higher education. It called for the institution of an open-admissions policy and special admittance programs beneficial to Third World students. Second, the TWLF demanded that the school establish a School of Ethnic Studies and a curriculum more relevant to the needs of Third World students in America. Third, the group wanted a prominent role for ethnic voices in the development of a new ethnic studies curriculum with courses taught by ethnic instructors. This particular demand flowed from the assertion of "self-determination," the right of each ethnic group to shape its own educational agenda and hire its own faculty in an effort to bypass the traditional, Eurocentric versions of history and modern world issues typically taught.

To make its point, the militant TWLF staged rallies and marches involving thousands of students, skipped classes, and sent teams of students into classrooms to promote the strike. As the general policy of disruption progressed, classes were suspended, prompting California state authorities, led by Governor Ronald Reagan, to demand a crackdown and the restoration of order. Police forces were called in to suppress the strikers; protestors were beaten by police, many severely, and hundreds of demonstrators were arrested.

Making matters worse for the strikers was the selection in late 1968 of faculty member S. I. HAYAKAWA as the new president of the college following the dismissal of the existing administration. The conservative Hayakawa was personally opposed to the strike and soon after his appointment imposed a campuswide prohibition against political gatherings of any sort. In early December, as students assembled on campus in defiance of the order, he climbed up onto the sound truck and ripped out the speaker wires of the public-address system. He also refused to negotiate with any students or with faculty sympathetic to them and brought in even more police. His election was also viewed as controversial among the Bay Area's Japanese American community, and not a few community members publicly opposed his appointment and supported the strikers. Additional support arrived when the American Federation of Teachers (AFT), a faculty labor union, began picketing the school's administration building. Ultimately, however, Hayakawa did end the strike and in so doing became a well-known public figure in California.

The compromise settlement that ended the strike in March of 1969 included the creation of the mandated School of Ethnic Studies. Among American universities, it is still the largest program in terms of the number of faculty and the classes available.

In September, San Francisco State College (now University) became the first college in the world to open an ASIAN AMERICAN STUDIES department. At American college and university campuses, the institution of Asian American Studies programs has been called the most significant legacy of the ASIAN AMERICAN MOVEMENT. In the wake of the strike, an Asian American Studies program was established at the University of California, Berkeley, the setting for a second successful student strike launched in early 1969. The concessions won by the strikers influenced students and activists at other schools to demand ethnic studies classes, programs, and departments and forced administrators to accede to such demands. As a result, Asian American Studies programs have been established at sister schools in the University of California and California State University systems and such schools as the Universities of Washington and Hawaii and the City College of New York (CCNY). Over the years, what began as experimental curricula have become fully accredited degree programs.

San Francisco Taiko Dojo: The original *taiko* (Japanese word for "drum") group in the United States is located in San Francisco, California. Its goal is to "rediscover, popularize, and revolutionize" *taiko* from a primitive folk art to a sophisticated version of contemporary rhythm, martial arts stances, and dance movements. Regarded as sacred in ancient Japan, the drum was used to drive away evil spirits and pests during planting seasons and to give thanks during harvest times.

San Jose Taiko: Asian American musical group utilizing Japanese instruments to communicate an Asian American cultural experience. The San Jose Taiko was founded in San Jose, California, in 1973 by Asian Americans, particularly Sansei. The original members had grown up in the United States and were Buddhists. The performers, most of whom are women, have been innovative in incorporating African, Latin, and American jazz rhythms and theater and dance. The group has also collaborated with other Asian American performers such as jazz musician Mark Izu and storyteller Brenda Wond Aoki. They have performed in Japan and have toured with the internationally known *taiko* group Kodo. They have also performed with the San Jose Repertory Theater in one of its productions.

The San Jose Taiko reflects the efforts of Asian Americans to articulate and maintain their heritage.

Taiko *drums.* (Ben Klaffke)

The *taiko* is a Japanese drum. There are three sizes of *taiko* used. The largest drum, used for bass sounds, is the *odaiko*. Originally an oak cask, both ends of the drum are covered with calfskin. It is perched on a stand. The top of the drum measures more than seven feet above the floor. The second largest drum, or *josuke taiko*, is also made from an oak barrel with calfskin attached at both ends. It provides the tenor sounds. The third and smallest drum is the *shime taiko*. The performers use *bachi*, sticks made of wood such as oak or maple, to strike the drums. Performing with the *taiko* has allowed the performers to maintain a sense of their Asian heritage. Through rehearsals, physical conditioning, and performances, members of the group work toward creating a unity of action.

The San Jose Taiko has received worldwide recognition. The group was awarded a grant from the National Endowment for the Arts (NEA) and an award from the Irvine Foundation. It has performed at many community functions, festivals, and celebrations such as the annual O-bon celebrations throughout California and including Hawaii.

San Juan, E. [Epifanio], Jr. (b. Dec. 29, 1938, Manila, Philippines): Scholar, critic, and writer. San Juan is Professor of English and Comparative Literature at the University of Connecticut, having taught there since 1967. He came to the United States in 1960 and took a Ph.D. degree at Harvard University in 1965. The widely published author of numerous books and articles appearing in many languages, San Juan has attracted worldwide renown for his work in comparative cultural studies. His *Racial Formations/Critical Transformations: Articulations of Power in Ethnic and Racial Studies in the U.S.*, which strives to define the central role of race and racism in American discourse and practice, was published in 1992. It won the National Book Award of the Association for Asian American Studies the following year. Other academic honors include a Fulbright lectureship at the University of the Philippines in 1987-1988 and an honorary fellowship at the University of Edinburgh in 1993.

San Pedro: Region of southwestern Los Angeles housing one of the area's busiest seaports. It was the site of the Japanese American Terminal Island fishing community, one of the first communities uprooted when Japanese Americans were interned during World War II.

Sand Island: Camp used by the U.S. Army, in the aftermath of the Pearl Harbor bombing, to house pro-Axis suspects. In Hawaii, the Army Counter Intelligence, assisted by the Federal Bureau of Investigation (FBI), the Office of Naval Intelligence, and the Honolulu Police Reservists, began rounding up pro-Axis suspects at 11 in the morning on December 7, 1941, about an hour after the Japanese had broken off their attack on Pearl Harbor and the military installations of Oahu. Most of the suspects were officers or members of pro-Japanese organizations and persons holding high positions in firms believed to be subsidized by the Japanese government.

The first day, the authorities picked up about two hundred suspects and lodged them at the Honolulu Immigration Building. On December 8, the Army activated Sand Island for use as an internment center. A fan-shaped island in Honolulu harbor, its semicircular top faces Honolulu and is connected to it by a bridge; the handle of the fan points seaward. Within a week, about three hundred Japanese were transferred from the immigration station to Sand Island.

On September 9, 1942, John R. Sulzer of the International Committee of the Red Cross, in accordance with the privilege granted to that organization by the Geneva conventions, investigated the internment camp. He reported that of the civilian prisoners held there, there were fifty-two citizens of Japan, including four women; two German males; three Italians, including one woman; and 267 American citizens, fifteen of them women. There were also thirty-six Japanese prisoners of war, four of them officers. Sulzer found that the camp consisted of several wooden barracks of excellent construction. Married couples were authorized to live in well-constructed tents. He rated lodging, food, clothing, hygiene, and sanitary installations satisfactory. From all viewpoints, he graded the camp excellent.

The Army used the camp for fifteen months. During that time, it spent about five hundred thousand dollars on additions and improvements. Most of the aliens were eventually sent to mainland detention centers. On March 2, 1943, the Army moved the camp to Honouliuli, Oahu.

Sangha: Order of Buddhist monks who study, teach, and preserve the teachings of the Buddha. The *sangha* has its origin in the mendicant lifestyle, common in ancient India, of those who had left their homes to seek out a teacher who could offer a meaningful explanation of existence and provide a doctrine of salvation. Those who were attracted by the Buddha's teachings in his lifetime followed him as he wandered throughout northeastern India. During the rainy season, the Buddha and his followers would cease their wanderings and settle for a time near a village where they could beg daily for their needs.

The disciples of the Buddha continued the practice of yearly rain retreats after his death in c. 483 B.C.E. Within several centuries, the temporary retreats were replaced by a permanent monastic settlement. The monasteries were supported by local villagers who donated land and buildings for the use of the monks and provided them with their daily sustenance. Gradually, the monasteries became centers of Buddhist learning for the villagers. The *sangha* guided the laity in studying the scriptures and provided opportunities for lay participation in religious observances.

The monks of the *sangha* follow a strict code of discipline (*Patimokkha*) consisting of 227 rules of conduct. Every two weeks, at the time of the full and new moons, the local *sangha* monks gather to recite the *Patimokkha*. The daily life of a *sangha* monk in Southeast Asia begins at dawn with a round of begging in the nearby village or town. The Buddhist laity gladly pro-

vides the monks with food, perceiving the act of giving as an opportunity for earning merit. When the monks return to the monastery, they eat their one meal of the day before noon, as prescribed by the *Patimokkha*. The rest of the time, the monks engage in the study of sacred texts and meditation.

Entrance into the *sangha* requires the aspirants to undergo a public ceremony in which they are required to shave their heads and recite the Threefold Refuge: "I go to the Buddha, *Dhamma* [doctrine] and *Sangha* for refuge." With this ceremony, the aspirant becomes a novice in the monastery and a member of the *sangha*.

Regarded by the laity as models of the ideal Buddhist life, *sangha* monks provide a constant source of example and inspiration and remain the focal point of Buddhist communities throughout Asia.

Sano, Roy (b. June 18, 1931, Brawley, Calif.): Bishop. A Japanese American, he became affiliated with the Los Angeles area United Methodist Church in 1992. He previously led the Denver area church (1984 to 1992) and served in various pastoral roles for nineteen years (1950 to 1969) in California and New York City. He received his M.Div. at Union Theological Seminary, New York, taught at the Pacific School of Religion in Berkeley, California, and wrote the books *From Every Nation Without Number: Racial and Ethnic Diversity in United Methodism* (1982) and *Outside the Gate: A Study of the Epistle to the Hebrews* (1982).

Sansei: Third-generation Japanese Americans. Japanese Americans employ distinctive generational terms that connote age and cultural characteristics. Because restrictive immigration laws such as the IMMIGRATION ACT OF 1924 terminated immigration from Japan, the population growth of Japanese Americans began with the second generation, the Nisei, the children of Issei (first-generation) women who had arrived before 1924. The third generation, the Sansei, were products of the baby-boom era following World War II.

Unlike their parents, the Nisei, many Sansei were not reared in Japanese American ethnic communities. The Sansei did not experience the institutionalized discrimination of segregated neighborhoods and the limited economic opportunities that had prevailed before World War II. Their parents had been raised in ethnic communities, attending Japanese-language schools and churches. Many Sansei, born after World War II, grew up having little awareness of the early Japanese American communities and the concentration camp experience. When the Sansei came of age,

Sansei have been especially active in helping to organize social programs to benefit the older Issei population. (Michael Yamashita)

entered college in the 1960's, and learned of the internment, they began to ask their parents why Japanese Americans had not resisted being placed in the relocation centers. Realizing that they knew little of the history of Japanese Americans and other ethnic minorities, and that these histories had been omitted from their schooling, a number of Sansei participated in the student movements of the 1960's and 1970's in support of issues such as the teaching of ethnic studies (see ASIAN AMERICAN MOVEMENT).

Marriage patterns among Sansei have indicated a high rate of outmarriage: More than 40 percent of Sansei men and women married someone other than a person of Japanese ancestry in the 1970's. Social scientists who have researched cultural attitudes in the 1970's and 1980's, however, find that some Sansei continue to display certain values and behavioral styles that are rooted in Japanese cultural patterns.

In addition, the Sansei have been actively involved in addressing the needs and concerns of the Japanese American community. For example, in expressing concern for the Issei, the first-generation immigrants,

the Sansei established centers and nutrition programs in the 1970's for Japanese American seniors (see PIONEER CENTERS). In addressing the concern for social justice, many Sansei became actively involved in the redress movement in the 1970's and 1980's. Sansei attorneys volunteered their time to challenge the constitutionality of the internment. The Sansei organized forums, known as Days of Remembrance and observed on February 19, discussing the significance of EXECUTIVE ORDER 9066, which was issued on that day in 1942.

Sanskrit: Classical language of India. "Sanskrit" means "purified," "adorned," and "cultured." It is the source of all modern Indo-Aryan languages spoken on the Indian subcontinent. So great is the impact of Sanskrit on the psyche and intellectual makeup of India that it is often called *deva-vaNii* (the voice of the gods). Although Sanskrit is not a living language, it nevertheless preserves an Indic religious way of life. In addition, it continues to serve as the single most important source of creativity and modernization in modern Indo-Aryan languages in South Asia. New words such as "radio" and "television" are coined from Sanskrit. Its influence on Southeast Asian countries (Thailand, Cambodia, Indonesia, Malaysia) is self-evident from the fact that even Islamic names in Malaysia and Indonesia contain Sanskrit elements.

The oldest form of Sanskrit is attested in the Vedic literature (c. 1500-c.1200 B.C.E.). The variety of the Sanskrit language found in the Epic literature (fifth century B.C.E.-second century C.E.) is quite distinct from its classical variety. The discovery of the Sanskrit language in the late eighteenth century is credited to Sir William Jones, an eminent British scholar of Indology. He summed up his finding in his 1786 address to the Royal Asiatic Society in which he stated that the "Sanskrit language, whatever be its antiquity, is of a wonderful structure; more perfect than the Greek, more copious than the Latin, and more exquisitely refined than either." This discovery led to a new era of historical-comparative linguistics that established Europe's racial, linguistic, and literary kinship with Vedic Hindus and Sanskrit literature.

European philosophers, thinkers, and literary giants (such as Johann Wolfgang von Goethe, Johann

German literary figure Johann Wolfgang von Goethe was among those Europeans who were favorably influenced by Sanskrit literature and other elements of Eastern culture. (Library of Congress)

Gottfried Herder, Arthur Schopenhauer, and Edwin Arnold) were overwhelmed by the beauty of Sanskrit literature. Consequently, Sanskrit set the stage for the entire Romantic movement, which found in the East all the mysticism and mystery that seemed to have died in the West following the approach of science and enlightenment. In addition to the dazzling impact of Sanskrit literature on Western literature and thought, Sanskrit also inspired great grammatical and phonetic literature of depth and diversity considered unmatched in the world. A case in point is Panini's grammar (c. fourth century B.C.E.), which is described as "one of the greatest monuments of human intelligence" by one of the founders of American linguistics.

Santa Fe (N.Mex.): One of four U.S. government internment camps used to detain Japanese enemy aliens during World War II. The camps were run by the Immigration and Naturalization Service (INS) of the U.S. Justice Department. Santa Fe was one of the largest of these installations; most of the internees were Issei males.

Under U.S. law, during time of war the government was empowered to round up all citizens or nationals of hostile nations and to detain or expel them as enemy aliens. Following news of the surprise air assault by Japan on Pearl Harbor, Honolulu, successive declarations issued by President Franklin D. Roosevelt implicated Japanese, German, and Italian aliens as potential security risks subject to imprisonment or deportation. The day of the bombing, December 7th, the Federal Bureau of Investigation (FBI), armed with presidential arrest warrants, began taking into custody hundreds of aliens classified as possibly dangerous (mostly Issei). By that evening, between twelve and fifteen hundred Issei had been apprehended. By March of 1942, more than four thousand enemy aliens were in temporary INS custody, where they were interrogated and either released, paroled, or sent to an internment camp.

The camp at Santa Fe occupied a tract of twenty-eight acres at an elevation of seven thousand feet. The Justice Department originally envisioned the installation as a holding pen for aliens awaiting a hearing on their cases. The first arrival of 426 Issei men occurred in mid-March, 1942. That number swelled to 826 a few months later but dropped precipitously as those arrested were released or paroled (more than 520) or consigned to Army prisons (more than 300). By September, the camp facilities were idle. The following March, 1943, a group of 357 new male civilian internees arrived at Santa Fe after being transferred by the

Army into the custody of the INS for the duration of the war. By August the population had risen to 1,783, climbing to a high of 2,100 in June of 1945.

The administration and quality of life inside Santa Fe were regulated by the standards set forth in the Geneva Convention of 1929, concerning the humane treatment of prisoners of war. Accordingly, basic needs—food, clothing, shelter—were in general adequately supplied, and, until the arrival of prisoners from TULE LAKE in late 1944 and early 1945, camp life proceeded peacefully. Surveys indicated that the physical conditions at the Santa Fe internment camp were at least as good as those at other camps. The grounds included a nineteen-acre farm, run by the internees, that supplied fresh vegetables, as well as a poultry farm; specialty food items from Japan were sold at the camp store. There was also a bakery, recreation hall, library, and athletic facilities. Films were shown, and a theater troupe composed of internees provided another source of diversion. Moreover, as many as forty-five visitors were permitted to enter the camp daily, and the inmates were allowed to travel to the relocation centers to see family members.

When the war ended, most of the internees were either freed or repatriated to Japan. By mid-1946, the camp had closed.

Santos, Bienvenido N. (b. Mar. 22, 1911, Manila, Philippines): Novelist, short-story writer, and poet. Set in both the Philippines and the United States, Santos' work explores the Filipino search for identity and community.

Santos has published many novels, including *Villa Magdalena* (1965), *The Praying Man* (1982), *The Man Who (Thought He) Looked Like Robert Taylor* (1983), and *What the Hell for You Left Your Heart in San Francisco* (1987); several short-story collections, including *You Lovely People* (1955), *Brother My Brother*, (1960), *The Day the Dancers Came* (1967), *Scent of Apples* (1979), *Dwell in the Wilderness* (1985); the poetry volumes *The Wounded Stag* (1956) and *Distances in Time* (1983); and the one-act plays *The Bishop's Pets* (1966) and *The Long Way Home* (1967).

Santos received a B.S.Ed. degree from the University of the Philippines in 1932 and an M.A. degree from the University of Illinois in 1942. He attended Harvard University from 1945 to 1946 and the University of Iowa from 1958 to 1961.

In 1941, Santos first came to the United States as a cultural envoy and was forced to remain there during World War II (1939-1945). After the war, he went back to the Philippines and became president of Legazpi College. He returned to the United States as a Rockefeller Foundation Fellow in 1958, a Guggenheim Fellow in 1960, and an Exchange Fulbright Professor at the University of Iowa in 1966. In 1972, he was teaching as a lecturer in the creative writing program at the University of Iowa when martial law was declared in the Philippines; he remained in the United States and in 1973 joined the faculty at Wichita State University, Kansas, as professor of English and distinguished writer-in-residence. He became a naturalized American citizen in 1976, retired from Wichita State University in 1982, and returned to the Philippines in 1986.

Santos has received numerous awards and honors for his writing. In the United States, he is known primarily for his finely crafted short stories about the "old-timers," Filipino bachelors who came to the United States between the 1920's and 1940's and were prevented by various circumstances from returning to the Philippines. The men's loneliness and nostalgia for their homeland are sensitively portrayed in *Scent of Apples*, which was published in the United States and was the 1981 winner of the Before Columbus Association Foundation's American Book Award.

Sargent, Frank Pearce (Nov. 18, 1854, East Orange, Vt.—Sept. 4, 1908, Washington, D.C.): Labor leader and government official. Sargent was commissioner-general of the U.S. Bureau of Immigration from 1902 to 1908. During the period when Chinese exclusion legislation was passed and prejudice, harassment, and violence against Chinese occurred, he campaigned vehemently for restrictions and controls curtailing immigration from Southern Europe and Asia.

Sargent was the son of Charles E. and Mary C. Sargent, who traced their ancestors back to Massachusetts as early as 1633. Sargent attended local schools and the Northfield Academy, Massachusetts, for one year until health problems forced him to move to Arizona in 1878. He enlisted in the U.S. cavalry, seeing action in the Geronimo campaign against the Apache Indians. In 1880 he was honorably discharged and went to work for the Southern Pacific Railroad. In 1881 he married Georgia M. McMullough; he was also initiated into the Brotherhood of Locomotive Firemen. This began Sargent's long career in the American labor movement, in which he led several major labor strikes.

President Theodore Roosevelt appointed Sargent commissioner-general of the Bureau of Immigration, succeeding Terence V. Powderly. This brought the ties between labor and immigration closer. Sargent was committed to the establishment of laws to prevent illegal and undesirable immigrants from coming to the United States, while favoring immigrants from Northern Europe. In 1904 he published two articles revealing his prejudice. The first, "The Need of Close Inspection and Greater Restriction of Immigrants," stated his views on setting higher standards for immigration with placement to sections of the country in need of labor. In the second article, "Problems of Immigration," he claimed that U.S. immigration laws provided for the "selection" of the best immigrants—not exclusion.

While in office Sargent gave special attention to the Chinese by strongly enforcing the Chinese exclusion laws and preventing the illegal migration of Chinese from Mexico and Canada. In 1904 he implemented the Bertillon system for the identification of Chinese adults. He also encouraged immigration officials to harass and abuse the Chinese in the United States, wrongly arresting or deporting many Chinese.

Sari: Primary outer garment worn chiefly by the women of India but also by women from all regions of South Asia. Purchased as nine yards of brightly colored or embroidered silk or cotton cloth, it is intricately wrapped around the waist, with one half falling as a skirt and the other half folding over the shoulder. Historical evidence verifies the use of the *sari* as early as the second century B.C.E., at which time the garment apparently covered only the lower body. In the twelfth century C.E., Muslim invaders of north and central India mandated that the entire body be covered up with cloth.

Sato, Eunice N. (b. June 8, 1921, Livingston, Calif.): Educator and city government officer. Sato attended Columbia University, earning her M.A. degree in 1948. During the 1940's and early 1950's she held several teaching posts, including a spell as an educational missionary in Yokohama, Japan, from 1948 until 1951. For more than ten years she served the city of Long Beach, California, first as a member of the city council (1975-1986) and then as mayor (1980-1982). Her career in public service has brought her a slew of civic honors and awards. She has, in addition, formerly served as president of the American Red Cross and the National Conference of Christians and Jews.

Satow, Masao (Feb. 14, 1908, San Mateo, Calif.— Mar. 3, 1977): Community leader and administrator.

Satow was best known as the dedicated leader of the JAPANESE AMERICAN CITIZENS LEAGUE (JACL) who helped to stabilize the organization after the Japanese American and alien internment of World War II. His frugal handling of the group's finances was legendary as he and his wife, Chiz, were credited with keeping the JACL afloat for more than a quarter century.

Satow was born to Shuzo and Kiyose Satow and was reared in Los Angeles, where his father worked as a domestic. Masao Satow earned his bachelor's degree from the University of California, Los Angeles (UCLA) in 1929 and later was graduated from Princeton Theological Seminary. In 1932 Satow returned to Los Angeles to begin his career in the Los Angeles Little Tokyo Young Men's Christian Association (YMCA) as its general secretary. Soon after accepting the YMCA position, Satow joined the JACL at its 1932 Los Angeles convention. Immediately he made an impression with the young Nisei organization and was named the convention's deputy registrar. This was his first step in a steady rise within the JACL national leadership.

While working in Little Tokyo, Satow met Chiz Uyeda at the Iwaki drugstore, where she worked at the lunch counter, and married her shortly before their internment at the Granada relocation center in 1942. While at Granada, he continued his leadership role in the JACL and represented the camp at a 1942 Salt Lake City JACL convention. By 1944 Satow was out of camp and working in Milwaukee, where he was the YMCA national field board representative.

At the JACL's 1946 Denver convention, Satow continued his rise through the ranks and was elected the group's second vice president. When, however, JACL national secretary Mike MASAOKA was appointed as the organization's lobbyist in Washington, D.C., Satow was asked to temporarily replace him for one year. It was a difficult decision, but Satow gave up his job at the YMCA to accept the JACL position. Eventually the position was retitled "executive director," and the job that was supposed to last for only one year continued for more than a quarter century. During his tenure he and Chiz, who ran the office, made a formidable team that helped to guide the JACL through some very lean financial years.

On February 14, 1973, his sixty-fifth birthday, Satow decided to retire from his position. Soon thereafter, he became senior adviser to the president of the Sumitomo Bank of California. A year after Satow's death, the JACL headquarters was rededicated as the Masao Satow Memorial Building.

Saund, Dalip Singh (Sept. 20, 1899, Chhajalwadi, near Amritsar, India—Apr. 23, 1973, Hollywood, Calif.): U.S. representative. The first Asian and the first native of India to become a U.S. congressman, Saund stands out as a rarity, one of the few political figures in the Asian Indian community to have held a high government office. He was a Democratic representative from January 3, 1957, to January 3, 1963, and as a member of the House Foreign Relations Committee, he traveled to India and several other Asian countries on a fact-finding tour and a goodwill mission for American democracy.

Agrarian Beginnings. Saund was born into a well-to-do Sikh family of landowners and contractors and was educated in boarding schools in Amritsar. He was graduated from the University of Punjab with a B.A. degree but saw no future for himself in an India repressed by British rule. Inspired by the ideals of Mahatma Gandhi, Abraham Lincoln, and Woodrow Wilson, he decided to travel to the United States to further his studies. In the fall of 1920, he enrolled at the University of California, Berkeley, where he studied food preservation. He went on to graduate with an M.A. degree in mathematics in 1922 and a Ph.D. degree in 1924.

Like a number of other Indian immigrants of his time, Saund became a lettuce farmer in Southern California's fertile Imperial Valley. Farming was an unpredictable and risky business, and when the Depression came, it hit Saund hard, as it did so many other farmers. Unlike them, however, he did not declare bankruptcy, because in India bankruptcy carries a moral stigma. Instead, he chose to pay off his debts over the course of seven years.

In 1928, Saund married Marian Z. Koza of Massachusetts, a University of California student of Czech parentage who became a teacher in Los Angeles. They had three children—one son, Dalip, who became a veteran of the Korean War (1950-1953), and two daughters, Julie and Eleanor. Soon Saund became active in organizing the Indian community at a time when Indians were barred by law from seeking U.S.

Dalip Singh Saund as a congressional candidate in 1956. (AP/Wide World Photos)

citizenship. He published a work titled *My Mother India* in 1930 with the purpose of presenting India in a favorable light to Americans. He helped form the India Association of America and became its president in 1942. He also journeyed to Washington, D.C., to lobby for the granting of citizenship rights to Indians in the United States.

Entry into Politics. After World War II (1939-1945), when the immigration law was amended and Indians living in the United States became eligible for U.S. citizenship, Saund applied for naturalization and became a citizen in 1949. He immediately became a member of the Central Committee of the Democratic Party in Imperial County. Within a year, he was elected judge in the court of Westmoreland Judicial District but was ineligible to take the position since he had not been a citizen for a full year. In 1952, he was reelected to the same position and served as a judge until 1957. He also set up his own chemical fertilizer company, called D. S. Saund Fertilizers in Westmoreland.

When Saund spoke of running for Congress in 1956, the odds were weighted heavily against him. He was a Democrat running in the Twenty-ninth Congressional District of Imperial and Riverside counties, which had always voted Republican. He was also pitted against the well-heeled and famous aviatrix Jacqueline Cochran Odlum, the Republican candidate. He rejected suggestions that he give up his Sikh religion and join the Church to please the voters. He also refused to be discouraged by the possibility of color prejudice among the voters. As it happened, Saund impressed the voters with his honesty and straightforwardness. He won a surprising victory by a margin of four thousand votes and went to Washington as a member of the Eighty-fifth Congress.

Triumph of Democracy. In his very first term as congressman, Saund was appointed to the powerful House Committee on Foreign Relations, a singular distinction for a freshman. He was asked to survey the effectiveness of the government's foreign-aid program in Asia and undertook a two-and-a-half-month tour of the Asian continent. He was a little apprehensive about how he would be received in India as an American citizen, after a gap of thirty-seven years, but everywhere he went, he was greeted with a tumultuous welcome, especially in his native village. Wherever he went, he presented himself, in his own words, as a "living example of American democracy," chosen by the American people in a free election. Thus, he helped counter allegations of discrimination against Indians in the United States and presented America as a land of opportunity for everyone. The high point of his trip was his address to the joint session of India's Houses of Parliament, an honor usually accorded only to visiting heads of state.

After his visit, Saund came to the conclusion that in order to maximize the effectiveness of its foreign-aid programs, the U.S. government should improve its public relations with Asia, investing more time and money explaining American motives and the United States' commitment to democracy. He also recommended an exchange program involving teachers and journalists. In 1958, he won an award for making "perhaps the most effective tour of India by an American on record."

Saund was reelected to the Eighty-sixth and Eighty-seventh Congresses and campaigned for yet another term in 1962. A massive stroke, however, disabled him, and though he continued to campaign from the hospital, he lost his bid for reelection. He never recovered fully and died an invalid in 1973.

During his terms as congressman, Saund supported many foreign-affairs bills, including the Mideast Doctrine (January, 1957) and an increase in U.S. subscriptions to the International Monetary Fund and the World Bank (March, 1959). On the domestic front, he voted for, among other things, an increase in Social Security benefits (July, 1958) and an extension on the life of the Civil Rights Commission (September, 1959).

Saund was both an idealist and a shrewd politician, and it was this combination of qualities that enabled him to go from lettuce farmer to U.S. congressman. He was also fortunate to have lived in the United States at a time when restrictive immigration laws and strong prejudice against Asians gave way to a more liberal politics of democracy and civil rights.—*Padma Rangaswamy*

SUGGESTED READINGS: • Bruce J. Campbell. "Our Congressman from India." *Reader's Digest* 73 (September, 1958): 175-177. • MacKaye, Milton. "U.S. Congressman from Asia." *The Saturday Evening Post* 231 (August 2, 1958): 25. • Moritz, Charles, ed. *Current Biography, 1960*. New York: H. H. Wilson, 1960. • "Obituaries." *The New York Times*, April 24, 1973, p. 44. • Saund, Dalip Singh. *Congressman from India*. New York: E. P. Dutton, 1960.

Saxton, Alexander P. (b. July 16, 1919, Great Barrington, Mass.): Scholar. Graduated with a Ph.D. degree from the University of California, Berkeley in 1967, he was professor of history at the University of California, Los Angeles until his retirement in 1991.

The recipient of a distinguished National Endowment for the Humanities Fellowship and author of the pioneering study *The Indispensable Enemy: Labor and the Anti-Chinese Movement in California* (1971), he has published widely in *Amerasia Journal, American Quarterly, Marxist Perspectives, Pacific Historical Review*, and other journals.

Say, Allen (b. Japan): Writer and illustrator. A prizewinning writer and illustrator of books for children and young adults, Say received the Caldecott Award for his book *Grandfather's Journey* (1993). The son of a Korean father and a Japanese American mother, Say spent his childhood in Japan. He came to the United States for the first time as a teenager in the early 1950's; since then he has spent time in Japan but has mostly lived in the United States. Among his other books are *The Ink-Keeper's Apprentice* (1979), *El Chino* (1990), and *Tree of Cranes* (1991).

Scholar gentry: Gentry landowners in imperial China who were the rulers and leaders until the demise of old China in 1911. Their status was gained by their educational qualifications, not by birth or wealth. As the literati, they were the bearers of Confucian ideology, playing important roles in state and society by taking advantage of numerous privileges.

The scholar gentry consisted of 1.5 percent of China's population during the last imperial dynasty. A fraction of the 1.1 million scholar gentry monopolized twenty-seven thousand positions in the government, and the rest were in teaching or other professions. To gain membership in the gentry, one had to pass at least one of three civil service examinations: the district, provincial, and national examinations; successful examinees were given the titles of *shengyuan* (government student), *juren* (selected scholar), and *jinshi* (advanced scholar), respectively. During the nineteenth century, the financially pressed Qing Dynasty (1644-1911) allowed a few unsuccessful candidates with considerable scholarly distinction to purchase the titles of *jiansheng* (students of the Imperial College) and *gongsheng* (imperial student). Purchased-degree holders, however, were generally less respected than and less successful as members of the scholar gentry.

The examinations were open to all people except to outcasts (who, until their legal emancipation, constituted less than 1 percent of the people). Education was private, however, and many poor people were unlikely to pass the competitive government examinations. Nevertheless, one-third of the scholar gentry failed to succeed because of incompetent offspring, while the common people rose to power by becoming officials in government and to glory by becoming teachers or leaders in society through success in the examinations. The scholar gentry were set apart from the commoners in style of dress and embellishments. They wore black gowns, with silver or gold buttons on their hats. The commoners cleared the way out of respect when the scholar gentry walked in the street. When a crime was committed, the scholar gentry could not easily be prosecuted or given corporal punishment unless stripped of their status, because they were social equals to the official gentry. They were also exempted from degrading and unpaid labor service and military conscription, and, more important, they paid little or nothing when it came to certain taxes.

The scholar gentry, though privileged, were not part of the ruling bureaucracy; they were the intermediary agents between the local officials and the common people because the commoners had no access to the officials. They also settled disputes between the parties involved, the individuals or the communities, by means of persuasion and arbitration. The scholar gentry's moral leadership resulted in few litigations. For these services rendered, they were handsomely paid, and they acquired enormous wealth in land and money. In times of crises, natural or otherwise, the scholar gentry volunteered to maintain law and order by teaching the public to adhere to Confucian morality, practiced charity for the poor by organizing food distribution centers, trained a militia to defend their community, and even organized an uprising to protest against government mismanagement. Through their monopoly on Confucian learning, they shaped the patterns of political, economic, and social life.

Schoolboy: Term for a male Issei who became a live-in domestic servant to earn a living in America while attending school. What such jobs lacked in pay and prestige they made up for in shelter, exposure to American life, and the chance to stay overseas. These elements made the jobs a popular choice among new arrivals. Moreover, in the first decade of the twentieth century, the Japanese schoolboy was apparently in great demand: At one point the number of schoolboys in San Francisco households exceeded four thousand. Following the GENTLEMEN'S AGREEMENT (1907-1908) between the United States and Japan, with Japan agreeing to stop issuing passports to laborers who wished to immigrate to the United States, the number of schoolboys began to decline.

Schoolgirl: Term for female Issei and Nisei who became live-in domestic servants to earn a living in America while attending school. For the new arrivals, these jobs were a popular means of making a living in America and learning the various aspects of American life. The schoolgirls were preceded by the schoolboys, Issei males who also had worked as domestics.

Scott Act of 1888: Amendment to the CHINESE EXCLUSION ACT OF 1882, which prohibited the immigration of Chinese laborers to the United States for a period of ten years (extended by subsequent legislation). Under the terms of the 1882 act, Chinese workers who were already in the United States and who wished to visit their homeland and then return to the United States were issued federal certificates guaranteeing their readmission. The 1888 amendment discontinued the issuing of such certificates and canceled all existing certificates. Several thousand Chinese im-

migrants who had gone back to China with the intention of returning to the United States were denied readmission.

The Scott Act was passed during a presidential election year. Its passage came on the heels of an aborted U.S.-China treaty and was motivated by presidential politics and the vying for the anti-Chinese vote in California and the western United States.

Prior to its passage, anti-Chinese proponents in California and the western United States had been protesting the alleged ineffectiveness of the Chinese Exclusion Acts in curbing the growth of the Chinese immigrant population. Then, in 1885 and 1886, anti-Chinese violence broke out in the region. Soon after, President Grover Cleveland renewed immigration negotiations with China.

By early 1888, the Chinese government and the Democratic administration of Cleveland had signed a new immigration treaty, providing for an indemnity for

Daguerreotype reproduction of Chinese and white gold miners in the western United States, entitled "Head of Auburn Ravine, 1852." The number of immigrant Chinese laborers in the United States had risen considerably since the California gold rush, a development that prompted Americans to demand more restrictive immigration rules. (California State Library)

the recent violence and restricting the reentry of Chinese laborers into the United States. The treaty was then forwarded to the U.S. Senate for ratification.

Republicans in the Senate, anxious to enhance their own anti-Chinese credentials for the coming presidential election, amended the treaty's prohibition (on reentering Chinese laborers) and made it immediately effective. The Senate then ratified the amended treaty, and the Cleveland Administration sent it back to the Chinese government for approval.

That summer, the Republicans in Congress, in another effort to bolster their anti-Chinese image, initiated legislation to implement the unsigned treaty. Then, in the fall, an unconfirmed news dispatch from London reported that China would not approve the amended treaty. Democrats in Congress, nervous over the effects of the treaty problems on Cleveland's reelection bid, immediately passed the Scott Act, which had been quickly drafted and introduced by Representative William L. Scott, head of the Democratic presidential election committee, in response to the London rumor.

The new law prohibited the reentry of Chinese laborers as of November 1, 1888, if the amended treaty had not been approved by China. As a result of the act, several thousand Chinese laborers were denied reentry to the United States. The Chinese government protested the act as a violation of existing treaties, and the Chinese in the United States mounted a constitutional challenge. In 1889 the U.S. Supreme Court upheld the act as being within the scope of congressional powers.

Sea cucumber: Dark-colored, spiny marine mollusk, of which there are about eleven hundred species. Its soft cylindrical body can measure from an inch to more than six feet long and from less than an inch to almost eight inches wide. Sea cucumbers are considered to be a delicacy and are sometimes served at Chinese banquets.

SEATO. *See* **Southeast Asian Treaty Organization**

Secret societies: Clandestine Chinese organizations that arose both in China and in overseas communities, particularly in the United States. Responding to social oppression by the Qing Dynasty (1644-1911), reformers largely from Guangdong and Fujian provinces arose to protest the injustices of local and state officialdom. The first and most widespread of these societies was the Triad, whose members were loyal to the preceding Ming Dynasty (1368-1644). Many members eventually migrated to San Francisco and established there the first Triad lodge. This lodge and other rival lodges, modeled after those in southeastern China, became centers for political and social reform, while dispensing benevolent services to the Chinatown community. As in China these secret societies in overseas communities degenerated into criminal activities as well.

Political Reform. The Qing Dynasty eroded to one of extravagant waste, embezzlement, and corruption. At this twilight of a despotic regime, emboldened commercial interests and governments led to the First Opium War (1839-1842), resulting in the Treaty of Nanjing (1842). Subsequent indemnities and levies upon imperial China resulted in high taxation for its citizens at a time of drought and famine. Shamed by the futility of its leaders and by defeat, goaded by civil unrest, irate citizens formed factions of Triad resistance and White Lotus Society revolt. The dream of establishing a wholly new and democratic republic was espoused by SUN YAT-SEN. It was embraced by the Triad secret society along with its counterpart in San Francisco. The Chinese Republic was established in 1912, marking the overthrow of the Qing Dynasty.

In ensuing years the Triad association in San Francisco was deeply concerned with and involved in the looming Communist-Guomindang disagreements in China. In 1923 its representatives held an international conference in China to mediate the differences. With little improvement, in 1947 the association, now known as the Chinese Freemason Democratic Party, issued a call for a cease-fire and demanded a coalition government in an effort to unify and pacify the country. Unheeded again, it later supported a "third force" movement that called for broad representation at the highest levels in a nonideological, vaguely democratic system. Surfacing with momentary appeal, this movement soon sunk into oblivion. Overseas societies could not affect the political fortunes in China. Such were the early efforts of the Triad secret society, along with others including the White Lotus Society and the Gelaohui (elder brother society).

Social Reform. The secret societies also provided the base and muscle for protest and reform against individual and collective oppression. They provided a check against clan and territorial-speech associations, the power elite that exploited and controlled smaller clans and entities. They served to voice complaint against government nepotism and favoritism in office seeking. They resisted and critiqued unfair state examinations that favored the privileged and doomed the career goals and advancement of the less privileged.

Sun Yat-sen (seated center) spearheaded the movement on the Chinese mainland to overthrow the wasteful and corrupt Qing government. (Library of Congress)

They sided with frustrated persons against monopolies of every kind.

Secret society members were those who saw their legitimate means to wealth and power blocked. Clan, territorial, and imperial protocol being what it was, forming another body politic with voice and influence was the required antidote. Such models of fraternal protection were imported to San Francisco by the immigrants as clans and territorial-speech associations again vied for advantage and jurisdiction. Smaller, weaker clans bundled together as adversarial movements in the face of any and all monopolies. The Chinese Six Companies (see CHINESE CONSOLIDATED BENEVOLENT ASSOCIATIONS) were just such a monopoly and controlled the destiny of many in Chinatown. Failing to gain the help of the courts, the societies flourished in this vacuum of authority. Mock Wah, receiving an unfavorable hearing from the Six Companies, formed the Kwong Duck Tong in retaliation. Num Sing Bark established the Hip Sing Tong to take revenge against the powerful clans responsible for his "failure" as a scholar-intellectual.

Criminal Activities. Secret societies drew high-minded citizens and reformers at the start. They also attracted the alienated and outcast with no legitimate avenues to wealth and status. They drew adventurers as well, individuals seeking a quick fix to their accomplishments and well-being.

The secret societies in China entered a stage of deterioration and degeneration, as societal muscle was now deployed in dishonest enterprise. Thievery, extortion, and prostitution constituted the business agenda. The same was true in San Francisco as reformers turned into or were replaced by renegades. The Hip Sing Tong engaged in gambling. The On Leong and Kwong Duck *tongs* maintained the brothels. In 1870, of more than seventeen hundred females over age fifteen, more than fourteen hundred of them were living as sing-song entertainers and prostitutes held in virtual slavery. Few wives had accompanied the men from China. Later exclusion served to compound the need as nuclear families were rare.

Meanwhile other *tongs* trafficked in extortion of shopkeepers in Chinatown and in the dispensing of drugs. In the face of such lucrative markets, *tong* rivalries and conflicts first occurred in 1875 as each *tong* vied for control. Rivalries spilled over into other cities across the United States wherever lodges existed. The Chinatown populace lived in constant terror. The more powerful clans and territorial-speech associations sought to subvert the illegal goods and services of the *tongs* but to no avail. The former lacked extraterritorial rights over Chinese criminals in the United States. Witnesses were hard to come by as they were easily bribed or intimidated.

The CHINESE EXCLUSION ACT OF 1882 excluded Chinese from the United States. Moreover subsequent attrition, the aging of present sojourners, and public outrage at such happenings took their toll as the TONG WARS went into decline and were of little significance after 1927. Societal leaders and their hatchet men were no longer in demand.

With the passage of the IMMIGRATION AND NATU-RALIZATION ACT OF 1965, opening the sluice gates to immigration from East Asia, membership in both *tongs* and youthful gangs began to rise. Delinquent youths from Hong Kong and other large cities of Southeast Asia migrated to Chinese communities in the United States. As marginal persons, alienated from their respective clans of blood and kinship ties, these disaffected toughs became a militant force for the revived *tongs*. Outcasts with no knowledge of English, school dropouts with no salable skills, they became mercenaries for hire. These "salaried soldiers" were, moreover, protected by the *tongs*, which assisted them in the event of imprisonment with assurances of financial aid.

Having tasted power and wealth, many delinquent youths formed their own secret societies rivaling that of their predecessors. Gangs such as the Black Eagles and Flying Dragons are known and feared. In a land where ruling power is completely alien to them in terms of race, language, manners, and customs, the staying power of such gangs is assured. Their needs unanswered by civil institutional arrangements, they have found kinship, assistance, and even spiritual content by way of ritual and corporate bond.

Charitable Involvement. Along with reform and criminal efforts, the secret societies simultaneously

Headquarters of the Hip Sing Association, in the old Chinatown district of Seattle, Washington. (Wing Luke Museum)

1326 — *Seicho no Ie*

engaged in benevolent assistance to the Chinatown communities. Secret societies were often the sole organizational basis for a governed community within the walls of Chinatown. This was especially true after the Six Companies lost favor and control, having failed to stem the anti-Chinese movement in the late 1800's. Taking the place of weakened clans and territorial-speech associations, the secret societies provided arbitration with civic authorities. They mediated intramural disputes as well as business covenants and legal regulations. Societies provided lodging for members newly arrived in the United States. Their disabled were given charitable aid, and free medical care was offered to their sick. A death benefit of several hundred dollars was given to the bereaved by some lodges. Several secret societies collaborated to foster Chinese schools, Chinese festivals, and celebrations to ensure the passage of culture and identity. Secret societies served as governing bodies, mediating entities, and sociocultural agents as a whole.—*Hoover Wong*

SUGGESTED READINGS: • Chen, Jack. *The Chinese of America*. San Francisco: Harper & Row, 1980. • Freedman, Maurice. *Chinese Lineage and Society: Fukien and Kwangtung*. New York: Humanities Press, 1966. • Lee, Betty S. *Mountain of Gold: The Story of the Chinese in America*. New York: Macmillan, 1967. • Lyman, Stanford. *Chinese Americans*. New York: Random House, 1974. • Yee, Min. "Chinatown in Crisis." *Newsweek* 75 (February 23, 1970): 57-58.

Seicho no Ie (House of Growth): One of the newly arisen Japanese religious movements, founded in Kobe in 1930 by Taniguchi Masaharu. As a young man Taniguchi led a tumultuous life and joined Omoto-kyo, one of the Sect Shinto movements, in his spiritual search. Finally, after much searching in Western philosophy, spirituality, Buddhism, and American New Thought, in 1929 Taniguchi is said to have received divine revelation that the material reality does not exist; rather the only reality is the divine life of the mind, the essential and original human character. Following this, he began publishing the journal *Seicho no Ie*, in which he applied the principles of mind to practical life for healing and happiness. Subsequently Taniguchi's writings amounted to more than forty volumes, as the fundamental teaching of Seicho no Ie.

Basic teachings of Seicho no Ie include the idea that humans by nature are children of the divine (God or Buddha), naturally pure. Since the phenomenal world is only the manifestation of one's mind, it is originally free from sickness and evil. Unnatural thoughts, however, give rise to illness and unhappiness; these have no reality in themselves but are symptoms of distortions of the relationship with the divine. Through right understanding of the "life of reality" and through developing an attitude of gratefulness, sickness and suffering can be healed. Included in Seicho no Ie's practices are prayerful recitations and a special type of meditation called *shinkosan* to help instill the right attitudes. Since World War II Seicho no Ie has generally been associated with patriotic and conservative causes. It appeals to middle- and upper-class Japanese, including a good number of intellectuals, with its claim of expressing truth common to all religions.

The organization of Seicho no Ie is highly centralized and hierarchical, revolving around Taniguchi's own family, with headquarters in Tokyo. As of 1993 the movement claims some three million adherents. Seicho no Ie came to the United States in 1938, when several leaders began work among Japanese Americans on the West Coast. After the war a church was opened in Los Angeles (later moved to suburban Gardena), and others were founded in Seattle, San Jose, Vancouver, and Honolulu.

Self-Help for the Elderly: Chinese American non-profit social service organization established in 1966 as a War on Poverty program in San Francisco, California. Serving more than twenty-five thousand seniors annually, the organization offers a comprehensive multiservice program that includes home-delivered meals; in-home support and licensed home health care; vocational training and job development; day care for Alzheimer's patients; home repairs and construction; residential board and care; and other social, educational, and recreational activities.

Self-Realization Fellowship (SRF): American spiritual society founded in 1925 to promulgate the teachings of the prominent Indian yogi Paramahamsa Yogananda. The fellowship is concerned primarily with spreading the practice of kriya yoga, a system of harnessing life energy through deep meditation in order to experience direct consciousness of God.

The SRF traces its origin back to the revival of kriya yoga in 1861 by Lahiri Mahasaya, the lay disciple of the mysterious spiritual master Mahavatar Babaji. The technique was given to Yogananda's master Swami Sri Yukteswar, under whose urging Yogananda established the Yogoda Sat-Sanga of India in 1917.

In 1920, Yogananda traveled to the United States to attend the International Congress of Religious Liberals and founded a branch of the Yogoda Sat-Sanga in Boston, Massachusetts. Later, after extensive lecturing throughout the United States, he founded the SRF headquarters in Los Angeles, California. In 1935, the SRF was incorporated as an international society, and in the following decades other centers were established in several California cities, along with smaller groups around the country. By the 1990's, there were eight temples, or ashrams, with more than one hundred smaller centers, or meditation groups, throughout the United States.

After Paramahamsa Yogananda's death in 1952, his disciple James Lynn (Swami Rajasi Janakananda) headed the fellowship, with Sri Daya Mata becoming the leader after Lynn's death in 1955.

In India, the SRF operates several schools, a free medical dispensary, and a hospital. Its activities in the West involve mostly the teaching of its devotional meditation technique, which is transmitted through a series of lessons lasting three-and-a-half years.

The stated aims of the SRF include teaching the fundamental unity of science and religion, and of Christianity and yoga; spreading the systematic techniques for attaining God-consciousness; establishing SRF temples worldwide for God-communion; disseminating the idea of the alliance of human beings based on their unity with God; and encouraging cultural understanding between East and West.

Senanayake, D. S. [Don Stephen] (Oct. 20, 1884, Colombo, Ceylon, now Sri Lanka—Mar. 22, 1952, Colombo, Ceylon): First prime minister of Ceylon after independence in 1948. Senanayake was a Ceylonese legislator for thirty years (starting in the 1920's) and held government ministerial posts for more than twenty. As minister for agriculture and lands (appointed in 1931), he instituted land development measures, attempted agricultural modernization, and urged the development of cooperatives. Under his leadership as prime minister, the country initiated efforts toward the development of hydroelectric power. Other ministerial seats occupied by Senanayake included defense, external affairs, and health and local government.

Seoul: Largest city and capital of the Republic of Korea, or South Korea. The city is the political, economic, educational, and cultural center of the country, containing more than 10 million of the nation's 43

The Han-gang River, which winds its way through the heart of Seoul, is a popular tourist and recreational spot on weekends.
(Korea National Tourism Corporation)

million people. Government ministries, major corporations, leading colleges and universities, museums, and financial markets are centered in Seoul.

The site was occupied as early as the Paekche Kingdom (18-660 C.E.). But the city truly began to flourish with the establishment of the Yi (CHOSON) Dynasty in 1392, when it was designated the capital. The city was surrounded by a ten-mile fortress wall with nine major gates. Five of the great gates and sections of the old wall have been restored and are now important national monuments and tourist attractions.

It is not known precisely when the city was first referred to as Seoul. It is one of the few metropolitan areas in South Korea whose name cannot be written in Chinese characters. There is speculation that the name "Seoul" is derived from the ancient word "Sorabol," the name given to an early capital of the Silla Dynasty, founded in 57 B.C.E.

At the beginning of the twentieth century, Seoul was a feudal city of mainly single-storied houses and a population of about 150,000. From 1910 to 1945 the city was the seat of the Japanese colonial government, under which the population increased to more than 500,000. In 1948 the Republic of Korea was proclaimed and Seoul was declared the official capital. During the Korean War (1950-1953) it was fought over by United Nations and Communist armies on four separate occasions and was devastated. As a consequence the contemporary city is almost entirely a product of post-Korean War reconstruction.

Located less than thirty miles from the demilitarized zone (DMZ) separating North and South Korea, Seoul is one of the largest cities in the world and a major source of Korean immigration to the United States. It is a city not only of beautiful ancient architecture but also of modern skyscrapers and bustling commercial districts. In 1988 the city hosted the twenty-fourth Summer Olympic Games.

Seth, Vikram (b. June 20, 1952, Calcutta, West Bengal, India): Poet, novelist, and travel writer. Seth has lived in India, England, China, and the United States; consequently, he brings to his writing an insider's understanding of diverse cultures.

Seth was trained as an economist and received his master's degree in philosophy, politics, and economics from the University of Oxford in 1978. He was senior editor at Stanford University Press and pursued graduate studies in the economic demography of China at Stanford. He lived in China as a student at Nanjing University from 1980 to 1982. Among the many awards he has received for his work are the Commonwealth Poetry Prize and a Guggenheim Fellowship (1986).

Seth's first work, *Mappings: A Chapbook of Poems*, was published in 1981. He received international recognition as a travel writer with *From Heaven Lake: Travels Through Sinkiang and Tibet* (1983), an account of his hitchhiking journey home from China to India in the summer of 1981. The book won the Thomas Cook Travel Award for 1983. His next collection of poems, The Humble Administrator's Garden (1985), was followed by The Golden Gate (1986), a novel in verse about life in San Francisco in the 1980's. Gore Vidal described it as "the Great Californian Novel," and the book was well received, enjoying both commercial success and critical acclaim. A Suitable Boy (1993) is a novel of manners set in postindependence India. It is a monumental story about the lives of four large, extended families, Hindu and Muslim, who are caught up in the political and social changes through which India goes after the departure of the British. Seth's other works include *Three Chinese Poets* (1993), a volume of translations, and *Beastly Tales from Here and There* (1993), fables in verse.

Seth writes in an elegant and graceful style, marked by gentle irony. His multiculturalism gives him the ability to see things from many angles, and he can be both wryly humorous and deeply compassionate. Notwithstanding his international background and the fame he has received abroad, he is strongly committed to the idea of indigenous recognition and chose to publish *A Suitable Boy* in India first, before publication in the West.

With his significant work in fiction and poetry, Seth has secured a prominent place in the list of Indo-Anglian writers who have lived abroad and retained their Indian identity.

Shamakami: South Asian Indian lesbian and bisexual women's support group, based in San Francisco. The organization is part of a network of other South Asian women's groups and similar gay and lesbian groups scattered across the world.

Shamanism: Shamanism in the broad sense of the term is an almost universal cultural phenomenon, still found throughout the world. The basic idea of shamanism is the spiritual/ritual leadership of a small community by a person who is recognized to have special abilities of divination, extrasensory perception, or connection to the forces of nature.

Hmong shaman in Atwater, California. (Eric Crystal)

Shamanism is often associated with the belief systems of "hunter-gatherer" societies. For the members of these closely knit and often fiercely independent societies, physical survival often depends on the ability to act in harmony with nature. Through a process of selection that sometimes involves the practice of austerities (fasts and vision quests, for example), a group member is singled out as being responsible for certain aspects of the group's well-being. Often this is someone who demonstrates his or her special qualities by having elaborate dreams, being able to predict the movements of grazing animals and changes in weather patterns, demonstrating the ability to heal sickness through touch, and so forth.

Shamanistic traditions represent an important cultural link between the peoples of Asia and the American Indian nations. The general features of shamanism are shared by many cultures, but the term itself is often applied more specifically to nomadic cultures of Siberia, East Asia, and the Americas.

In East Asia shamanism represents the most ancient cultural "layer" in a complex overlapping of several belief systems and religions, including Taoism (Shinto in Japan), Confucianism, and Buddhism. Shamanistic practices tend to be strongest in isolated rural areas. In part because of Korea's long period of relative cultural isolation, a richly developed shamanistic tradition persists in Korean folk culture. While there is a great deal of syncretism of shamanism with the natural philosophies of Taoism and with the deistic forms of Buddhism, Confucian traditionalists have often regarded shamanistic practices as "superstitious."

In American popular culture the most familiar examples of shamanism are from American Indian traditions. Authors such as Joseph Campbell and Roger Walsh, however, have adopted a more universalist view of shamanism as a path to the unconscious, stressing universal themes such as transformative death and rebirth and altered states of consciousness. For many people shamanism remains important not as a remnant of ancient superstition but as an essential dimension of life.

Shanghai Communique (1972): Document issued jointly by both the United States and the People's Republic of China on February 28, 1972, at the end of U.S. president Richard M. Nixon's visit to China. It set forth the positions of China and the United States on questions regarding Taiwan and announced their mutual desire to normalize relations. The American government officially recognized the Communist and Nationalist assertion that Taiwan was part of China and agreed in principle to remove all U.S. military forces from Taiwan. Following the issuance of the communique, liaison offices were opened in both Washington, D.C., and Beijing; after full diplomatic relations were established in 1979, these offices became the official embassies of the two powers.

Shankar, Ravi (b. Apr 7, 1920, Varanasi, Uttar Pradesh, India): Sitarist and composer. Perhaps the most internationally well-known of twentieth century Indian classical musicians, he is regarded not only as a virtuoso soloist and a versatile composer but also as a cultural ambassador. Son of a Bengali statesman and scholar, Shankar grew up in Varanasi and first traveled to Europe in 1930 as a member of a performing arts troupe led by his elder brother Uday Shankar. During this time, he acquired a basic knowledge of several instruments and of two classical dance genres, *kathak* and *kathakali*. He later studied music with maestro

Ravi Shankar plays an Indian raga on the sitar at New York's Madison Square Garden. (AP/Wide World Photos)

Allauddin Khan, from whom he received six years of rigorous training in the traditions of Hindustani (North Indian) classical music. Through Allauddin Khan, Shankar traces his artistic lineage all the way back to Tansen (one of the founders of North Indian classical music) of the sixteenth century. During this time Shankar grew close to Allauddin Khan's son, sarodist Ali Akbar, and also to Khan's daughter, Annapurna, who became his wife.

In 1948, Shankar began working for All-India Radio as a composer and performer. In addition to his interpretations of classical *ragas* within the Hindustani system, he has also been active in the exploration of new forms. His compositions, which often fuse Indian melodic styles with European orchestrational concepts, include film scores, symphonic works, and chamber music.

Shankar is featured as a sitarist on countless recordings, often accompanied by Alla Rakha on *tabla* drums. Shankar has often collaborated with European musicians, most notably with violinist Yehudi Menuhin and with Andre Previn, who conducted the London Philharmonic's recording of his sitar concerto. His students have included some from outside the sphere of Indian traditional music, including composer Phillip Glass and ex-Beatle George Harrison. Shankar's son, sitarist Shubho Shankar, has joined his father in public performances of sitar duets.

Shankar has also authored a book, *My Music, My Life*, published in 1969. He has also been active in the incorporation of musical material and theoretical concepts from the Karnatic (South Indian) system into the North Indian system. His awards include two honorary doctorates, the Presidential Padma Bhushan Award, and many others.

Shen, Catherine (b. Oct. 31, 1947, Boston, Mass.): Publisher. As publisher of *Star Bulletin*, a major daily afternoon newspaper in Honolulu, Hawaii, she became the first Asian American publisher of a mainstream daily. She has also served as assistant managing editor of the "Life" section of *USA Today* and associate publisher of *Marin Independent Journal* in California. She holds a B.A. degree from Wellesley College in Massachusetts and an M.A. degree from Claremont Graduate School in California.

Shigeta, James (b. 1933, Territory of Hawaii): Actor and singer. At a time when Asian American men were not given leading roles, even for parts that clearly called for an Asian actor, Shigeta was a notable excep-

tion. He starred or had a major role in films such as *The Crimson Kimono* (1959), *Walk Like a Dragon* (1960), *Cry for Happy* (1961), *Bridge to the Sun* (1961), and *Flower Drum Song* (1961). Among his many other credits are *The Yakuza* (1975) and *Die Hard* (1988). Before beginning his film career in the United States, Shigeta had enjoyed great success as a singer, entertainer, and actor in Japan, where he went after serving in the U.S. Marine Corps in the Korean War.

Shima, George (Kinji Ushijima; 1864, Kurume, Japan—1926, Los Angeles, Calif.): Potato farmer and community leader. Shima's pioneering agricultural efforts in the difficult Sacramento delta earned for him millions of dollars, making him one of the richest and most successful Issei farmers ever and probably the first Issei millionaire. Prospering amid the rising tide of anti-Japanese agitation in California, he was both a target of the exclusionists and a spokesman for the Japanese community.

Shima grew up near Fukuda, a port city in northern Kyushu, in a family of landowners and farmers. His formal schooling did not begin until about age eleven. In 1885, with plans to become a Chinese classical scholar, he traveled to Hitotsubashi University in Tokyo, hoping to enroll. After failing the entrance exam, he sailed for the United States in hope of learning English. Throughout his life he remained actively interested in poetry and philosophy and composed and published poems. He also maintained a strong interest in education, later using his wealth to assist many Japanese at Stanford University and the University of California.

Landing in San Francisco in 1889, he found a job as a schoolboy, which among other things afforded him the chance to learn English. The same year he moved to the Stockton-Sacramento delta, where he began as a simple field worker before rising to the position of labor contractor. The delta region was flourishing agriculturally, but Shima was more impressed by the abundance of less-desirable marsh and swamp lands that were overrun by the periodic flooding of the Sacramento and San Joaquin rivers. Such acreage sold for very little money, and he and some friends were able to purchase a small tract of land. Ten years later they were among the first to farm potatoes successfully for the California market and had added another four hundred acres of marshland to their land holdings.

In an effort to tame such a large expanse of fertile but swampy acreage, Shima supervised the construction of a system of dikes, pumps, and drainage ditches that would remove the excess water and expose the land surface for planting. This extensive undertaking turned out to be one of the largest land reclamation projects in California history. By 1909, with thousands of acres of potato crops under his control, he had been dubbed the "Potato King" by the California press. His own Empire Delta Farms would eventually span six thousand acres. Twenty-four years after arriving at the delta, Shima had managed to reclaim almost twenty-nine thousand acres of uncultivated land. A newspaper report published in 1920 estimated that he controlled 85 percent of the California potato market, worth in excess of $18 million.

Shima's ingenuity inspired others. At the University of California, a graduate student submitted a research thesis in 1913 explaining Shima's sophisticated operations in the delta. His empire, in addition to the many thousands of acres under his direct control, included commercial contracts with other largely ethnic growers in the region under which he distributed their produce for them. By this time, Shima employed more than five hundred agronomists, engineers, riverboat pilots, foremen, and field workers. Moreover, his mostly Japanese workforce included South Asians and Caucasians.

In addition to bringing him wealth and reputation, Shima's success as an entrepreneur attracted the resentment of California exclusionist groups driven by fear of economic competition. Such nativist associations as the Native Sons of the Golden West and the Asiatic Exclusion League vindictively portrayed him and all other Issei, particularly the successful ones, as representative of the Japanese swarm that, if left unchecked, would soon overrun the entire state. Japanese economic success, these groups warned, threatened the livelihood of the state's white landowners and farmers and would supplant white control of the state's agricultural industry.

Forced to respond to the movement to expel them, and unwilling to leave the United States, the Japanese community found ways to fight back. In 1909 Shima became the first president of the newly formed Japanese Association of America, an organization that among other things both encouraged and assisted the

In the wake of the successful Shima farms operation, potato plantations owned and operated by Japanese Americans have appeared in other states as well. Here the Wada family inspects potatoes grown on its Idaho farm. (Michael Yamashita)

George Shima. (San Joaquin Delta College)

process of Japanese assimilation in America and backed the Issei in their drive for American citizenship and civil rights. Shima personally felt the wrath of the exclusionists when, in 1909, he encountered severe public opposition after he bought a house in a well-to-do section of Berkeley. As president of the Japanese Association of America, he lobbied California governor Hiram Johnson to prevent enactment of what became the ALIEN LAND LAW OF 1913. The bill proposed to ban the Issei from buying or owning agricultural land anywhere in the state while limiting to three years the length of any agricultural land lease entered into by an Issei. Shima launched a similar appeal to stop passage of the 1920 amendment to the statute, under which the Issei would not even be able to lease agricultural land or engage in sharecropping, but he was unsuccessful.

Shima suffered a fatal stroke while on a business trip to Los Angeles in 1926. Posthumously, he was awarded the Fourth-ranking Rising Sun Medal by the emperor of Japan.

SUGGESTED READINGS: • Daniels, Roger. *Asian America: Chinese and Japanese in the United States Since 1850*. Seattle: University of Washington Press, 1988. • Hata, Don, and Nadine Hata. "George Shima: 'The Potato King of California.'" *Journal of the West* 25 (January, 1986): 55-63.

Shimoda, Yuki (early 1920's, Sacramento, Calif.—May 21, 1981): Actor. Shimoda achieved fame as one of the busiest Japanese American actors of his time, appearing in Broadway plays and more than two dozen feature films. He grew up in Sacramento, where his parents ran a hotel and restaurant. During World War II the family was interned at the Tule Lake relocation center in Northern California. After his release he accepted a teaching job at the University of Chicago and studied accounting there as well.

Subsequently, Shimoda entered the world of entertainment, dancing for the Chicago Opera and in various New York stage shows. From there he won roles in such long-running Broadway productions as *South Pacific* (1949), *The King and I* (1951), *Teahouse of the August Moon* (1953), and *Auntie Mame* (1956) before traveling to California to film the 1958 screen version of *Auntie Mame*. Deciding to remain out West to work in motion pictures, he was cast in such feature films as *A Majority of One* (1961), *Midway* (1976), and *MacArthur* (1977). He also filmed commercials and appeared in television series such as *Ironside* (1967-1975), *Hawaii Five-O* (1968-1980), and *Kung Fu* (1972-1975). Many people know Shimodo best for his role in *Farewell to Manzanar*, a dramatization of the internment experience written by Jeanne Wakatsuki HOUSTON and broadcast by NBC in 1976. One of his last roles was that of an Issei railroad foreman in *Hito-Hata: Raise the Banner* (1980), the first feature film about the Japanese experience in America produced entirely by Japanese Americans.

Toward the end of his career, Shimoda helped lead the way in lobbying the Hollywood film studios and industry leaders to hire more Asian Americans as writers and actors. During his career he remained active in the EAST WEST PLAYERS (EWP) and the JAPANESE AMERICAN CITIZENS LEAGUE (JACL).

Shin-issei: Japanese term for those emigrating from Japan after World War II. *Shin* means "new."

Shin shukyo (new religion): New and popular religious movements in Japan that experienced phenomenal growth during the nineteenth and twentieth centuries. These movements, despite being called "new," actually appear to be "renewed" offshoots of primarily Shinto and Buddhist traditions. Japanese folk religion, Confucianism, Taoism, and Christianity have all had some influence also.

These new religions are messianic, utopian, revitalistic, and eschatological lay movements. Their teaching is simple, easy, practical, profitable, and optimistic. These religions also emphasize the importance of their headquarters and encourage regular pilgrimages. The founders were typically charismatic leaders and ably mixed some Christian teachings with Shinto and Buddhist ideas. Followers often believe the founders to be divine. Distinction, however, between the leader and followers is weak. Ministry is open to all. Personal faith is strongly emphasized—with faith, they believe, nothing is impossible. Faith healing is also widely practiced and firmly believed. Women members usually constitute the majority of these groups.

In the nineteenth century the Nyoraikyo, Kurozumi-kyo, Tenri-kyo, Butsuryukyo, Konko-kyo, Rengekai, and Omoto-kyo sects appeared. In the twentieth century the Reiyu-kai, Soka-gakkai, Seicho no Ie, Sekai Kyuseikyo, and Rissho-Kosei-kai sects were founded. After World War II the Tensho-kotai-jingu-kyo, Zen-rinkai, Ananaikyo, PL Kyodan, and Kyuseishukyo sects were organized.

In 1951 a union of the new religious organizations was founded with eighty-four member groups. Together they represent a strong political force with significant influence in Japan.

The Soka-gakkai organization has about sixteen million members, a daily newspaper, and a complete educational system from elementary school through the university level. It also has close relations with the Komeito (clean government party), Japan's third largest political party.

These new religions present a common worldview and promote unity of the family and respect for age and tradition. They already have become part of the social and political scene in contemporary Japan. In addition, some of these religious movements have become active in the United States and elsewhere outside Japan.

Shinran (Matsuwaka-Maru; 1173, near Kyoto, Japan—Nov. 28, 1262, Kyoto, Japan): Buddhist philosopher and religious reformer. Shinran founded the Jodo Shinshu (True Pure Land) sect, the largest school of Buddhism in modern Japan, in 1224. A descendent of a minor aristocratic family, Shinran entered the Tendai monastic order at the age of nine and was trained in Buddhist philosophy and disciplines for twenty years at its headquarters atop Mount Hiei, northeast of present-day Kyoto. His spiritual yearnings, however, were unfulfilled until he encountered Honen, who had founded an independent Jodo, or Pure Land, school in 1175 (see PURE LAND SECTS). Unlike the traditional

schools of Buddhism, which were basically monastic, the Pure Land school attracted people from all classes who were deemed evil and depraved in the eyes of society. These included fishers and hunters, who violated other forms of life, a cardinal sin in Buddhism; merchants and peasants, who took advantage of others; monks and nuns who had violated the precepts; and women of all classes. Such people, Honen taught, were the primary concern of the Primal Vow, manifesting the great compassion of Amida Buddha, which is directed to both laity and clergy, transforming the lowest to the highest, the evil into the good.

Because of the radical nature of this teaching, which traditional Buddhism claimed violated the time-honored precepts and disrupted society, the government outlawed the Pure Land movement. Honen and his disciples, including Shinran, were exiled to remote provinces as common criminals.

Although they were pardoned after a few years, Shinran, who had by then gotten married, remained in the provinces and spread the Pure Land teaching in the outlying areas of eastern Japan. In order to correct the deviations and misinterpretations of the teaching by others, he returned to Kyoto and entered a period of prolific writing, his most creative period being between the ages of seventy-five and eighty-five. Although he never intended to establish a school separate from his teacher Honen, Shinran's following grew eventually to become known as Jodo Shinshu. The majority of Japanese American Buddhists are affiliated with this school.

Shinto: Literally the "way of the gods," the religion that is most closely associated by the Japanese with their nation and culture. Although it combines elements from the Asian mainland, Shinto predates any other religion in Japan and is therefore the most indigenous. Shinto expresses itself not only as a national religion but also as an individual and communal faith. In both Japan and the United States, the history of Shinto has been determined by these two aspects.

Individual and Communal Faith. Shinto is primarily a religion of the people, who turn to the gods with their petitions, prayers, and expressions of gratitude for all good things. A variety of rituals and observances allow participants to purify themselves in body and spirit, to mark the important rites of passage, and to invite the blessings of the gods for their families, school work, businesses, and personal relationships. The emphasis is on matters concerning life; death and its rituals are left to Buddhist temples.

When Japanese immigrants brought Buddhism and Shinto with them to the United States, they, like most Japanese, made little distinction between the two and did not think that believing in the one should exclude the other. The gods and the buddhas belonged to one large pantheon, and appeals were made to whichever deity seemed the most appropriate for particular tasks. Japanese families of the first and second generations usually maintained household altars for both Shinto and Buddhist deities. Despite this dual allegiance, most Japanese immigrants identified themselves institutionally as Buddhists, and Shinto shrines consequently are far fewer than Buddhist temples.

Being a religion of rituals for the attainment of pragmatic results, Shinto is relatively free of extensive, complicated philosophies and theologies. Doctrinal explanations were developed primarily in response to the challenge posed by Buddhists and their sophisticated philosophies, but the ordinary believer is mostly uninterested in metaphysics. Japanese Americans of the third and younger generations, however, seek intellectual understanding of Shinto in addition to the benefits of rituals and prayers. They ask to know the meaning of what is being done and said, and priests find themselves challenged to provide philosophical explanations in English.

Shinto shrines reached the height of their popularity in Hawaii during the first thirty years of the twentieth century. In response to criticisms leveled against PICTURE BRIDES by Christian moralists, who did not think it proper for marriages to be so casually arranged, couples were eager to be married by Shinto priests, some of whom performed up to thirty weddings a day. Shrines were built throughout the islands, and many operated language schools, Sunday schools, and night classes.

National Religion. The writing of the early myths of Shinto dates back to the eighth century C.E. with the appearance of the *Kojiki* (record of ancient matters) and the *Nihongi* (chronicles of Japan). These stories tell of the creation of the world and of Japan by the gods, or *kami*, who are also the progenitors of the imperial line. The emperor, therefore, was believed to be a descendant of the gods and justified his rule by his

Shinto shrine in Japan. (Diane C. Lyell)

The Shinto temples of Japan, such as the one shown here, are less popular than before and are becoming mainly places of historical curiosity rather than devout worship. (Diane C. Lyell)

divine birth and not, as was the case with the Chinese emperor, according to his acquired virtue and righteousness. Throughout its history Shinto was associated with the imperial house and thus had a political role and identity.

In Hawaii, Shinto maintained its identity with Japan and its national goals before World War II. Major ceremonies, such as the celebrations for the emperor's birthday, drew large crowds. During Japan's invasion of China during the 1930's, Shinto shrines were active in soliciting money and good luck charms for Japanese soldiers and sponsored popular victory celebrations after the conquest of Hankou and Canton. The modernization of Japan since the late nineteenth century had included a reassertion of Shinto's association with the emperor and the nation, and this nationalistic aspect was retained by Shinto in the United States.

During World War II. Japanese imperialism in Asia during World War II was buttressed by the use of Shinto to instill loyalty and obedience to a divine emperor, and Shinto came to be nearly synonymous with Japanese militarism. Shinto was explicitly attacked in American society as being nothing but a tool in the service of Japan's war effort. In 1942 Shunzo Sakamaki of the University of Hawaii published in the *Honolulu Star-Bulletin* a series of articles entitled, "Shinto: Fake Religion." Sakamaki "exposed" Shinto for being "not a true religion but a Japanese nationalist and propaganda cult . . . aimed to assist in Japanese military and economic domination." Such accusations led to official government decisions to deport priests to relocation camps, to force congregations to disband "voluntarily," and to confiscate shrine properties. Fewer in number than Buddhist temples to begin with, Shinto shrines suffered serious setbacks during the war years with the loss of patrons and property because of its explicit association with Japanese imperialism.

Shinto survived the war, but only a few shrines remained active. In the 1950's and 1960's the shrines legally managed to regain their properties but never were able to attract a significant number of people back into the fold of their activities and beliefs. In addition to the wartime association with Japanese militarism, the steady loss of a Japanese cultural identity among younger Japanese Americans also contributed to the demise of Shinto. For the individual worshipper Shinto shrines were community centers preserving the traditional rituals and observances that were an integral part of the culture of the immigrants. With the shift of cultural knowledge and identity from Japan to the United States taking place among younger Japa-

nese Americans, Shinto shrines, still the largely unaccommodated centers of Japanese religion and traditions, faced a future primarily as places of historical interest.—*George J. Tanabe, Jr.*

SUGGESTED READINGS: • Hardacre, Helen. *Shinto and the State, 1868-1988.* Princeton, N.J.: Princeton University Press, 1989. • Holtom, Daniel C. *The National Faith of Japan: A Study in Modern Shinto.* London: Kegan Paul, 1938. • Kitagawa, Joseph M. *Religion in Japanese History.* New York: Columbia University Press, 1966. • Mulholland, John F. *Hawaii's Religions.* Rutland, Vt.: Charles Tuttle, 1970. • Ono Sokyo. *Shinto the Kami Way.* Rutland, Vt.: Charles E. Tuttle, 1962. • Ross, Floyd H. *Shinto, the Way of Japan.* Boston: Beacon Press, 1965.

Shiomi, Rick A. (b. May 25, 1947, Toronto, Ontario, Canada): Playwright, screenwriter, and theater director. A Sansei Japanese Canadian, Shiomi wrote for Canadian television. He also authored works that became Asian American theater standards, *Yellow Fever* (1982) and *Rosie's Cafe* (1987). Other works include *Play Ball* (1989), a comedy based on Gordon Hirabayashi's refusal to enter a World War II internment camp, and *Uncle Tadao* (1992), about a Japanese Canadian family and the issue of redress. As artistic director of Minneapolis' Theatre Mu, a post he assumed in 1993, Shiomi was instrumental in nurturing young Asian American playwrights, actors, and designers.

Shirota, Jon (b. 1928, Peahi, Maui, Territory of Hawaii): Writer. Born to Nisei parents, he was graduated from Brigham Young University in 1952, moved to Los Angeles, and worked as a treasury agent for the Internal Revenue Service (IRS). He finished his first novel at the Louwney Handy Colony, a writing-school retreat in Marshall, Illinois, and has published the novels *Lucky Come Hawaii* (1965) and *Pineapple White* (1972).

Shivers, Robert L. (1894?, Ashland City, Tenn.—June 28, 1950, Honolulu, Territory of Hawaii): Government official. Shivers worked for the U.S. Justice Department after serving during World War I. When tensions between the United States and Japan began escalating in the late 1930's, the Federal Bureau of Investigation (FBI) appointed him agent-in-charge of its Honolulu office. He was to determine how Hawaii's large Japanese population should be handled in the event hostilities occurred. He ran the office from August, 1939, until April, 1943, when a heart ailment resulting from overwork forced him to return to the U.S. mainland. Following the December 7, 1941, attack on Pearl Harbor by Japan, he remained at his office continuously for more than a week, and for the first month almost never left his office.

Shivers' handling of the Japanese in Hawaii was vastly different from how the Japanese on the West Coast of the United States were handled by mainland authorities. While 120,000 Japanese Americans on the West Coast (the majority of Japanese living there) were interned in inland camps, by contrast only 980 were detained in Hawaii—out of a population of 160,000. During his tenure as Honolulu FBI director, his approval was required for any person to be interned or released from internment. He developed a deep faith in the loyalty and patriotism of Hawaii's Japanese and was supported by military leaders on the islands.

Shivers vigorously disputed claims by some high-level military officials, such as Admiral Husband E. Kimmel, steadfastly maintaining that Hawaii's Japanese were never involved in "fifth column" activity following the bombing of Pearl Harbor. Shivers was assisted by people such as businessman Charles Hemenway, a member of the University of Hawaii Board of Regents, whose contacts with members of the Japanese American community helped Shivers realize how loyal and committed Hawaii's Americans of Japanese ancestry were to the United States.

After returning to the mainland in 1943, Shivers headed the FBI's office in Miami, Florida. The following year, President Franklin D. Roosevelt appointed him collector of customs for Honolulu. He was reappointed to the post by President Harry S Truman. He died in Honolulu while serving as collector of customs.

Shogun: Title given to the de facto ruler of Japan during the three military regimes that dominated the country from 1192 until 1867, when the last shogun, Tokugawa, resigned. The word is a shortened form of *sei-i tai shogun*, which means "barbarian-quelling generalissimo." The term first arose to designate Japan's chief military commanders from the eighth to the

Japanese actors re-create a sword fight between two shogun warriors during the Cherry Blossom Festival in San Francisco, California. (Michael Yamashita)

twelfth centuries. As the military class grew in power from 1192 onward, the shogun, whose office was hereditary, became the actual ruler of Japan. The emperor did, however, continue to retain formal sovereignty. The era of the shogun was popularized in America through James Clavell's *Shogun: A Novel of Japan* (1975) and a network miniseries based on the novel and broadcast in 1980.

Shoong, Joe (1879, Longtouhuan Village, Zhongshan, Guangdong Province, China—Apr. 13, 1961, San Francisco, Calif.): Businessperson and philanthropist. Shoong arrived in the United States around 1899 and worked as a garment worker. In 1901 he and three partners founded Sang Lee dry goods store in Vallejo. Two years later he bought out his partners and moved to Fillmore Street in San Francisco. Around 1905 the store, now named "China Toggery, J. Shoong Company," moved downtown to Market Street. Its Chinese name became Zhongxing (resurgence of China; Chung Hing in Cantonese), a name that was kept after the English name was changed to "National Dollar Stores."

In 1916 Shoong established his first branch store in Sacramento. By 1920 there were eight branches, and the store became a California corporation. Shoong managed the business until 1959, when he handed the presidency over to his son. At the time of his death, the corporation had fifty-four outlets in California, Hawaii, Nevada, Arizona, Washington, and Utah.

Shoong also invested in real estate and was successful on the stock market. Around 1926 he acquired 51 percent interest in National Shoe Company, which by 1961 operated thirty-two Reeves Shoe Stores on the West Coast. He was one of the wealthiest Chinese in the continental United States during the first half of the twentieth century.

In 1928 Shoong built the Joe Shoong Primary School in his native village and from 1928 to 1949 donated $230,000 for operating expenses. In 1936 he contributed $20,000 to beautify the village. He also contributed $8,000 annually to support the Longdu Middle School near his village. In 1931 his contribution paid off construction debts of San Francisco's Chinese Central High School. He established a $60,000 scholarship fund for needy Chinese students at the University of California in 1938. Around 1946 Shoong established the Joe Shoong Foundation with an original contribution of $1 million. The foundation increased the University of California scholarship fund to $100,000 and dropped racial restrictions. Other major recipients of contributions included Oakland's Chi-

nese Community Center and Chinese School (1949), Locke's Joe Shoong Chinese School (1952), Sacramento's Chung Wah School (1960), San Francisco's Chinese Hospital, San Francisco's Cumberland Church, Oakland's Presbyterian Church, and Berkeley's Chinese Community Church.

Shridharani, Krishnalal (Sept. 16, 1911, Umrala, Bhavnagar, Republic of India—July 23, 1960, New Delhi, India): Writer and activist. Shridharani was a major voice for the India independence movement in the United States. When Shridharani was eight, his father died unexpectedly. The latter had been a successful lawyer and had left his widow with property to manage in addition to overseeing the education of their five children. The younger son, Krishnalal, became too much to handle, so she sent him to live under her mother's care at her brother's house. During a pilgrimage a few years later, Shridharani's mother experienced the fervor of Gandhi's rise to popularity and decided to send him to a nearby, nationalist boarding school. She died when Shridharani was fourteen. Soon afterwards he chose to go to Gandhi's National University at Ahmadabad.

In 1930 Mahatma GANDHI asked sixty of his followers including Shridharani to accompany him on his "March to the Sea" to protest the British government's salt monopoly. On their way to Port Dandi, Shridharani was one of the marchers chosen to address laborers and farmers. Before the protesters were able to raid the government salt depots, they were arrested and taken to prison. After his release from prison, Shridharani went to study at the International University of poet Rabindranath TAGORE in Ahmadabad, earning a degree in history and philosophy.

Shridharani came to the United States on a scholarship in 1934 and earned three degrees: an M.A. degree in sociology from New York University and, from Columbia University, an M.S. degree in journalism and a Ph.D. degree in sociology and political theory. During his twelve years in the United States, Shridharani addressed groups throughout the country on behalf of India's independence movement. In his efforts to publicize India's cause he received assistance from the successful Asian Indian entrepreneur G. J. Watumull. In 1945 Shridharani and two other students traveled by car across the United States. At points along the way he gave lectures on India, its culture, its nationalist movement, and his prediction that the independence struggle would spread to other Asian countries. After receiving considerable acclaim,

Shridharani returned to India in 1946.

Shridharani wrote several books—some in English and others in his native tongue, Gujarati. While he was a political prisoner in 1930, he wrote *The Banyan Tree*. Among his other works in Gujarati are a short novel, *I Shall Kill the Human in You* (1932), also based on his experiences in prison; *Spring Flowers* (1933), three plays for children; and a collection of poems, *These Earthen Lamps* (1934). Later he wrote several books in English including *War Without Violence* (1939), *My India, My America* (1941), and *The Mahatma and the World* (1946). He also contributed many articles to *The New York Times* as well as to Indian newspapers.

Shufeldt, Robert W. (Feb. 21, 1822, Red Hook, N.Y.— Nov. 7, 1895, Washington, D.C.): Commodore. As U.S. special representative, he, along with Li Hongzhang, China's foreign-relations representative, initiated and directed the Treaty of Chemulpo (1882), Korea's first treaty with the West.

Shushin: The teaching of moral conduct in the schools of Japan, as mandated by the Japanese Meiji government in the Education Act of 1872. After a period of experimenting with Western liberal democratic ideas, the government instituted the *shushin*, or "morals," course of instruction. The *shushin* was to be taught in primary and secondary schools as a key component of the curriculum.

Originally derived from the *Analects* (c. late sixth or early fifth century B.C.E.) of Confucius, the essence of the *shushin* remained Confucian. By the late Meiji period (1868-1912), however, *shushin* came to embody strong nationalistic elements as well. By 1890, in the Imperial Rescript on Education, moral conduct had come to embody such concepts as absolute loyalty, filial piety, and an absolute willingness to sacrifice one's self for the emperor. Following the Russo-Japanese War (1904-1905), the *shushin* became increasingly chauvinistic.

Despite the ultranationalist elements, however, the aim of the *shushin* was to produce law-abiding citizens with a highly developed moral sense. To that end, the Japanese Ministry of Education incorporated into elementary school primers *Aesop's Fables* (fourth century B.C.E.), Benjamin Franklin's *Poor Richard's Almanack* (1733-1758), and tales from the life of Abraham Lincoln.

It was this moral element, along with the unremitting Confucian themes, that were brought to the United States from Japan by the Issei in the early 1900's.

During Japan's educational reforms of the late 1800's, Japanese educators cited writings by American inventor Benjamin Franklin (shown here) as pointing the way toward good moral behavior. (Library of Congress)

In the more or less mandatory Japanese-language schools that flourished on the West Coast in the prewar period, the *shushin* was a vital part of the curriculum. Indeed many Nisei credit their success to the moral education given at home and reinforced in schools. Many believe that the great emphasis on discipline, duty and obligation, and the importance of the family is a direct result of the "moral" education they received.

Because of its militaristic and ultranationalistic teachings, the *shushin* was among the first targets of reform during the U.S. occupation of Japan and was quickly abolished. Although a modified "ethics" course was reintroduced in the school curriculum in the mid-1950's, most senior Japanese mourned the loss of discipline, morality, and common purpose that the old *shushin* imparted.

Sidewalk Ordinance (1983): San Francisco city ordinance, signed by Mayor Dianne Feinstein, that required merchants in the city's Chinatown and North Beach areas to apply to the city for permits in order to display merchandise in front of their stores. The intent of the ordinance was to keep sidewalks clear for pedestrian traffic. Many of the merchants objected to the ordinance.

Sikh holidays: Sikh tradition recognizes a number of holidays, according to the lunar calendar. Particular celebrations may continue for as long as fifteen days. Three of the holidays are universal, three are celebrated on a local level, three represent Sikh and Hindu celebrations, and nine are local fairs (*melas*) or special commemorations. The three universal commemorations are *gurpurbs*. The first honors the birthdate of Guru NANAK in November, the fifteenth century mystic, ascetic, and founder of Sikhism to whom all Sikhs ascribe superlative adoration as one who demonstrated all that was good and lofty in human nature. It is especially celebrated in Gurdwara Sri Nankana Sahib, Pakistan, the site of his birth in 1469. Then follows in December the celebration of the birth of the tenth and last guru, GOBIND SINGH, who gave the Sikh community its present form in the Khalsa, or militant Sikh theocracy and brotherhood. The third holiday recalls the martyrdom of the fifth guru, Arjan Dev, in May, the compiler of the sacred *Adi Granth* and the founder of Amritsar. Featured during these holidays is the Akhand Path, or forty-eight-hour continuous reading of the *Guru Granth Sahib*; the sharing of *karah parshad*, a flour-sugar-ghee preparation; and recitation of the Ardas prayer at the conclusion of the reading. December also witnesses the commemoration of three martyrdoms on the local level, that of the ninth guru, Teg Bahadur, in 1675, at the Rikab Ganj Gurdwara in Old Delhi, and two separate holidays honoring the martyrdom of the sons of Gobind Singh, at Fategarh Sahib and Chamkaur Sahib. Three festivals are also celebrated by the Sikhs: Hola Mohalla, or Holi, during February-March marking the start of spring, Vaisakh (Baisakh) during April-May as New Year's Day, when Gobind Singh instituted the Khalsa, and Diwali, or the Festival of Lights, during October-November. Nine local fairs are also celebrated throughout India honoring various events significant to Sikh culture and history. These include historical battles, events in the life of Nanak, and the death or martyrdom of significant Sikh leaders.

Sikh Studies programs in North America: Sikh Studies programs in the United States and Canada focus on Sikh religion, history, literature, and the study of Punjabi language, literature, and culture. As of 1993, five universities had established or were in the process of raising funds to establish Sikh Studies programs. Three factors that have influenced the evolution of these programs are the large numbers of Sikhs residing in North America, the fact that Sikhs constituted the majority of first-wave immigrants from South Asia at the beginning of the twentieth century, and the dearth of scholarship devoted to Sikhism in North America.

During the mid-1980's the University of Michigan, Ann Arbor, together with the local Sikh community began building an endowment to support a chair in Punjabi and Sikh Studies. The volume *The Sikh Diaspora: Migration and the Experience Beyond the Punjab* (1989), edited by N. Gerald Barrier and Verne A. Dusenbery, is based on papers delivered at the 1986 conference. In 1988 Michigan began offering Punjabi language courses at the beginning and intermediate level.

A formal Sikh Studies program has not been instituted at the University of California, Berkeley, but scholars at the university and members of the California Sikh community have hosted several presentations focusing on the subject. The university has been the site of several international conferences since the mid-1970's. The university has also presented lecture series featuring eminent Sikh and Punjabi scholars such as Harbans Singh of Patiala University, Punjab; W. H. McLeod of the University of Otago, Dunedin, New Zealand; and Christopher Shackle of the University of London. In the fall, 1993, Berkeley began offering a course on Punjabi language and literature.

Columbia University in New York had begun to build an endowment for a Sikh Studies program by the late 1980's. While courses in Punjabi language and literature had been offered earlier, since 1988 the religion department has presented an annual course on Skikhism. Columbia's program, coordinated by Gurinder Singh Mann, has sponsored two major conferences on the state of Sikh Studies. Proceedings from the 1989 conference were published in the 1993 volume *Studying the Sikhs: Issues for North America*, edited by Mann and John Stratton Hawley.

Two major projects dealing with Sikh Studies have been developed in Canada at the University of Toronto and the University of British Columbia. At Toronto scholars in religious studies and languages have taught courses on Sikhism and Punjabi since 1986. In 1987 the university hosted an international conference on twentieth century Sikh issues. The proceedings from this conference, *Sikh History and Religion in the Twentieth Century*, were published in 1988. This volume, edited by Joseph T. O'Connell and others, provides a multidimensional view and analysis of twentieth century political, social, and religious developments in the Punjab.

In 1987 the University of British Columbia became the first institution fully to establish a chair in Punjabi and Sikh Studies in North America. The Sikh and Punjabi community in Canada raised funds to match a government of Canada grant designated to endow chairs in ethnic studies at Canadian universities. The university recruited Harjot Singh Oberoi, a graduate of the Australian National University at Canberra, for the position in 1988. Since 1988 Oberoi has offered courses in Sikh history, religion, and Punjabi language and literature.

Sikh Studies programs in the United States and Canada are, in part, a reflection of the efforts of the Sikh American community to articulate its identity. Many Sikhs see themselves as a distinct ethnic group within the larger South Asian American microcosm. These programs also respond to the dearth of courses available on Sikhism and the Punjabi language in the United States and Canada.

Sikh temples: Often the centers of Sikh religious and social life. The Sikh temple is more correctly called a *gurdwara* (the Anglicized spelling of the Punjabi term *gurduara*) and can be translated both literally as "the guru's door" or more poetically as "by means of the guru's [grace]." Historically, the Sikh *gurdwaras* have functioned not only as houses of worship but also as the nexus of community social and political life.

From earliest times, Sikhs have gathered together in "communities of pious Sikhs" (*satsangs*) to sing sacred songs (*kirtan*), particularly those composed by the gurus and eventually compiled by the fourth guru, Arjun, as their holiest book, the *Adi Granth*. Upon the death of their tenth guru, GOBIND SINGH, the belief that the mystical presence and guidance of all the gurus resides in this text bestowed a special status on the *Adi Granth*, thereafter being referred to as the *Guru Granth Sahib*. The presence of the book alone is considered to constitute a *gurdwara*. Even a room in a

Sikh temple in El Centro, California, acquired by the Sikh community in 1942. (National Archives)

Sikh household enshrining the *Guru Granth Sahib* is a sacred place, but the designation *gurdwara* is normally reserved for public buildings dedicated to religious services.

An assembly of believers in the presence of the holy book is called the *Panth* (the path, or way). This corporate assembly, according to Sikh doctrine, constitutes the continuation of religious authority after the passing of the last of the ten human Sikh gurus. The normal pattern of worship consists of singing *kirtan*, distributing sanctified food (*karah-prasad*), and commenting on the scriptures (*katha*), which is most often delivered by the *granthi* (reader of the Granth), a religious officiant who is in charge of the daily operations of the *gurdwara*.

A feature of *gurdwaras* everywhere is their practice of preparing and serving food (*langar*) and offering temporary shelter to any traveler. This custom exemplifies the idea of service to the community (*sewa*) and the active involvement of Sikhs in providing for temporal as well as spiritual needs. For those Sikhs who left the Punjab to travel overseas, locating a *gurdwara* in a new place was an important initial step because this institution often functioned as the focal point of the local Sikh community and was a source of information, assistance, food, shelter, and fellowship. There are now thousands of *gurdwaras* located in more than sixty countries worldwide. They are an important factor in the maintenance and celebration of the Sikh religion and culture outside Punjab, India.

Sikhism: Indian religion. The word "Sikh" is derived from Pali or Sanskrit and means "disciple." Sikhism was founded by Guru NANAK in the Punjab in the late fifteenth century. The Sikhs, as its members are called, are a religious group that developed in the Punjab, a region now divided between India and Pakistan, where Hindus and Muslims had long coexisted. Although Guru Nanak taught that truth transcends all religious rivalries, his disciples have increasingly forged their own sectarian identity, shown outwardly by their turbans, uncut hair, and distinctive dress. For the past several hundred years, the Sikhs have formed a potent third force in the ethnic and religious struggles of North India.

History. Nanak was born in 1469 in a village near Lahore (in modern-day Pakistan). Traditional Sikh sources state that he was an unusually bright and curious child who questioned many of the religious practices, both Muslim and Hindu, of his day. At the age of thirty, Nanak disappeared while bathing in a river.

This 1952 photograph shows a U.S. Army private and full-blooded Asian Indian American who received special permission from the government to keep his hair long as required by Sikh tradition. (National Archives)

Three days later, he reappeared, transformed, and began preaching devotion to the one true God. For several decades, Guru (teacher) Nanak traveled widely, from Assam to Mecca, singing devotional hymns and teaching men and women of all castes and social stations. Around 1520, he established the village of Kartarpur and spent the rest of his life looking after his growing religious community. When Nanak died in 1539, his designated successor, Guru Angad, became the second of what were eventually to number ten gurus of the Sikh religion.

In the next 169 years, guided by the succession of gurus, the Sikh community took on an increasingly distinct identity, partly in response to intermittent persecution by the Mughal rulers of North India. In this process, some gurus were more important than others.

In front of the Bangla Sahib Sikh temple in New Delhi, angry Sikh demonstrators shout antigovernment slogans days after the Indian army stormed the Golden Temple, killing many. (AP/Wide World Photos)

One of the first steps was the creation of a Sikh scripture, the *Adi Granth* (also known as the *Guru Granth Sahib*). This scripture began under the second guru, who collected hymns composed by Nanak and earlier teachers of devotional religion (*bhakti*), and was finished by the tenth guru in 1706, when the book was given its final form. The sixth guru began arming his followers after his father, the fifth guru, died in captivity. The tenth guru created a militant fraternity called the Khalsa (pure ones). Members of the Khalsa undergo a rite of baptism and wear the "5 Ks"—uncut hair, comb, sword, steel bracelet, and short pants—so known because each item begins with the letter *K* in Punjabi. Males in the Khalsa substitute Singh (lion) and females Kaur (princess) for their "caste" names,

symbolically indicating their equality and commitment to defend the Sikh community. With the tenth guru's creation of the Khalsa in 1699 and his deathbed installation of the *Adi Granth* as the final Sikh guru, the process of development slowed, and the salient features of the modern Sikh religion were established.

In the nineteenth century, the Sikhs fought valiantly to defend the Punjab from the British. Recognizing the Sikhs' military talents, the British army recruited large numbers of them, stationing them throughout the Empire, thus beginning the emigration that by 1980 had led to perhaps one million Sikhs, out of a total of twelve million, living outside India.

Doctrines. Nanak's primary message is rigorously monotheistic: God is one, without form, the ultimate reality. He is not present in statues and never takes on human or animal forms, he does not care for the religious labels humans adopt, and he judges worshippers by their purity, sincerity, and devotion. Nanak rejected the authority of the Vedas and traditional teachings on caste, female inferiority, ritual purity, and sacrifices. He criticized the professional ascetics and "holy men" of India, who abandon all worldly responsibilities to seek liberation. For the Sikhs, liberation is found through meditation, worship, and ultimately grace, in the midst of the obligations of work and family, and moral conduct is essential.

Nanak accepted the traditional Indian doctrine of *samsara*, the belief that unenlightened souls are reincarnated into different bodies, based upon their *karma*. Liberation comes when the heart is so full of God that all sense of separate identity disappears. When liberated human beings die, their souls dwell in God's presence eternally, never again to take birth.

The hymns and sayings of Nanak show that he placed great importance on the human guru as essential to spiritual growth and eventual liberation; however, since the death of the tenth guru, orthodox Sikhs have viewed the *Adi Granth* as the guru. The role of priest and teacher (*granthi*) can be assumed by any adult Sikh who can read the *Adi Granth*, but the *granthi* does not have the spiritual authority held by gurus in the early Sikh tradition.

Practices. Though Sikhs may worship and meditate at home, congregational worship in a *gurdwara* (temple) is extremely important. Wherever a number of Sikhs reside, they will establish a *gurdwara*; many European and North American cities have several. Services tend to be long but informal, including short readings from the *Adi Granth*, scriptural explanations, hymn singing, prayers, and the sharing of a simple meal. The Golden Temple, which is a *gurdwara* in AMRITSAR, India, is viewed as especially holy and is a major pilgrimage site.

Early morning is considered an excellent time for home scripture reading and meditation, which often consists of repeating the name of God, but there is no set time for daily devotions. The Sikhs have no special day set aside for worship, but those living in the West often attend Sunday services at a *gurdwara*. Sikhs generally participate in the major Hindu religious festivals and observe a number of holy days of their own.

Modern Developments. With the partition of India and Pakistan in 1947, the Sikhs' homeland was divided. While Hindus and Muslims received their own countries, the Sikhs suffered significant hardships and loss of property; millions fled to the Indian side of the Punjab. Sikh leaders soon regretted not demanding a separate country for themselves and have sought varying degrees of autonomy ever since.

When Sikh separatists occupied the Golden Temple in 1984, Indira Gandhi sent in the Indian army. A massacre resulted, the temple was desecrated, and many Sikhs were deeply offended. Prime Minister Gandhi was assassinated by her Sikh bodyguards soon afterward. Radical separatists have made the creation of a Sikh nation one of the most pressing issues in Indian politics, often resorting to violence to emphasize their demands.

As a group, immigrant Sikhs have prospered. Sikh professors teach at most Western universities, and many Sikhs are successful in business and other professions. In the 1960's, several Punjabi teachers of Sikh-based spirituality became prominent in the West, developing large followings.—*Scott Lowe*

SUGGESTED READINGS: • Cole, W. Owen. *The Guru in Sikhism*. London: Darton, Longman & Todd, 1982. • Cole, W. Owen, and Piara Singh Sambhi. *The Sikhs: Their Religious Beliefs and Practices*. London: Routledge & Kegan Paul, 1978. • McLeod, W. H. *The Evolution of the Sikh Community*. Oxford, England: Clarendon Press, 1976. • McLeod, W. H., ed. and trans. *Textual Sources for the Study of Sikhism*. Totowa, N.J.: Barnes & Noble Books, 1984.

Sikhs in Canada: Sikhs were first attracted to Canada in 1897, when several Sikh soldiers passed through British Columbia while returning from Queen Victoria's Diamond Jubilee in London, England. They were favorably impressed with the region, which had many similarities to their home state of Punjab, and a few remained in Vancouver. Overcrowding and economic problems in India also provided justification for migration, as most immigrants came with the intent of earning their fortune and returning to their homelands.

While the early immigrants were mostly soldiers, those that followed usually came from farming backgrounds and took on farming work. They had heard that wages were much higher in North America than in India. They were not, however, told that the cost of living was also much higher in North America and that the high wages were for skilled workers, not unskilled laborers, such as the vast majority of those that left South Asia for Canada.

Despite the fact that they were citizens of the British Empire, the immigrants encountered a great deal of opposition to their arrival in Canada from those that wanted to keep British Columbia as a land for white people only. Facing racist attacks from the media as well, they suffered a great deal of discrimination in many areas including those of housing, wages, and restrictive immigration legislation. Despite the opposition, there were also strong interests in British Columbia that hoped to retain the Sikh laborers, because the latter were willing to work for less money than white laborers.

As a matter of government policy, there were very few Sikh families in Canada until the early 1930's. After the lifting of restrictive legislation, however, a number of families were reunited and began the formation of a vibrant, dynamic community in Canada. The first *gurdwara*, or Sikh temple, in North America was established at Port Moody, British Columbia, in 1907. This became a central point for the community's cultural, religious, social, and political activity. As the community grew, it became relatively successful—even affluent—and these immigrants spread throughout Canada, forming large concentrations in most major Canadian cities.

Sikhs in the United States: No official census of Sikhs in the United States exists, but estimates range from 150,000 to 200,000 out of a 1990 census total of 815,000 "Asian Indians." Although Sikhs make up only about 2 percent of the population of India, they have always been disproportionately represented among overseas Indian communities, living in some sixty countries around the world. Contemporary American Sikhs are among the most educated, professionally trained, and economically successful immigrant groups in the United States, most having arrived after 1950, the majority in the 1970's and 1980's. They are permanent residents who fully participate in the economic and political life of American society while largely maintaining their unique religion and social life. Their status stands in stark contrast to their early history in America.

The First Waves. East Indians in America are sporadically mentioned in historical documents beginning in colonial times through the gold rush in California (1849-1850). Prior to 1900, however, the total of all people from India in North America was considerably less than one thousand, consisting mostly of transient sailors, religious figures, or businesspeople. The earliest Sikh immigration of any significance in the United States began between 1901 and 1923 with the arrival of Punjabi male agricultural laborers. South Asian immigration to North America from that time until the

Gurdip Singh, Sikh priest at a temple in Hollywood, California. "Singh," translated into English as "lion," is a common Sikh last name. (Martin A. Hutner)

independence of India (1947) was largely a Punjabi affair; at least 90 percent of those from Punjab were Sikhs, the remainder being Punjabi Hindus and Muslims. The total population during this period was relatively small, never exceeding ten thousand individuals, the majority of whom were Jat Sikhs from the Malwa and Doab regions of Punjab, India.

Northwestern India since the 1880's had suffered a series of plagues, famines, and droughts, making employment opportunities scarce. Early Sikhs were "passenger" migrants from the Indian subcontinent, initially seeking only an economic stake and not intending to settle in the United States. They were drawn by a variety of circumstances, such as advertisements by steamship companies, recruitment to work on the Canadian Pacific Railroad, and their own international experiences earned as part of their military service under the British. Although the bulk of early Sikhs arrived prior to World War I (1914-1918), legal immigration continued throughout the first two decades of the twentieth century, with illegal immigration through the Panama Canal and Mexico between 1923 and the late 1930's adding perhaps three thousand more Sikhs.

The Sikhs entered North America at a time of strong and growing anti-Asian feelings and suffered severe social and economic discrimination, including a series (1910-1917) of exclusionary acts ranging from state alien land laws to congressional immigration restrictions. This discrimination culminated in 1923 with the U.S. Supreme Court decision (*United States v. Bhagat Singh Thind*) that declared South Asians ineligible for citizenship because they were not "white," rendering many Sikhs "stateless" under the law, able to leave but not return to the United States. In addition, many Sikhs were involved in political activities (see GHADR MOVEMENT) to overthrow the colonial British Raj in India, and they returned to India to fight. Between 1911 and 1920, nearly fifteen hundred East Indians, most of them Sikhs, left the United States. This outflow, coupled with legal encapsulation, an aging male population, and legal barriers to immigration, left an Indian population of only about fifteen hundred by the end of World War II (1945), at least half of whom lived in rural California.

West Coast Intermarriage. The majority of early Sikhs in the United States (perhaps as many as 70 percent) were concentrated on the West Coast, particularly in California's Central Valley, an agricultural heartland stretching north from the Imperial Valley on the Mexican border to the orchards and rice fields of the San Joaquin and Sacramento valleys. Employment in agriculture provided an outlet for their cultivation skills and allowed them to keep a lower profile. Because there were fewer than a dozen Sikh women in the United States, and no possibility of importing brides or reuniting with Indian families, over the years many Sikhs married Spanish-speaking women. By the 1950's, there was a small biethnic community of some four hundred couples who were termed, erroneously, "Mexican-Hindus" (also "Mexidus"), who, along with their children, briefly formed a subculture in the 1910-1950 period. This unusual group, which formed a loose network, was the sole social center for many Punjabi men for up to four decades. These families gradually lost their ethnic distinctiveness as their "half-and-half" offspring chose to marry non-Indians. Numerically, they soon became a minority as immigration resumed between the United States and newly independent India.

The Second Wave: The Professionals. Changes in immigration laws allowed resumption of two-way

Sikh priest and follower outside a temple in Sacramento. (Ben Klaffke)

From a limousine, a Sikh candidate for civil court judge seeks the support of fellow New Yorkers. (Richard B. Levine)

immigration and family reunification. Between 1947 and 1965, some six thousand Indians entered the United States, again mostly Sikh, but with many more non-Punjabis represented. The elimination of national quotas in 1965 set the stage for the most dramatic increase of South Asian immigration in U.S. history. Sikhs were no longer the largest South Asian segment by 1970, when the U.S. census reported some fifty-one thousand foreign-born and twenty-five thousand native-born Americans of Indian descent. By 1980, the U.S. South Asian population totals were more than 360,000, increasing to 815,000 by 1990. By then, Sikh socioeconomic profiles revealed the emergence of a highly visible, largely urban-based, often professionally trained or entrepreneurial group. Sikhs constitute some 25 percent to 30 percent of the total South Asian population in the United States. Sikhs make up approximately one-quarter of the Asian Indian population in the state of California, reflecting both a continuing regional preference by Sikh immigrants and the existence of what may be the largest and most prosperous Sikh farming community outside India—in Yuba and Sutter counties, about sixty miles north of Sacramento.

Moving Out and Moving Up. Sikhs now reside in every state in the United States, with concentrations in California on the West Coast, the New York/New Jersey areas of the Northeast, and Chicago and Michigan in the Midwest. Sikhs are found in educational institutions, scientific research centers, and anywhere retail business and restaurant opportunities present themselves. They have built more than 150 *gurdwaras* (Sikh houses of worship); established foundations, cultural societies, and charities; organized Sikh political groups; endowed university chairs for Sikh and Punjabi language studies; and maintained active English/Punjabi press and media operations; in addition, they are prominently represented in many areas of engineering, medicine, public health, and commerce. Their status and achievements are in marked contrast to the long and often difficult path followed by their coreligionists during the first half-century of their residence in the United States.—*Bruce La Brack*

SUGGESTED READINGS: • Barrier, N. Gerald, and Verne A. Dusenbery. *The Sikh Diaspora: Migration and the Experience Beyond Punjab*. Columbia, Mo.: South Asia Publications, 1989. • La Brack, Bruce. *The Sikhs of Northern California, 1904-1975*. New York: AMS Press, 1988. • Leonard, Karen. *Making Ethnic Choices: California's Punjabi Mexican Americans*. Philadelphia: Temple University Press, 1992.

• Gibson, Margaret A. *Accommodation Without Assimilation: Sikh Immigrants in an American High School*. Ithaca, N.Y.: Cornell University Press, 1988. • Takaki, Ronald. "The Tide of Turbans—Asian Indians in America." In *Strangers from a Different Shore: A History of Asian Americans*. New York: Penguin Books, 1990.

Sikhs in Yuba City: Beginning in 1904, small numbers of Sikh laborers from the Punjab region of India entered North America through Canada and moved slowly southward through Washington and Oregon, eventually arriving in the Imperial Valley of Southern California by 1908. During this period, a small core of Sikhs became established in the areas of Yuba and Sutter counties in the northern Sacramento Valley of California. From 1907 to 1947, they constituted only a tiny presence in the lands surrounding Yuba City, but after World War II (1939-1945), and particularly after the late 1960's, a growing influx of Sikhs to the region eventually resulted in the establishment of what is probably the largest (up to ten thousand at certain periods), most successful, and best-known Sikh agrarian community outside South Asia.

The Sikhs were undoubtedly attracted to the area for three related reasons. First, even in 1900, this location had been an important agricultural center for more than

CALIFORNIA

■ Yuba City
★ Sacramento
San Francisco
Los Angeles
San Diego

a century and was able to provide for the immediate employment of Sikh irrigation and labor skills either as workers attached to a farm or as migrants working with other Punjabis as part of a "gang." Second, the physical setting was remarkably familiar. In climate and geography, this area closely resembles the Sikh homelands of northwestern India, being well watered by five rivers, possessing rich alluvial soils, and having hot summers and cool winters. Third, the area was rural and therefore out of the mainstream of the anti-Asian sentiments and movements that racked the West Coast for most of the first half of the twentieth century.

Of the six thousand legal Sikh immigrants entering the United States between 1907 and 1923, approximately 10 percent (around six hundred) eventually settled in Yuba City, Marysville, and the surrounding areas. By 1947, despite California's ALIEN LAND LAWS, restrictive immigration laws, the decline of their population to less than four hundred, and many hardships, thirty-four Sikhs had acquired some one thousand acres of land. Following the independence of India (1947), the area's Sikh population began to grow slowly, reaching four thousand by the early 1970's, as new immigrants arrived and long-separated families reunified. Founded on an economic base of ten-to-thirty-acre family farms, the community has grown to nearly ten thousand people owning many thousands of acres. Three *gurdwaras* (Sikh temples) have been built since 1969 to serve the spiritual needs of the area's Sikhs. The community also supports a full range of Punjabi cultural and social activities, including public parades and participation in multicultural community events. It is known throughout the world as the agricultural center for Punjabi Sikhs in the United States.

Silla Dynasty: (668-935): The line of hereditary rulers in the Silla Kingdom founded in 57 B.C.E., one of the three kingdoms in ancient Korea. According to tradition Silla was founded by Pak Hyokkose in southeast Korea. With the aid of the Chinese Tang Dynasty (618-907), Silla managed to destroy the two rival kingdoms, Paekche in southwest Korea in 660 C.E. and Koguryo in the northern half of Korea in 668, thereby unifying all three kingdoms under Silla rule. Korea thereafter was a united country throughout its history until 1948, when it was divided into North and South Korea. Silla's victories in the wars of unification were possible because of superior military and political leadership provided by the members of the Hwarangdo (flower of youths corps). The Hwarangdo was made up of youthful warriors drawn from the noble class.

They emphasized comradeship, military training, loyalty to the monarch, and bravery in battle. The Silla Dynasty, with fifty-six monarchs, dominated Korea from its capital, Kyongju, for nearly ten centuries.

During the second half of the seventh century, the Silla rulers undertook a wholesale introduction of Chinese culture and institutions. They reorganized their government along the lines of the Tang Dynasty, establishing central and provincial government administration, adopting a bureaucratic system of seventeen ranks of officials, and instituting the civil service examination system as a means of recruiting officials. Following the Chinese manner they divided the country into nine provinces, which were in turn subdivided into prefectures and districts. Silla rulers also adopted a Chinese calendar (674), established a national university (682) to teach the Confucian classics, and instituted a medical school to teach medicine and acupuncture. Chinese writing characters were extensively used in the government, in schools, in temples and in monasteries. The Silla aristocrats began to use a name system patterned after the Chinese: a one-character Silla surname, such as Kim, Yi, and Pak, followed by a two-character given name.

In order to monopolize their powers in government, the aristocrats retained their traditional Kolpum (bone-rank) system, a hereditary caste system based on birth. The highest caste of this system was the Songgol (sacred bone), the royal family. The next was the Chingol (true bone), which was made up of cadet branches of the royal family, the families of the king's consort, and the powerful elite families. The Songgol and the Chingol monopolized the top government posts. Below the aristocratic caste were the elite, the commoners, and the slaves, whose lives were strictly regulated by the government.

The Mahayana form of Buddhism was officially adopted as the state religion of Silla in 528. Buddhism flourished among the common people in the next two centuries. Under royal patronage Silla artisans constructed many temples and monasteries. They created stone stupas and bronze Buddha images, displaying splendid artistic skills and genius. In the early ninth century Son (Zen in Japanese) Buddhism became popular.

After the late eighth century Silla began to decline. The Hwarangdo lost their fighting prowess, the aristocrats weakened the government by engaging in power struggles among themselves, and in the midst of struggle, the king was assassinated (789). In the late ninth century numerous peasant uprisings ensued, leaving the countryside in chaos. In 918 Wang Kon established the state of Koryo. In 935 he overran Kyongju, the Silla capital, and finally established a single government again on the Korean peninsula (the Koryo Dynasty, 935-1392).

Sin Hanguk po (also, *New Korean News*): Publication created by Korean Americans supporting the Korean independence movement to communicate information about Korean nationalist activities in the United States and in Korea. Other newspapers and magazines devoted to this purpose included the *Shinhan Minbo* (*New Korea*), the *Kongnip Sinmun* (*Korean News*), and the *Taipyongyang Chubo* (*Korean Pacific Weekly*). Such news organs became an important means of maintaining public awareness and patriotic zeal during the push for independence.

Sindo haksaeng: Term used by Korean Americans to refer to "recently arrived" students from Korea, chiefly during the period from 1910 (when Japan annexed Korea) to 1945.

Sing, Lillian K. (b. Nov. 13, 1942, Shanghai, China): Judge. She became a San Francisco municipal court judge in 1981 and the first Asian American woman judge in Northern California. She cofounded Chinese

Lillian Sing. (Asian Week)

for Affirmative Action, Wah Mei Bilingual Pre-School, and the Chinese Elected Officers Association; served as board member of the Chinese Newcomers Service Center and the Chinese Cultural Foundation, and as president of the Chinese American Democratic Club; and cochaired the Asian American Task Force on University Admissions.

Sing Tao Jih Pao: Hong Kong-based Chinese-language daily newspaper, founded in 1938. In 1961 the paper began shipping an overseas edition by air to San Francisco. Around 1964 offices were established in San Francisco and New York. Local editions were eventually published in San Francisco, New York, Vancouver, Toronto, and Los Angeles. One of the most widely distributed Chinese newspapers in the world, *Sing Tao Jih Pao* also publishes editions in Sydney, Australia, and in London. All this expansion has taken place under the guidance of Sallie Aw Sian, who inherited the paper from her father, Aw Boon Haw. Because it contains more complete coverage of Hong Kong than other community dailies, the paper has been particularly popular among recent Hong Kong immigrants.

Singapore, Republic of: Metropolis and independent nation in Southeast Asia, not a part of China (as many Westerners mistakenly believe). It is an island city-state located at the southern tip of the Malaysian Peninsula and north of Sumatra (Indonesia) in the strategic Strait of Malacca connecting the Indian and Pacific oceans.

Land and Economy. Lying some ninety miles north of the equator, Singapore has a tropical climate of year-round heat (78 to 95 degrees Fahrenheit) and high humidity (100-inch annual rainfall). The main land mass is the diamond-shaped Singapore Island, covering only 221 square miles, its greatest extent being twenty-seven miles east to west and fourteen miles north to south. A causeway connects Singapore and Malaysia. Despite its size, Singapore is home to 2,800,000 people (1993 estimate), and its excellent harbor and shipyards made it the busiest port in the world in the late 1980's, serving more than 36,000 ships annually; during that period, its airport also saw 11 million passengers yearly, traveling on some fifty airlines.

A hub of international finance and industry, Singapore is also the world's third largest oil refining center. Economically, Singapore is prosperous and energetic, one of the "little dragons" of Asia: Its 1990 per capita gross national product was $12,310, and Singaporeans enjoy a living standard unsurpassed in Asia except in Japan and Brunei. A campaign to limit popu-

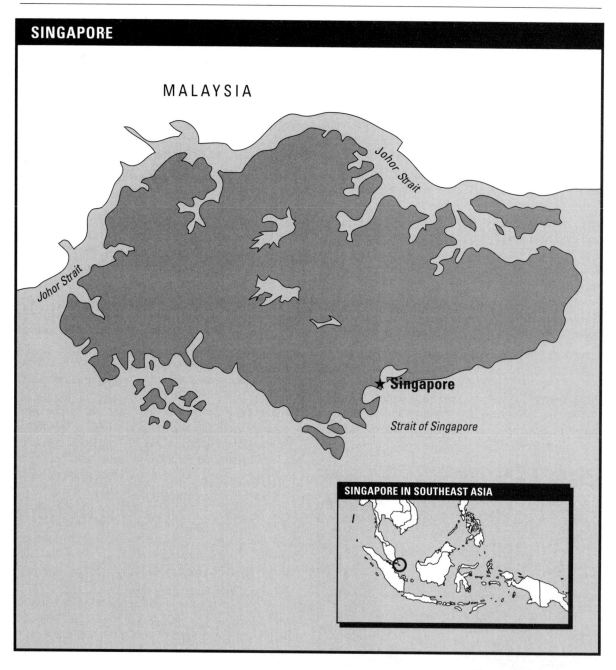

SINGAPORE

MALAYSIA

Johor Strait

Johor Strait

★ Singapore

Strait of Singapore

SINGAPORE IN SOUTHEAST ASIA

lation growth in the 1970's was so successful that the government decided during the 1980's to offer incentives to college-educated women bearing more than two children.

History. Records of the existence of Singapore (previously named Temasek) survive from the fourteenth century. Modern Singapore, however, came into being only after 1819, when Sir Thomas Stamford Raffles of the British East India Company envisioned its potential as a trading center and British colony. From a few

fishing villages, Singapore grew into the administrative seat of Britain's Straits Settlements (including Malacca and Penang). During World War II (1939-1945), Singapore, supposedly an impregnable fortress, was swiftly captured and occupied by the Japanese, reverting to British control in 1945.

Singapore gained internal self-government in 1959 and became a part of Malaysia in 1963, from which federation it was ejected in 1965. After that, Singapore remained a republic with a parliamentary democ-

Fruit market along a busy city street in Singapore. (Eric Crystal)

racy modeled upon the British. From 1963 to 1966, Singapore successfully weathered Indonesia's "Confrontation," an effort to harass and terrorize Singapore (by military coercion) into joining a "Greater Indonesia." To discourage such overtures, Singapore built a credible armed deterrence with the help of Israeli advisers.

In 1959, Singapore began to be ruled by the popularly elected People's Action Party, with Lee Kuan Yew as its prime minister and guiding force for three decades. While pursuing a policy of economic development under close government stewardship, the People's Action Party has shaped Singapore into a meritocracy with a skilled and compliant labor force.

The People. The people of Singapore form a multiethnic society of several languages, religions, and cultures. Its four official languages are English, Chinese (Mandarin), Malay, and Tamil (a south Indian language). All children are educated in English and learn an Asian mother tongue, and Singapore's literacy rate exceeds 90 percent. Ethnically, 77.7 percent of Singaporeans are Chinese, 14.2 percent are Malay, and 7.1 percent are Indian (South Asian). Other significant ethnic groups are Eurasians, Europeans, Jews, Arabs, and Armenians. All Singaporeans are immigrants or descendants of immigrants. The most popular religions are Buddhism (28 percent), Christianity (18 percent), Islam (16 percent), Taoism (13 percent), and Hinduism (5 percent); in the 1980's, the Singapore government encouraged a Confucian ethic.

The Chinese, Singapore's majority group, arrived in numbers during the nineteenth century Chinese diaspora. They originated primarily from southeastern China, from several different dialect areas, most speaking either Hokkien (from Fujian Province) or Teochew (from Shantou). Cantonese formed the third most populous subgroup, followed by Hainanese and Hakkas. (This diversity contrasts with the makeup of pre-1965 Chinese immigrants to the United States, who were predominately Cantonese.) In the 1980's, the government instituted a policy of Chinese education in Mandarin (the official language of China), hoping to eradicate dialect differences and build a more cohesive Chinese community.

In the nineteenth and early twentieth centuries, a hybridized type of Chinese evolved known as Baba, Peranakan, or Straits(-born) Chinese. These are second- or third-generation Chinese settlers, some the children of Chinese men and native women; they no longer speak Chinese but Malay (laced with Hokkien) or English (mingled with so much Singaporean diction

and syntax that it has evolved into "Singlish"). Their hybrid culture blends Chinese, Malay, and European influences, producing distinctive styles of dress, decor, rituals, and a piquant cuisine comparable to Louisiana creole.

The Chinese are to be found in all the economic and social classes of Singapore, from laborer to tycoon, and have come to dominate government and politics as well as the professions, businesses, and industries. Singapore Chinese are said to have developed a distinctive trait (upon which Taiwanese and mainland Chinese have remarked) known as *kiasu* (Hokkien for "fear of losing"); it manifests itself in an overanxiety not to be last (preferably to be first), not to lose out on anything (preferably to get more than one's money's worth), and not to admit defeat (preferably to win, or at least to have known all along that the prize was not worth winning).

The Malays are descendants of immigrants from Malaya or Indonesia (primarily Java). They speak Malay, and almost all are Muslims. Economically and educationally, the Malays have not been as high achievers as the majority group; but in the 1980's, the Malay community's self-help foundation, Mendaki, with government cooperation, began to make advances in this regard.

Singapore's Indians, originating mostly from south India, generally speak Tamil and practice Hinduism. Many Indians in Singapore, however, have adopted English as their primary language. Although there is considerable relaxation of the Indian caste system, the more menial jobs within the Indian community are held by the lower castes, and the professional, business, and banking positions by the higher castes.

Interracial and interfaith marriage is not uncommon in Singapore, but the melting pot is not part of the society's ideology. Each ethnic community preserves its identity, cultural traditions, and artistic expression, and the society as a whole attempts to foster equality of opportunity for all. To ensure minority representation in parliament, Singapore designated a number of combined electoral constituencies that must be contested by teams of three candidates, one of whom must be non-Chinese. Singapore's government encourages its population to imbibe the best from Western and Asian traditions. Drawing from the West, it encourages pragmatism, technological advance, and rationalism. Drawing upon Asian tradition, it encourages strong family values, emphasizes education and work, and promotes the good of the community above self-interest.—*C. L. Chua*

SUGGESTED READINGS: • Hassan, Riaz, ed. *Singapore: Society in Transition*. New York: Oxford University Press, 1976. • Krause, Lawrence B., Ai Tee Koh, and Yuan Lee. *The Singapore Economy Reconsidered*. Singapore: Institute of Southeast Asian Studies, 1987. • LePoer, Barbara Leitch, ed. *Singapore: A Country Study*. Washington, D.C.: Government Printing Office, 1991. • Quah, Jon S. T., Heng Chee Chan, and Chee Meow Seah. *Government and Politics of Singapore*. Singapore: Oxford University Press, 1985. • Singapore Ministry of Communications and Information. *Singapore Facts and Pictures, 1989*. Singapore: Information Division, Ministry of Communications and Information, 1989. • Turnbull, Constance M. *A History of Singapore, 1810-1975*. Kuala Lumpur, Malaysia: Oxford University Press, 1977.

Singh: Translated into English as "lion," a common Sikh last name. Originating from Rajasthan and Punjab states, this name is prevalent throughout north India and Nepal.

Singh, Gurdit (1859?, Sarhali, Amritsar District of Punjab State, India—July 24, 1954, Calcutta, Republic of India): Merchant and activist. Although he received little education as a child, leaving school at a very young age out of dislike for the unkind manner of his teacher, Singh became a wealthy and powerful representative and spokesperson for the rights of South Asians as citizens of the British Empire, as well as the lower classes.

Going to Malaya in the early twentieth century, Singh developed a prosperous business through railway contracts and by planting rubber. Upon returning to India in 1909, he actively protested against the practice of *begar*, or forced labor. He petitioned the colonialist government in protest of the British practice of forcing impoverished peasants to work on public works without pay. When his call for reform was rebuffed by the government, Singh urged his fellow villagers to unite and refuse subjugation.

In 1914 he chartered the Japanese ship *Komagata Maru*, renamed *Guru Nanak Jahaj*, to test the Canadian government's anti-Indian immigration laws. The journey climaxed seven years of protest in both Canada and the United States over discriminatory treatment of South Asian immigrants.

Singh arranged the voyage so as to comply with the many requirements placed upon South Asians by the Canadian government, in order to receive legal admittance into Canada. The ship left Hong Kong with 376 Punjabi passengers, 340 Sikhs, 24 Muslims, and 12 Hindus, arriving in Vancouver on May 22, 1914. The ensuing battle to keep the ship's passengers out of Canada exposed the palpably racist nature of Canada's exclusionary immigration legislation, as well as the subordinate nature of Indians' citizenship in the British Empire. This incident aroused great resentment against the British, from Indians in both Canada and India.

After returning to Calcutta following the failure of the *Komagata Maru* to gain admittance into Canada, Singh fled from the British authorities ruling India at the time. He remained underground until 1921, when he gave himself up on the advice of Mohandas K. Gandhi. Singh spent five years in jail before retiring to Calcutta, where he died.

Singh, Jane: Scholar. She specializes in Asian Indian American history at the University of California, Berkeley. She is descended from one of the original Sikh families that immigrated to California in the early 1900's and settled in the Sacramento Valley. Her other responsibilities have included serving as coordinating editor of *South Asians in North America: An Annotated and Selected Bibliography* (1988), sitting on the editorial board of *Making Waves: Writings By and About Asian American Women* (1989), and serving as curator of "People of South Asia in America," a national pictorial exhibit.

Singh, Jawala (1859?, Thatian, Amritsar District of Punjab State, India—1938?): Farmer, activist, and revolutionary. Born to a poor, peasant family, Singh left India in search of better economic opportunity, eventually becoming one of the wealthiest farmers in America. His arrival in California enabled him to take advantage of the low price of land, by joining with another Sikh farmer—Wasakha Singh—in a joint farming venture. Jawala Singh's eventual success earned him the nickname "the potato king."

In 1912 Singh joined with other Sikh settlers in the area in organizing the building of the first *gurdwara*, or Sikh temple, in the United States. This temple—built in Stockton, California—was particularly important to the settlers because it served both as a focus for their solidarity and religious faith and as a center in which to discuss affairs of interest to the small community, which had formed in a hostile, alien environment. The *gurdwara* later became a center of revolutionary activities aimed at the expulsion of British imperialism from India.

Singh was among the founders of the Ghadr Party, a group working toward armed revolution against the British in India. In fact, he was one of the leaders of the first group of Ghadr revolutionaries that went to India to try to foment rebellion in 1914. This joint venture of Sikhs, Hindus, and Muslims failed, as most of the revolutionaries were arrested immediately upon arrival in Calcutta. Singh was arrested and sentenced to life in prison. He served eighteen years, obtaining his release in 1933. While in jail in the Andaman Islands, he went on a hunger strike in protest of the cruel treatment of prisoners there.

Upon returning to India, Singh again ran afoul of British authorities as a result of his work on behalf of peasant farmers. Because of his activities, he served a year in jail. He remained an activist until his death in 1938 while traveling to a conference in Bengal.

Sinhalese: People of Indo-Aryan origin who immigrated to SRI LANKA from northern India in the fifth century B.C.E. Composing roughly three-fourths of a total population of almost seventeen million people (1990 figure), they are the largest ethnic group in the country. They are for the most part farmers, and their society is based on the caste system. The great majority of Sinhalese are Theravada Buddhists; a few are Christians. Residing mostly in the central, south, and southwestern regions of Sri Lanka, the Sinhalese also hold most of the political and governmental power. Their ongoing racial and religious conflicts with the next-largest ethnic group, the Tamils, who constitute 18 percent of the country, have produced a mass exodus of Tamil refugees. Sinhalese is also the name for one of two official languages in Sri Lanka, the other being Tamil; the former is the majority language.

Sinhan Minbo (*New Korea People's Press*): Newspaper published in the United States by overseas Korean nationalists during the Japanese protectorate of Korea. Particularly with the signing of the Protectorate Treaty of 1905, it became essential to fan the flames of Korean public opinion and outrage against Japanese aggression by giving the general public means of speaking out. The *New Korea People's Press* was only one of many newspapers devoted to this purpose. Those periodicals published in Korea (the majority of them) did so in an atmosphere of increasing censorship by the Japanese Residency-General, which enacted a law in 1907 that further restricted newspaper production. By 1908 most if not all newspaper circulation in Korea had been prohibited.

Sinitic languages: The principal family of Chinese languages spoken in mainland East Asia. The major languages in this family include Cantonese, Hakka, Fukienese, Suchow, Taiwanese, and Hsiang, as well as standard Mandarin Chinese, the official language of both the People's Republic of China and Taiwan. Some scholars also include the Bai languages of China's Yunnan Province near the Burmese border as members of the Sinitic family.

The label "Chinese" has been used for hundreds of years by Europeans as a general term to name the variety of languages and dialects spoken in mainland

The Major Sinitic Languages, 1990			
Language Group or Family	Principle Language/Dialects (common names)	Primary Locations	Number of Speakers (in millions)
Yue	Cantonese	Hong Kong, Macau, Guangdong	54.0
Xiang	Hsiang	Hunan	50.0
Wu	Suchow, Shanghaiese	Shanghai, Suzhou, Anhui, Zhejiang	84.0
Gan	Kan	Hebei, Shanxi, Jiangsu	24.0
Kejia	Hakka	Guangdong, Fujian, Guangxi	42.0
Beifanghua	Mandarin	north and northwest China, Beijing, Taiwan	713.0
Min	Taiwanese, Fukienese	Taiwan, Hainan, Fujian	45.0
Bai	Pai, Minchia	Yunan	1.1

Notes: (1) Shanghai, Hong Kong, Macau, Suzhou, and Beijing (Peking) are cities; other places are territories or provinces. (2) Geographical features and language families are given in pinyin romanization, while language names are cited in the form by which they are best known.

China and parts of Southeast Asia. Linguists, however, often use the more precise term "Sinitic" when referring to these languages, especially when contrasting them with the closely related Tibetan and Burman language families (see SINO-TIBETAN LANGUAGES). Also, what many people generally call Chinese dialects are actually different languages in the technical sense. For example, Cantonese, Hakka, and Mandarin are for the most part mutually unintelligible (and are as different as French, Spanish, and Italian).

There are many specific linguistic properties that each Sinitic language or dialect may share or lack, but almost all have the following important features in common. First, tonality is used to indicate differences in meaning. For example, the Mandarin word *ma*, when said with a rising pitch, can mean "hemp," when said in a flat tone can mean "mother," when said with a falling pitch can mean "to scold," and when said in a rising-falling pitch can mean "horse." Sinitic languages may have from three to eight different tone patterns. Second, most morphemes are monosyllabic, that is, individual words are made up of single syllables (or of compound words, themselves made up of single syllables). Third, prefixes and suffixes on root words are absent; grammatical relationships are generally indicated by word order. Fourth, the order of the parts of speech in a sentence in a Sinitic language is subject-verb-object (the same as in English). Fifth, adjectives and modifiers tend to come before the noun they modify, as they do in English. Finally, numeral classifiers are generally required to count things. In the Sinitic languages, one counts by adding a special word that reflects some property of the class of the noun being counted. For example, one must say, "two *animal* dogs," "one *person* teacher," "three *cylindrical-object* pencils." Few such classifiers exist in English (for example, "*head* of cattle," "*cups* of coffee," or "*pairs* of jeans"), but these are compulsory in the Sinitic languages.

Around 1900, with the decline of the Qing Dynasty, intellectual reformers and educators realized a need for a national *lingua franca* to unite China linguistically. A spoken version of literary Chinese was eventually chosen to be the common language, based largely on the grammar of the northern dialects with a Beijing accent. This became known as *putong hua* (the common language) in China, *guo yu* (the national language) in Taiwan, and Mandarin Chinese in the West.

Sinmin-hoe (New People Society): *Dong-hoe* (village council; also *tong-hoe*) founded in 1903 by Korean im-

migrants in Hawaii chiefly to protest Japanese interference in Korea. Distrustful of outsiders, and mistreated by them, plantation immigrants established these *dong-hoe* as improvised forms of self-government. These democratically elected councils set down rules to help settle disputes and preserve order among the various Korean plantation communities. About four years later the various *dong-hoe* became one large representative body, the Hanin Hapsong Hyop-hoe (United Korean Society), headquartered in Honolulu.

Sino-Japanese War of 1894-1895: War between Japan and China, which brought Japan into the modern world of imperialistic expansionism. Japan's swift, total victory also catapulted it into the first rank among Asian nations.

The war's immediate causes lay in domestic turbulence in Korea. Japan had maintained a strong presence there after the Treaty of Kanghwa (1876), which began trade relations between the two nations. Chinese troops also had been brought in during internal political disputes in the mid-1880's, with the result that both Japan and China became enmeshed in Korea's domestic affairs. When China was asked to help quell Korea's quasi-religious Tonghak Rebellion of 1894, Japan sent its own troops and used the ensuing unrest as a pretext for declaring war on China.

The war's fundamental causes lay in Japan's larger domestic and foreign goals. Many Japanese saw a more aggressive foreign stance as necessary to counter continuing Western incursions in Asia. Others saw increased military activity as a useful tool in Japan's drive to secure equal treaties with the Western powers. The domestic political leaders saw war with China as a way of uniting the public and strengthening the government.

War was declared on August 1, 1894, and, within seven months, Japan had won totally, having defeated the Chinese at Pyongyang, Port Arthur, at Weihaiwei, and on the Yalu River. The peace treaty, signed April 17 in Shimonoseki, gave Japan nearly all it had sought: cession of Taiwan and the south Manchurian peninsula of Liaodong, commercial and industrial privileges in China, and a two hundred million tael indemnity (approximately $278 million).

Public enthusiasm over the settlement was unbounded, until Russia, Germany, and France delivered a note two weeks later, admonishing Japan to return Liaodong to China so as not to threaten Asian stability. The real motive for this triple intervention—Russia's own designs on the region—was barely veiled, and when the Japanese government felt obliged to give in (accepting thirty million more taels in return), the enthusiasm turned to outrage.

Historians regard the war as a turning point in Japan's history. Besides demonstrating the effectiveness of its modernization policies of the previous twenty-five years, the conflict marked Japan's first serious move as an imperialist nation, presaging further territorial acquisition after war with Russia in 1904-1905. It also stimulated the early stages of Japan's first industrial revolution and allowed Japan to go onto the gold standard.

Sino-Korean People's League: Korean left-wing political group in Hawaii. Formed in 1938, and dissolved in 1945, the league's objectives were to promote anti-Japanese activities in the United States and to assist Chinese fighting against Japanese aggression in China.

Sino-Tibetan languages: The world's most widely spoken language—Chinese—belongs to this language family. The other two major languages of this family are Burmese and Tibetan. Chinese is spoken by approximately one billion people in the People's Republic of China and in such countries as Hong Kong, Taiwan, Singapore, Malaysia, and Thailand. A significant number of the Chinese-speaking community is also found in North America. Although often many languages of China are conveniently labeled as Chinese because of the shared writing system, they are as different as French and German. A case in point are Cantonese and Mandarin. Although Cantonese (the language of Macao and Hong Kong) is considered a dialect of Chinese, Cantonese and Mandarin are not mutually intelligible. The Chinese writing system is derived from a pictorial writing system and it is written primarily from top to bottom and right to left. One of the striking features of Chinese is its tonality. Although pitch changes are employed by almost every language in the world, tonal languages such as Chinese use changes in pitch to bring about changes in meaning. Mandarin, which is spoken in the northern (it is the language of Beijing), central, and eastern parts of China, is considered the standard variety of Chinese. Among the other varieties of Chinese are Hakka (Hong Kong), Hunan (Hunan region of China), Min (Fujian), and Wu (see Sinitic languages).

Burmese is spoken by more than twenty-five million people both inside and outside Myanmar (formerly Burma). The written records of Burmese date back to the eleventh century. The number of speakers of Tibetan is quite uncertain. It is estimated that at least three to four million speak this language as their native tongue. After the occupation of Tibet by China, the Dalai Lama fled to India accompanied by a large segment of Tibetans, who now live in exile in India. Therefore, a significant number of speakers of Tibetan now reside in India. The written records of Tibetan go back to the eighth century. The Buddhist influence on Tibet can be seen in the Tibetan writing system, which is more similar to the writing system of the languages of India than those of China.

The number of minor languages of Tibeto-Burman is approximately three hundred. These languages are spoken in Thailand, Laos, and Vietnam, in addition to the major geographical areas covered by this language family.

Snake River massacre (1887): One of the worst outbreaks ever of anti-Chinese violence in the Old West, resulting in the murder of more than thirty Chinese miners. A major U.S. river, the Snake originates in west Yellowstone National Park, flows a thousand miles through the plains of southern Idaho, irrigating six million acres of farmland, plunges into Hells Canyon, the deepest gorge in North America, then joins the Columbia River as its major tributary near Pasco. Chinese immigrants were attracted to the area at first because of railroad construction, mining, and farming. In 1870 25 percent of Idaho's population and more than half the state's almost sixty-six hundred miners were Chinese. Small, widely scattered Chinese communities sprang up along the Snake River to service these predominately placer miners. Their large numbers in relationship to the rest of the population and their visibility led to numerous anti-Chinese movements in the late 1870's through the 1880's. Partially as a result of the anti-Chinese movements and the increase in the white population, the Chinese comprised only 10.4 percent of the population in 1880, 1.9 percent in 1890, and .7 percent in 1900.

The Rock Springs, Wyoming, massacre of twenty-eight Chinese miners on September 2, 1885, probably had a catalytic effect upon anti-Chinese movements in the Pacific Northwest. That month at the mining camp at Orofino, Idaho, a "citizens committee" arrested, imprisoned, and then hung five Chinese men for the alleged murder of a white restaurant owner. The Chinese men, including the merchant Lee Kee Nam, who had angered white miners because he would not sell them goods on credit, were not allowed legal counseling or a trial.

This political cartoon from the 1880's exemplifies the stridently anti-Chinese public sentiment that characterized San Francisco at the time. (Asian American Studies Library, University of California at Berkeley)

The worst violence, however, was at a site immediately north of Hells Canyon on the Snake River in May, 1887. Thirty-one Chinese miners were shot, beaten, or hacked to death by a gang of "cowboys" who had heard that Chinese miners were accumulating great quantities of gold through their frugality and were cleverly hiding their gold because they did not trust Western banks. Some of the Chinese miners were tortured in an attempt to learn where the caches of gold were. The bodies were then thrown into the river.

Society for Establishment of Righteousness and Personal Perfection Through Fellowship (Rissho Koseikai): One of the Japanese new religions, founded by Niwano Nikkyo and Naganuma Myoko in Tokyo in 1938. The sect was formed originally as the Dai Nippon Rissho Koseikai (Great Japan Society for Establishment of Righteousness and Personal Perfection Through Fellowship); the name was shortened following World War II. Like the Society of Companions of the Spirits (Reiyukai), another new religion, this cult is one of Japan's largest lay religious associations. Although inspired by Nichiren Buddhism, it has no clergy and no formal affiliation with any Buddhist sect. Emphasis is placed on daily recitations of the *Lotus Sutra* and on ancestor worship. This religion,

which claimed more than five million members in 1980, is popular in the United States.

Society of Companions of the Spirits (Reiyukai): One of the Japanese new religions, founded in 1925 by Kubo Kakutaro, his brother Kotani Yasukichi, and Kotani's wife, Kimi. The sect is also one of the country's largest lay religious associations. Derived from the Nichiren sect of Buddhism, it centers on ancestor worship based on daily recitation of the *Lotus Sutra*. The rites are carried out at home without the need for priestly mediation. The sect has branches in at least seventeen countries, including the United States. Roughly 2.8 million members belonged to this cult as of 1978.

Soga, Yasutaro (1873—1957): Soga rose to prominence as publisher of the *Nippu Jiji*, a Japanese-language daily newspaper in Hawaii. He also installed, in 1919, an English-language section in the newspaper—the first such section to appear in any Japanese newspaper the world over. Arriving in Hawaii in 1896, he began working for the *Hawaii Shimpo* a few years later. Taking control of the *Yamato Shimbun* in 1905, he changed its name to the *Nippu Jiji* the following year and used the publication to advance support of the prolabor movement in Hawaii. Under his tutelage the newspaper remained highly influential for many years. Soga also implemented detailed news coverage of foreign affairs—particularly those involving Japan. During World War II he was imprisoned in various internment camps.

Sojourners: Individuals who leave their native countries to find better economic opportunities elsewhere. Unlike immigrants who intend to become permanent residents, however, sojourners regard themselves as visitors who plan to return home as soon as circumstances allow. Consequently, sojourners typically avoid assimilating into the larger society and may instead deliberately isolate themselves.

Historically the early Chinese and Japanese immigrants to the United States have been described as primarily sojourners. While that remains the majority view, some scholars in the field of Asian American Studies argue that the traditional interpretation is misleading, and that many of the early immigrants came with the intention of putting down roots. In any case it is important to note that the sojourning phenomenon can be found among immigrants from many different nations, regions, and ethnic backgrounds. For example, many Italian immigrants to the United States in the early twentieth century were sojourners.

Soka-gakkai (Value Creation Society): Lay Buddhist association that is one of Japan's largest new religious movements, linked with the Nichiren-shoshu sect. In 1930 a schoolteacher named Makiguchi Tsunesaburo founded Soka-Kyoiku-gakkai (Value Creation Educational Society) to promote his theories for educational reform integrated with Nichiren religious teachings. Soka-Kyoiku-gakkai grew slowly during the 1930's, and there were about three thousand members in 1942. Makiguchi and some associates were jailed in 1943 for opposing governmental war policy and advising followers not to venerate Shinto. Makiguchi died in prison in 1944, but his chief disciple, Toda Josei, reconstructed the movement after the war (renaming it "Soka-gakkai"); it grew rapidly, claiming a membership of 750,000 family units by 1958. In 1960 Ikeda Daisaku became association president, and under his leadership Soka-gakkai expanded greatly, with more than ten million families by the mid-1980's. As president of Soka Gakkai International, Ikeda also promoted Soka-gakkai in North America, Europe, the People's Republic of China, India, and the former Soviet Union.

Soka-gakkai, as a lay organization, is really part of the Japanese Buddhist sect founded by Nichiren's disciple Nikko. Emphasis is on faith in the teachings of Nichiren as the Buddha for the present age. The central practice is chanting the *daimoku-namu Myoho rengekyo* (adoration to the Lotus of the perfect law) before the *gohonzon*, the *mandala* designed by Nichiren and placed on the altar. Soka-gakkai regards the Buddha nature as the power that can change one's bad karma into good. Since the Buddha nature is identical with the ultimate law of the *Lotus Sutra*, by chanting the *daimoku* the Buddha nature is active within to change individuals and society.

Soka-gakkai has continued Nichiren's emphasis on aggressive promotion of faith (*shakufuku*). The organization carries on a broad range of religious, educational, cultural, and social programs to transform its adherents. It founded a political party, Komeito, which now is separate from the religious organization. This movement came to the United States through immigration of its members to Hawaii and the West Coast after World War II. An important leader in America has been George Williams (born Masayasu Sadanaga), who moved to the United States in 1957 and later became director of Nichiren Shoshu of America, as Soka-gakkai is known there. There are now some 300,000 adherents in America.

Sokabe, Shiro (June 26, 1865, Fukuoka Prefecture, Japan—July 3, 1949): Christian minister. A pastor in Hawaii, Sokabe established a Christian school and led the Honomu Church for almost fifty years. The son of a samurai, he became a Christian sometime in the 1880's and began active church work in his native Japan. In the years that followed he also studied theology at various schools before leaving for Hawaii in 1894 to pastor a church in Honomu on the Big Island of Hawaii. One of his earliest achievements there was to build an adequate school for the children of the town's impoverished plantation workers. The Honomu Gijuku (school), a Christian Japanese-language boarding school, opened sometime after 1897 and, with the full support of the local Japanese American population as well as the sugar planters, soon began to thrive. Sokabe's favorable disposition toward the planters, however, later became a point of contention among some of the laborers, since he had been urging the latter not to stage strikes despite their poor treatment at the hands of the planters.

Sokuji Kikoku Hoshi-dan (Organization to Return Immediately to the Homeland to Serve): Japanese ultranationalist organization founded at the TULE LAKE relocation center in late 1944. Tule Lake was the segregation internment camp for Japanese earmarked for deportation or who had refused to serve in the U.S. military and their families. Members were those internees who had pledged absolute loyalty to Japan and wished to return there immediately in order to serve that country. In concert with the Hokoku Seinen-dan, the Hoshi-dan coerced other camp internees to renounce their rights as American citizens or residents in order to serve Japan. When the U.S. Department of Justice began accepting petitions for renunciation, thousands of Japanese applied (see DENATIONALIZATION ACT OF 1944).

Son Pyong-hui (1861-1922): Religious and political leader. During his lifetime he served as the third leader of the Tonghak (Eastern learning) religious movement, as a Korean independence movement activist, and as chairman of the thirty-three signatories to the Korean Declaration of Independence (1919). He was also elected chief executive of the Korean left-wing Manchuria group, one of three provisional governments established following the 1919 March First uprising.

Sone, Monica (b. 1919, Seattle, Wash.) Her autobiographical narrative, *Nisei Daughter* (1953) became the first published account of the Japanese American search for identity and the World War II internment experience as seen through a Nisei woman's eyes.

Sone's father originally had come to the United States to study law. Her mother, a daughter of a Japanese Christian minister, was an accomplished poet of *tanka*, traditional Japanese poetry. Born of such unusual Issei parents, Sone was raised in an intellectual and cultured environment. Living in Seattle's Carrollton Hotel, which her parents owned and operated for white dockworkers, Sone had more contact with white society than with other Nisei children, who stayed mainly within the Japanese community. Such a unique childhood, along with her internment experience, compelled her to write *Nisei Daughter*.

The narrative portrays Sone's childhood identity crisis in a Seattle Japanese American community that suffered from hostility and prejudice from Anglo society before the war, and the evacuation that divided and destroyed the community. Reflecting the low political consciousness of Japanese Americans in the 1950's, Sone's personal account did not really articulate the bitterness and hardship experienced by Japanese Americans, and it ended with her happy assimilation into the mainstream Anglo culture.

The book was reprinted in 1979 at a critical time in Japanese American history, the beginning of the redress campaign. In the preface to the 1979 edition, Sone more explicitly stated her stance as follows:

> So that their story will not be forgotten and lost to future generations, the Nikkeis are telling the nation about 1942, a time when they became prisoners of their own government, without charges, without trials. . . . The Nikkeis hope that this redress movement may discourage similar injustices to others.

Sone graduated from Hanover College in Hanover, Indiana, and received a master's degree in clinical psychology from Western Reserve University in Cleveland, Ohio, in 1949. She married Geary Sone, a Nisei veteran from California, and has four children.

Song, Cathy (b. Aug. 20, 1955, Honolulu, Territory of Hawaii): Poet. Song, who is of Korean and Chinese ancestry, grew up in Hawaii, and much of her poetry reflects her childhood experiences there. She attended the University of Hawaii and later Wellesley College, where she received a B.A. degree in 1977. She completed an M.A. degree in creative writing at Boston University in 1981. In 1987, she returned to Hawaii with her husband, daughter, and son.

Song's first book of poetry, *Picture Bride* (1983), won the prestigious Yale Series of Younger Poets Award in 1982. Her second volume, *Frameless Windows, Squares of Light*, was published in 1988, followed by *School Figures* in 1994. Her poems have appeared in a number of journals and magazines, including *Amerasia Journal, The American Poetry Review, The Cream City Review, Dark Horse, The Greenfield Review, Michigan Quarterly Review, Ploughshares, Poetry, Prairie Schooner,* and *Seneca Review.* Her work has also appeared in the anthologies *Breaking Silence: An Anthology of Contemporary Asian American Poets* (1983), *Poetry Hawaii: A Contemporary Anthology* (1979), and *Talk Story: An Anthology of Hawaii's Local Writers* (1978). In addition to writing poetry, she has published a short story, "Beginnings (for Bok Pil)," in the Spring, 1976, edition of *Hawaii Review* and coedited with Julia Kono the volume *Sister Stew: Fiction and Poetry by Women* (1991), an anthology of short fiction and poetry by women from Hawaii.

In her poetry, Song explores the themes of intimacy and human relationships, particularly within the family. Her poems portray the experiences of her immigrant Korean grandparents, memories of her own childhood, and relationships among spouses, parents, and children, siblings, lovers, and friends. Her work often depicts the personal histories and daily lives of Asian American women. For example "Beginnings (for Bok Pil)" compares a young woman's abortion in a modern hospital to her grandmother's failed attempt to abort a child.

Song's poetry has been praised for the beauty and immediacy of its imagery and for its ability to freeze a particular moment in time. Her poems are highly sensual, highlighting the special and memorable in everyday experience and revealing a keen perception of the natural world.

Sonjinkai: Type of organization formed by Japanese immigrants to the United States, specifically one consisting of people from the same village back home. The *sonjinkai* was only one type of organization among numerous ones established by these immigrants. Other similar locality clubs were based on sub-village, township, subtownship, city, subcity, or prefectural associations.

In the early years the *sonjinkai* and other locality clubs provided aid to members in times of need. When there was a death in the family or when a member was ill and wished to return to Japan, the locality club pooled its resources and provided assistance. Help was also provided at other times, such as at weddings. Furthermore a number of locality clubs paid attention to the needs of the children and sponsored activities, including speech contests and baseball games, that aided their assimilation into the larger society.

Locality clubs met the needs of the Issei (first generation) well. As the Issei became too old to remain active, however, clubs tended to disband, except for prefectural locality clubs and all-Japanese organizations. Within the Okinawan American community in Hawaii, however, many locality clubs based on associations below the prefectural level, including *sonjinkai*, remain active, with leadership handed over to the second and third generations. As members of the United Okinawan Association of Hawaii, these locality clubs participate in the cultural activities of the association. For its own members, one of the most important functions of the locality clubs is to help bereaved families with funerals. When a death occurs club leaders offer help with the ceremonies and the collection of the monetary gifts that friends give the family of the deceased. The main social functions of most locality clubs are a picnic during the summer and an end-of-the-year or New Year's party. Picnics are a gala affair with a variety of races for all age groups and prizes for all participants. At New Year's parties the feeling of belonging together is renewed, especially among the Issei and Nisei (second generation).

Sonno-joi: Japanese movement of the late Tokugawa period (1600-1867). *Sonno* means "doctrine of reverence for the emperor," and *joi* means "doctrine of expulsion of foreigners." The *sonno-joi*, "revere the Emperor! Drive out the barbarians!," movement, existed around the time of Commodore Matthew C. Perry's arrival in Japan for his mission to open Japan's ports. The ideological foundation for *sonno-joi* was provided by the nineteenth century Japanese thinker Hirate Atsutane, who was the leader of the Restoration Shinto school and who strongly believed in Japan's natural superiority and divinity, and by the seventeenth century Japanese tradition Mitogaku, or school of Mito, which was influenced by Neo-Confucianism.

Soo, Jack (Goro Suzuki; b. 1915, Oakland, Calif.—Jan. 11, 1979): Actor. A successful performer on the West Coast before World War II, Soo, born Goro Suzuki, was incarcerated for two years at the Topaz relocation center. Subsequently he adopted a Chinese stage name to secure employment in the anti-Japanese atmosphere that prevailed after the war. Soo appeared

Jack Soo. (AP/Wide World Photos)

in the original production of Rodgers and Hammerstein's 1958 Broadway musical *Flower Drum Song*. Although Soo landed roles in such motion pictures as *Thoroughly Modern Millie* (1967), *Flower Drum Song* (1961), *Who's Been Sleeping in My Bed?* (1963), *The Oscar* (1966), *The Green Berets* (1968), and *Return from Witch Mountain* (1978), he is best remembered as Sergeant Yemana on the popular television series *Barney Miller*, which premiered in 1975.

Soong, T. V. (Song Ziwen; Dec. 4, 1894, Shanghai, China—Apr. 25, 1971, San Francisco, Calif.): Chinese financier and nationalist government official. Soong was the eldest son of Song Jiashu (or Charles Jones Soong), progenitor of the legendary Soong family. His sisters were married to three of the most powerful men in Republican China: SUN YAT-SEN, H. H. Kung, and CHIANG KAI-SHEK. He himself rose to be the president of the Executive Yuan (or cabinet) in the government of Chiang.

Soong was part of the first wave of Chinese to be educated abroad after 1900, when China finally realized the need for fundamental change. He was born and bred in Shanghai, China's most cosmopolitan city, where his father had become a wealthy businessman. After attending the middle school attached to St. John's University in Shanghai, he went to the United States in 1912 and was graduated from Harvard University in 1915 with a B.A. degree in economics. (As a student, he was exempt from the CHINESE EXCLUSION ACT OF 1882, which otherwise prevented most Chinese from entering the United States.) On his return to Shanghai in 1917, he followed his father's example and proceeded to amass a fortune as a banker and entrepreneur. He eventually became one of the wealthiest persons in the world.

In 1923, Soong began a twenty-five-year career as an official in the Chinese Nationalist regime that was founded by Sun in Canton and extended throughout the country by Chiang. His brothers-in-law first utilized his financial talents to straighten out and strengthen the economy. As minister of finance (1928-1933), Soong helped to centralize the country's finances, standardize the currency, and regain control over the tariff from the foreign powers. Subsequently, during China's war with Japan (1937-1945), Soong, who was fluent in English and comfortable with foreigners, shifted his attention to international relations. As minister of foreign affairs, he secured a great amount of foreign aid for beleaguered China. In 1943, he not only negotiated an end to the foreigners' right of

T. V. Soong. (AP/Wide World Photos)

extraterritoriality (by which they were exempt from Chinese law) but also saw the United States repeal the much-resented Chinese Exclusion Act. After the war, he served (until 1947) as president of the Executive Yuan and was the equivalent of a prime minister.

When the Communists took over the Chinese mainland in 1949, they listed Soong along with Chiang as among their top enemies. Despite his personal and official ties to Chiang, he was not always on cordial terms with his brother-in-law. Thus, he did not follow Chiang to Taiwan. He went instead to the United States, as did many others fleeing the Communists. Despite his enormous wealth, he lived quietly and unobtrusively in New York City. He died in San Francisco in 1971, while visiting old banking associates.

South Asia: Region consisting of the contemporary nation-states of India, Pakistan, Nepal, Bangladesh, Sri Lanka, Bhutan, and Maldives. One of the most diverse areas of the world, South Asia contains more than 20 percent of the world's population. India's population alone will reach one billion sometime in the early decades of the twenty-first century, and South Asia as a region has already exceeded one billion, with its population showing no signs of slowing its birthrate.

SOUTH ASIA

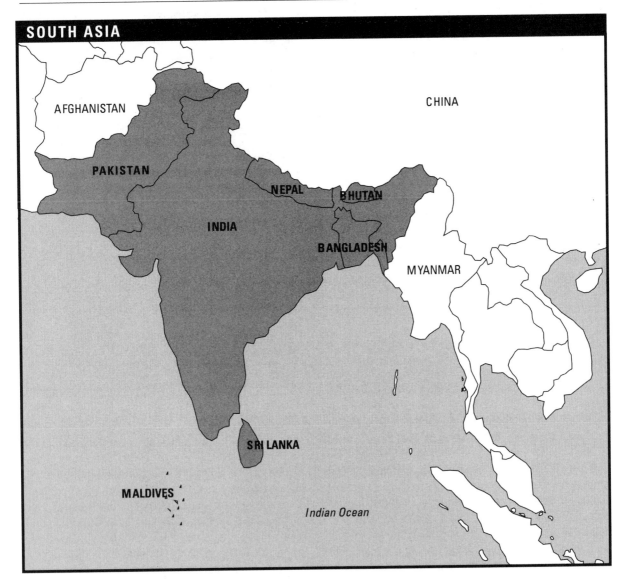

Dominated by a monsoon climate, South Asia is geographically a study in contrasts: It contains desert areas (Thar in Rajasthan) that receive little rain; tropical forests (Assam) that receive more than four hundred inches per year; some of the world's highest mountain ranges and peaks (Mount Everest, K2); fertile, flat alluvial plains (Indus Valley, Bengal Delta) that are the historic breadbaskets of South Asia; and tropical coastlines of coconut palms and fishing villages.

Early Civilizations and Invasions. Containing some of the oldest civilizations on earth, South Asia's cultural continuity is exceeded only by China. The region has been characterized by cycles of conquest and complex social interaction throughout the past four and a half millennia of its history. It originated with the founding of the Indus Valley civilization (c. 3000-1550 B.C.E.) and continued through the Aryan invasions (c. 1500-1000 B.C.E.), Alexander the Great's short-lived Greek conquests (326 B.C.E.), the early Buddhist and classical Hindu kingdoms (300 B.C.E.-600 C.E.), the Muslim invasions (900-1200), and the Mogul Dynasty (early sixteenth to mid-eighteenth century). During the seventeenth century, frequent European contacts began, and by the eighteenth century, Western powers (Dutch, Spanish, Portuguese, French, and English) became both contesting and consolidating forces on the subcontinent.

Great Britain eventually dominated the area starting around 1757 and added most of South Asia as colonies to the imperial British Empire, which lasted until the

Mosque in India. (Library of Congress)

mid-twentieth century. After World War II (1939-1945), the states of South Asia gained their freedom. India was partitioned in 1947, and Pakistan was created as a separate nation with two territories (East Pakistan and West Pakistan). In 1971, Pakistan itself was further split as East Pakistan rebelled and became the independent nation of Bangladesh. Later, India and Sri Lanka began experiencing a variety of separatist movements demanding autonomy, especially among the Sikhs of Punjab, the Muslims of Kashmir, and the Tamils of Sri Lanka.

Home of World Faiths. The primary organizing principle and cultural institution throughout South Asia is religion. The area is the birthplace of two world faiths: Hinduism, which, for more than two and a half millennia and until the twentieth century, was almost wholly restricted to the subcontinent and formed the rationale of the caste system; and Buddhism, which, although founded in India in the sixth century B.C.E., had its greatest influence upon Southeast and East Asian society and religion. Five additional major religions are practiced in South Asia: Christianity, Islam (11 percent of the population in India), Jainism, Sikhism, and Zoroastrianism, as well as countless subgroups, sects, and animistic groups.

Racial and Linguistic Diversity. This diversity is

Young Kashmir girl. (Government of India Tourist Office)

Houseboats anchored along a waterway in Kashmir, India. (Government of India Tourist Office)

reflected again in the racial and linguistic composition of the area. Descendants from both the early Aryan incursions and the medieval Muslim invaders live throughout northern South Asia, particularly the northwest. Physically, they are classified as Caucasian, being lighter-skinned, taller, and more solidly built than southern populations. They speak primarily Indo-European languages derived from Sanskrit but written in many different scripts.

The indigenous Dravidians, somewhat darker and of slighter physique than northern Indians, are now concentrated in the southern tip of India and northern Sri Lanka. They speak four related Dravidian languages. In the northeast, many South Asian Tibeto-Burman tribal groups exhibit Mongolian traits, including rounder faces and the epicanthic fold, and speak a wide variety of languages. India alone recognizes fourteen official languages and more than sixteen hundred major dialects.

Independence and Economic Progress. Since their independence, these South Asian states, always crossroads of trade and commerce, have been working hard to raise their standards of living and to distribute income more equitably. These region's economies have

historically been agriculturally based, with about 70 percent of the population economically dependent on farm production. Urbanization, skilled crafts of all varieties, and trade have been important features of South Asian life for millennia. Three-quarters of all South Asians live in rural areas, although the remaining one-quarter represents huge numbers of urban dwellers who live in metropolitan areas containing some of the largest cities in the world (Calcutta, Bombay, Delhi, Madras).

At once very large and relatively poor, these less developed countries have attempted since the 1950's to balance critical food production activities with industrialization. Although India now ranks among the most industrialized nations and has one of the largest and best-trained technical labor pools in the world, like the rest of South Asia it is still heavily dependent on agriculture for about one-third of its gross domestic product.

Starting in the 1970's, and mainly through the "Green Revolution" (which utilized high-yield crop varieties, irrigation, fertilizers, and insecticides), India, Sri Lanka, and Pakistan have been able to keep food supplies slightly ahead of population growth, although

Bangladesh has been less successful. Food grains (wheat, millet, rice), vegetables, and dairy products (milk, butter) remain the core of the South Asian diet.

Many of these local economies have had considerable external assistance through the remittances sent home by South Asians living overseas (in the United States, Canada, England, Australia, and more than sixty other countries) or by those working as temporary labor (such as South Asians in the Arabian Gulf States).

New Global Immigrants. South Asia has always had internal migrations, but the movement overseas was accelerated during the British rule, as South Asians were recruited as railroad or plantation laborers or sent abroad as part of military forces. They were followed by voluntary migrants who established hundreds of South Asian communities and settlements abroad. After independence, the migration of professionals to first-world nations of the industrialized north increased, as did the reunification of families overseas.

Crowded bank along the Jumna River in Agra, Uttar Pradesh, India. (Government of India Tourist Office)

The result was that a large number of South Asians (perhaps fifteen million immigrants and/or their descendants) have become permanent members of societies around the world, maintaining a wide range of distinctive South Asian cultural values and religious orientations while actively participating in the economic and political life of their adopted countries.—*Bruce La Brack*

SUGGESTED READINGS: • Cohn, Bernard S. *India: The Social Anthropology of a Civilization.* Englewood Cliffs, N.J.: Prentice-Hall, 1971. • Maloney, Clarence. *Peoples of South Asia.* New York: Holt, Rinehart and Winston, 1974. • Schwartzberg, Joseph E., et al. *A Historical Atlas of South Asia.* Chicago: University of Chicago Press, 1978. • Singer, Milton. *When a Great Tradition Modernizes: An Anthropological Approach to Indian Civilization.* New York: Praeger, 1972. • Tinker, Hugh. *The Banyan Tree: Overseas Emigrants from India, Pakistan, and Bangladesh.* New York: Oxford University Press, 1977. • Wolpert, Stanley. *A New History of India.* 4th ed. New York: Oxford University Press, 1993.

South Asian American writers: South Asian American literature reflects not only the diversity of America but also the long-standing complexities and diversities of South Asian languages and literary (both oral and written) traditions.

The Language of Landscapes. Although this essay will focus on the different landscapes (physical and philosophical) in South Asian American literature written in English, one needs to be aware that there are many South Asian American writers who publish in the different South Asian languages and who enjoy a substantial audience of readers in South Asia and America. The selection of geographical, historical, and conceptual contexts by South Asian American writers for their works is important and falls mainly within three categories: The first two involve South Asia itself (Bangladesh, India, Pakistan, Sri Lanka) presented through two different perspectives; the third is the landscape of the Americas.

South Asian Narratives in South Asia. In this category are works by writers who live and write in America but who place their narratives explicitly and entirely in South Asia. Within the narrative there is no acknowledgment of the author's own physical distance from South Asia, or even of the author's possible emotional or intellectual dislocation from the landscape of the work. At its weakest, it becomes obvious that the author is translating the story, the characters, the land-

scape of one culture, Asian, mainly for another culture, Western. In this task of translating, the author often falls into the temptation of awkwardly explaining words, phrases, ideas, events, and even people in parentheses, footnotes, and appendices. At its best, a work in this category adds to the presence of the already existing multiplicity of cultures and landscapes in American literature.

Meena Alexander's works definitely belong to the latter group. For example, she wrote the poems and prose pieces that appear in *House of a Thousand Doors* (1988) in the United States, yet the locations and narratives of the central works are Indian. The volume is an homage to her grandmothers, but at no time does she intrude into their portraits and stories as an alien, Westernized granddaughter, introducing them with translations and glossaries for her Western audience.

In her novel *Cracking India* (1991), Bapsi Sidhwa, a Pakistani American, tells the story of the struggle for independence and the partition of the subcontinent as observed and narrated by an eight-year-old girl, Lenny, who lives in Lahore (part of India and later Pakistan) surrounded by Parsis, Hindus, Muslims, and Sikhs.

The Canadian author Rohinton Mistry, in his *Tales from Firozsha Baag* (1987), portrays the residents of an apartment building in the city of Mistry's birth, Bombay. His novel *Such a Long Journey* (1991) presents the relatively modern story of one man and his family in Bombay during the India-Pakistan war of 1971. Shashi Tharoor in his *The Great Indian Novel* (1989) uses the ancient stories and actors from the epic *Mahabharata* within the context of contemporary India. "President Sahib's Blue Period" (1989), a satire on Pakistani politics by the Pakistani American Javaid Qazi, is set in "Pakypoor." The only Western character in the story is Ambassador Burford.

Stories of the Return to South Asia. In this category are works that present the stories and emotions of South Asians who live in the West and who return to their ancestral land either as visitors or as residents. A sense of living in disturbingly discontinuous landscapes, where memory does not help the protagonists to be comfortable in the once-familiar South Asian landscape, pervades many of these works.

Santha Rama Rau, born in Madras in 1923, educated in England and the United States, and later a resident of the United States, published *Home to India* in 1945. It is an autobiographical account of her return to her family in India after ten years of education in the West. In *East of Home* (1950), she discovers herself and India as part of the vast landscape of Asia as she travels through post-World War II Japan, China, Indo-china, and Indonesia. Echoes of Santha Rama Rau can be heard in Bharati Mukherjee's early works. Her first novel, *The Tiger's Daughter* (1971), is about the frustrations and fears of Tara Banerjee Cartwright, a Western-educated, well-to-do Bengali woman, married to an American, on a visit to her family in Calcutta. In Tahir Naqvi's short story "Hiatus" (1989), Fatima, who is visiting Pakistan, grapples with the weather, argues with her family, and bursts into tears as the blind prophet in her grandmother's recitation begins to resemble Charlton Heston "Hollywood" Moses.

A fascinating novel within this literature of the return to South Asia is Boman Desai's science-fiction and historical work *The Memory of Elephants* (1988). A young Parsi scientist from India invents a memory machine and tries to reexperience happiness with his lost American love. The machine malfunctions, however, and activates the memories of his family and his ancestors in Iran, India, England, and Scotland.

Sara Suleri's literary autobiography, *Meatless Days* (1989), Meena Alexander's lyrical memoir, *Fault Lines* (1993), are set within the framework of their present lives in the United States, but their experience in the United States is described, explored, and discussed primarily through their memories of their lives in South Asia and other parts of the world. In Bharati Mukherjee's novel, *The Holder of the World* (1993), the two American women protagonists travel from America to India not only in the context of geographical place but also, and much more important, in the context of historical time.

The American Landscape. These are narratives and poems that are located not on the soil of Asia but within the physical and cultural landscapes of America. It is a landscape where, to paraphrase the South Asian Canadian poet Uma Parameshwaran in *Trishanku* (1987), many South Asian Americans remain suspended between cultures like the ancient sage Trishanku suspended upside-down in the sky unable to enter heaven or earth. Chitra Ban Divakaruni is another Indo-American poet who describes life in America in works such as *The Reason for Nasturtiums* (1990) and *Black Candle* (1991). Bharati Mukherjee's second novel, *Wife* (1975), begins in Bengal, but the main story takes place in a series of apartments in New York, where Dimple Basu tries to make sense of her life among other Americans. The protagonists of Mukherjee's collection of short stories *The Middleman and Other Stories* (1988) live in America, but most of them have arrived from places such as India, Pakistan, Sri

Calcutta-born author Bharati Mukherjee became a naturalized U.S. citizen in 1988. (AP/Wide World Photos)

Lanka, Afghanistan, Cuba, the Philippines, and Vietnam. Her novel *Jasmine* (1989) could be called a South Asian American picaresque novel in which an Indian woman travels from her village in India to Florida, to Manhattan, and onward.

Feroza Ginwalla, the young protagonist of Bapsi Sidhwa's *An American Brat* (1993), is sent off by her family to the United States to visit her uncle in order to remove her from the alarming influence of the growing fundamentalism in Pakistan. Feroza decides to stay in the United States to begin her university studies. She discovers freedom and love in her new life—much to the dismay of her mother, who is visiting her.

Javaid Qazi's "The Ski Trip" (1988) is a Pakistani man's encounter with skiing, American poetry, and an American woman. "Slouching Towards San Hozay" (1982) deals with the violence in urban California without explicitly mentioning any ethnic group. Vikram Seth's *The Golden Gate* (1986), a twentieth century California epic constructed entirely of a series of sonnets, also bears no trace of South Asia in either the story or the characters.

The poetry and novels of Zulfikar Ghose involve the landscapes of South Asia and the Americas. His "Brazilian" novels such as *The Incredible Brazilian* (1972),

A Different World (1978), *A New History of Torments* (1982), and *Don Bueno* (1983) have as the central character a man who reappears with different identities at different times of Brazilian history. Although the physical landscape of these works is in South America, the abstract, internal landscape regarding configurations of time and space, of complex causalities, and of reincarnation, *Karma*, and dharma (righteous duty) owes much to South Asian philosophies and traditions.

Regardless of their choice of the physical or conceptual landscapes, South Asian American writers have made important contributions to American literature. By introducing their particular diversity of landscapes and literary traditions in their works, they actively participate in the revisioning, renewing, and expanding of American literature.—*Roshni Rustomji-Kerns*

SUGGESTED READINGS: • Katrak, Ketu H., and R. Radhakrishnan, eds. Special issue. "Desh-Videsh: South Asian Expatriate Writing and Art." *The Massachusetts Review* 29 (Winter, 1988-1989). • Mukherjee, Bharati. "Writers of the Indian Commonwealth." *The Literary Review* 29 (Summer, 1986): 400-401. • Rustomji-Kerns, Roshni, ed. Special issue. "South Asian Women Writers: The Immigrant Experience." *The Journal of South Asian Literature* 21 (Winter/Spring, 1986). • Vassanji, M. G., ed. *A Meeting of Streams: South Asian Canadian Literature.* Toronto: Toronto South Asia Review Publications, 1985. • Women of South Asian Descent Collective, eds. *Our Feet Walked the Sky: Women of the South Asian Diaspora.* San Francisco: Aunt Lute Books, 1993.

South Asian diaspora: By 1990, South Asians were two-thirds of the population of Mauritius; more than one-half of the population of Fiji; one-half of the population of Guyana; and one-third of the population of Trinidad. They were also still a significant section of the South African population; and they were the third-largest ethnic group in Malaysia, after the Malays and the Chinese. In addition, there were South Asian colonies in Great Britain, Australia, the Middle East, Kenya, Nigeria, the French islands of the Caribbean, and even Hong Kong. The scattering of South Asians outside the subcontinent had begun in the nineteenth century, long before the first South Asians arrived in large numbers in the United States and Canada. There were two spurs to the nineteenth century export of South Asian labor: the abolition of black slavery in the European colonies of the Caribbean and the acquisition of new colonial lands in Africa and Asia by the major European powers.

Abolition of Slavery as One Cause of the Diaspora. Black slavery was abolished in the British colonies in the years from 1834 to 1838, in the French colonies in 1848, and in the Dutch colonies from 1863 to 1873. In some Caribbean islands, such as Barbados, the extreme shortage of land forced the newly freed slaves back into plantation labor. In those Caribbean lands where land abounded relative to population, such as Guyana (formerly British Guiana), Surinam, and Trinidad, many freed slaves simply took up independent subsistence farming on previously unoccupied land. Hence, the plantation owners needed a new source of labor.

The Indentured Labor System. Thus began the system of indentured labor, often called the "coolie" system. Natives of India would pledge themselves to work in a distant colony for a fixed term of years, in return for the provision of housing by the employer and a meager wage. Most coolie laborers came from northcentral and northeastern India, especially Bihar, Uttar Pradesh, and Bengal; the latter two provinces supplied most of the indentured laborers of Trinidad. A sizeable minority of the coolies came from the Telugu and Tamil-speaking areas of southern India. Most coolies were Hindu; a minority were Muslim; none were Punjabi Sikhs, the group that played such a big role in migration from India to the United States between 1905 and 1924. Although the indentured laborers were heavily male, women composed a much larger proportion of this immigrant stream than of the pre-1924 South Asian immigration to the United States.

The Pattern of Migration to the Caribbean, Africa, the Indian Ocean islands, and the Pacific Ocean Islands. In the 1840's, South Asians began to come to the British colonies of Trinidad (in the Caribbean), Guyana (in South America), and Mauritius (in the Indian Ocean, near Africa) to work on the sugar plantations. South Asian indentured sugar cane laborers also started coming to the Dutch colony of Surinam in the 1870's; to the island of Fiji in the 1880's (following the British annexation in 1874); and to the British South African colony of Natal in the 1860's. Not until 1920 was the indenture system finally ended by the British government; immigration to colonial areas, however, often continued.

The Pattern of Migration to Other Asian Lands. Not all South Asian migrants went far from India. Sri Lanka, like India under the rule of the British Empire, attracted Tamils from southern India to work the tea plantations. South Asians went to tap rubber in the British colony of Malaya, in southeast Asia, in the last

Asian Indian residents shop in Nadi town, Fiji—for many South Asian immigrants, a popular destination. (John Penisten, Pacific Pictures)

quarter of the nineteenth century. Indian Muslims and Hindus likewise migrated to neighboring Myanmar (Burma) to work the plantations, to function as money-lenders, and to perform various menial jobs. Most of these migrants were not indentured laborers but short-term contract laborers. The migrant flow to other lands of Asia, which drew heavily from southern India, continued even after the abolition of the indenture system.

Migrants Who Were Neither Indentured Laborers Nor Contract Laborers. In general, the South Asians who flocked to the British East African colonies of Kenya, Uganda, and (after 1919) Tanganyika did not become plantation workers. They came first in the late 1890's, to build a railway; later, they filled various intermediary roles in the local economy, as lower civil servants, professionals, merchants, and businesspeople (often small shopkeepers). These people were largely free immigrants; many of them hailed from the western Indian province of Gujarat; some were Sikhs from the Punjab; a few were Christians from Goa (Portuguese India). In addition, the 1880's and the 1890's saw the migration to South Africa of South Asian merchants, who paid for their own passage; they augmented the community that had been originally formed by indentured laborers.

Culture Change in the South Asian Diaspora. The crossing of the seas was a harrowing experience, and working conditions of the indentured laborers were often so brutal as to verge on slavery. The extent to which the culture of the immigrants was altered by the coolie experience has been a matter of dispute; it is certain, however, that their culture was not as radically uprooted as was that of African slaves in the United States. The South Asian indentured laborers, unlike African slaves in the United States, generally kept their original religious beliefs. The extent to which the original languages were retained varied; in the Caribbean colonies, Creole languages made serious inroads on South Asian tongues. Morton Klass, an American anthropologist, shows how the traditional Indian joint family survived in Trinidad, but not in Guyana, because of differences in the pattern of rainfall and crop production between the two countries. Caste was drastically weakened among the South Asian Hindus of the Caribbean plantation colonies; it survived with much greater vigor among the South Asians of East Africa. Although most of the descendants of indentured laborers probably remained farm workers, some South Asians in the plantation colonies were eventually able to rise in the world by dint of education, thrift, and hard work.

The Political Fate of the Nineteenth Century Diasporas in an Era of Decolonization. After the Indian Ocean island of Mauritius became independent in 1968, South Asians, who formed the majority of the population, gained control of the government. Once Fiji and Guyana became independent (in 1970 and 1966, respectively), a seesaw struggle for political power erupted between two ethnic groups. In Fiji, in May, 1987, native Fijians resorted to military force to prevent a South Asian takeover. In Guyana, blacks managed to gain and keep power despite the existence of the bare majority of South Asians among the population. In Trinidad, the South Asians, who constituted about 40 percent of the population, never got to enjoy much political power. Barely suppressed tension between the black and South Asian communities persisted for a long time after independence was achieved in 1962. In 1970, in the course of an abortive Black Power rebellion, some of the shops in Port of Spain destroyed by black rioters were owned by South Asians.

In the Asian diaspora lands, South Asians rarely had even the slightest chance of gaining political power; sometimes they even had difficulty simply surviving as a separate group. In Malaysia (formerly Malaya), the Indians, outnumbered by both the indigenous Malays and the ethnic Chinese, enjoyed relatively little political influence after the achievement of independence in 1957. After Sri Lanka gained independence in 1948, descendants of the nineteenth century Indian immigrants to Sri Lanka, the Indian Tamils, like the so-called Ceylon Tamils (indigenous to the island since time immemorial), began to experience discrimination at the hands of the Buddhist Sinhalese; this treatment worsened in the 1980's. The presence of Hindu and Muslim South Asians in Myanmar had stirred animosity from the Buddhist Burmans even before the end of the British colonial era. After Myanmar attained its independence in 1948, successive Burman-dominated governments exerted various pressures (including discriminatory economic legislation) to induce the South Asians to leave; after General Ne Win came to power in 1962, he ordered their expulsion. By 1990, only a small fraction of the colonial-era South Asian population remained in Myanmar.

The people of South Asian descent in Africa were regarded with hostility and suspicion by both white settlers and black African natives. In August, 1972, the dictator of Uganda, Idi Amin, suddenly ordered all those of South Asian ancestry expelled from the country; these unfortunates were accepted as refugees by

Pakistani student (right) at the University of Dubuque, Iowa. (James L. Shaffer)

Britain, Canada, and the United States. After Kenyan independence was attained in 1963, a steady emigration of South Asians began. In August, 1982, the many Asian-owned businesses in Nairobi, the capital of Kenya, were attacked by mobs in the course of an abortive putsch. Even in South Africa, where all nonwhite groups were submerged under apartheid until the early 1990's, there was unrest; in 1949 anti-Asian rioting by blacks broke out in Durban, the capital of the province of Natal. Nevertheless, many of South Africa's South Asians, from the 1960's onward, lent at least passive support to the more moderate wing of the black antiapartheid movement, the African National Congress; since the South Asians were only about 2.9 percent of the total population of South Africa, they could not achieve power on their own.

The Late Twentieth Century Diaspora in the Middle East. As a result of the post-1973 oil boom, the oil-rich Arab states of Saudi Arabia and the Persian Gulf emirates attracted Pakistani, Bangladeshi, and Sri Lankan migrant laborers (as well as laborers from some other Third World countries) to do the menial labor the na-

tives no longer would perform. Newspaper stories indicate that some of these migrants have been shamefully exploited.

The Late Twentieth Century Diaspora in Europe and Australia. In Great Britain in the 1960's, South Asians, at first largely Sikhs from the Punjab, began to appear as factory laborers in the industrial towns. Here they were greeted with resentment by native-born, working-class white Britons. Pakistani and Bangladeshi Muslims also came to work in Britain. Because they were initially drawn to Britain by the promise of blue-collar employment, the South Asians who settled there in the 1950's and early 1960's tended to form concentrated urban ghetto neighborhoods. In this respect they differed markedly from the heavily professional post-1965 South Asian immigrants to the United States, who tended to be dispersed in comfortable (and mostly white) suburbs. By the mid-1980's, South Asians composed slightly more than half of the entire nonwhite population of Britain.

By the 1980's, Germany and Austria, on the European continent, were attracting South Asian immigrant

The majority of American Sikhs arrived after 1950, largely in the 1970's and 1980's. Here a Sikh displays his pride in being an American during a Sikh Day celebration in New York City. (Frances M. Roberts)

professionals. After the early 1980's, Germany was, because of its liberal asylum laws, particularly attractive to Sri Lankan Tamils fleeing their country's violent Tamil-Sinhalese strife. Some South Asians also settled in Australia, an English-speaking country in the Pacific, after that country liberalized its immigration laws in the 1960's, which modified its previously discriminatory policy.—*Paul D. Mageli*

SUGGESTED READINGS:

• Clarke, Colin, Ceri Peach, and Steven Vertovec, eds. *South Asians Overseas: Migration and Ethnicity*. New York: Cambridge University Press, 1990. Includes essays on South Africa; East Africa; Fiji; Southeast Asia (including Myanmar, Malaya, and Singapore); Trinidad; and the French overseas departments of Guadeloupe, Martinique, and Reunion. One essay on the United States and six essays on Great Britain. The economics and sociology, as well as the politics, of the diasporas are discussed. Tables; maps; references at end of each chapter; contributor information; index.

• Gregory, Robert G. *South Asians in East Africa: An Economic and Social History, 1890-1980*. Boulder, Colo.: Westview Press, 1993. Organized topically rather than chronologically. Makes use of interviews with East African Asians, Africans, Arabs, and Europeans, as well as published and unpublished documents and various books written by Asians. Maps of British East Africa and of South Asian sources of emigration; bibliographical references; index.

• Gupte, Pranay. *The Crowded Earth: People and the Politics of Population*. New York: W. W. Norton, 1984. Written by a South Asian American journalist. One chapter has some comments on the South Asians of East Africa; another deals with the South Asian (Sri Lankan and Pakistani) and other diasporas in Saudi Arabia and the Persian Gulf States; yet another discusses, among other things, the South Asian community in Britain. Glossary; index. For the general reader.

• Helweg, Arthur W. "The Indian Diaspora: Influence on International Relations." In *Modern Diasporas in International Politics*, edited by Gabriel Sheffer. New York: St. Martin's Press, 1986. An excellent general essay, with illuminating remarks on the various regional origins of the different South Asian diasporas. Combines historical and social science perspectives. Provides a good brief history, for the general reader, of the indenture system. Notes at end of essay are informative. Map showing origins of various diasporas; references.

• Kotkin, Joel. "The Greater India." In *Tribes: How Race, Religion, and Identity Determine Success in the New Global Economy*. New York: Random House, 1993. Emphasizes the role of Diaspora Indians as entrepreneurs, especially in Great Britain and the United States; ignores the experience of South Asians as migrant laborers, past or present. Pays particular attention to Gujaratis and Sindhis. Good for comparison with other far-flung ethnic groups. Chapter notes at end; index.

• *Migration and Modernization: The Indian Diaspora in Comparative Perspective*. Williamsburg, Va.: Department of Anthropology, College of William and Mary, 1987. Includes essays on the religious life of South Asians in the United States; the Indian Tamils of Sri Lanka; the Indians of Australia; and the Indians of South Africa both in the distant past and in the 1980's. References at end of book; notes on contributors; no index.

• Tinker, Hugh. *The Banyan Tree: Overseas Emigrants from India, Pakistan, and Bangladesh*. New York: Oxford University Press, 1977. Organized topically rather than chronologically or by country. The emphasis is on more recent times, and on the political side of interethnic relations, although economics and sociology are not completely neglected. Discusses Sri Lanka; Myanmar; Malaya; Kenya, Tanganyika, and Uganda; South Africa; Rhodesia (Zimbabwe after 1979); Mauritius; Trinidad; Canada; Great Britain; and the United States. Tables; footnotes; index. For the general reader.

• Tinker, Hugh. *A New System of Slavery: The Export of Indian Labour Overseas, 1830-1920*. New York: Oxford University Press, 1974. The best history, for the general reader, of the indentured labor system of the nineteenth century, by which South Asians were recruited to toil on foreign plantations around the world. Relies heavily on British written sources, especially the reports of commissioners. Contains diagrams; maps; bibliography; index.

South Asian immigration to Canada: South Asians first migrated to Canada at the start of the twentieth century, in relatively small numbers. By 1990 South Asians had become one of the largest nonwhite ethnic groups in Canada. There are interesting parallels, as well as important differences, between the pattern of South Asian migration to Canada and that of South Asian migration to the United States.

Beginnings of Immigration. South Asian migration to Canada did not assume significant proportions until the years 1907 and 1908. In Canada, as in the United States, the overwhelming majority of these early immigrants were Sikhs from Punjab, driven by the same economic motives that impelled their compatriots in the United States. In Canada, as in the United States, the earliest South Asian immigrants settled on the Pacific Coast: California and Washington in the American case, the province of British Columbia in the Canadian case. In Canada, it was the sawmill industry, rather than agriculture, that provided employment for the South Asian immigrants. By 1908 about 5,000 South Asians had entered Canada; there, as in the United States, the South Asian influx aroused the hostility of the white population.

Early Restrictions on Immigration. In response to the clamor from white Canadians, the Canadian government adopted new regulations designed to discourage South Asian immigration. Since Canada and India were then both parts of the British Empire, South Asian immigrants could not simply be banned outright. In 1908, therefore, the Canadian government ordered that no immigrants could enter Canada unless they came by continuous voyage directly from their native country. Since, at that time, there were no shipping lines taking passengers directly from India to the Pacific Coast, this measure effectively reduced to al-

Sikh man. The early years of South Asian migration to Canada were dominated by Sikhs from the Punjab. (Richard B. Levine)

most nothing the number of South Asians who could get in. Between 1909 and 1920, only 118 South Asians entered Canada.

Severe restrictions on South Asian entry into Canada remained in force until after World War II. Between 1920 and 1943, only 760 South Asians were allowed entry. Unlike the U.S. government, however, the Canadian government did, after 1919, allow South Asian immigrants a reasonable time period during which they could return to India and bring back a spouse and all children under age eighteen, while still enjoying residence rights in Canada. South Asians in Canada, unlike their counterparts in the United States, did not have to marry outside their ethnic group in order to start a family. By 1941 there were still only 165 South Asian women over age nineteen in Canada, and 747 men; 424 of Canada's 1,465 South Asians, however, had been born in Canada.

Gradual Liberalization of the Immigration Laws. In Canada, as in the United States, the post-World War II years brought a loosening of immigration policy regarding South Asians and greater rights for those South Asians who had migrated already. In 1947 South Asians in British Columbia were finally given the right to vote. In 1951 the Canadian government, desiring better relations with the new members of the British Commonwealth of Nations, established minuscule immigration quotas for India, Pakistan, and Ceylon (now Sri Lanka). Truly substantial liberalization of the immigration laws did not come, however, until the acts of 1962 and 1967. These new laws, like the American immigration law of 1965, opened the door wider for South Asians, while favoring the professional over the unskilled laborer; skilled blue-collar workers arrived in greater numbers after 1972.

Post-1962 Immigration. In 1951 there were only 2,148 South Asians in Canada (721 of them female); 1,937 of them lived in British Columbia. In 1961 there were only 6,774. Between 1962 and 1967, however, more than 20,000 South Asians arrived in Canada; between 1968 and 1975, more than 90,000 entered the country. By 1975 the number of South Asians in Canada had risen to more than 175,000; in 1982 their numbers were estimated at 310,000.

The new immigration, more balanced between the sexes than the heavily male pre-World War II wave, was also spread more evenly across Canada. South Asians now settled not only in Vancouver and other parts of British Columbia but also in other major Canadian cities: Montreal, Quebec; Toronto, Ontario; Calgary and Edmonton, in Alberta; and Winnipeg in Man-

Young boy with traditional Muslim cap. The post-1962 South Asian migration to Canada has included a number of Muslims. (Richard B. Levine)

itoba. The majority came to reside in Toronto.

The new South Asian immigration was much more diverse in its regional origins and religious makeup than the older influx had been. The new South Asian immigration included not merely Sikhs from Punjab but also orthodox Hindus from Gujarat, Bombay, and the Delhi area; Sunni Muslims from West Pakistan and from Bangladesh (East Pakistan until 1971); Ismaili Muslims; Christians from Kerala in southern India; Parsis (Zoroastrians) from the Bombay area; and even Buddhists from Sri Lanka. There was also a secondary migration from the South Asian diaspora communities in the West Indies, Fiji, Malaysia, East Africa, and Mauritius. Canada took in, for example, many of the South Asians expelled from Idi Amin's East African state of Uganda in 1972.

The impact of the South Asian migration to Canada after 1962 can be better understood by Americans if Canada's overall ethnic makeup is compared with that of the United States. In the United States of the 1980's, Asian Indians, numbering 312,000, were heavily outnumbered by African Americans, who constituted 12 percent of the population. In Canada during the same decade, the total nonwhite population (South Asians, East Asians, and African Canadians) was only 6 percent of the total population; the number of South Asians was nearly equal to the number of African Canadians (most of whom were from the West Indies). Hence, Canada's South Asians stood out much more among white Canadians than did the United States' South Asians among white Americans.

After the early 1970's, South Asians who arrived in Canada encountered not only opportunity but also intolerance. Harassment by white Canadians, most of them young adult males, became widespread; the epithet "Paki" was hurled at South Asians regardless of their place of origin on the subcontinent. Overt acts of violence, some of them resulting in deaths, took place in the cities of Toronto and Vancouver. The harassment of South Asians reached its peak between 1976 and 1978 but died down gradually after the latter year. The intolerance of this period was probably harder for blue-collar immigrants to deal with than it was for immigrant professionals.

There were various reasons for the hostility. South Asians differed from white Canadians in customs, mother tongue, and food habits, and often in skin color, religion, and dress habits as well. The women often wore saris; the Sikh male's insistence on wearing a beard and a turban was often a bone of contention. White Canadians, like white Britons and unlike many white Americans, tended to see the South Asian as colored rather than white, even though the latter's complexion ranged from black to light olive. Finally, the recession that hit Canada in the early and mid-1970's caused white Canadians to view the immigrants as unwelcome competitors for jobs and housing.

Although Canada's government tightened regulations in 1975 in response to white anxieties, it did not revert to a policy of exclusion. In 1986 a boatload of Tamils, refugees from the strife between Sinhalese and Tamils in Sri Lanka, arrived on Canada's shores, claiming the right of asylum; they were allowed in. Canada was for some time more generous than the United States in granting asylum to Sri Lanka Tamils.

Status of South Asian Canadians in 1990. By the end of the 1980's, South Asians had been able to achieve a secure economic foothold in Canada despite the persistence of employment discrimination. They did this by accepting downward occupational mobility, putting every adult in the family to work, and working two jobs. Great sacrifices were made in pursuit of the goal of home ownership. The high value placed by South Asian Canadian parents on education as a means of upward mobility for their children boded well for the community's future.

Yet even in the 1980's, many South Asians still had considerably greater difficulties assimilating into mainstream Anglo-Canadian or French Canadian culture than did such European immigrants as the Italians or the Portuguese. Particularly thorny problems in this regard were experienced by the Sikhs of British Columbia, many of whom (including the post-1962 immigrants) were blue-collar workers rather than professionals. Some South Asian parents tried to preserve their children from corruption by the surrounding culture by insisting on a traditional arranged marriage, but this seemed to be a losing strategy in the long run: A growing tendency to seek love and marriage outside the ethnic group could be perceived by the 1980's among the Canadian-born.—*Paul D. Mageli*

SUGGESTED READINGS: • Buchignani, Norman, Doreen M. Indra, and Ram Srivastiva. *Continuous Journey: A Social History of South Asians in Canada.* Toronto, Ontario, Canada: McClelland and Stewart in association with Dept. of the Secretary of State and the Govt. Pub. Centre, Supply and Services, Canada, 1985. • Chadney, James G. *The Sikhs of Vancouver.* New York: AMS Press, 1984. • Johnston, Hugh J. M. *The East Indians in Canada.* Ottawa, Ontario, Canada: Canadian Historical Association, 1984. • Joy, Annamma. *Ethnicity in Canada: Social Accommodation and Cultural Persistence Among the Sikhs and the Portuguese.* New York: AMS Press, 1989. • Kanungo, Rabindra N., ed. *South Asians in the Canadian Mosaic.* Montreal, Quebec, Canada: Kala Bharati, 1984. • Ramcharan, Subhas. *Racism: Nonwhites in Canada.* Toronto, Ontario, Canada: Butterworths, 1982.

South Asian immigration to the United States: The pattern of immigration from the Indian subcontinent to the United States historically has been shaped as much by the vagaries of American immigration law as by conditions in South Asia itself. Hence, the pattern of immigration from South Asia can be represented by two main waves: one lasting from about 1907 to 1924, and another, much larger wave, which began in 1965 and was still continuing in the early 1990's. The first wave was overwhelmingly Punjabi and mostly Sikh, with some Muslims; the second wave drew on people from all regions of India and was predominantly Hindu. From an extremely tiny ethnic group in 1960, Asian Indians had become, by 1990, the fourth-largest Asian American community, outnumbered by Chinese

Americans, Japanese Americans, and Filipino Americans but outnumbering Vietnamese Americans and Korean Americans.

Early Immigrants to the United States, 1907-1924: A Comparative Perspective. Aside from an occasional Hindu teacher or Parsi merchant, there was almost no immigration to the United States from the Indian subcontinent before 1900. Beginning in 1907, a large number of immigrants from rural Punjab arrived on the West Coast of the United States; many of them had originally migrated to Canada, America's neighbor to the north. The total immigration to the United States from the Indian subcontinent before 1924 is estimated at no more than sixty-four hundred. This immigration was dwarfed by the total number of indentured South Asians who migrated to the Caribbean colonies and

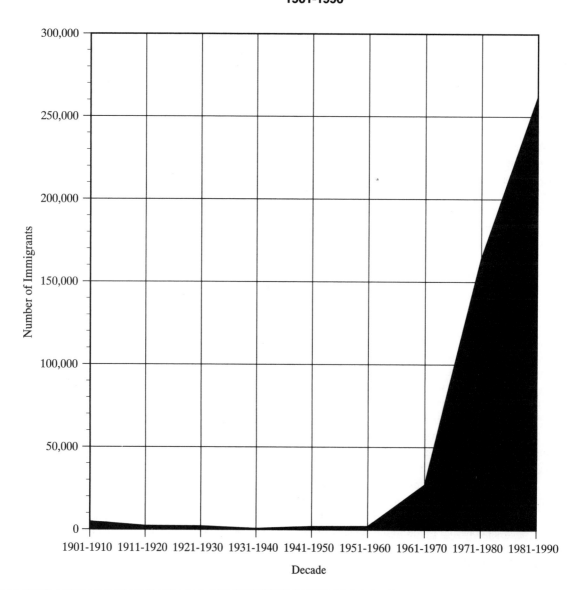

Asian Indian Immigration to the U.S., 1901-1990

Source: Susan B. Gall and Timothy L. Gall, eds., *Statistical Record of Asian Americans.* Detroit: Gale Research, Inc., 1993.

Hindus living in the United States pose for a group shot, 1910. (California State Library)

Mauritius during the nineteenth and early twentieth centuries. Furthermore, the South Asian immigrants were, before World War II, far outnumbered—even in California, the area of heavy Punjabi immigration—by Japanese, Chinese, and Filipino immigrants. Because both the Canadian and the U.S. governments frowned on the use of indentured labor by Canadian or American employers, Punjabi immigrant laborers had to finance their passage to North America with their own or their families' resources; hence, the Punjabi immigrants were overwhelmingly male, like many pre-1924 immigrant streams from southern and eastern Europe. Also, like many southern and eastern European immigrant streams active at the start of the twentieth century, the pre-1924 South Asian inflow was predominantly working-class: Students, merchants, and professionals were always in the minority.

Change in Occupational Profile, 1907-1910. At first the South Asians had tried to gain a foothold in the lumber and sawmill industries. This strategy, which was successful in Canada, did not work in the United States. After rioting in 1907 in Bellingham, Washington, by white workers, most South Asians went south to California, where they became part of the agricultural labor force. Over time, through hard work and a frugal lifestyle, some became landowners. Since American law never permitted Indian immigrant males the extended departures necessary to find a wife in India, most either remained unmarried or married Hispanic women living in California.

Increasing Restrictions on South Asian Immigration, 1910-1924. The early South Asian immigrants had begun to encounter, by 1910, considerable animosity from some white Americans. Immigration began to taper off after 1910 because of the imposition of harsher restrictions on entry by the executive branch of the U.S. government. The entry of Indian immigrants into the ranks of leaseholders and farm operators, es-

Dalip Singh Saund (center, with Mrs. Saund to the right) came to the United States to attend an American university in the 1920's and later won election as the first Asian Indian American congressional representative. (AP/Wide World Photos)

pecially during the World War I boom, lessened their appeal to white farmers as a source of cheap labor. The involvement of some Indian immigrants in the GHADR MOVEMENT for Indian freedom in 1917-1918 (when the United States was allied with the colonial power in India, Great Britain, against Germany) also seems to have turned opinion against them. A law passed by the U.S. Congress in 1917 included India in the so-called barred zone that included most Asian countries, from which further immigration to the United States was not permitted. University students from India attending American schools were still permitted entry between 1917 and 1924; this group of immigrants, although nowhere near as large as it would be after World War II, produced such individuals as Dalip Singh SAUND, the first Indo-American representative in Congress. The IMMIGRATION ACT OF 1924 barred further immigration from India.

The Question of Eligibility for Naturalization, 1907-1923. After 1870, "whites" and persons of African origin were eligible for American citizenship. A long train of court cases was necessary to determine whether South Asians were "white" under the meaning of the

law; the variety of physical types and skin colors among the South Asian population made answering the question difficult. At first, some South Asian immigrants, usually well-educated merchants or professionals, were able to secure naturalization. The decision of the U.S. Supreme Court in the 1923 case of UNITED STATES V. BHAGAT SINGH THIND that immigrants from India were Asian rather than white made it impossible for such immigrants who were in America already to gain citizenship; it also meant that those South Asians who had been naturalized already might see their naturalization revoked, although this in fact did not happen in all cases.

The Low Point of South Asian Immigration, 1924-1946. Between 1924, when all Asian immigration was barred, and 1946, what little Indian immigration to the United States there was took the form of illegal entry via Mexico; the coming of the Great Depression in 1930 put an end to most such activity. In the 1920's, a good number of South Asians returned to the Indian subcontinent. Some were undoubtedly disillusioned by the new bars on naturalization and (as a result of California's ALIEN LAND LAW OF 1913) on property holding; others had never intended to settle permanently in North America in the first place and seized the opportunity to go home once their income targets had been achieved in the United States. By 1946 there were less than fifteen hundred South Asians in the whole United States.

The 1946 Immigration Law and Its Effects. Change did not come until 1946, after World War II. The war, which raised the specter of Nazi racism, caused many white Americans to question the morality of excluding Asian immigrants simply on the basis of race. Hence, the Luce-Celler Bill of 1946 instituted a small quota (one hundred per year) for immigrants from India; after the partition of India in 1947, a small quota was established for Pakistan also. The 1946 law also gave

South Asian immigrants the right to apply for naturalization. The Immigration Act of 1952, although restrictive of immigration from southern and eastern Europe, retained small quotas for the Asian countries, including India and Pakistan.

The immediate effect of the 1946 liberalization was not great. In California, women finally began to arrive from the Punjab. Immigrants from Gujarat began to arrive in substantial numbers to work in the hotel industry. Students from India and Pakistan, attracted by the lead in technology and science that the United States possessed in the 1950's, began to attend American universities in greater numbers; some of them stayed on to become permanent residents. Between 1947 and 1965, there were about six thousand immi-

India-born Har Gobind Khorana shared the Nobel Prize in 1968 for his investigation of the genetic code. Khorana, who arrived in the United States in 1960, is shown here at work in his laboratory at the Massachusetts Institute of Technology. (AP/Wide World Photos)

grants from India to the United States.

The 1965 Immigration Reform. The real turning point in the history of South Asian immigration to the United States was the enactment of the IMMIGRATION AND NATIONALITY ACT OF 1965, passed in October of that year. Quotas as such were abolished; the limit on the number of immigrants from India was effectively raised from one hundred (under the 1946 law) to twenty thousand (the maximum number of immigrants from any one country under the 1965 law); and the key criteria for admitting immigrants became the applicant's possession of professional skills, on the one hand, and kinship with a legal immigrant who could offer sponsorship, on the other hand.

Increase in Immigration After 1965. During the 1970's, there was an upward spurt in the number of immigrants from the Indian subcontinent to the United States. Between 1965 and 1974, immigration from India to the United States increased by more than 2,000 percent; immigration from Pakistan increased by more than 1,000 percent. Immigration from Bangladesh steadily increased after that country became independent in 1971. By 1990, the number of Asian Indians in the United States had increased to 815,447; that of Pakistanis, to 81,371; that of Bangladeshis, to 11, 838; and that of Sri Lankans, to 19,970.

Comparisons Between Pre-1924 and Post-1965 Immigrant Waves. A noticeable difference between the post-1965 immigration and the pre-1924 immigration lay in the gender and age composition of the former. At least one-third of all post-1965 Asian Indian immigrants were women, usually wives of male immigrants; a good proportion were also children, the dependents of adult immigrants. This fact bode well for the creation of a stable family life among the new immigrants.

The majority of pre-1924 immigrants had been laborers; in the post-1965 South Asian migration, by contrast, educated professionals predominated. Many

As of 1990, Asian Indians are the fourth-largest Asian American group in the United States. (Martin A. Hutner)

South Asian Immigration to the U.S., 1981-1991	
Bangladesh	25,867
India	306,905
Pakistan	81,719
Sri Lanka	7,502

Source: Susan B. Gall and Timothy L. Gall, eds., *Statistical Record of Asian Americans*. Detroit: Gale Research, Inc., 1993.

post-1965 South Asian immigrants were physicians, engineers, and college professors. Between 1966 and 1972, more than 80 percent of the occupationally active immigrants from India arriving each year were professional or technical workers. According to the 1980 census, 52 percent of Asian Indians above age twenty-five in the United States had at least four years of college education.

Nevertheless, there were enough blue-collar immigrants to rejuvenate the Sikh communities of California. These Sikh ethnic communities, which had come to support themselves primarily by orchard farming, now consisted of entire families rather than simply bachelor males. In the 1980's the proportion of non-professionals in the immigrant stream from India, which had been increasing gradually since 1972, grew larger still; blue-collar Asian Indian immigrants, especially those in New York City, often took jobs as taxicab drivers or went into business for themselves as gas station owners.—Paul D. Mageli

SUGGESTED READINGS:

• Bagai, Leona B. *The East Indians and the Pakistanis in America*. Minneapolis: Lerner, 1972. Although written for young audiences, this book is more original and informative than usual for one of this type. As a white Euro-American woman who married into an Indo-American family, the author has uniquely personal insights into the topic. Provides much information on pre-1924 immigration; is of less value on post-1965 immigrants. Photographs.

• Helweg, Arthur W., and Usha M. Helweg. *An Immigrant Success Story: East Indians in America*. Philadelphia: University of Pennsylvania Press, 1990. Although its focus is on South Asians' adaptation in America in the 1980's, the book also provides much information on the history of the immigration movement itself. Useful maps indicate immigrants' regions of origin. The appendices are a mine of facts and figures, in tabular form. Tables in text also. Bibliography; index.

• Jensen, Joan M. *Passage from India: Asian Indian Immigrants in North America*. New Haven, Conn.: Yale University Press, 1988. This book is informative on the origins of South Asian immigration; anti-South Asian violence; immigration and naturalization law as applied to South Asian immigrants up to 1924; and exile anti-British nationalism. Contains almost nothing on post-1965 immigrants. Uses government documents, supplemented occasionally by the testimony of surviving immigrants. Endnotes; bibliography; list of unpublished sources and court cases; index.

• Leonhard-Spark, Philip J., and Parmatma Saran. "The Indian Immigrant in America: a Demographic Profile." In *The New Ethnics: Asian Indians in the United States*, edited by Parmatma Saran and Edwin Eames. New York: Praeger, 1980. Somewhat dated, but still useful as of 1993. Gathers together and interprets data from the reports of the U.S. Immigration and Naturalization Service and the authors' own investigation of Asian Indians living in the New York City area. Includes seven tables. For college students.

• Mazumdar, Sucheta. "Punjabi Agricultural Workers in California, 1905-1945." In *Labor Immigration Under Capitalism: Asian Workers in the United States Before World War II*, edited by Lucie Cheng and Edna Bonacich. Berkeley: University of California Press, 1984. Provides a useful survey of pre-1924 working-class Punjabi migration; the pre-1924 immigration to America of educated, upper-, and middle-class South Asians is also examined. Based partly on oral history interviews. Five tables; references (abbreviated in text; complete at the end of essay). Index at end of book.

• Mazumdar, Sucheta. "South Asians in the United States with a focus on Asian Indians: Policy on New Communities." In *The State of Asian Pacific America: A Public Policy Report, Policy Issues to the Year 2020*. Los Angeles: LEAP Asian Pacific American Public Policy Institute and UCLA Asian American Studies Center, 1993. Ably exploiting data from the 1990 census, Mazumdar points out trends in immigration from India, Pakistan, Bangladesh, and Sri Lanka during the 1980's and discusses the darker side of the post-1965 South Asian immigrant experience. Notes at end of essay are a mine of bibliographical information. For both the scholar and the general reader.

• Melendy, H. Brett. *Asians in America: Filipinos, Koreans, and East Indians*. Boston: Twayne, 1977. Still useful in 1993, this book contains a good overview of the course of South Asian immigration up to 1974. Provides an illuminating discussion of the difficulties historians face in trying to count pre-1946 South Asian immigration to America. Tables in text and in appendix are especially helpful. Endnotes; index.

• Takaki, Ronald. Strangers from a Different Shore: A History of Asian Americans. Boston: Little, Brown, 1989. This highly readable book is somewhat disappointing in its coverage of South Asian immigration. Pre-1946 immigration gets a separate (and rather brief) chapter, based on oral history sources and published materials. The 1946 immigration reform, and post-1965 South Asian immigration, are buried in broad thematic chapters. Photographs include one of a Sikh farm laborer in California. Endnotes; index.

South Asian immigration to the United States, sources of: It often happens that immigrants of a particular nationality come from one particular region of the home country; this tends to be the case if they are unskilled laborers rather than highly educated professionals. Thus, most early Chinese immigration to the United States, consisting primarily of migrant laborers, came almost exclusively from a narrow region of southern China. The same pattern can be found with South Asian immigration to the United States.

Punjab as an Early Source of Immigrants. Early (1905 to 1924) South Asian immigrants to the United States overwhelmingly hailed from the Punjab province and from select districts (Malwa and Doab) of the Punjab; members of the Sikh faith, a minority in the subcontinent, were a majority of these early immigrants. Muslims were the second-largest religion represented; Hindus, the overwhelming majority in the subcontinent, were a tiny minority of the immigrants to America.

Both push-and-pull factors made Punjab the source of the majority of working-class South Asian immigrants before 1924. After British annexation of the Punjab, there had been growth in agricultural production, but also an ever-increasing mortgage burden on the peasantry. Because emigrant remittances by a male offspring could help a family hold on to or expand its landholdings in this province, family resources would be mobilized to pay the migrant laborer's passage to North America. The Sikhs were the first to discover the benefits of migration to the United States and Canada: Their traditional soldierly virtues caused them to be overrepresented in the British Indian army, which deployed them outside as well as within the Indian subcontinent.

Early Student, Merchant, and Professional Immigrants. Before 1924, when all Asian (and hence Indian) immigration was barred, American universities were already attracting some adventurous Indian students. The University of California, Berkeley, was a special magnet for such elite Indians, some of whom became permanent immigrants. The first university students from the subcontinent arrived in 1901. Students, merchants, and professionals, who settled in the cities of the East Coast and the Midwest as well as

Golden Temple in Amritsar, Punjab district of India—the source of numerous immigrant Sikhs to America and elsewhere. (Government of India Tourist Office)

those of California, constituted less than one-fourth of pre-1924 South Asian immigration to the United States. The few student, merchant, and professional immigrants who came to America at this time were more representative of the subcontinent as a whole in regional origin than were the working-class immigrants.

Gujarat as a Source of Immigrants. After 1946, when India was granted a tiny immigration quota to the United States, a new region of South Asia began to send a stream of immigrants: Gujarat, in the southwest. This immigration, of the Patels, was Hindu rather than Sikh. They found an economic niche in California, and later in the rest of the United States, as hoteliers, buying up decaying establishments, renovating them, and operating them with the help of cheap family labor.

Post-1965 Immigrants from India. The liberalized American immigration law of 1965, which would raise the number of Asian Indians in the United States to 815,447 by 1990 (according to the U.S. census of that year), favored those with professional skills. Consequently, the highly educated have been overrepresented among all immigrants from India, and urbanites have probably been overrepresented compared with rural people. By 1980 the census showed that 52 percent of all Asian Indians in the United States over age twenty-five had at least four years of college. It was not until the 1980's that the high proportion of professionals in the immigrant stream began to decline somewhat.

Because of the preference given to immigrants with skills, the post-1965 immigration from India was not as heavily drawn from a single region and a single religious group as the pre-1924 immigration had been. Estimates of the proportions of post-1965 immigration from each of the different regions of India vary somewhat from scholar to scholar. Major regional sources of immigration were southern India (especially Kerala, on the Malabar coast), Uttar Pradesh, the Calcutta area of West Bengal, Gujarat, and, of course, Punjab. In

Competitors in an Onam snake boat race in Kerala, southern India. Kerala has been a major source of Indian immigration to the United States since 1965. (Government of India Tourist Office)

religious makeup, too, the new immigration was more representative of India as a whole than the pre-1924 immigration had been. It is estimated that about 65 percent of the Asian Indians in the United States in the 1980's were Hindus, 16 percent were Muslims, 10 percent were Sikhs, and almost 5 percent were Christians (largely from Kerala).

One motive for emigration from India by professionals was unemployment: As late as the 1980's, some of the country's physicians could not find jobs. In other cases, the motive to emigrate was not lack of a job but lack of opportunity for job advancement or simply a belief that America offered more chances for the ambitious than India did.

Immigration from Other South Asian Countries After 1947. The Muslim republic of Pakistan contributed to the post-1965 South Asian immigrant stream. Pakistani immigrants initially tended to be students and professionals. The greatest number of them were either Punjabis (the province was split between Pakistan and the new Republic of India in 1947) or Urdu-speakers from the city of Karachi; others were Pathans from North-West Frontier Province or Sindhis. The 1990 census noted 81,371 Pakistanis living in the United States; the fact that students entering on visitor's visas later decide to stay makes determining the exact number difficult.

Another predominantly Muslim republic, Bangladesh, is also a rich source of South Asian immigrants. Immigration from Bangladesh to the United States was not officially counted until the former became independent in 1971, although immigration from what was East Pakistan (and, before the partition of British India in 1947, eastern Bengal) did occur. Independence, by cutting longstanding economic ties with West Pakistan, provided a spur to emigration. By the early 1990's, Bangladeshi immigration, although still containing a large professional component, probably included more individuals with lower levels of education than that from India; the 1990 immigration lottery had made possible this lowering of the educational levels. More than other South Asians, Bangladeshis, many of whom settled in New York City, supported themselves by the restaurant trade. The 1990 census noted 11,838 Bangladeshis in the United States.

One South Asian country that is often neglected in studies of immigration is Sri Lanka. Since the immigration quota for Sri Lanka in the early 1990's was relatively low, its level of legal immigration to the United States was correspondingly low; the potential for Sri Lankan immigration, however, was great. Sri Lanka has long been simultaneously blessed with relatively high (for an underdeveloped country) levels of education and cursed with appallingly high levels of chronic unemployment; among the highly educated Tamil minority, unemployment has been exacerbated by government policies favoring the Sinhalese majority. Professionals and artisans have sought new lives in Europe, Canada, the United States, and Australia; with the rise in petroleum prices in the 1970's, unskilled Sri Lankans sought work in the oil-rich Persian Gulf States. The eruption of violence between Sinhalese and Tamils in 1983 was a further spur to emigration.

The census of 1990 noted a total of 10,970 Sri Lankans living in the United States. Most seem to have been either university students or former university students who had found jobs and decided to stay. The Boston area (where the Massachusetts Institute of Technology had drawn Sri Lankan students) was one major Sri Lankan center; a sizable minority of them settled on the West Coast. The U.S. government has, since 1983, consistently refused to grant blanket refugee status to the Sri Lankan Tamils. Canada has been more generous in admitting members of this group. Liberalization of the U.S. asylum regulations in 1991, however, allowed those who claimed asylum to stay indefinitely until their case could be adjudicated by the immigration authorities; hence, a number of Sri Lankans, which cannot be determined with any assurance, were probably living in the United States illegally in the early 1990's. At that time, some Sri Lankan asylum-seekers were staying in the Buffalo area in western New York, sustained by local religious charities, while awaiting the chance to cross the border into Canada.

Another source of South Asian immigration to the United States is the South Asian diaspora outside the United States. In 1972, for example, the U.S. government admitted 2,000 South Asians who had been expelled from Uganda by dictator Idi Amin. In 1983, 35 percent of all those recorded in the census as being of Asian Indian origin had been born in Guyana, Trinidad and Tobago, and the United Kingdom, not in India. In 1990, there were in the United States around 50,000 Guyanese Indians, more than 7,000 Fijian Indians, and a small number of Trinidadian Indians.

A look at the foreign languages spoken in America indicates both the number and the variety of South Asian immigrants. The 1990 census listed five South Asian tongues among the fifty foreign languages most commonly spoken. There were 331,484 Hindi speakers (from Uttar Pradesh), 102,418 Gujarati speakers (from Gujarat), 50,005 Punjabi speakers (from both Pakistan and India), 38,101 Bengali speakers (from Bangladesh and from West Bengal), and 33,949 speakers of Malayalam (largely from Kerala).—*Paul D. Mageli*

SUGGESTED READINGS: • Bagai, Leona B. *The East Indians and the Pakistanis in America*. Minneapolis: Lerner, 1972. • Jensen, Joan M. *Passage from India: Asian Indian Immigrants in North America*. New Haven, Conn.: Yale University Press, 1988. • La Brack, Bruce. *The Sikhs of Northern California, 1904-1975*. New York: AMS Press, 1988. • Larmer, Brook. "Sri Lankan Ethnic Strife Troubles Tamils in the U.S." *Christian Science Monitor* 78 (May 9, 1986): 1, 36. • Lorch, Donatella. "Between Two Worlds: New York's Bangladeshis." *The New York Times*, October 10, 1991, p. B1, B10. • Malik, Iftikhar Haider. *Pakistanis in Michigan: A Study of Third Culture and Acculturation*. New York: AMS Press, 1989. • Mazumdar, Sucheta. "Colonial Impact and Punjabi Emigration to the United States." In *Labor Immigration Under Capitalism: Asian Workers in the United States Before World War II*, edited by Lucie Cheng and Edna Bonacich. Berkeley: University of California Press, 1984. • Mazumdar, Sucheta. "South Asians in the United States with a Focus on Asian Indians: Policy on New Communities." In *The State of Asian Pacific America: A Public Policy Report, Policy Issues to the Year 2020*. Los Angeles: LEAP Asian Pacific American Public Policy Institute and UCLA Asian American Studies Center, 1993.

South Asian languages: South Asia (India, Pakistan, Nepal, Bangladesh, and Sri Lanka) represents a dazzling array of linguistic diversity, unique linguistic characteristics, and the pattern of communication. For these reasons, this region is often described as "the linguistic laboratory of the world." Despite the extensive history of indigenous and European research, it is a common belief of linguists that much still needs to be learned about the nature of human communication in general and the parent language of the Indo-European languages in particular, that is, Proto-Indo-European.

Diversity and Linguistic Complexity. Because numerous languages (about two thousand) are reported to exist in South Asia, there is a common misperception in the Western world that South Asia is a Balkanized version of Asia. Such a perception, however, has no merit, because if one considers the formula of the number of speakers per language, Europe is more fragmented than South Asia. Approximately one-fourth of humanity speaks South Asian languages, and at least two languages of the region—HINDI and BENGALI—are ranked among the ten most-widely spoken languages in the world. Even by most conservative estimates (excluding the speakers of URDU, the Bihari dialects), the native speakers of Hindi rank fourth highest in the world. The number of Punjabi speakers matches, if not exceeds, the number of speakers of French. Other languages such as Telugu, Tamil, and Marathi are among the twenty most widely spoken languages.

There are four notable aspects of the linguistic complexity in South Asia. First, the census data reveal the presence of extremely high numbers of languages in the region. Often, however, these languages are alternative names of the same language. The main reason for this complexity is that the speakers unconsciously use different labels to reveal their religious, social, ethnic, or caste identity. For example, Hindu and non-Muslims may report their language as being Hindi, but Muslims will use the same language but give it a different label. Similarly, among Hindus, Hindi may be identified as Khatri, because for the persons in question their caste identity is more important than their linguistic identity. Second, in some cases, the question of dialect and language has yet to be settled. For some speakers, Bihari is a dialect of Hindi; for others, it is a separate language. It is interesting to note, however, that three speakers reporting their languages separate from one another (Hindi, Urdu, or Bihari) will have absolutely no problem understanding one another's language. Third, the degree of bilingualism is extremely high in the region. Fourth, in spite of South Asia's linguistic diversity, there is a considerable amount of unity.

Language Families. South Asian languages belong to the four language families: Indo-European, Dravidian, Munda, and Tibeto-Burman. The first two families are the most significant and the major ones in terms of the number of speakers and the power represented by their languages.

It is now clear beyond the shadow of any doubt that the Indo-European languages of South Asia are cousins of most languages of Europe. The credit of this finding goes to Sir William Jones, who startled Europe with the discovery of the Sanskrit language. In his presidential address to the Asiatic Society in 1786, Jones declared that the Sanskrit language was related to Latin and Greek, which in turn revolutionized European linguistic studies. Sixteen major modern Indo-European (also called Indo-Aryan) languages are reported to have stemmed from Sanskrit, with intervening middle Indo-European languages (Pali, Prakrits, and Appabhramshas; 1000 C.E.-1500 C.E.). Sixteen languages of this genetic stock, however, figure prominently in South Asia. These languages may be divided into various groups based on geographical grounds. The midland group mainly includes Hindi-Urdu, Bihari, and Rajasthani. The broad view of Hindi includes the Bihari and Rajasthani languages as the modern dialectal variants of the standard Hindi-Urdu. The eastern group contains three major languages: Bengali, Assamese, and Oriya. The western and the southwestern groups include major languages such as Marathi, Gujarati, and Sinhalese, and minor languages such as Konkani and Maldivian. The northwestern group contains Punjabi, Sindhi, and the Dard languages, such as Kashmiri.

The second major language family is the Dravidian language family. About twenty languages of this family are spoken. The four major languages are Tamil, Telugu, Kannada, and Malayalam. These languages are predominant in the southern part of India and are descendants of the old Tamil language (200 B.C.E. to 700 C.E.). Genetically speaking, the Indo-Aryan languages spoken in northern India, Pakistan, and Nepal are more related to their European cousins than their neighboring Dravidian languages. Approximately 150 million people speak Dravidian languages, 95 percent of whom use one of the four major languages. Only one minor language of this family—Brahui—is found in Pakistan.

The third family is the Munda language family. More than 7 million people speak these languages including the group's two main languages, Mundari and Santali. These languages are spoken primarily in the northeastern region of India. The fourth group of languages found in South Asia belongs to the Tibeto-Burman family. About 7 million speakers in the northeastern part of India, Nepal, Bhutan, and Bangladesh use the languages of this group. The two prominent languages of this group are Bhotia and Newari (Nepal).

Literary Tradition. The Indo-Aryan and Dravidian languages have a long literary tradition, going back to Vedic Sanskrit (1600 B.C.E.) and old Tamil (third century B.C.E.), respectively. The modern Indo-Aryan and Dravidian languages have their own history to add to the literary tradition, ranging from eight to four centuries back. The Munda languages are often called languages with nonliterary tradition, that is, they do not have an attested literary tradition, but this should not be interpreted as a lack of literary tradition. Languages with literary traditions are written in a wide variety of scripts that are ranked as the most scientific writing systems among the existing writing systems of the world. These scripts, such as the Devanagari, are written from left to right and are descendants of the Brahmi script, which was well established in India before 500 B.C.E. These scripts are phonetic in nature, and there is a fairly regular correspondence between the letters and their pronunciation.

Migration from South Asia from ancient to modern times led to the establishment of South Asian languages in Southeast Asia, Fiji, Mauritius, East and South Africa, Guyana, Trinidad, and various other Caribbean countries, and recently in Europe (England) and North America. One such unique variety is the Gypsy language in Europe.—*Tej K. Bhatia*

SUGGESTED READINGS: • Bhatia, Tej K. *A History of the Hindi Grammatical Tradition.* Leiden, The Netherlands: E. J. Brill, 1987. • Bhatia, Tej K. "Transplanted South Asian Languages: An Overview." *Studies in the Linguistic Sciences* 11, no. 2 (Fall, 1981): 129-134. • Masica, Colin. *The Indo-Aryan Languages.* Cambridge, England: Cambridge University Press, 1991. • Zograph, G. A. *Languages of South Asia: A Guide.* London: Routledge & Kegan Paul, 1982.

South Asian press in the United States: South Asians began publishing newsletters and small journals shortly after their arrival in the United States and Canada during the first decade of the twentieth century. Although printed sporadically, these periodicals helped link the small, widely dispersed community. Articles in these publications discussed the major concerns of South Asians in North America such as restrictive immigration laws, local economic and working conditions, prejudice and the struggle to survive, and news from South Asia. Besides serving the needs of the local community, the immigrant press also became a vehicle for expressing South Asian nationalism. Among the early immigrants were political dissidents, some of them journalists, who had been forced to leave South Asia because of their opposition to British colonial rule. With support from the wider immigrant community, these activists launched journals that advocated independence for the South Asian region. The political importance of the press endured until 1947, when Britain withdrew from South Asia and when India and Pakistan became independent nations.

By 1920, the size of the South Asian community in North America had diminished as the result of exclusionary immigration laws and other regulations that limited the rights and opportunities of aliens. Although there were fewer South Asian periodicals, they continued to provide an important channel of communication and information for the community. After 1965, new U.S. immigration laws allowed South Asians to enter the United States in significant numbers. This led to the reemergence of an active South Asian press to address the concerns of this expanding ethnic group.

The Early Press. The fledgling journals of this period reflect the limited resources and itinerant nature of the immigrant community. One of the earliest publications, *Circular-i-Azadi* (circular of freedom), was issued first from San Francisco, then from Oakland, California, in 1907. Although it was called a monthly, it was published sporadically for about one year. Editor-publisher Ram Nath Puri lithographed the periodical in the Urdu language and script. It was circulated throughout the Southern Asian community on the west coast of the United States and Canada. In early 1908, Tarak Nath Das began publishing the *Free Hindustan* in Vancouver, British Columbia. By the middle of the year, he had moved the journal to Seattle, Washington, and by the end of the year he had resettled in New York. Das continued to publish his periodical intermittently from New York until 1910. This English-language journal was aimed at a North American audience as well as the immigrant community.

Both the *Circular-i-Azadi* and the *Free Hindustan* were primarily nationalistic in tone. They denounced the British colonial government in South Asia and advocated independence for the region. Both were banned in South Asia by the colonial government. These journals ushered in a series of periodicals that addressed the political situation in South Asia and that covered local events and developments that affected the immigrant community. Stories in these papers described the increasing anti-immigrant sentiment in North America. They also discussed the restrictive immigration measures that were being imposed on South Asians who were trying to enter the United States and Canada. The stories of local discrimination frequently ended with a condemnation of the British Indian government for its unwillingness or inability to prevent the ill treatment of its citizens abroad.

The Ghadr Party (party of revolution) developed a relatively large and steady publications program, printing several periodicals from 1913 to the 1940's. It also published political tracts in English and several South Asian languages calling for the end to British colonialism in South Asia. During the 1920's, the party issued two English-language monthlies, the *Independent Hindustan* and the *United States of India*, to win American

public support for the South Asian nationalist movement. Another periodical aimed at an American audience was *Young India*, published by the Home Rule League of India in New York from 1918 to 1920.

After South Asians in the United States won their citizenship and property rights in 1946 (the Luce-Celler Bill) and India and Pakistan became independent in 1947, the emphasis of the South Asian press changed. As the number of South Asians in the United States grew, particularly after the passage of the 1965 immigration law, the press shifted its focus to give more attention to the immigrant community itself.

The Contemporary South Asian Press. From 1965 to 1980, the South Asian American population in the United States increased from approximately 15,000 to nearly 400,000. This fourth-largest Asian American community has settled throughout the United States with population concentrations in New York, Illinois, Florida, California, and Texas. Several nationally circulated weekly newspapers such as *India Abroad, India-West, News India-Times,* and *Pakistan Link* connect the widespread South Asian community. While many of the major weeklies are in English, there are several widely read newspapers printed in languages such as Bengali, Punjabi, and Urdu.

South Asians also publish numerous cultural, religious, literary, and educational journals in various South Asian vernacular languages and English. South Asian social, professional, and religious organizations frequently publish newsletters for their members.

The national weekly papers, and many of the local journals, carry stories about the immigrant community, news of South Asia, and articles on South Asian art and culture as well as on aspects of American culture and history. Much of the South Asian press is devoted to cultural events, community calendars, and advertisements. Shops and businesses run display ads that illustrate their goods and describe their services. Professionals such as doctors and lawyers often advertise their practices. Many of the weekly and monthly periodicals include matrimonial columns in their classified sections.

In spite of the community's large size, which in 1993 approximated 800,000, many South Asian publications are short-lived. Each year several newspapers and journals are launched but frequently are not sustained beyond a few issues. Among the older, more established periodicals are *India Abroad* and *India-West*, founded in 1970 and 1975 respectively. The former has a weekly circulation of over 40,000, while the latter's weekly distribution is 13,000. A West Coast-based monthly, India Currents, was established in 1987 and has a circulation of 23,000. This entertainment-oriented news magazine concentrates on providing a calendar of performances and community events. It also includes short literary selections, interviews, reviews, and articles focusing on South Asian American issues. A Canada-based literary journal, *The Toronto Review of Contemporary Writing Abroad*, has been distributed in both the United States and Canada for more than a decade.

The contemporary press still covers events in South Asia. This news remains important because many readers are relatively recent immigrants and because the U.S. media has a lack of news on Asia. U.S. relations with countries of the South Asia region also receives regular attention.

South Asian American journalists have not yet produced a daily newspaper. There is only one semiweekly, the *India Monitor*, which primarily serves the New York area. While most South Asian Americans turn to the U.S. mainstream press for their daily news, they continue to rely on ethnic publications for community information and alternative perspectives on topics such as immigration and minority issues. Increasing circulation figures and the consistent appearance of new publications indicate the vitality and importance of the South Asian press.—*Jane Singh*

SUGGESTED READINGS: • Siddiqi, Mohammed A. "Indian Ethnic Press in the United States and Its Function in the Indian Ethnic Community of the U.S." *Gazette* 39 (1987): 181-194. • *South Asians in North America: An Annotated and Selected Bibliography*, edited by Jane Singh. Berkeley: Center for South and Southeast Asia Studies, University of California, Berkeley, 1988.

South Asian Studies centers: Prior to World War II (1939-1945), international studies in the United States were left primarily to missionaries, foreign-service agents, and some news organizations. This limited interest left some serious gaps in the understanding of the world outside some selected European countries. This situation began to change radically, however, during and after World War II with the perception that knowledge about other countries is not only critical for foreign policy but also intimately tied to economic and business growth. Although some scattered attempts were made to promote South Asian Studies in the United States, such as the establishment of the professorship of Sanskrit at Yale University (1844) and similar positions at Harvard and Columbia universities and

other universities in Pennsylvania, Chicago, and California, the largest and most vigorous attempts had to wait until the passage of the National Defense Education Act in 1958. With this act, Foreign Language and Area Studies (FLAS) mushroomed in American universities.

In the 1960's, a number of South Asian Studies centers at various universities, including the University of California, Berkeley; the University of Washington, Seattle; the University of Texas, Austin; Columbia University; and Cornell University, offered a wide variety of programs, among them summer school and India-Year Abroad programs at both the undergraduate and the graduate levels. The University of Wisconsin, Madison, offered specialized courses on India and had the only department of Indian Studies. This department and others that followed offered an FLAS Fellowship that enabled students to study languages and other subjects (history, literature, linguistics, humanities, anthropology, geography, religion, sociology, political science) dealing with South Asia. Extensive language training was the major factor distinguishing FLAS Ph.D.'s from nonarea specialists. Among the South Asian languages studied by FLAS Ph.D.'s in the 1970's, the following were the most popular: Hindi-Urdu, Sanskrit, Tamil, Bengali, Telugu, Marathi, and Prakrits. South Asian Studies got further impetus with the emergence of the American Institute of Indian Studies, which opened new avenues for research and language studies for the faculty as well as for graduate and undergraduate students specializing in South Asia. In the 1980's and 1990's, South Asian Studies underwent roller-coaster growth. Old centers gradually became sluggish whereas new institutions filled the gap by developing new diversified and innovative programs dealing with South Asia. One such success story is the joint Syracuse University-Cornell University South Asia Center in the 1980's, which aimed at combining professional studies with the traditional language and area offering of South Asian Studies centers.

South Asian women: South Asian women exhibit a diversity of lifestyles depending on where they live (India, Pakistan, Bangladesh, Sri Lanka, Nepal, or Bhutan), their social class (or caste), and the religion that they practice.

Region. In the southern regions of South Asia (southern India and Sri Lanka), women have higher status relative to their male counterparts than is the case in the northern regions (northern India, Pakistan,

Bangladesh, and Bhutan). In the south, rice, which is the predominant grain crop, requires constant tending. Women there have a history as laborers in rice-paddy fields; thus, they are viewed as important producers. By contrast, in the north, the predominant crops are dry ones such as wheat and millet. Cultivating dry crops requires more physical strength than paddy agriculture, so there is less demand for female labor. The exclusion of women from productive labor in the northern regions often leads to the exclusion of women from the right to inherit land. This difference may account for the strong preference for male offspring among many groups in the north.

Class/Caste. South Asian women's lives are patterned by the class/caste into which they are born. Class/caste affects not only material standard of living but also life options such as opportunities for education and employment as well as influence and decision making. Much of Indian society, for example, is characterized by a rigid, hierarchical caste system. A woman's position within this system is determined at birth and usually influences whom she marries, her occupation, and her economic well-being. Economically privileged women obtain higher levels of formal education and may delay marriage to seek a career. Upper-caste women in India are, however, more often bound by religious traditions, which may require the seclusion of women or prohibit the remarriage of widows. Impoverished lower-class women must focus on providing basic necessities for themselves and their families. In India, the most extreme deprivation exists among women in the scheduled castes and scheduled tribes, groups designated as particularly disadvantaged in the Indian constitution. These women must often struggle for basic survival. The higher work participation rate of lower-caste women, however, results in their having somewhat higher status and in greater egalitarianism between husband and wife.

Religion. The predominant religions practiced by South Asian women are Hinduism, Islam, and Buddhism. In India a large majority of women are Hindu. Hindu law books from the second century B.C.E. state that the position of women is one of complete dependence on men—on fathers in childhood, on husbands as adults, and on sons in old age. This emphasis on a wife's subordination to her husband may serve to limit women's opportunities for decision making and influence within their families. At the same time, there are

South Asian women worshiping at a Hindu temple. (Martin A. Hutner)

Women of the Delhi Pradesh Congress Committee stage a mile-long procession through the streets of New Delhi in 1955 to protest the reported military alliance between the United States and Pakistan, India's neighbor to the northwest. (National Archives)

many female deities worshiped by Hindus, and the religious tradition views women as possessing special female energy and power, Shakti. In Bangladesh and Pakistan, the majority of women practice Islam, as do about fifty million women in India. This religion also stresses women's subservience to men, and Islamic religious laws in Bangladesh and Pakistan strongly favor men. The Islamic holy book, the Quran, emphasizes that men must care for their sisters, wives, and mothers and guarantees property and inheritance rights for women. Traditional Muslim families practice purdah, which involves limiting the interaction between men and women. It is accomplished by secluding girls past puberty and requiring that, when in public, they wear a garment that conceals the head and face. Purdah is also practiced among certain Hindu groups. In Sri Lanka, Buddhism is practiced by the majority of the women. It differs from Islamic and Hindu religions in that it places far less emphasis on women's subservience to men. Buddhism recognizes women as individuals with functions other than wife and mother and allows women to join Buddhist orders. In Sri Lanka, Buddhist nuns are less visible and less politically active than monks and are held to more strict standards of behavior.

Sex Ratio. South Asian countries are among the few in the world where men outnumber women. Not only does the sex ratio in these countries favor men, but also it has become increasingly so through the twentieth century. The differential mortality of women in these nations is a manifestation of their disadvantage. The lower life expectancy of women is a result of discrimination and neglect. Studies show that daughters are more likely to be malnourished and receive fewer health services than sons. Among certain groups in South Asia, it is common for women to eat only after other family members are fed. In lower class/caste families, this may mean that there is little food left for women. The practice of female infanticide—the killing of female babies—may also contribute to the imbalanced sex ratio in India. This practice, while more common in the eighteenth century, reportedly still occurs in some regions of contemporary India. The poverty of the population, combined with religious customs that favor sons, are the primary reasons for female infanticide. The practice of dowry—payment in money, goods, or land by the bride's family to the husband's family—may also contribute to the practice of female infanticide. The practice of dowry is quite harmful for women in that each daughter represents a significant expense at the time of marriage. Low-income families may have great difficulty bearing this expense; thus, sons are preferred to daughters.

Women's Movements. The disadvantages faced by many South Asian women have served to fuel the development of a number of reform movements for women. As a result, women's issues have received considerable attention in the media and political systems of these countries. The United Nations' Decade for Women in 1975 spurred the investigation of the conditions for women in countries worldwide. In India, reports of the findings of this investigation revealed serious problems for women and galvanized Indian women into organizing to improve their opportunities. Tens of thousands of women's organizations exist in India today. These organizations work to promote equal work opportunities and other reforms for women. Similar activities exist, though on a smaller scale, in other South Asian nations.—*Dana Dunn*

SUGGESTED READINGS: • De Souza, Alfred, ed. *Women in Contemporary India.* Delhi: Manohar Book Service, 1975. • Duley, Margot, and Mary I. Edwards, eds. *The Cross-Cultural Study of Women.* New York: Feminist Press, 1986. • Everett, Jana Matson. *Women and Social Change in India.* Delhi: Heritage, 1979. • Gross, Susan Hill, and Mary Hill Rojas. *Contemporary Issues for Women in South Asia: India, Pakistan, Bangladesh, Sri Lanka, Nepal, and Bhutan.* St. Louis Park, Minn.: Glenhurst, 1989. • Jahan, Rounaq, and Hanna Papanek, eds. *Women and Development: Perspectives from South and Southeast Asia.* Dacca: The Bangladesh Institute of Law and International Affairs, 1979. • Sakala, Carol. *Women of South Asia: A Guide to Resources.* Millwood, N.Y.: Kraus International, 1980.

South Asians in the United States: South Asians refers to those immigrant populations originally from the Indian subcontinent. Early twentieth century historical documents often labeled these groups as "East Indians" and "Hindus" (the latter term is correct only if they are followers of the religion Hinduism). Modern South Asians comprise the peoples of India, Pakistan, Nepal, Bangladesh, Sri Lanka, Bhutan, and Maldives. The total population of these Asian nations is more than one billion, with an additional fifteen to twenty million South Asian immigrants and/or their descendants living outside their ancestral homelands, often overseas.

Although significant immigration from South Asia to the United States did not begin until shortly after the beginning of the twentieth century, by 1990 more than 815,000 Asian Indians had been recorded in the U.S.

Distribution of South Asians in the U.S., 1990

Group	Region	Percent
Asian Indian	Northeast	35%
	Midwest	18%
	South	24%
	West	23%
Bangladeshi	Northeast	58%
	Midwest	10%
	South	20%
	West	12%
Pakistani	Northeast	34%
	Midwest	19%
	South	27%
	West	20%
Sri Lankan	Northeast	25%
	Midwest	15%
	South	22%
	West	38%

Legend: Northeast, Midwest, South, West

Source: Herbert Barringer, Robert W. Gardner, and Michael J. Levin, *Asians and Pacific Islanders in the United States.* New York: Russell Sage Foundation, 1993.

census. South Asian populations in the United States are composed of a complex mix of culturally varied groups who maintain many of their traditional socioreligious practices. They constitute an expanding and relatively successful segment of U.S. society and are likely to retain a substantial amount of their social distinctiveness while increasing their active participation in the nation's economic and political life.

Early Punjabi Immigration. South Asians constitute one of the most ethnically and linguistically diverse peoples in the world including great variations in racial features, language, religion, and social structure. This degree of variation was not reflected in American society until after 1965, when changes in previously restrictive immigration policies allowed the resumption of large-scale, two-way travel between South Asia

and the United States. Although occasional references to a South Asian presence in the United States have been found since colonial times, the first half of the twentieth century was dominated by Punjabi Sikh immigration from northwestern India. The early period (1904-1947) saw fewer than ten thousand immigrants enter the United States, legally or illegally. By the end of World War II there were no more than fifteen hundred persons of South Asian descent in the United States, most of them residing in California. The current situation, in which South Asian immigrants represent all the countries and states of South Asia, began in the late 1960's and accelerated throughout the 1970's and 1980's.

Religious Diversity. A primary organizing principle, social identity, and cultural institution throughout

South Asia is religion. This area is the birthplace of two of the world's oldest faiths: Hinduism and Buddhism. Hinduism, which can trace its origins back some twenty-five hundred years, was almost wholly restricted to the subcontinent until the late nineteenth century. It is the Hindu worldview of stratified and sanctified social relationships that formed the rationale of the Indian caste system. Buddhism, although founded in India in the sixth century B.C.E., ceased to be a major Indian influence more than a millennium ago. Buddhism made its greatest impact in Southeast Asia, China, and Japan. Five other major religions are practiced in South Asia: Islam (11 percent of the population in India but representing less than 5 percent among all South Asian immigrants), Jainism, Sikhism, Christianity, and Zoroastrianism. Often subdivided into myriad subgroups and sects, all these faiths are practiced by South Asians in contemporary American society, and Hindu temples, Sikh *gurdwaras*, and Muslim mosques are now common in American cities. Hinduism numerically dominates there as it does in India (82 percent of Indians are Hindus), with signifi-

South Asian girl waves the flags of both the United States and Pakistan during a Pakistani Day parade in New York City. (Richard B. Levine)

cant numbers of Sikhs, Muslims, Jains, and Parsis.

Race and Language. Although there are substantial physical differences between and among South Asian groups, the majority of this variety is derived from only three macrogroups: the Caucasian or Indo-Aryans of the northern areas, including the Gangetic Plains; the Dravidians in the south of India; and the Mongolians of the Himalayan borders, including Bhutan and Sikkim. The majority of U.S. immigrants are from Aryan or Dravidian populations. Physically, Aryans are somewhat more lighter-skinned, taller, and more solidly built than the peoples of southern India. In India almost three-quarters of the entire population speak one or more languages from the Indo-European language family, which is primarily derived from Sanskrit but written in many different scripts. The main Indo-European languages spoken by U.S. immigrants are Gujarati (60 percent), Punjabi (30-35 percent), and Hindi-Urdu.

Almost a quarter of India's population speaks one of four related Dravidian languages, historically concentrated in the southern portion of India and northern Sri Lanka. In the United States speakers of Malayalam (from Kerala State) and Tamil (from Tamil Nadu) constitute the greatest number. The most recent immigrants are well educated and speak English, which was the medium of education during the British colonial period and remains an official language in India. English serves as a common language in India as well as between South Asian U.S. groups. In addition to direct immigration from the subcontinent, many South Asians hail from other areas such as Hong Kong, Fiji, England, and East and South Africa, where communities had been established in the past.

Contemporary Society. The most substantial concentrations of South Asians in the United States are on the East and West coasts and in the Midwestern states of Illinois and Michigan. The New York tristate metropolitan area and California contain large and growing populations of South Asians, with significant numbers in Ohio, Pennsylvania, Maryland, Massachusetts, and Texas. Because of their largely professional or business backgrounds they are usually urban-based and frequently affiliated with colleges, universities, and research/technology centers. Some groups are associated with specific businesses, such as the Gujarati Patel hotel and motel owner/operators; other South Asians generally are associated with occupations in engineering, medicine, and mathematics.

The current economic and political status of South Asian communities reflects the more educated and

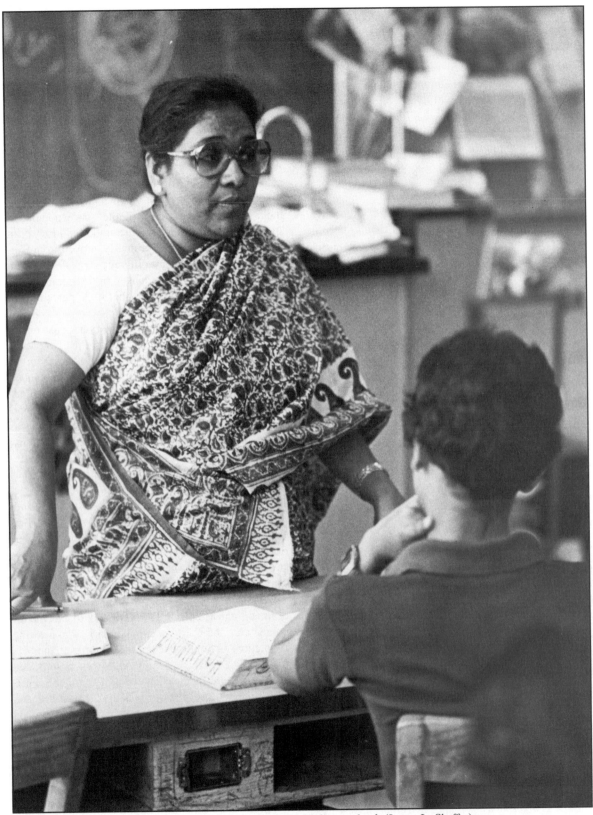

South Asian American teacher at a Midwest school. (James L. Shaffer)

cosmopolitan nature of their recent immigrants. These people have established and participate in a wide range of cultural and religious organizations dedicated to celebrating their heritage and preserving their faiths. Several large Pan-Indian national associations are concerned with more political issues such as immigration regulations, discrimination, and U.S.-India relations. South Asians, once a tiny and isolated component of U.S. society, have become a growing, visible, and quite successful part of the American multicultural mosaic.—*Bruce La Brack*

SUGGESTED READINGS: • Chandrasekhar, S., ed. *From India to America: A Brief History of Immigration, Problems of Discrimination, Admission, and Assimilation.* La Jolla, Calif.: A Population Review Book, 1982. • Helweg, Arthur W., and Usha M. Helweg. *An Immigrant Success Story: East Indians in America.* Philadelphia: University of Pennsylvania Press, 1990. • Jensen, Joan M. *Passage from India: Asian Indian Immigrants in North America.* New Haven, Conn.: Yale University Press, 1988. • Saran, Parmatma. *The Asian Indian Experience in the United States.* Cambridge, Mass.: Schenkman, 1985. • Singh, Jane, et al. *South Asians in North America: An Annotated and Selected Bibliography.* Berkeley: Center for

South and Southeast Asia Studies, University of California, Berkeley, 1988.

South Korea. *See* **Korea, Republic of**

Southeast Asia: Southeastern corner of the Asian landmass. Southeast Asia includes the geographical areas bounded by the states of Myanmar, Thailand, Malaysia, Singapore, Brunei, Indonesia, Laos, Cambodia, Vietnam, and the Philippines. It is the homeland of many of the newest Asian American groups.

Land and Sea. Southeast Asia is a region of great geographical diversity. The broad region occupies the margin of the Asian landmass and the vastness of the Pacific Ocean. The region is composed of a series of islands and peninsulas. Except for Laos, no country is without a shoreline and adequate anchorage for ocean-going ships. In fact, the Strait of Malacca is one of the world's great shipping corridors, and most maritime traffic between Europe and eastern Asia passes through it. Thus, accessibility ranks high among the assets of Southeast Asia; the seas that separate the various countries and islands are much more a link than a barrier.

Southeast Asia can be divided as two regions. Main-

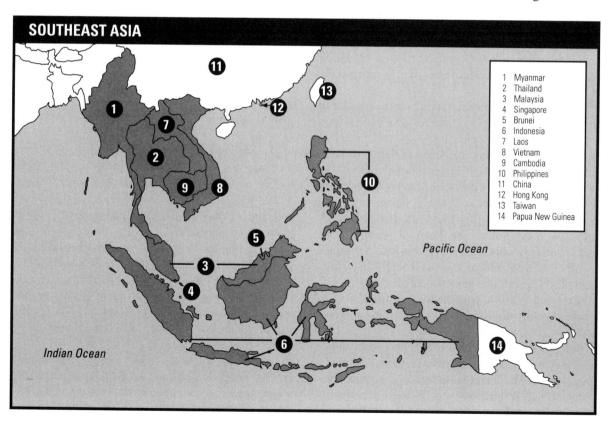

land Southeast Asia includes Myanmar, Thailand, Laos, Cambodia, and Vietnam, the latter three nations being collectively called "Indochina." Insular Southeast Asia refers to Malaysia, Singapore, Brunei, Indonesia, and the Philippines. Indonesia comprises more than 13,000 islands, fewer than 1,000 of which are inhabited; the Philippines comprises an estimated 5,000 to 7,000 islands. Mainland Southeast Asia is noted for its diverse mountain ranges and rivers running north-south, most of them originating in Tibet.

People. Even as Tibet is the source of major rivers of mainland Southeast Asia, southern China and eastern Tibet were the source of the region's population. As the Han Chinese expanded, they drove most of the other ethnic peoples southward, and eventually across the mountain ranges into Southeast Asia. The largest ethnic element are the brown-skinned Malay from southern China, now inhabiting Malaysia, Brunei, Indonesia, and the Philippines.

Population in Southeast Asia has become concentrated in three kinds of natural environments. The first are the valleys and deltas of Southeast Asia's major rivers. The second are the volcanic soils, especially across much of Java. The third base for population concentration is the plantation economy along the western coast of the lower Malay Peninsula. Compared with neighboring regions, mainland Southeast Asia's population densities remain relatively low. Rapid population growth has prevailed in the island regions, notably in the Philippines, during much of the twentieth century.

A Colonial Past. Southeast Asia has been penetrated by many outside forces. Centuries ago traders from India arrived, as did settlers from China. From across the Indian Ocean came the Arabs in search of commerce and the Europeans in pursuit of empires. From the Pacific came the Americans. Southeast Asia was dominated by European colonial powers until the Japanese invasions during World War II. The individual countries, except for Thailand, gained independence only after the war. As a result, the region exhibits intense cultural fragmentation, reflected by complex linguistic and religious differences.

Colonialism was responsible for the growth of large-scale industries that required both skilled and unskilled laborers. Because the local peasants preferred their traditional way of life, the colonists imported Chinese and Indians to work in factories, tin mines, and rubber plantations. The Chinese and Indian communities, through their connections with Western imperialism, thus enjoyed and continue to enjoy economic power in

Southeast Asia far beyond their numbers.

Cultures. Southeast Asia's indigenous culture was developed in the mainland deltas and the fertile low-lying plains of Java. Long ago the region's inhabitants had created their own means of organizing their society, based on irrigated cultivation, sharing the benefits and problems common to the inhabitants. Large-scale penetration by Indian and Chinese cultures began around the commencement of the Christian era. China succeeded in making a great impact upon all of Southeast Asia in the political sphere. Yet with the exception of the Vietnamese, most of Southeast Asia followed India's cultural patterns, its rituals, customs, laws, language, and religion.

Major religions in Southeast Asia include Buddhism, Hinduism, Islam, and Christianity. Myanmar, Thailand, Laos, and Cambodia follow Hinayana Buddhism and exhibit more extensive cultural borrowing from India than does Vietnam, which is culturally Chinese-oriented and mostly follows Mahayana Buddhism. Malaysia and Indonesia (except for Bali, which follows Hinduism) are overwhelmingly Muslim. The Philippines is predominantly Catholic.

Environment and Economic Development. The entire region of Southeast Asia is characterized by tropical climates, vegetation, and animals. The uniformly high temperatures and heavy rainfall of the tropical environment produced a fragile ecological condition that requires careful management to prevent serious and perhaps irreversible damage to the natural resource base. As a result of agricultural expansion, one of the most serious problems in the Southeast Asian rain forests has been the forest loss and grassland invasion.

Three major types of agriculture are practiced in Southeast Asia. Over large areas of the humid tropics, shifting agriculture is widespread. The most common type of agricultural cultivation is, however, paddy-rice agriculture, which provides the primary food grain for most of the population. The third type is estate, or plantation, agriculture, which is commercialized and involves the use of considerable capital. Because of its association with money and international trade, this third form of agriculture is a dynamic force for modernization and economic progress in the region. Important plantation crops include sugarcane, rubber, coconuts, coffee, and oil palm.

Southeast Asia also possesses some important mineral resources. The best known are tin and petroleum, which generate capital and assist economic development in the region.

Grandmother and granddaughter, Ha Son Binh province, Vietnam. (Eric Crystal)

A variety of approaches to development have been attempted in Southeast Asia, ranging from communism to socialism to free enterprise. No one approach has succeeded. Some countries of Southeast Asia have become industrialized, whereas others remain among the least industrialized. Regional disunity is apparent. Interregional communications in Southeast Asia remain poor. External connections are often more effective than internal linkages. Nowhere in Southeast Asia are the problems of dual economy so conspicuous as they are in the great cities of the region. The great capitals of Southeast Asia—Rangoon, Bangkok, Jakarta, and Manila—are the largest cities of their countries, as well as the greatest ports and commercial trade centers. Each contains the major international airport and accounts for a major share of the nation's industrial output. Yet the division between city and countryside in Southeast Asia is a division between a modernizing economy and society and a traditional economy and folk society.

The U.S. involvement in Southeast Asia during the region's postindependence period was traumatic. The United States, which had carried out a long, costly, and controversial war in Indochina and developed patron-client relationships with the noncommunist countries, was integrally involved in the region's affairs. By the 1990's Southeast Asia was dominated by economically vital, anticommunist nations, and it sheltered no adversarial superpower that threatened U.S. interests. At the same time, the nations of Southeast Asia were moving in the direction of greater national resilience and self-reliance. Their prospects rested on each nation's internal capacity to meet the needs of its people and to assure them of a higher standard of living.—*Lee Liu*

SUGGESTED READINGS: • De Blij, Harm J., and Peter O. Muller. *Geography: Regions and Concepts.* 6th ed. New York: John Wiley & Sons, 1992. • Fisher, James S., ed. *Geography and Development: A World Regional Approach.* 4th ed. New York: Macmillan, 1992. • Neher, Clark D. *Southeast Asia in the New International Era.* Boulder, Colo.: Westview Press, 1991. • Osborne, Milton. *Southeast Asia: An Illustrated Introductory History.* Exp. ed. Boston: Allen & Unwin, 1988. • Rigg, Jonathan. *Southeast Asia: A Region in Transition.* Boston: Unwin Hyman, 1991. • SarDesai, D. R. *Southeast Asia: Past and Present.* 2d ed. Basingstoke, England: Macmillan, 1989.

Southeast Asia, Christianity in: As Europeans came into Southeast Asia, they brought their varieties of Christianity with them. Roman Catholicism became the major religion of the Philippines and an important part of the Vietnamese religious life. Protestantism was accepted by numerous minority groups, particularly in the highlands.

Europeans in Southeast Asia. The first major European groups to enter the region were the Portuguese and the Spanish during the sixteenth century. The Portuguese, while Catholic, were more interested in blending into the commercial and cultural patterns of the region than in mass conversions. Their Christian impact tended to be on a scattered, individual basis. The Spanish, by contrast, tied Christian conversion strongly into the expansion of their power and administration through the Philippines.

The seventeenth century saw the arrival of other European powers, especially the Dutch, the English, and the French. Only the Dutch gained major territorial control (in Indonesia). Yet they were initially not interested in conversions to their Protestant form of Christianity. The only other area to have conversions before 1800 was Vietnam, where French and other European priests had an impact, including the romanization of the language.

The nineteenth and twentieth centuries saw the Protestant missionary movement enter the region, particularly in those areas of British and American contact. While China and India were these missionaries' main targets, some of the effort came to Southeast Asia, beginning with America's first foreign missionary, Adoniram Judson, who worked among the Karen hill people of Burma from 1813. Such missionaries also had contact with King Mongkut of Siam (Thailand) in the mid-nineteenth century.

French missionaries had continued to work in Vietnam even before French control of Indochina late in the nineteenth century. Simultaneously, Dutch missionaries became active in the outer islands of Indonesia and the British on the Malay Peninsula and Borneo and in Burma. When the United States took the Philippines from Spain, American missionaries played a key role in the colony. American Protestants became increasingly involved throughout the entire region, particularly after World War II. Thailand, Vietnam, and the Philippines were their main targets, until the fall of Indochina to the Communists in 1975, when much effort shifted to Indonesia.

Catholicism in Southeast Asia. When the Spanish entered the Philippines, they found its northern and central islands not yet exposed to Islam, unlike its southern islands. This fact allowed the Spanish to

Vietnamese bearing food offerings observe the lunar New Year at a Catholic church in Iowa. (James L. Shaffer)

spread Roman Catholicism throughout the lowland population of these areas. Churches run by Spanish priests (divided among the various orders) were established in the indigenous communities, and Catholicism blended with local beliefs. In the process the Philippines has become the only Christianized nation in Southeast Asia with more than 90 percent of the population Catholic (more than 40 million). Remnants of the Portuguese Empire exist in East Timor and its Catholics as well as around Malacca on the west coast of the Malay Peninsula. Overall, Indonesia has 2.5 to 3 million Catholics, while Malaysia, Myanmar, and Thailand each have between 200,000 and 300,000.

Vietnam, as with its East Asian neighbors (China, Korea, and Japan), has had a significant number of its population accept Christianity. Even before the beginning of French colonial control, Catholic villages and districts had come to exist in different parts of the country, and during the colonial period the Catholics were able to function and thrive as a community, constituting more than a tenth of the population. When the Communists took control of the north, most of the 900,000 who moved south were Catholic. The head of the Republic in Saigon, Ngo Dinh Diem, and his fam-

ily were strongly Catholic, and educated Catholics thrived in his administration until his fall in 1963. During the years after the collapse of the Republic in 1975, many Catholics became refugees abroad, being twice as likely to leave as other religious groups. Nevertheless, the Catholic community in Vietnam remains sizable through the early 1990's.

Protestantism in Southeast Asia. Where Catholicism gained converts among lowland populations (except where the latter were Muslims or Theravada Buddhists). Protestantism saw its main appeal among minority groups, especially in the mountains. The Dutch, British, and American missionaries worked to bring their faith to peoples out of the mainstream of their state.

In Indonesia, Dutch missionaries brought their Reformed belief to non-Muslim areas in the outer islands, such as the Minahasa, central Sulawesi, and Toradja peoples. A German missionary started the great Christian movement among the Bataks of northern Sumatra. American and English work tended to be among Chinese or scattered among minority groups in the outer islands. This pattern would intensify only in the 1970's as the missionary effort in Indochina shifted to eastern

Indonesia. Overall more than 8 million Protestants live in this Muslim nation.

British missionary activities have taken place mainly among either Chinese and Indians in the cities (as extensions of the China and India missions) or upland tribal groups. The Muslim population of Malaysia and the Theravada Buddhists of Myanmar have had little interest in conversion. In Sarawak, East Malaysia, on the island of Borneo, for example, mission work started with immigrant Chinese and then moved inland to influence the upland Iban. Then, with the fall of Chinese mainland to the Communists in 1949, much more effort went toward the work among the overseas Chinese. In Malaysia, Singapore, and Brunei, the percentage of Protestant Chinese is higher than any other group. In addition, smaller minority groups, as the urban Indians and various mountain peoples, have their share of converts. These countries have almost half a million Protestants.

In Burma, mission work, while active in the cities, has had a major impact in the highlands among such peoples as the Karen, the Kachin, the Chin, and the Lahu. In recent decades, Christian groups have moved into Myanmar from Assam in northeast India and from southwest China. The total number of Protestants exceeds three quarters of a million.

Much of the mission effort in Myanmar has been American, and this effort may also be seen next door in Thailand. Here the emphasis was originally on Bangkok and the north around Chiengmai. Since the closure of China, the greater number of missionaries has spread Christian influence more widely. Nevertheless, little Christianity exists among the Theravada Buddhist lowlanders.

The Philippines became the main ground for American Protestant missionary work. Again, however, the lowland religions, Catholicism and specifically Islam, prevented much conversion, and it was in the highlands and the cities that the many denominations had their success. Thus, the Chinese and the hill peoples, together with some lowland Filipinos, form the Protestant movement in the Philippines. Since World War II, an increasing number of fundamentalist missionaries has arrived; at one point more than two hundred Protestant denominations with 1.5 million members existed throughout the islands.

The area of Southeast Asia most recently influenced by Protestant Christianity has been Indochina. Since World War II, and particularly during the period of direct American involvement (1954-1975), much missionary work, mainly fundamentalist, has occurred.

Once again the cities and the highlands have seen the most success, as Catholicism is the Christianity of choice among the lowland Vietnamese and Theravada Buddhism the religion of the Khmer and the Lao. Elements of the Chinese in the cities and of groups such as the Stieng, the Mnong, and the Hmong in the mountains have accepted Protestant Christianity.

Thus, Catholicism is the largest Christian religion in Southeast Asia. The Philippines is heavily Catholic, Vietnam has a significant minority, and from the missionary effort of almost five hundred years millions of Catholics are scattered across other countries of the region. Protestantism is mainly a twentieth century phenomenon for Southeast Asia. Though some conversion has occurred among lowland populations (Muslim, Theravada Buddhist, and Catholic), particularly during traumatic times, much higher percentages of acceptance exist among city dwellers (particularly Chinese) and scattered highland peoples. Since World War II, a very active, fundamentalist brand of Protestantism has had a continuing impact on the region.— *John K. Whitmore*

SUGGESTED READINGS: • Anderson, Gerald H. *Studies in Philippine Church History*. Ithaca, N.Y.: Cornell University Press, 1969. • Harrison, B. *South-East Asia: A Short History*. London: Macmillan, 1954. • Hoke, Donald, ed. *The Church in Asia*. Chicago: Moody Press, 1975. • Manikam, R. B., and L. T. Thomas. *The Church in South-East Asia*. New York: Friendship Press, 1956. • Moffett, Samuel Hugh. *A History of Christianity in Asia*. Vol. 1, *Beginnings to 1500*. San Francisco: Harper San Francisco, 1992.

Southeast Asia Treaty Organization (SEATO): Regional defense organization formed by ratification of the Southeast Asia Collective Defense Treaty (1954). SEATO arose in response to Communist expansion in the region. The group maintained no standing military or naval forces but relied on the striking ability of the original signatories to the treaty—the United States, the United Kingdom, Australia, France, New Zealand, Pakistan, the Philippines, and Thailand. SEATO was formally ended in June, 1977.

Southeast Asian American educational issues: After the end of the Vietnam War in 1975, the United States received a significant number of Southeast Asian immigrants/refugees into its public schools. In their attempt to adjust to their new lives in the United States, these refugees have had to learn to cope with an educational system that is fundamentally foreign to them. The refugee population is made up of numerous minority groups (such as Hmong, Mien, Vietnamese, and Cambodians), and each of these groups has had differing historical experiences with formal learning. Moreover, American educators have had to make adjustments in curriculum and instructional approaches in order to accommodate the presence of Southeast Asian students.

Education Prior to Arrival in the United States. In viewing Southeast Asians as a culturally diversified population and with varying degrees of exposure to formal education, three distinct refugee populations emerge: those who have had no formal education, those who have had some formal education (typically obtained in refugee camps in Thailand), and those who have had extensive formal education. Most Vietnamese fall in the latter category, while other Southeast Asian minority groups make up a majority of the other two. Many Vietnamese refugees came from middle-class or aristocratic backgrounds where access to formal education was nearly universal. Even those Vietnamese refugees from lower socioeconomic family

backgrounds typically had some exposure to formal education. In contrast, for the hill groups of Laos (primarily Hmong and Mien) most adults had not received any formal education prior to their arrival in the United States. Younger members of these groups, however, received varying degrees of formal education in small barracklike schools that had been set up by various agencies in refugee camps in Thailand. The Worldwide Christian Relief Organization, the United Nations, the Thai government, and the refugees themselves supported these educational programs.

Education in the United States. A number of relevant forces have affected the education of Southeast Asian refugees in the United States. Perhaps the most obvious has been in the area of communication and language. Most Southeast Asians, when they arrive in the United States, do not speak English. Languages spoken by refugee groups differ significantly from English in grammatical and semantic structures. As a consequence, translation, interpretation, and communication in general have been problematic. For example,

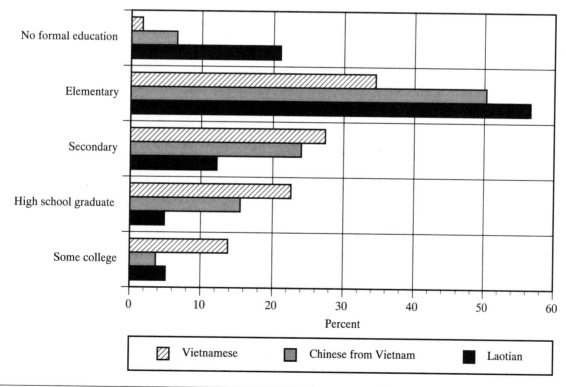

Educational Attainment of Southeast Asian Refugees, 1978-1982

Legend: Vietnamese / Chinese from Vietnam / Laotian

Percent

Source: Susan B. Gall and Timothy L. Gall, eds., *Statistical Record of Asian Americans.* Detroit: Gale Research, Inc., 1993.
Note: Data are for refugees 17 years and older who arrived in the U.S. 1978-1982.

With the massive exodus of Southeast Asian refugees from their homelands to the West beginning in the 1970's, large numbers of Southeast Asian schoolchildren have entered the public schools of America. Here a Cambodian refugee boy studies geography with two schoolmates. (Skjold Photographs)

Students in an English as a Second Language class in the Midwest. (James L. Shaffer)

the Hmong language has no equivalent terms for such words as "economics," "psychology," "mathematics," and other abstractions. Thus, translations have had to be constructed through descriptive-concrete representations of terms (for example, "economics" might translate to "ways of handling and allocating goods," "history" to "talking about past generations," and so forth).

Programs designed to teach English to Southeast Asian students have arisen largely out of existing bilingual/multilingual approaches. Because of the increased linguistic diversity resulting from higher numbers of Southeast Asian students in American classrooms, however, educators have had to modify these programs significantly. Also, ethnolinguistic studies have shown that second-language acquisition occurs in informal situations (for example, on playgrounds or in cafeterias and hallways) as well as in classrooms; as a

result, educators have shifted second-language acquisition instruction away from grammar rule memorization to more natural approaches (such as teaching English through informal conversational channels).

Cultural differences among various Southeast Asian refugees have also played a significant role in the educational process. Too often, policymakers and educators in the United States have treated Southeast Asians as if they were members of a single cultural group. Although there are a significant number of culture traits that are generalizable for Southeast Asians, differences between such groups as the Hmong, Mien, Lao, Vietnamese, and Khmer in language, religious belief, and social behavior need to be taken into account.

Other problems concerning education have stemmed from cultural differences between Southeast Asians and the dominant Anglo-American culture. For example, Southeast Asian parents have, in general, been

Southeast Asian American football player at a Chicago suburban school. (Jim Whitmer)

reluctant to involve themselves with school activities. This reluctance stems from cultural differences concerning traditional views on the division of labor. Southeast Asian parents tend to view school personnel as "caretaker/teacher" specialists, and to interfere with the business of these school functionaries is considered impolite and disrespectful.

Some concerns have been raised regarding Southeast Asian gang activity. Although the raw number of Southeast Asian students exhibiting gang behavior remains relatively low, the number appears to be growing. Educators and law enforcement officials have begun to work together in an attempt to curtail this trend.

Not all the adjustments to the American educational system have been problematic. Studies have shown that many Southeast Asians, especially the Vietnamese, perform above the national norm across a number of academic areas. The number of Vietnamese valedictorians graduating from high school has been significantly higher than other minority or nonminority populations. This high level of performance has been attributed to traditional family support and a cultural emphasis on effort. It is generally the case that Southeast Asians value collective effort over individual achievement, and this has had an overall positive effect on academic performance. In addition, the Vietnamese experience

with public schools in Vietnam (a system combining French, Chinese, and indigenous Vietnamese educational policies) reflects these cultural values of hard work, collective effort, and perseverance.

Adaptations by American Educators. To accommodate Southeast Asians in their classrooms, teachers have relied on a combination of instructional approaches and techniques that have been developed to accommodate multilingual conditions. Some districts have used "sheltered" classes at the middle- and high-school levels. Sheltered classes utilize monolingual teachers who instruct students of varying linguistic backgrounds in a number of subjects (such as math, government, economics, and science). At the primary level, bilingual pull-out approaches still dominate. During the 1980's teachers in general began to rely more and more on cooperative instructional strategies. This approach has generally worked well with Southeast Asian students given their cultural preference for cooperation.

Some school districts have developed "outreach" programs that attempt to get Southeast Asian parents more directly involved in public education. Southeast Asian college students working in conjunction with American educators have formed local associations designed to bring Southeast Asian parents and public schools closer together. Educators have assisted in the development of these associations and have also contributed to the development of Southeast Asian resource centers. These adaptations represent a significant step forward in educating students who are linguistically and culturally different from the mainstream student population. Despite these adaptations, however, many problems remain.—*Michael S. Findlay*

SUGGESTED READINGS: • Caplan, Nathan, John Whitmore, and Marcella H. Choy. *The Boat People and Achievement in America: A Study of Family Life, Hard Work, and Cultural Values.* Ann Arbor: University of Michigan Press, 1989. • Gibson, Margaret. "The School Performance of Immigrant Minorities: A Comparative View." *Anthropology & Education Quarterly* 18 (December, 1987): 262-275. • Haines, David W., ed. *Refugees as Immigrants: Cambodians, Laotians, and Vietnamese in America.* Totowa, N.J.: Rowman & Littlefield, 1989. • Nguyen, Ngoc Bich. "Can the Southeast Asian Americans Play a Leading Role in the Current Revolution in American Education?" The 13th Annual Conference on Indochinese Education and Social Services, San Francisco, April, 1992. • Smith-Hefner, Nancy J. "Education, Gender, and Generational Conflict Among Khmer Refugees."

Anthropology & Education Quarterly 24 (June, 1993): 135-158.

Southeast Asian dance. *See* **Southeast Asian music and dance**

Southeast Asian diaspora: The movement of Southeast Asians abroad resulted from the political activities of the modern world. From the mid-nineteenth to the mid-twentieth century, European and American colonialism led people to take up residence in various lands. Later, decolonization brought many colonial supporters to Europe and America. Finally, conflict in Indochina during the late 1970's caused hundreds of thousands of Vietnamese, Cambodians, and Laotians to move to Asian countries of first asylum and then to resettle in Western lands.

Colonialism and Decolonization. Southeast Asians first moved abroad during the colonial period, when European empires divided Southeast Asia and linked each segment to the home country. The Philippines, for example, was first tied to Spain, then to the United States; Indonesia to The Netherlands; Burma (now Myanmar), Malaysia, Singapore, and Brunei to Great Britain; and Indochina to France. As colonialism developed, indigenous elite, as well as poorer elements of the society, established neighborhoods in the metro-

Hmong refugee in California with photograph of parents left behind in Laos. (Eric Crystal)

poles. They also made links with the colonizing countries, but the number of those leaving their homeland was small until after World War II (1939-1945). The decolonization process, however, fed these communities, as supporters of the colonial powers left their homelands.

The fall of French Indochina had a particularly dramatic impact. The mid-1950's and mid-1970's saw many Indochinese, mainly Vietnamese, go abroad, in the first instance to France and the second to the United States, though some continued on to France.

Asian Asylum. The major diaspora of Southeast Asians began in the late 1970's. Many Lao and upland Hmong had already crossed the Mekong River to camps in northeast Thailand. Few Khmer, however, had left the Cambodia of the Khmer Rouge. Then, in 1978, the eruption of regional politics sent hundreds of thousands fleeing. This occurrence arose out of two developments, one regional, one internal to Vietnam. The radical nationalism of the Khmer Rouge led to a conflict with Vietnam and to support from the People's Republic of China, as the Vietnamese made major changes in their urban economies. The Chinese of Vietnam were caught in the pincer of the two developments. Whether forced or encouraged, thousands left, many aboard old boats apparently arranged through overseas Chinese networks. These people were followed in the 1980's by hundreds of thousands of anti-communist Vietnamese.

These "boat people" moved across the South China Sea and the Gulf of Thailand (where many fell prey to Thai pirates) to first-asylum camps in Malaysia (such as Pulau Bidong) and Indonesia. From northern Vietnam, Chinese and Vietnamese also fled to China, Macao, Hong Kong, and Japan. At the end of 1978, Vietnam invaded Cambodia, and thousands of Khmer fled to Thai camps. Unlike the other ethnic groups, many Khmer remained classified as "displaced persons," not "refugees," because of the Thai worry of being permanently burdened with them.

By 1986-1987, a total of almost seven hundred thousand refugees had arrived in Thailand. They went into camps along the Thai eastern border. Malaysia accepted two hundred thousand refugees and Indonesia one hundred thousand, in both cases Vietnamese and Chinese from Vietnam. The refugees reached the east coast of the Malay Peninsula and islands south of Singapore. In addition, refugees from other countries came to processing camps in Indonesia (Galang Island) and the Philippines (Bataan). Hong Kong received more than one hundred thousand, Japan eight thousand. Thus, in ten years, more than one million refugees, not to mention a quarter of a million displaced persons, left Indochina.

Asian countries were generally not interested in absorbing these huge numbers of refugees into their societies. Southeast Asian nations were leery of adding more Chinese, China and the overseas Chinese were not happy with each other, Hong Kong was too crowded, and Japan was too insular. In some cases, boats were pushed back to sea, and the Thai wanted to be able to return Cambodians across the border. The Indochinese were kept in camps on islands and other remote locations. While China did resettle at least one hundred thousand refugees in the far south, the main solution for refugees in Asia has been movement to Western countries. Therefore, international agencies processed applications for immigration and sought lands to take the Southeast Asians.

Western Resettlement. While the majority of these refugees went to the United States, many were taken into European and former British Commonwealth countries. (The numbers cited are generally from 1986-1987.) France was a natural destination and took about twelve thousand per year. In addition, it allowed eight thousand Cambodians to enter France during 1981. The Indochinese community in France grew by almost 150,000 after 1975, about half coming from Thailand. While most Indochinese are in the Paris region, others have been sent out to provincial centers.

Germany, since World War II, has seen itself as a place of asylum for refugees, taking in thirty-five thousand Indochinese, mainly Vietnamese. The largest number (ten thousand) live in Germany's North Rhine-Westphalia (Nordrhein-Westfalen), but they are also scattered through ten other formerly West German states. Other European countries that accepted Indochinese, generally from one thousand to several thousand, are Switzerland, Belgium, The Netherlands, Austria, and Italy. Scandinavia, Norway, Denmark, and Sweden also received such numbers.

The other major group of countries accepting refugees from Indochina consists of members of the British Commonwealth. Great Britain has taken in more than twenty thousand, almost entirely from Vietnam

In 1978 Malaysia denied these Vietnamese refugees temporary asylum, insisting that other countries accept them directly. (AP/Wide World Photos)

but split between Vietnamese and Chinese. Two-thirds of them came from Hong Kong. While the British government attempted to disperse refugees throughout England, they have become concentrated in big cities. London is naturally the main area, but 10 percent live in Birmingham, and others have gone to Manchester and Bradford.

Canada has made an effort quite out of proportion to its size, accepting 125,000 refugees, which is more than 10 percent of the U.S. total (the ratio of Canadian to U.S. population). Three-quarters are from Vietnam and an eighth each from Cambodia and Laos. They came from countries of first asylum, though proportionately about double arrived from Hong Kong. The Indochinese have fit well into the multicultural Canadian scene.

The entry of the refugees into Australia, by contrast, played a major role in the change of Australia's immigration policy. Of the one hundred thousand refugees entering, 80 percent came from Vietnam, 13 percent Cambodia, and 7 percent from Laos. While they, too, arrived from various first-asylum countries, Indonesia was a proportionately larger source. Australia, too, attempted to disperse the Indochinese, but again they moved toward the cities, especially Sydney and Melbourne; they have, however, settled in the suburbs. New Zealand has a much smaller Indochinese community, totaling about eight-thousand, fairly evenly split between those from Vietnam and those from Cambodia (less than 10 percent from Laos). These small numbers have been easily absorbed.—*John K. Whitmore*

SUGGESTED READINGS: • Chantavanich, Supang, and E. Bruce Reynolds, eds. *Indochinese Refugees: Asylum and Resettlement.* Bangkok: Institute of Asian Studies, Chulalongkorn University, 1988. • Grant, Bruce. *The Boat People: An "Age" Investigation.* Harmondsworth, Middlesex, England: Penguin Books, 1979. • St. Cartmail, Keith. *Exodus Indochina.* Auckland, New Zealand: Heinemann, 1983. • Tepper, Eliot L., ed. *Southeast Asian Exodus: From Tradition to Resettlement, Understanding Refugees from Laos, Kampuchea and Vietnam in Canada.* Ottawa: The Canadian Asian Studies Association, 1980. • Viviani, Nancy. *The Long Journey: Vietnamese Migration and Settlement in Australia.* Carlton, Victoria: Melbourne University Press, 1984.

Southeast Asian exodus to the United States: The presence of the United States in Southeast Asia during the twentieth century has led to a movement of Southeast Asians into the United States. First, American

Southeast Asian Refugees in the U.S. by Country of Origin, 1992

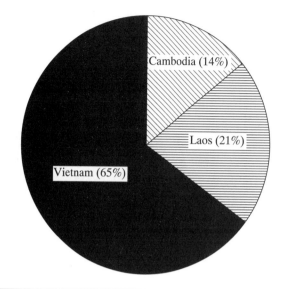

Source: Refugee Resettlement Program, U.S. Department of Health and Human Services, *Report to Congress,* 1993.

control of the Philippines brought in Filipinos, then, after mid-century, American involvement in the anti-Communist struggle in Vietnam led Vietnamese to enter, particularly after the fall of Saigon in 1975. The upheavals of Indochina during the late 1970's sent a more diverse second wave to the United States, which continued through the 1980's. Between 1975 and 1990, more than one million immigrants from Vietnam, Laos, and Cambodia arrived in the United States; more than 90 percent of these were classified as refugees.

The United States in Southeast Asia. The involvement of the United States in Southeast Asia began during the colonial era and continued through the years of decolonization. Southeast Asians came to the United States as a direct result of this political involvement. Such involvement began at the end of the nineteenth century during the Spanish-American War, when American forces took control of the Philippines. Over the next half century, American colonial control led to Filipino immigration across the Pacific, including members of the elite classes as well as less prosperous members of the society. Many who served in the armed forces became American citizens. This flow of Filipinos continued through the second half of the century, forming a large community in California.

The major influx of Southeast Asians into the

Southeast Asian Refugee Arrivals by Nationality, 1975-1991

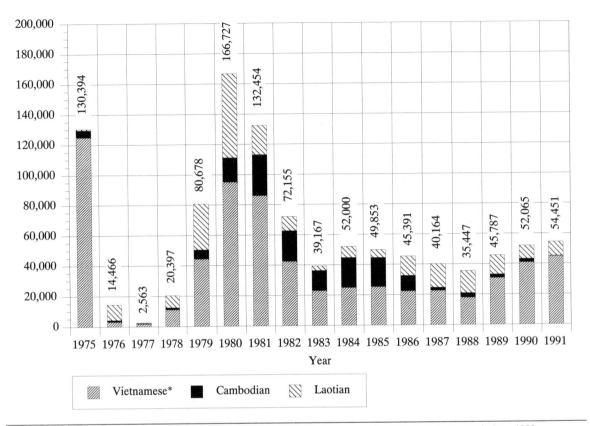

Source: Susan B. Gall and Timothy L. Gall, eds., *Statistical Record of Asian Americans.* Detroit: Gale Research, Inc., 1993.
* Includes 38,885 Amerasians and family members after 1988.

United States, however, came as a result of American participation in the Vietnam struggle. As the anticolonial efforts of the Viet Minh turned into a conflict over Communism, the American government joined the French in the fight. From the mid-1950's, students, government officials, and military officers came to the United States from Indochina. Increasingly, the United States supported governments in Saigon, Vientiane, and eventually Phnom Penh. American civilians and military worked closely with their counterparts in South Vietnam, Laos, and Cambodia. Many of these Indochinese would come to the United States after the collapse of their governments in 1975, joining the few who had already taken up residence in North America.

With the fall first of Phnom Penh in mid-April, 1975, and then Saigon at the end of the month, and with Vientiane shifting to the Communists later in the year, the movement of Indochinese to the United States reached much larger proportions. About 130,000 Viet-

namese fled southern and central Vietnam, going to the Philippines and Guam and then to four processing centers in the United States. Simultaneously, Lao and upland Hmong and Mien moved across the Mekong River into northeast Thailand and its camps. Few were able to escape the Khmer Rouge in Cambodia. Little changed for three years.

Regional Conflict. From the years 1977-1978, tensions rose among the Communist governments of Beijing, Hanoi, and Phnom Penh. The People's Republic of China and Vietnam had a falling out, the Khmer Rouge attacked the Vietnamese border, and Hanoi changed its internal economic policy. From Hanoi's perspective, China challenged Vietnam on the north and backed the Cambodians in the south. In addition, Chinese merchants were seen to work against the government's economic effort. These external and internal pressures triggered a flood of "boat people" from Indochina. Chinese from both northern and southern Vietnam, whether forced or encouraged, started to leave. Thousands took to the seas, many using boats set up via contacts with overseas Chinese elsewhere.

As these boat people moved across the South China Sea and the Gulf of Thailand, many fell prey to pirates. Those who landed on Thai, Malaysian, Indonesian, or Philippine shores were often give a poor reception, if they were not turned away, and segregated on islands such as Pulau Bidong off the Malay coast. The first-asylum countries had little interest in resettling the refugees, particularly if they were Chinese. Interna-

tional agencies took up to two years to set up a system whereby eligible refugees moved from these countries to regional processing centers (mainly Galang Island in Indonesia and Bataan in the Philippines) before going on to their countries of resettlement.

In this two year period, 1978-1980, the Vietnamese attacked the Khmer Rouge and drove them west. China then attacked Vietnam on the north. The result was thousands of Cambodians in Thailand and more refugees taking to the seas. The United States began to take Lao, Hmong, and Mien from northeast Thailand

Southeast Asian Refugees in the U.S., Selected Labor Characteristics, 1985-1992

Labor Force Participation

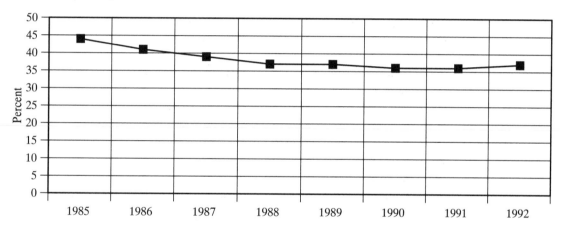

Occupational Status, 1992

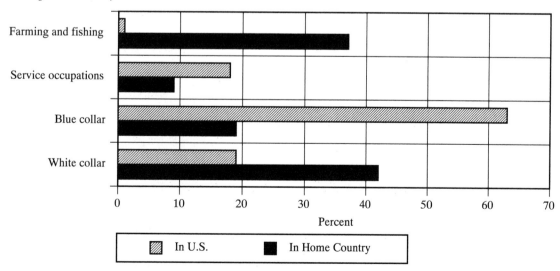

Source: Refugee Resettlement Program, U.S. Department of Health and Human Services, *Report to Congress,* 1993.

Top 10 States of Southeast Asian Refugee Residence, 1992

State	Number of Southeast Asian Refugees
California	409,800
Texas	76,900
Washington	47,800
Minnesota	37,700
New York	36,000
Massachusetts	32,200
Pennsylvania	31,600
Illinois	31,000
Virginia	26,100
Oregon	22,200

Source: Refugee Resettlement Program, *Report to Congress.* Washington, D.C.: U.S. Department of Health and Human Services, 1993.

in an effort to relieve pressure on the Thai government. The latter wanted the Cambodians labeled "displaced people," not refugees, thus allowing the Cambodians to push them back across the border legally. Negotiations between Washington and Bangkok led in 1981 to thousands coming to the United States. In the meantime, the composition of the boat people fleeing Vietnam shifted from Chinese to Vietnamese.

Refugees in America. The major destination of the refugees was the United States. The handling of the ever-increasing second wave differed from that of the first wave in that the processing centers were outside the United States. From Galang and Bataan, the refugees went directly to local sponsors with no general state-side orientation.

Other major differences exist between the first wave and the second. Those in the first were Vietnamese who tended to be of higher social class and with more education, better job skills, greater English proficiency, and more extensive contacts with the Western world. The second wave had much greater ethnic diversity—

Southeast Asians Receiving Aid to Families with Dependent Children (AFDC), 1991

Percent of recipients who are female: 52%*
Percent of recipients who are unmarried: 16%*
Average number of children per family: 3.5*

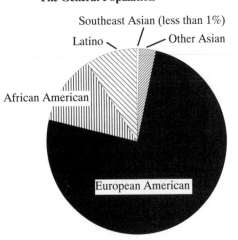

Welfare (AFDC) Recipients, Comparative

Southeast Asian
Other Asian (less than 1%)
Latino
European American
African American

The General Population

Southeast Asian (less than 1%)
Latino
Other Asian
African American
European American

Source: The New York Times, "National." May 19, 1994.
* 1989 figures.

the Chinese came first, then the Lao, Hmong, and Mien, the Cambodians, and finally many more Vietnamese. They were of lower class and generally had less education and job skills, poor (if any) English proficiency, and fewer Western contacts. The Lao were less urban, with the greatest number of farmers. The Chinese were mainly urban and had held city occupations—commercial, construction, manufacturing, and service. The Vietnamese had more professionals and fishers and were more likely to have had a higher education. The Chinese tended to have secondary education and the Lao primary education. The Cambodians had survived four horrible years of the Khmer Rouge, and the Hmong and Mien had come out of the mountains.

In February, 1994, the United Nations High Commissioner for Refugees announced that Vietnamese who fled their country would no longer be automatically entitled to consideration for asylum as refugees from persecution. Instead, "boat people" from Vietnam will be evaluated as are asylum-seekers from any nation. This announcement brought the nineteen-year exodus of the boat people to a close.—*John K. Whitmore*

SUGGESTED READINGS: • Barkan, Elliott Robert. *Asian and Pacific Islander Migration to the United States: A Model of New Global Patterns.* Westport, Conn.: Greenwood Press, 1992. • Caplan, Nathan, John K. Whitmore, and Marcella H. Choy. *The Boat People and Achievement in America: Family Life, Hard Work, and Cultural Values.* Ann Arbor: University of Michigan Press, 1989. • Grant, Bruce. *The Boat People: An "AGE" Investigation.* Harmondsworth, Middlesex, England: Penguin Books, 1979. • Haines, David W., ed. *Refugees as Immigrants: Cambodians, Laotians, and Vietnamese in America.* Totowa, N.J.: Rowman & Littlefield, 1989. • Haines, David W., ed. *Refugees in the United States: A Reference Handbook.* Westport, Conn.: Greenwood Press, 1985.

Southeast Asian gangs: As with many immigrant groups to the United States, parents of Southeast Asian youths have encountered difficulties in bringing up their children in their new country. One unfortunate result has been the rise of youth gangs among Vietnamese, Laotian, and Cambodian children. In the absence of supervision from either the parents or the schools, some of these gangs commit crimes leading to the arrest and incarceration of their members. In the late 1980's, such gang activity became particularly common in the Southeast Asian communities of California and was a source of major concern both to the leaders of these communities as well as to the police.

Talks with Southeast Asian parents and officials indicate that most of the gang activity is conducted by youth who have had trouble in school and have poor relations with their parents and elders. Most gangs are informal groups of such boys ages thirteen to twenty-five who "hang out" together and develop a small subculture for their group. Elements of this subculture may include practices borrowed from Latino or African American-oriented gangs such as hand signals, tattoos, gang names, and gang related clothing such as Los Angeles Raiders jackets. Unlike the gangs from which such symbols are borrowed, however, the Southeast Asian gangs generally do not have neighborhood "territories" or engage in drug trafficking.

Types of Crimes. When Southeast Asian gangs do commit crimes, they are often the "specialties" of that particular gang. For example, in the late 1980's and early 1990's, some Vietnamese gangs were known for violent "home invasions" committed against other Southeast Asian refugees. These gangs took advantage of the fact that many Southeast Asians did not trust banks, kept large sums of money at home, and were afraid to report crimes to the authorities. Using information gathered through the refugee community's rumor mill, the gangs would hear about a family that had recently received a large sum of money. They would then break into the house and threaten to kill the occupants unless the money was surrendered. Similarly, "protection" payments were often extorted from the many small Southeast Asian businesses that sprang up in the late 1980's and 1990's.

The police have had great difficulty investigating the robberies and extortion rackets. The victims often do not speak English or have any familiarity with American police procedure or the courts. Typically, victims are unwilling to testify in open court about the crimes because of the threats of gang members who are released on bail or not caught. While some individuals and merchants were starting to report the crimes to the police in the early 1990's, many such crimes continued to go unreported.

Although Laotian and Cambodian youth were occasionally associated with the Vietnamese gangs, more often they formed gangs from within their own ethnic group. This was particularly true of Mien, ethnic Lao, and Cambodian youth living in California's Central Valley. Fewer Hmong youth were involved. The Laotian and Cambodian gangs were occasionally involved with home invasion-type crimes; auto theft and joy riding were, however, more common.

Analysis. Why did California's Southeast Asian communities experience such violent gang activity during the 1980's? Theories about gang activity with immigrant groups provide a partial explanation. Clifford R. Shaw and Henry D. McKay wrote in 1942 about the conditions that led to much gang activity in Chicago's European immigrant communities during the early twentieth century. Perhaps not coincidentally, many of the conditions that Shaw and McKay described were similar to those found in California's Southeast Asian communities in the 1980's. For example, it was observed that gang activity was likely in poor inner city areas that are areas of first immigrant settlement, areas whose inhabitants move frequently, areas that are so ethnically mixed that no one group exerts "social control" over the youth, and, in general, communities that are "disorganized" for whatever reason. Shaw and McKay go on to note that in such communities, young boys tend to become disconnected from either the parents' society or that of their American schools. Instead, they group together in cliques and form "subcultures" in which the acquisition of goods by illegal means is perceived as being legitimate. Notably, this "subculture" is not a unit of either the home culture (Vietnamese, Laotian, or Cambodian) or the host American culture. Rather it has its own unique traditions, beliefs, and activities.

The above description fits the circumstances encountered by the later Southeast Asian refugees. As with the European groups, Southeast Asians quickly found themselves living in blighted areas with low rents. American policies dealing with the dispersal of the refugees also meant that family movement was frequent during the first few years of resettlement as families regrouped. Finally, in no American city is the Southeast Asian population large enough to develop the means of social control necessary to police itself. Rather, the Southeast Asian refugees live in the same neighborhoods as immigrants from other countries, in quarters that include Eastern Europeans, Latino Americans, African Americans, and poor white Americans. From Shaw and McKay's perspective, then, it is not surprising that gang activity should be common in the Southeast Asian communities.

Prognosis. What does this mean for the future of Southeast Asian youth in the United States? Oddly, the answer is mixed. For while the focus of this essay has been on the problems encountered by Southeast Asian youth, it should also be noted that unusually large numbers of Southeast Asian children are successfully attending universities. The irony is that these youth are the same age as the gang members and are often the siblings or cousins of gangsters in prison for various crimes. In other words, at least for some youth, refugee parents are able to transmit the values that lead to success in American society. It can be expected that the longer Southeast Asians have to adjust to the new society, the more capable they will be of transmitting the kind of values to their children that can steer the latter away from gangs. Another factor that will continue to a lower rate of gang activity is that as Southeast Asian families accumulate the capital necessary to purchase homes in the United States, they will move out of the area of first settlement and into more stable suburbs where gang activity is less of a problem.— *Tony Waters*

SUGGESTED READINGS: • Arax, Mark. "Lost in L.A." *Los Angeles Times Magazine,* December 13, 1987, pp. 10-16. • Dannen, Fredric. "Revenge of the Green Dragons." *The New Yorker* 68 (November 16, 1992): 76-99. • Kifner, John. "New Immigrant Wave from Asia Gives the Underworld New Faces." *The New York Times,* January 6, 1991, p. 1. • Shaw, Clifford R., and Henry D. McKay. *Juvenile Delinquency and Urban Areas: A Study of Rates of Delinquency in Relation to Differential Characteristics of Local Communities in American Cities.* Rev. ed. Chicago: University of Chicago Press, 1972. • Waters, Tony, and Lawrence E. Cohen. *Laotians in the Criminal Justice System.* Berkeley, Calif.: California Policy Seminar, 1993.

Southeast Asian languages: Approximately eight hundred or more different languages are spoken in Southeast Asia. This region includes the nations of Myanmar (formerly Burma), Cambodia, Laos, Thailand, Vietnam, and Malaysia in mainland Southeast Asia, and Singapore, Indonesia, and the Philippines in insular Southeast Asia. While these nations are all independent and sovereign political entities, there is great ethnic and linguistic diversity within each of these countries (even though there may be one or two dominant ethnic majority populations).

The number of speakers of each of the Southeast Asian languages ranges from only a few dozen to well into the millions. There are at least one hundred major language and/or cultural groups. The languages in this area are extremely diverse, and linguists generally classify them into four different language families.

Austroasiatic. There are between 100 to 150 Austroasiatic languages, with most of them spoken in mainland Southeast Asia and parts of eastern India. They are divided into two main branches: the Munda languages of India and the Mon-Khmer. Among the languages in the Mon-Khmer branch are Cambodian (Khmer) and Vietnamese. Vietnamese and Cambodian are the official national languages of Vietnam and Cambodia, respectively. The other languages in this branch generally are those of nonurban ethnic minority groups.

Sino-Tibetan. Most of the Southeast Asian languages from the Sino-Tibetan family fall into either the Sinitic or Burman branch. The Sinitic (or Chinese) languages are spoken mostly in Singapore and parts of Malaysia, as well as by hundreds of thousands of overseas Chinese in Indonesia, the Philippines, and the Indo-Chinese subcontinent. The most well known is Mandarin Chinese (the national language of the People's Republic of China). The second branch includes Burmese, the official language of Myanmar, spoken by more than twenty-five million people. Other important Sino-Tibetan languages are Karen, Chin, and Kachin, all spoken by several million people. Hmong (Miao) is the language of the Hmong people, many of whom came to the United States as refugees after the Vietnam War (1965-1975).

Tai. The Tai linguistic family includes the national language of Thailand (standard or Central Thai), as well as the related minority languages of Red, White, and Black Tai. (These distinctions of "Red," "White," or "Black" are so named because of the color of the dresses worn by the local women.) Laotian, the national language of Laos, is closely related to Thai. For example, it is said that Lao people can understand most of Central (standard) Thai, though standard Thai speakers claim not to be able to understand Laotian and tend to regard Lao people as rustics. Lao culture, however, varies somewhat from Thai culture.

Austronesian. The Austronesian languages (which used to be called Malayo-Polynesian) include most of the languages of insular Southeast Asia and the Pacific Islands. Probably more than two hundred million people speak an Austronesian language, a spread that covers about a fifth of the world in geographical area stretching from Madagascar, off the African coast, to Easter Island, approaching South America. Six main branches of this family are represented in Southeast Asia: Sundic, the languages of Java, Bali, Sumatra, and the Malay-speaking areas of Malaysia; Bornean, most of the languages found on Borneo; Moluccan, the language found in the Celebes Islands; Northern Philippine, the languages of northern Luzon; Central Philippine, the languages of central and southern Luzon and the islands of Samar, Cebu, Panay, Negros, Min-

doro, Palawan, and Leyte; and Southern Philippine, the languages of Mindanao and the Sulu Archipelago. A seventh branch—Cham—is an isolated family of languages spoken in the interior of Vietnam, including by some Montagnards in the central highland plains.

One of the most widely spoken Austronesian languages in Southeast Asia is Javanese (in East Java) with fifty million speakers, followed by Sundanese (in West Java) with around thirty million. The two most important languages in this area, however, are Pilipino/Tagalog and Indonesian/Malay—the official languages of the Philippines and Indonesia—even though both have fewer native speakers. The reason for this is national identity.

When the Philippines became independent in 1946, it was obvious that for a national identity to be formed, one of the more than 159 different local languages would need to be selected as a lingua franca. English, though spoken by the middle classes and used as the language of instruction in the schools, was still believed to carry overtones of colonialism. Tagalog, an indigenous language spoken around the capital of Manila, was chosen instead. In the 1970's, a more standardized version of Tagalog was proposed to be the country's official language under the more impartial name Pilipino. Today, more than twenty-five million people speak Pilipino as a native language, and most Filipinos have at least some facility in it.

Indonesia faced even greater problems when it became independent in 1949. In a country with more than five hundred languages and thirty thousand islands, political and intellectual leaders realized that finding a tongue that everyone would agree upon would be almost impossible. For example, if the majority language—Javanese—became the national language, it would most likely alienate Sumatrans, Balinese, and others who would feel at a distinct disadvantage when applying for jobs, entering public service, or attending higher education. Thus, a neutral language—Malay—was selected. Pidgin Malay had been widely spoken throughout the islands as a trade language for centuries, so this was a logical choice as many already had at least some familiarity with the language. More important, however, by choosing Malay, almost everyone would be learning a second language and no one would be in a more privileged linguistic position.

Other Languages. There are at least three other important languages spoken in Southeast Asia, none of which is in the four families mentioned above. The Tamil language became entrenched in the area when people from south India were brought in by the British to work the Southeast Asian mines and plantations in the nineteenth century. Today, there are very large Indian minorities who speak Tamil in Malaysia and Singapore, as well as in Indonesia and other places. There are also sizable populations of speakers of French and English, the languages of the French, British, and American colonizers. The French controlled Indochina (the areas consisting of Vietnam, Laos, and Cambodia) from the 1860's until the 1950's. The British considered Singapore and Burma part of the British Empire and had quasi-official control of Malaysia via treaties with the various Malay sultanates. The Americans took control of the Philippines after winning the Spanish-American War in 1898 and did not grant independence until 1946. The former economic and military dominance of these Western powers assures that these languages will remain a presence for some time to come.—*James Stanlaw*

SUGGESTED READINGS: • Benedict, Paul. *Austro-Thai Language and Culture*. New Haven, Conn.: HRAF Press, 1975. • Huffman, Franklin. Bibliography and Index of Mainland Southeast Asian Languages and Linguistics. New Haven, Conn.: Yale University Press, 1986. • LeBar, Frank, ed. *Ethnic Groups of Insular Southeast Asia*. Vol. 1. New Haven, Conn.: HRAF Press, 1972. • LeBar, Frank, et al. *Ethnic Groups of Mainland Southeast Asia*. New Haven, Conn.: HRAF Press, 1964. • McFarland, Curtis. *A Linguistic Atlas of the Philippines*. Tokyo: Institute for the Study of Languages and Cultures of Asia and Africa, 1980. • Peacock, James. *Indonesia: An Anthropological Perspective*. Pacific Palisades, Calif.: Goodyear Publishing, 1973. • Provencher, Ronald. *Mainland Southeast Asia: An Anthropological Perspective*. Pacific Palisades, Calif.: Goodyear Publishing, 1975. • Voegelin, C. F., and F. M. Voegelin. *Classification and Index of the World's Languages*. New York: Elsevier, 1977.

Southeast Asian languages—prehistory of: The linguistic map of Southeast Asia is dominated by a small number of language families. On the mainland, the major families are Austroasiatic, Sino-Tibetan, Tai-Kadai (Daic), and Hmong-Mien (Miao-Yao). In insular Southeast Asia, the major language families are Austronesian and Papuan.

Language families are, by definition, groups of genetically related languages. Thus, each Southeast Asian language family evolved out of a single parent language spoken in a specific place at a specific time.

For each family, the questions concern the location of the original homelands and how these languages attained their present distribution.

Dispersal. Within recorded history, language spread often accompanies military or cultural dominance, but early expansion of Southeast Asian language families took place either in prehistory or at least in very early historical times. In these early times, the languages spread through forces perhaps less dramatic than military conquest but certainly as powerful.

Without question, some of the dispersal was the result of the migration of foraging hunter-gatherers. As Peter Bellwood, a prehistorian at Australian National University, notes, thirty to fifty thousand years ago seagoing foragers had already migrated eastward along the Malay archipelago to Sulawesi, New Guinea, Australia, New Ireland, and the Northern Solomons. These foragers were most likely the ancestors of the Aborigines of Australia and of many of the peoples of New Guinea. Undoubtedly, these foragers brought with them at least some of the Australian and Papuan language families. Much later, many of these peoples mixed with Austronesian speakers, adopting Austronesian languages while contributing their own genetic heritage to Melanesia.

Simple foraging only accounts for some of the language dispersal. Much more of it correlates with the development of agriculture in southwestern China in the last ten thousand years or so. At least four of the major language families of Southeast Asia—the Austroasiatic, Sino-Tibetan, Hmong-Mien, and Tai-Kadai language families—are still found in this area, with clear evidence that the precursors of the Austronesian people also came from this area. The archaeological record, supported by botanical and environmental evidence, shows that, under the population pressures caused by the agricultural revolution, there was a major movement of peoples outward from this region of southwestern China. Agriculture gave the first farmers an advantage over gatherers and foragers. Because of the regular food supply, the population increased rapidly; as a consequence of the rapid population explosion, there was a rapid growth in the need for land suitable for growing crops. As these peoples migrated, their languages moved with them—a movement accounting for much of the early dispersal of Southeast Asian languages into largely uninhabited regions.

In southwestern China, the archaeological record shows agriculture developed in two culturally related and geographically contiguous areas. Foxtail millet was domesticated in the basin of the Yellow River about eight thousand years ago, while rice was domesticated in the Yangzi basin. The domestication of these and other plants led to the systematic clearance of land and seasonal planting of crops, rapidly changing the way people lived. Scarcely three thousand years later, the rice-cultivating peoples were already living along the east coast of China and in northern Vietnam and Thailand.

Even among the farmers, however, there is a distinction between those practicing swidden, or slash-and-burn agriculture, and those practicing wet rice irrigation. Swidden agriculture basically involves clearing the land by cutting down and burning the vegetation. Then, when the land's fertility is depleted, the farmers move on to another plot of land, where they repeat the process. These seminomadic agriculturists certainly had an advantage over simple foragers.

Those practicing wet rice irrigation need a more sophisticated, more structured social organization, but the techniques do provide bigger and better crops. The population is no longer inherently nomadic, and thus, in the long run, the peoples using wet rice irrigation had an enormous advantage not only over their foraging neighbors but also over those who practiced slash-and-burn agriculture.

The implications for language spread are clear. Earlier foragers have been replaced by slash-and-burn agriculturists, with the latter being replaced at least in the lowlands by those practicing wet rice irrigation.

Austroasiatic. Austroasiatic speakers are among the very earliest inhabitants of Southeast Asia, having spread throughout the region before the other major language families. The earliest homeland, according to Gerard Diffloth, a leading expert on Austroasiatic languages, places the homeland of the Austroasiatic speakers in the Burmese-Yunnan border area, perhaps in the Salween basin, but it is possible that an even earlier homeland was located further back in China.

The major division within the Austroasiatic languages is between the Munda languages of India and the Mon-Khmer languages (Cambodian, or Khmer; Vietnamese; Mon; and so forth) of mainland Southeast Asia. This split of Austroasiatic into Munda and Mon-Khmer occurred early in the prehistory of the region.

Sino-Tibetan. Sino-Tibetan is an ethnic designation; "Sino" refers to the Chinese component of the family, while "Tibeto" refers to the Tibeto-Burman component—Tibetan, Burmese, and so forth. The oldest split in Sino-Tibetan languages is between Sinitic (the various Chinese dialects) and the Tibeto-Burman languages.

The Sino-Tibetan languages appeared on the scene after the Austroasiatic languages, as is often evident from the existence of small pockets of Austroasiatic speakers scattered among speakers of Sino-Tibetan languages. Within the last two thousand years, the Chinese speakers, particularly Han speakers, have come to dominate southern China.

Tai-Kadai. The Tai-Kadai language family includes Thai, Lao, Shan, and speakers of languages related to Thai. These languages are found from southern China to the northern half of the Malay Peninsula.

The historical evidence, the current distribution, and the linguistic evidence show that the Tai-Kadai speakers came down in almost a straight line from southern China in recent history, expanding continuously into areas where there was land suitable for wet rice irrigation. The modern descendants of this expansionary movement are the Thai, the Lao, and the Shan (of Burma), as well as various peoples on the island of Hainan and in Vietnam.

There is also evidence that there was intimate early contact between Tai-Kadai speakers and speakers of what was to become the Austronesian languages in southeastern China. Both the Tai-Kadai and the Austronesian languages show a residue of this contact in the presence of common words for "moon," "eat," "flower," and "louse."

Hmong-Mien. Hmong-Mien, like Sino-Tibetan, is an ethnic designation; in the older literature, this family is referred to as Miao-Yao, the Chinese names for these peoples.

The Hmong and Mien are scattered in small pockets over much of southern China (Hunan, Guangxi, and Yunnan provinces). Only in the past several centuries have the Hmong and Mien come into the northern part of Southeast Asia.

Austronesian. The Austronesian languages are the languages for which scholars have the most complete and most reliable picture of origin and subsequent spread. Here, the archaeological and the linguistic record are in essential agreement. The precursors of the Austronesian peoples began their journey in southeastern China about eight to ten thousand years ago. These speakers left the mainland for Formosa (Taiwan) about six thousand years ago, beginning their great sojourn that would take them throughout the Pacific, all the way from Easter Island in the east to Madagascar in the west.

The Austronesian family tree not only presents a graphical representation of the historical development of the Austronesian languages but also correlates quite

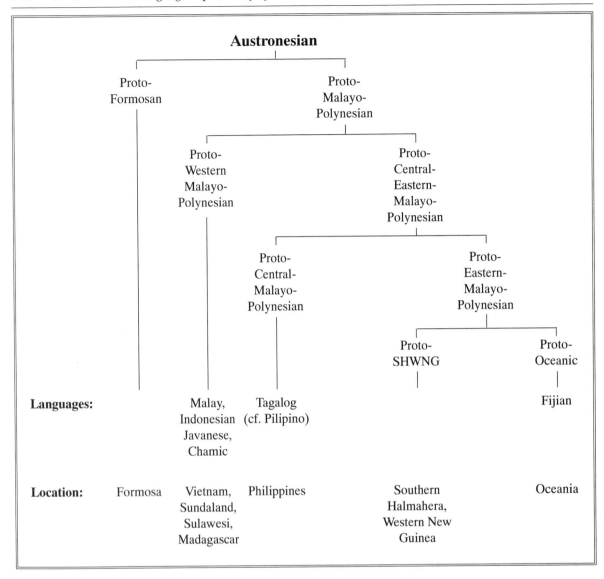

Austronesian

Proto-Formosan

Proto-Malayo-Polynesian

Proto-Western Malayo-Polynesian

Proto-Central-Eastern-Malayo-Polynesian

Proto-Central-Malayo-Polynesian

Proto-Eastern-Malayo-Polynesian

Proto-SHWNG

Proto-Oceanic

Fijian

Languages: Malay, Indonesian Javanese, Chamic — Tagalog (cf. Pilipino)

Location: Formosa — Vietnam, Sundaland, Sulawesi, Madagascar — Philippines — Southern Halmahera, Western New Guinea — Oceania

well with the migration of the Austronesian peoples through the islands of the Pacific and then back to the mainland. Although the ancestors of the Austronesians came from eastern China, the starting point for Austronesian proper is Formosa. From Formosa, some of the Austronesians branched off, moving down into the Philippines. From the Philippines, they split into two groups. Some moved into western Malayo-Polynesia; these seafarers moved into Sulawesi, Sundaland, Indonesia, Malaysia, and then as far west as Madagascar and back as far north as Vietnam. The other group moved from the Philippines into the rest of the Pacific, including western New Guinea, Fiji, Samoa, Hawaii, and Easter Island.

Papuan Languages of New Guinea. The Papuan peoples, although now intermixed with Austronesian peoples, appear to have arrived in New Guinea as part of an early migration of foragers from the mainland, as noted earlier. The Papuan people did not, however, remain foragers. The archaeological record makes it clear that agriculture was independently developed in this area about six thousand years ago, well before the Austronesian speakers arrived on the scene. The relative prosperity accompanying the discovery of agriculture undoubtedly helped make New Guinea perhaps the most linguistically diverse area on earth, with its seven hundred or so languages spoken in a relatively small area.

Recent History. Once the stage shifts from prehistory to historical times and the growth of nations and their armies, much of the dispersal has certainly come about through military conquest, and still more has come through cultural domination. These developments, however, belong to the histories of specific languages, of individual countries, and of the region was a whole.—*Graham Thurgood*

SUGGESTED READINGS: • Bellwood, Peter. "The Austronesian Dispersal and the Origin of Languages." *Scientific American* 265 (1991): 88-93. • Bellwood, Peter. "Southeast Asia Before History." In *From Early Times to c. 1800*. Vol. 1 in *The Cambridge History of Southeast Asia*, edited by Nicholas Tarling. Cambridge, England: Cambridge University Press, 1992. • Blust, Robert. "Austronesian Etymologies." *Oceanic Linguistics* 19 (1980): 1-2. • Burling, Robbins. *Hill Farms and Padi Fields: Life in Mainland Southeast Asia*. Englewood Cliffs, N.J.: Prentice-Hall, 1965.

Southeast Asian music and dance: Filipino Americans and political refugees and immigrants from Cambodia, Laos, and Vietnam constitute the bulk of Southeast Asians in the United States. Their music and dance forms show great vitality on the West Coast, on the Gulf Coast (Vietnamese), in Hawaii and Alaska (Filipinos) and in numerous American cities. The extent of continuity of the performing-arts traditions of a people is usually related to the amount of time that has passed since their arrival and settlement as well as the size of the local community. Southeast Asian music and dance function largely as entertainment or expressions of ethnic identity.

Filipino. Of the traditional Filipino music, the *rondalla* (string orchestra) is most commonly heard at weddings, reunions, religious holidays, Commonwealth Day (November 15), and Rizal Day (December 30). Its various sizes of lutes and fiddles are reminders of the Spanish influence in the Philippines. Ballroom dances that modify and paraphrase the steps of the waltz, polka, mazurka, *paso doble*, and quadrille are accompanied by the *rondalla*. Wind bands were established as dance bands during World War II (1939-1945), but while few wind bands remained active, *rondalla* ensembles are heard in Filipino communities in California, Texas, and Hawaii.

The folk-song style of Spanish influence is popular among Filipino Americans and is accompanied by the Spanish guitar. There is a large following of Filipino popular music, including jazz, rock, and beat, through radio, television, recordings, and videos imported and sold locally in stores in Filipino neighborhoods. Tagalog film songs and *kundiman* (love songs) reinforce not only the music but also the language. Touring choirs and concert tours by singers such as Freddie Aguilar and Jun Polistico are well supported by Filipino communities, and "pinoy rock" is preferred by younger immigrant and American-born Filipinos.

The indigenous Southeast Asian bamboo flutes, xylophones, and flat and knobbed bronze gongs are

A mixed Filipino chorus performs songs native to the Philippines. (Martin A. Hutner)

rarely heard in the United States. The Kalilang Ensemble of San Francisco performs *kulintang* (gong ensemble) music from the Maranao and Magindanao cultures, and several universities provide *kulintang* instruction, including the University of Hawaii and the University of Washington, Seattle. In their search for a Filipino American identity, some young people have produced neotraditional styles that stem from indigenous Southeast Asian and Islamic music and dance forms. Bamboo pole dances such as *tinikling* are popular and are modeled after those of touring groups such as the Bayanihan Dance Company.

Khmer/Cambodian. Because many highly trained musicians and dancers were murdered during the Pol Pot regime of the late 1970's, there are few Khmer artists to carry on the court-classical forms of Cambodia in the United States. The *pinn peat* (court orches-

tra) of wooden xylophones and gongs has been modified to include flutes, oboes, fiddles, and zithers of the *mahori* (folk ensemble). The *phleng kar* (wedding music) is heard at weekly ceremonies in Cambodian communities, featuring the spike fiddle, plucked lute, small oboe, and drums. Vocal music is continued by Buddhist monks who chant the Pali scripture in temples and by congregational singing of Khmer devotional poetry.

In comparison to the music, the court traditions are well preserved. Associations such as the Cambodian American Heritage in Maryland and the Cambodian Studies Center in Washington offer classes in the traditional choreographic arts. At the Cambodian New Year, classical dance dramas such as the *Ramayana* story are frequently performed by dancers, musicians, and chorus. Folk dances are also being maintained, and couple

Members of the Samahan Philippine Dance Company perform the Paypay de Manila. (Samahan Philippine Dance Company)

Cambodian American girls rehearse native Cambodian dance at a Los Angeles, California, studio. (Claire Rydell)

dances featuring the rhythmic tapping of coconut shells are especially popular at dance concerts.

Khmer rock music is popular in the United States as it was in Cambodia. Earlier styles that blend Latin American rhythms such as the bolero, the cha-cha, and the tango with traditional Khmer melodies are popular with older generations, while Cambodian American youths listen and dance to rock ensembles that may blend elements of rap with traditional rhythms and that use Khmer language to convey the sentiments of love, life, and resettlement. The *roam vung* and *saravann* are popular dances accompanied by the music of Khmer rock bands.

Lao. Two organized troupes of Lao classical musicians and dancers, patterned after the court traditions at Cambodia and Thailand, were resettled in Nashville, Tennessee, and Des Moines, Iowa. Despite supportive grants, neither is active today. Lao music genres that survive include Buddhist chants, the *basi* or *soukhouan* ritual of good wishes, *khene* (mouth organ) playing, repartee singing called *khap* or *lam* that is accompanied by *khene*, and Lao rock music.

The Lao New Year brings together the largest gathering of traditional and contemporary musicians. Excerpts from the *Ramayana* story are presented through a combination of court and folk dances, accompanied by the *pi phat* orchestra of xylophones, gongs, flute, and drum. The national instrument of Laos is the free-

Cambodian musician plays a traditional stringed instrument at a Buddhist ceremony in Stockton, California. (Eric Crystal)

reed bamboo *khene*, which is used during solo repertoires and serves as accompaniment for *mohlam* (expert) singers. Memorized and improvised verses of romantic subjects, or philosophical and humorous comments on current events, are performed by skilled singers in melodic contours that resemble exaggerated speech tones. Lao rock bands play popularized renditions of traditional styles and music for the *lamvong*, a dance in circle formation for couples.

The Hmong constitute the largest population of the tribal groups of upland Laos. Their sung poetry is heard in the United States, as are solo instruments such as *geng* (free-reed mouth organ), *nja* (jew's harp), and *ja* (side-blown bamboo free reed). The characteristic movements of the male *geng* player in performing funeral music is unique among traditions that blend dance and music. Hmong rock bands are prominent at dances and social gatherings.

Vietnamese. Although most Vietnamese refugees and immigrants have become well integrated into American society, their long-established forms of traditional music show great vitality throughout the United States. Folk or entertainment songs called *dan ca* were once peasants' songs; the vernacular texts and simple melodies are easily accessible to all. *Nhac tai tu*, or instrumental and vocal entertainment music, survives largely through house concerts that feature *dan tranh* (zither), *dan bau* (monochord), *dan ty ba* (pear-shaped lute), and *dan nguyet* (moon-shaped lute). The *dan tranh* is the most popular classical instrument for study or listening. While *chau van* (shamanist chanting and trance dancing) are infrequently found in several West Coast temples and in Texas, the Buddhist *sutra* is commonly chanted in about sixty Vietnamese temples.

Featured at the Tet festivals of the Vietnamese New Year is the *cai luong* of southern Vietnam. This form of modernized musical theater enjoys great popularity, partly because its many plots derive not only from

Vietnamese dancers at a lunar New Year celebration in Iowa. (James L. Shaffer)

Vietnamese legends and history but also from contemporary politics and religious beliefs. Instrumental music resembling either traditional *nhac tai tu* or a Western ensemble of piano, traps, bass, and organ, as well as singing and dancing are key to *cai luong* theater, as is the contemporary staging that includes scenery, lighting, and state-of-the-art sound amplification. Central to *cai luong* is a favorite song of Vietnamese immigrants, "Vong Co," (longing for the past); to many, "Vong Co" is *cai luong*. "Vong Co" is subject to extensive improvisation on the structural pitches of an original melody that was formulated around 1919, so that singers have great freedom of expression as several string instruments provide a heterophonic accompaniment. *Cai luong* has been widely disseminated on recordings and radio. The youngest generation favors "new wave" Vietnamese rock called *tan nhac*, although they are exposed to *cai luong* and other traditional genres at many family and community occasions.—*Patricia Shehan Campbell*

Suggested Readings: • Catlin, Amy. *Music of the Hmong: Singing Voices and Talking Reeds*. Providence, R.I.: Center for Hmong Lore, Museum of Natural History, 1981. • Manuel, Peter. *Popular Musics of the Non-Western World*. New York: Oxford University Press, 1988. • Miller, Terry E. *The Survival of Lao Traditional Music in America: Selected Reports in Ethnomusicology*. Vol. 6. Los Angeles: University of California Press, 1985. • Molina, A. J. *Music of the Philippines*. Manila: The Philippine Press, 1967. • Nguyen, Thuyet Phong, and Patricia Shehan Campbell. *From Rice Paddies and Temple Yards: Traditional Music of Vietnam*. Danbury, Conn.: World Music Press, 1990. • Sam, Sam-Ang, and Patricia Shehan Campbell. *Silent Temples, Songful Hearts: Traditional Music of Cambodia*. Danbury, Conn.: World Music Press, 1991.

Southeast Asian religions in the United States: Historical and social factors have had important impacts on the religious life of Southeast Asians who have relocated to the United States. These factors bear upon whether the newcomers maintain their religious traditions and pass them on to their descendants.

Early Worship and Influences in Southeast Asia. The majority of Southeast Asians today claim adherence to religions first developed in South or East Asia or in the Middle East. Hinduism, Buddhism, and Confucianism all originated in other parts of Asia, but each reached Southeast Asia more than a thousand years ago. Islam became firmly established in Southeast Asia only about seven centuries ago; however, it is now the state religion of two Southeast Asian nations and is embraced by more than 80 percent of the population in a third. Christianity is an even more recent introduction, yet is has become the dominant religion in one Southeast Asian country and is embraced by sizable minorities in several others. Prior to the widespread adoption of these religions, the inhabitants of Southeast Asia practiced varieties of animistic religions. These local faiths involved belief in nature spirits and sometimes ancestor worship. Shamans usually served as intermediaries between the natural and supernatural worlds. Unlike organized "book" religions such as Islam and Christianity, animist religions generally have no codified texts. Animist beliefs are usually passed down from generation to generation in the form of oral lore. As religious belief in Southeast Asia is often highly syncretic, elements of animism continue to find their way into religious observances throughout the region. Belief in spirits is widespread, and few Southeast Asians would find the contradiction between spirit worship and their adherence to one of the aforementioned religions problematic. As a result, one often encounters significant variation between "popular" and "doctrinal" religion in Southeast Asia. Animist religions per se, however, are increasingly rare. Their practice is usually confined to remote hill tribes or other isolated peoples.

Filipinos and Catholicism. The first Southeast Asians to arrive in the United States in significant numbers were Filipinos. Shortly before the beginning of the twentieth century, many Filipinos were contracted to work on sugarcane plantations in the Hawaiian Islands. As a result of hundreds of years of Spanish colonial domination in their own country, the Filipinos were largely Catholic. These temporary laborers found opportunities for worship in churches built near or on the plantations. Filipinos form the largest Southeast Asian group in the United States, and contemporary immigrants include large numbers of professionals. Like their forebears, these immigrants are usually Catholics, though there are significant Muslim minorities in the southern Philippines.

Theravada and Mahayana Buddhism. With the Immigration and Nationality Act of 1965 came the abolishment of national-origins quotas in the United States. As a result, increasing numbers of immigrants from other parts of Southeast Asia began settling in the United States. Many of the new arrivals were Theravada Buddhists. Some of these, such as the Thais, established Buddhist temples where monks and nuns

Catholic priests participate in a Vietnamese Lunar New Year celebration in Iowa. (James L. Shaffer)

could minister to the spiritual needs of adherents of that religion. With the fall of Saigon in 1975, a large number of Vietnamese refugees began relocating to the United States. About half of the refugees that arrived that first year were Mahayana Buddhists. They, too, established temples. The remaining half were Catholic, though Catholicism is embraced by only about 10 percent of the Vietnamese population. To serve these newcomers and the many other Vietnamese who have followed as part of the Orderly Departure Program, some churches in the United States have begun to offer special services in the Vietnamese language.

In addition to the influx of Vietnamese, displaced persons from Laos also began arriving in the United States in the late 1970's. These included Laotian refugees as well as hill-tribe peoples such as the Hmong and Mien. While the Laotians themselves were primarily Theravada Buddhists, the hill-tribes were mostly animists. A later group of refugees to reach the United States were Cambodians. Like their neighbors in Thailand, Myanmar, and Laos, Cambodians are primarily Theravada Buddhists.

Adapting to the New Land. As part of their adaptation to life in the United States, some immigrants and refugees have abandoned their traditional faiths and converted to Christianity. For those who do not convert, whether they are allowed to practice their traditional religions openly may depend upon circumstances in the communities in which they settle. In many parts of the United States, Southeast Asians and Asian Americans have been targets of acts of racial hostility. Attacks are sometimes leveled against their places of worship. An example is the repeated bombing of a Laotian Buddhist temple that occurred in Rockford, Illinois, in 1984. For refugees who are not part of organized religions, maintaining their religious traditions often poses special challenges. Some refugees report that they feel embarrassed about performing their ancestral rites in their new surroundings and that they do not want to risk disturbing their neighbors with the outdoor chanting and drumming that often accompanies worship. The establishment of cultural centers where refugees can go to worship with others who share their beliefs may contribute to the maintenance of their religions as well as their cultural identity. At the same time, however, many refugees wonder whether it is even possible to solicit the aid of spirits in their new land. As one young Hmong man observed, "In Laos we believed there were spirits in the mountains. Here, maybe the American Indians believe in spirits, but those (pointing in the direction of the nearby Laguna range) are *their* mountains, not ours."—*Anne Schiller*

SUGGESTED READINGS: • Hall, Daniel George Edward. *A History of South East Asia*. New York: St. Martin's Press, 1961. • Lemoine, Jacques. "Shamanism in the Context of Hmong Resettlement." In *The Hmong in Transition*, edited by Glenn Hendricks, Bruce Downing, and Amos Deinard. Staten Island, New York: Center for Migration Studies of New York, 1986. • Scott, George, Jr. "A New Year in a New Land: Religious Change Among the Lao Hmong Refugees in San Diego." In *The Hmong in the West: Observations and Reports*, edited by Bruce Downing, Bruce Olney, and Douglas Olney. Minneapolis: Center for Urban and Regional Affairs, University of Minnesota, 1982. Seigel, Taggart. *Blue Collar and Buddha*. San Francisco: CrossCurrent Media, 1987. Film. • Swearer, Donald. *Buddhism and Society in Southeast Asia*. Chambersburg, Pa.: Anima, 1981. • Takaki, Ronald. *Strangers from a Different Shore: A History of Asian Americans*. Boston: Little, Brown, 1989. • Velazquez, Elaine. *Moving Mountains: The Story of the Yiu Mien*. New York: Filmmakers Library, 1989. Film.

Southeast Asian return to homeland movements: When people are forced to flee from their homeland, they typically do so with the idea that they will return one day. Refugees in particular flee with the idea that they will return when political conditions change back to what they were "before." Often, this longing for return results in social movements that are taken advantage of by local refugee leaders or even foreign governments. The strength of these movements depends on a number of conditions encountered during exile, such as the harshness of the circumstances, the

Scores of Cambodian civilians and soldiers pass through Klong Had village, in neighboring Thailand, in 1979 to escape Vietnamese troops, who invaded Cambodia in late 1978. Many refugees remained in camps scattered along the Thai-Cambodian border until peace negotiations in the early 1990's enabled them to return home. (AP/Wide World Photos)

physical proximity to the home country, the ability to socialize refugee children (and perhaps grandchildren) into a desire to return, and the perceived chance for improvement in the conditions that precipitated flight in the first place.

In the case of the Cambodian, Vietnamese, and Laotian refugees in the United States and Southeast Asia, different conditions have meant that return to homeland movements have had different effects. For example, in the case of large numbers of Cambodian refugees living on the Thai-Cambodian border from 1980 to 1992, the harsh conditions, their isolation from the Thai people, and the United Nations-brokered peace of 1991-1992 has meant that large numbers have returned to Cambodia. By contrast, Cambodians living in the United States who are far from the Cambodian border and who live in more secure circumstances have not returned to their homeland even though older Cambodians may continue to express a desire to do so "when conditions improve."

In contrast, the relative stability of the Communist Vietnamese government and the absence of refugee camps on Vietnamese land borders have meant that Vietnamese refugees have not fulfilled their desire to return to their homeland permanently. Furthermore, large numbers of Vietnamese children have been socialized into the societies of the United States and other host societies and may not wish to return permanently. As a result of the relaxation of travel restrictions in the late 1980's and early 1990's, however, Vietnamese from the United States did begin to return as tourists to visit relatives.

Return to homeland movements among the Hmong in the United States have been powerful, although relatively ineffective. In the late 1980's, the Hmong resistance group Neo Hom sold airplane tickets redeemable upon the fall of the Communist government to homesick Hmong refugees as a fund-raising gimmick. As with the Vietnamese, however, it can be expected that such social movements will weaken as a generation of Hmong youth socialized by American schools becomes older.

Southern California Retail Produce Workers Union (SCRPWU): All-Nisei labor association established in Los Angeles in 1937 to champion the interests of Nisei retail produce workers among not only white labor unions but also Issei produce workers and operators. Its formation followed the unsuccessful attempt by a white-dominated union to recruit Nisei into its ranks. Already suspicious of white organized labor

to begin with, Nisei workers hoped instead to bridge the gap between Nisei and Issei and to press for Japanese ethnic solidarity in the industry. The new union was conceived with this in mind.

The SCRPWU was well received from the start, filling up its membership roll with a thousand members in the space of a week and earning recognition from the Retail Market Operators' Association, composed of Issei, not long after that. By 1938, this atmosphere of acceptance had begun to deteriorate, however, and in the face of internal disputes support by SCRPWU members for their union faded in the years following. The union was eventually rechartered as a member of the Fruit and Vegetable Store Employees (Japanese) Union but was dissolved in the wake of the Japanese internment of World War II.

Southern Mariana Islanders. *See* Guamanians

Spanish-American-Philippine War (1898-1902): What became a two-stage war for the United States began as a poorly managed diplomatic crisis with Spain over its rule in Cuba. Though the causes of the Spanish-American War (1898) were related to Cuba, some people in the American government saw an opportunity to detach the Philippines from the Spanish Empire and acquire a base of operations for American power, commercial interests, and influence in Asia. Even before hostilities began, Commodore George Dewey and the Asiatic Squadron of the U.S. Navy were ordered to prepare for action against the Spanish in the Philippines. In attacking the Spanish fleet in Manila Bay on May 1, 1898, Dewey put the United States on a collision course with the aspiration of many Filipinos.

Prewar Situation in the Philippines. Ever since the Spanish had acquired the Philippines in the 1500's, the Filipinos had launched numerous sporadic rebellions against Spanish rule. One such movement came from a militant secret organization called the Katipunan (meaning the "most respected and highest sons of the people"), which called for the end to Spanish rule in favor of an independent Filipino republic without class distinctions. In August, 1896, the Katipunan began an armed revolt. A young schoolteacher from a middle-class family, Emilio Aguinaldo, led Katipunan forces against the Spanish in Cavite Province and distinguished himself as a leader. In March, 1897, an assembly of revolutionaries gathered, proclaimed the Philippines a republic, and chose Aguinaldo as president. Eventually the war became a stalemate, and an armistice was signed in 1897. The Spanish agreed to insti-

Emilio Aguinaldo arrives in Malolos, the Philippines, the capital of the newly proclaimed First Philippine Republic, for his inauguration as president of the republic. (Library of Congress)

tute reforms and pay Aguinaldo for surrendered weapons and his departure from the islands. Intending to wait and see if the Spanish kept their promises, Aguinaldo went into exile in Hong Kong.

U.S. Intervention. Having received his orders, Dewey took his squadron to Hong Kong to get sup-

plies and information about the situation on the Philippines. There Aguinaldo met with Dewey and informed him of troops in the islands that could assist American operations. In these prewar discussions Aguinaldo got the impression that the United States and Dewey supported independence for the Philippines. Dewey accepted the concept that Aguinaldo and his movement might be useful if and when war came. Yet when the war did begin Dewey hurriedly left Hong Kong for Manila without Aguinaldo. The Americans easily defeated the Spanish fleet in Manila Bay, and the Spanish governor-general offered to surrender the colony at Dewey's convenience. Dewey's problem was that there were more than fifteen thousand Spanish soldiers in the islands. Dewey had no land forces to effect a smooth surrender, to guard Spanish prisoners, and to assure civil law and order after the removal of Spanish authorities. Moreover he had no idea about what the U.S. government's reaction to his victory would be or the ultimate resolution of the status of the Philippines. Considering these questions, Dewey sent a ship to Hong Kong to retrieve Aguinaldo and a dozen other revolutionaries and return them to the islands. Subsequently Aguinaldo, with Dewey's encouragement and material support, established himself at Cavite and organized a Filipino army while attacking outlying Spanish forces and pushing them into Manila. Meanwhile Dewey requested additional American soldiers so that he could assume complete control of the islands. It is unclear as to what both men thought of the other and what they perceived to be the relationship between the Katipunan independence movement and the United States. Aguinaldo always maintained that he had received assurances that by helping the United States the Filipinos would be advancing their cause toward independence. Dewey and other American commanders maintained that they did not think that the Filipinos had any real plans for independence and that Aguinaldo was not of much use to the Filipinos or the United States. Nevertheless, after U.S. Army forces arrived, Dewey accepted the Spanish formal surrender on August 13, 1898.

The United States Colonizes the Philippines. Having been defeated in Cuba and the Philippines, Spain sued for peace and in December, 1898, signed a peace treaty giving the United States the Philippines, Puerto Rico, and Guam. The decision of the McKinley Administration to take the Philippines under the American wing and to "civilize" them was unacceptable to the Filipino independence movement, and tensions soon developed between Aguinaldo and his former American allies and friends.

Filipino Resistance. In February, 1899, after the American Congress had ratified the imperialistic peace treaty, Aguinaldo and his followers began a second struggle for independence—this time against the United States. Aguinaldo revived the republic pro-

claimed in 1897, established his capital at Malolos, Bulacan Province, and called a constituent assembly that produced a written constitution for the islands in 1899. American commanders labeled Aguinaldo's movement an "insurrection" and began to suppress the revolutionaries.

The Filipino War. Hostilities raged in the Philippines from 1899 to 1902 between Aguinaldo's poorly equipped and largely citizen army and the forces of the United States. Facing superior American strength Aguinaldo and his army soon turned to guerrilla warfare tactics. In response to the complicated situation American commanders ordered reinforcements, and eventually seventy thousand American soldiers were directly involved in suppressing the insurrection. In various places American commanders sought to prevent the civilians from assisting the guerrillas by moving the former into what amounted to concentration camps. It became common for American troops to burn villages and crops in retaliation for guerrilla activities and ambushes. General Jacob F. Smith, later court-martialed for his severe prosecution of the war, ordered his troops on Samar to "[k]ill and burn, kill and burn, and the more you burn, the more you please me. This is no time to take prisoners." Asked if this order applied to children, the general replied, "Kill everything over ten."

Aguinaldo was captured in March, 1901, and all but sporadic fighting ended by 1902. The effort to subdue the Filipinos and give them the blessings of American democracy cost the United States five thousand soldiers killed and $160 million (more than the entire Spanish-American War). The Filipinos paid an even higher price in suffering, as estimated by one American general, perhaps as many as one million casualties brought on by battle, the policy of concentration camps, and diseases that raged through devastated districts.

Eventually the islands were "pacified," and the "American" phase of their history began creating numerous shared historical experiences, both positive and negative, between the citizens of both nations. The expense and horror of the suppression campaign helped to redirect the development of American foreign policy away from further American imperialism.—*P. Scott Corbett*

SUGGESTED READINGS: • Graff, Henry F. *American Imperialism and the Philippine Insurrection.* Boston: Little, Brown, 1969. • Grunder, Garel A., and William E. Livezey. *The Philippines and the United States.* Norman: University of Oklahoma Press, 1951. • Karnow, Stanley. *In Our Image: America's Empire in the*

Philippines. New York: Random House, 1989. • Linn, Brian McAllister. *The U.S. Army and Counterinsurgency in the Philippine War, 1899-1902.* Chapel Hill: University of North Carolina Press, 1989. • Miller, Stuart C. *"Benevolent Assimilation": The American Conquest of the Philippines, 1899-1903.* New Haven, Conn.: Yale University Press, 1982.

Spanish policies in the Philippines: Spain's policies in the Philippines were influenced for more than three hundred years by two factors: Spain's colonial experiences in Mexico and South America and by the Catholic church.

Ferdinand Magellan "discovered" the Philippines in 1521 (he was killed in Cebu by Lapulapu, a Filipino chief), and Spain officially took possession of that nation in 1573, when Manila was subdued. Spanish rule was ended in 1898 when U.S. admiral George Dewey defeated the Spanish armada in Manila Bay. Spain later ceded the Philippines to the United States over the objections of nationalist Filipinos, who sought independence. An independent Philippine government was finally established in 1946.

Filipino leaders had protested and fought against Spanish domination and policies since Magellan first landed on Cebu. Because of superior weaponry and lack of coordinated leadership by Filipinos, however, Spain's imprint on the Philippines continues to be lasting.

There were a number of policies that changed the future of that nation of more than seven thousand islands. Probably among the most important policies were converting the nation to Catholicism and the influence of the Catholic church in governing the Philippines. There was no separation of church and state in Spanish colonial policies. Since the Philippines did not have the riches of Mexico or other countries, Spain's main goals in the Philippines were twofold: to thwart the then-growing influence of Portugal in Asia and to spread Catholicism. Friars and Jesuits were not only representatives of the church but also agents of the Spanish king. Through the early 1990's roughly 85 percent of the population was Catholic.

In terms of colonial government, the Philippines was administered by the Council of the Indies, and all Spanish officials were appointed by the king of Spain. Government was centralized with the governor-general representing the Spanish king. Local and provincial government was headed by the "gobernadorcillo" (mayor).

There were two policies that Filipinos resented. One

was forced labor, which ordered Filipinos to work for the church and state to construct roads, bridges, and ships, sometimes splitting families and without pay. The other was the *encomienda*, in which the Spanish government, to reward Spaniards who had helped in the conquest and settlement of the Philippines, confiscated land and gave it to these loyal subjects. Lands were given to the church, private individuals, and the king.

Because the Philippines did not have the natural resources or gold of Spain's other colonies, Spanish officials introduced new crops for export: tobacco and sugarcane, which continue to play a role in the nation's economy. The Philippines played a key role in what was known as "the galleon trade," in which goods were imported from China and then shipped (by galleons) to Mexico. Filipino seamen worked in these ships, and some remained in Mexico and eventually made their way to the United States, becoming the first Asians to settle in North America.

Another policy involved education and language. Spanish (and Catholic) officials did not teach the Spanish language to Filipinos. Only later, when wealthy Filipino families could afford to send their sons to Europe for schooling, did they learn Spanish. Filipinos did have their own alphabet and language before conquest, but the Spaniards eliminated the written language. Spanish officials did create several colleges and universities, although the institutions were primarily to serve Spanish students.

Speer, William (Apr. 24, 1822, New Alexandria, Pa.—1904): Missionary. At a time of anti-Chinese riots and persecution, Speer served as an influential advocate for Chinese American concerns. He grew up in western Pennsylvania and was graduated from Kenyon College in 1840. He studied medicine under his father for three years, after which he studied at the Allegheny Seminary, receiving his license to preach on April 21, 1846.

The Reverend Speer then served as a missionary under the Presbyterian Board of Missions in Canton, China, from 1846 to 1850. He mastered the Cantonese dialect, only to see his mission service cut short because of poor health. He worked as a pastor in western Pennsylvania for the next two years. During this stint, the Presbytery of San Francisco sent a formal request to the board, drawing attention to the growing number of Chinese immigrants in the Bay Area. The board then asked Speer to open a mission in San Francisco, and he began his work in November, 1852. Knowing Cantonese and being sensitive to Chinese culture, he was admirably suited and qualified for this first effort to evangelize the Chinese in America.

Being a trained physician, Speer opened a dispensary in conjunction with the mission. Preaching services began in February, 1853, and on November 6 of that same year, the first Chinese church in America was established. It consisted of four charter members, all of whom had been communicants of a Presbyterian church in Hong Kong. Speer worked as the editor of *The Oriental* newspaper during this time, addressing the social issues pertaining to the Chinese immigrants and the anti-Chinese racist assaults. He was influential in the repeal of the California laws of 1854-1855 that excluded Chinese workers from the mines. His diversified ministry and work continued until 1856, when he was forced again to retire because of ill health. Yet his efforts provided the strong foundation that enabled other pioneers in mission work to succeed. In 1859, under his successor, A. W. Loomis, the first "public" school for the Chinese was opened.

Speer retired to itinerant evangelistic efforts in Wisconsin and Minnesota and served the presbytery as the corresponding secretary in the Department of Christian Education. He wrote *China and the United States* in 1870. During his career, he received the honorary Doctor of Divinity degree from Central College, Kentucky, and the honorary Doctor of Laws degree from Washington and Jefferson College.

The Presbyterian church was the first Protestant denomination to reach out to the Chinese in the United States in the last half of the nineteenth century. Speer was the first mission worker and pastor to serve the Chinese with compassion and influence.

Spivak, Gayatri Chakravorty (Gayatri Chakravorty; b. Feb. 24, 1942, Calcutta, West Bengal, India): Scholar, writer, and translator. Born into a Bengali Brahmin family, Chakravorty received her early education in a Bengali school in Calcutta and went on to take her B.A. degree at Calcutta University (1959). She came to the United States in 1961 to pursue her graduate studies and received her M.A. (1962) and Ph.D. (1967) degrees in English and comparative literature from Cornell University. In 1966, she became a permanent resident of the United States. She acquired the last name "Spivak" by marrying an American.

Starting her teaching career in 1965 at the University of Iowa, Spivak taught at the University of Texas, Austin, before moving to the University of Pittsburgh as Andrew W. Mellon Professor of English. In 1987, she was a visiting professor at the Centre for Historical Studies at Jawaharlal Nehru University, New Delhi, India.

Spivak's first critical book, *Myself Must I Remake: The Life and Poetry of W. B. Yeats*, was published in 1974, but it was her translation of the French philosopher Jacques Derrida's *De la Grammatology* (1967; *Of Grammatology*, 1976) that brought her into the limelight among literary critics in the United States. Her introduction, in which she expounded the historical context and the philosophical and critical import of Derrida's work, played a pivotal role in disseminating Derrida's ideas. In 1987, she published a collection of critical essays entitled *In Other Worlds: Essays in Cultural Politics*. In 1990, a collection of twelve interviews with Spivak, brought together and edited by Sarah Harasym, appeared under the title *The Post-Colonial Critic: Interviews, Strategies, Dialogues*.

Noted for her contributions to contemporary critical theory in the fields of Marxist, feminist, and deconstructive criticism and postcolonial studies, Spivak has been invited to many international conferences and symposia as a guest speaker and participant. As an advocate of international feminism, she has been instrumental in bringing the question of marginality to the forefront of critical discourse, and through her translations and deconstructive readings of the fiction of a modern Bengali woman writer, Mahasweta Devi, she has sought to integrate Third World women's literature with mainstream feminist criticism.

Spring Festival: Chinese (lunar) New Year. The Spring Festival is the most important traditional festival in the People's Republic of China as well as in overseas Chinese communities around the world.

Although China has had several changes in its calendar system for thousands of years, the lunar calendar remains in use today, especially in rural areas. After the Chinese Revolution of 1911, led by Sun Yat-sen, the nationalist government of China promoted the use of the Gregorian calendar and encouraged the celebration of the Western New Year. To distinguish the New Year based on the Gregorian calendar from the one based on the lunar calendar, the Chinese started calling the latter the "Spring Festival," because it usually falls at the beginning of spring. The Spring Festival is also called "Nian" or "Xin Nian." The Chinese character *Nien*, in ancient lexicons, means "a good harvest."

Chinese family associations, *tongs*, and benevolent associations in the United States continue to celebrate the lunar New Year. In some large Chinatowns, besides organizing many popular activities such as dragon

Early photograph of a Chinese mother and child dressed for the Chinese New Year observance. (Asian American Studies Library, University of California at Berkeley)

dances, lion dances, firecrackers, and parades, these organizations work out in their community a schedule to host Spring Festival banquets for their members. Some organizations must host their banquets in several Chinese restaurants at the same time in order to accommodate all their members. Representatives from other organizations may be invited depending on the size of membership. The representatives usually include officers from those organizations, and donations are given to the host organizations. The size of donations will reflect the number of representatives who will attend the banquet as well as the local practice in the community. Spring Festival banquets are usually held on the evenings of Friday, Saturday, and Sunday. It takes two to three months after the New Year's Day for these Chinese associations to complete hosting the Spring Festival banquets in their communities.

Square and Circle Club: Organization founded in 1924 in San Francisco, California, to serve the needs of those less fortunate. It is considered the oldest Chinese women's organization in the United States. The club's motto is derived from a Chinese couplet that when translated means, "In deeds be square, in knowledge be all-round."

Sri Lanka, Democratic Socialist Republic of: Formerly known as Ceylon, an independent island state in the Indian Ocean, off the southern tip of India. It is 25,332 square miles in area and contained a population of almost 17 million people in 1990. The administrative capital and largest city is Colombo (population of 615,000 in 1990); the legislative capital is Sri Jayewardenepura, in Kotte (population of 109,000). Sri Lanka, warm and humid throughout the year, is composed of coastal lowlands and a central highland. Except for the southwest portion, most of the island is dry, and farming depends primarily on irrigated agriculture.

The island is ruled by a parliamentary form of government headed by an elected president. It won its independence from Great Britain in 1948, when a British-style parliamentary system of government was instituted. In 1959 Sirimavo Bandaranaike of the Sri Lanka Freedom Party (SLFP) was elected the country's first prime minister. A French-style form of government, which recognized the president rather than the prime minister as chief of state, was established in 1978, and Junius Richard Jayewardene of the United National Party became the nation's first popularly elected president.

Sri Lanka's two major ethnic-linguistic groups are the Sinhalese, who constitute roughly three-fourths of the overall population and are mostly Theravada Buddhists, and the Tamils, who make up about 18 percent and are generally Hindus. Sinhalese and Tamil are the two official languages, the former being the majority language. In this multiethnic country, the relationship between the two groups began to deteriorate in 1948, when laws discriminating against the Tamils were passed. When peaceful resolution to the ethnic conflict failed, military confrontation between Tamil militants, who called for an independent Tamil state, and government forces killed hundreds of people and left thousands homeless. Muslims form a substantial minority. Sri Lanka was the center of Buddhist civilization in the third century B.C.E.

Although about 80 percent of the people live in rural areas, the national literacy rate is 87 percent, one of the highest rates among Asian nations.

The nation's agricultural economy is precariously dependent on the exports of tea, rubber, and coconut, all of which are subject to severe fluctuations in world

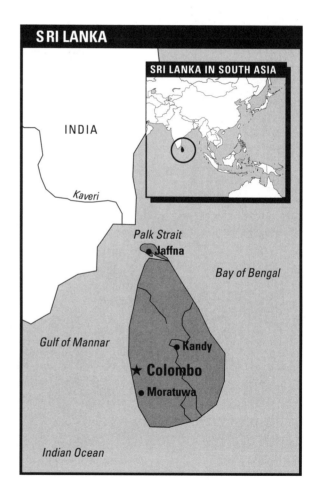

SRI LANKA

SRI LANKA IN SOUTH ASIA

INDIA

Kaveri

Palk Strait

Jaffna

Bay of Bengal

Gulf of Mannar

Kandy

★ Colombo

Moratuwa

Indian Ocean

market prices. Moreover, periodic droughts have necessitated the importation of rice. Manufacturing consists primarily of the processing of agricultural products, but in 1978 a free-trade zone was established north of Colombo, Sri Lanka's premier port, to promote the export of textiles and electronics. While the country has initiated a massive effort to cut birthrates and to improve agricultural production, economic development has been severely undermined by the raging ethnic conflict.

SS China: Passenger steamship, originally of the Pacific Mail Company, bought by Robert Dollar, who started a steamship line that later became the "American President Line" passenger ship company. In 1902 the ship first stopped in Yokohama, Japan, and then stopped in Hawaii, with more than a thousand people, most of them Japanese. It probably brought Issei laborers to Hawaii.

Statement of United States Citizens of Japanese Ancestry. *See* **Loyalty Oath**

Stevens, Durham White (Feb. 1, 1852, Washington, D.C.—Mar. 25, 1908, San Francisco, Calif.): Political figure. Stevens became a victim of the struggle for control of Korea. In order to gain a foothold on the Asian mainland in its 1904 war against Russia, the Japanese government forced Korea to sign an agreement that provided Japan with almost complete control over all domestic and foreign matters pertaining to Korea. The Japanese government demanded that Korea accept Japanese advisers in key Korean ministries as well as appoint a foreign affairs adviser empowered to handle all diplomatic affairs in consultation with Japanese officials. Stevens was named to the post of foreign affairs adviser in Korea and worked closely with other members of the puppet government installed by Japan. When he returned to San Francisco in 1908, he was confronted by a hostile Korean expatriate, Chang In-hwan. Chang, a former Hawaii plantation laborer who emigrated to the United States in 1905, had become part of a fervent coalition of Koreans in the Bay Area who were deeply concerned about Japanese influence in their homeland. On March 23, 1908, Chang shot Stevens, who was admitted to St. Francis Hospital and died of his wounds two days later.

Steward incident (1910): Race riot involving white farmers and workers who attacked Korean American orange-pickers working and living in Upland, California, on land owned by their white American employer, Mary E. Steward.

Stimson, Henry L. (Sept. 21, 1867, New York, N.Y.—Oct. 20, 1950, Huntington, N.Y.): U.S. secretary of war. In the service of five U.S. presidents of both political parties between 1911 and 1945, he strongly influenced American foreign policy in the 1930's and 1940's. He was admitted to the New York state bar in 1891 and then began, some years later, a long and varied career in federal service. Stimson was secretary of war under President William Howard Taft from 1911 to 1913 and secretary of state under Herbert Hoover from 1929 to 1933. From 1927 until 1929 he was governor-general of the Philippines. As secretary of war under Franklin D. Roosevelt from 1940 until 1945, he designed the government's World War II exclusion and internment orders pertaining to Japanese Americans. Although aware that the orders were unconstitutional and guided by racism, Stimson argued for their execution on the basis of "military necessity." As chief atomic policy adviser to Harry S Truman, he advocated dropping atom bombs on Japan.

Stockton fairgrounds: Located in Stockton, California, one of sixteen temporary assembly centers set up for the mass relocation of Japanese Americans during World War II. Under EXECUTIVE ORDER 9066 (1942), more than 110,000 Americans of Japanese ancestry were first relocated to temporary centers and later incarcerated in relocation centers administered by the WAR RELOCATION AUTHORITY (WRA). Other temporary centers were in Mayer, Arizona; Portland, Oregon; Puyallup, Washington; and California locations at Fresno, Manzanar, Marysville, Merced, Pinedale, Pomona, Sacramento, Salinas, Santa Anita, Tanforan, Tulare, and Turlock.

Stockton gurdwara: First Sikh house of worship in the United States, established in 1912 and located in Stockton, California. *Gurdwara* means "doorway to the guru, or guide." The Pacific Coast Khalsa Diwan Society, a Punjabi Sikh association formed originally in 1910, raised the necessary funds and established the *gurdwara* in 1912. The original two-story wooden structure was replaced in 1929 by a brick building of similar appearance that continues to serve the Northern California Sikh community.

Until World War II (1939-1945), the *gurdwara* was the major religious and social center for East Indians on the West Coast. In this early period of Sikh migration to the United States (1912 to the 1930's), the *gurdwara* served as the spiritual home for both the male migrant laborers who regularly traveled through the San Joaquin Valley as they followed the crop cycle and the Sikhs who had intermarried with Spanish-speaking women and settled in the surrounding area.

The *gurdwara* functioned as a primary channel for information on the Indian independence movement and conditions in India until 1947. It was also associated, sometimes reluctantly, with anti-British Ghadr political activity, especially after 1918, when the Ghadr Party became a predominantly Sikh organization. The *gurdwara* also assisted Sikhs moving north from the Mexican border to Northern California in the period of illegal Sikh immigration, which lasted from 1924 until the end of World War II.

From the beginning, the temple provided for a variety of needs, including acting as a recruiting center for contract laborers and work gangs, providing shelter and food to East Indians with no other resources, celebrating major Sikh commemorations and religious festivals, conducting funerals, and offering a social center for Punjabis of all backgrounds, including Hindus and Muslims. Although the full range of life-cycle rites (that is, marriages, and child-naming ceremonies) was not established until after Indian Independence (1947),

for more than three decades the *gurdwara* was the most visible formal institution on the Pacific Coast for pioneer Sikhs.

Although many *gurdwaras* have been constructed in California, the Stockton temple continues to play an active role in contemporary Sikh religious life in the Central Valley, often drawing Sikhs from throughout the West to worship on special religious holidays.

Stockton schoolyard incident (1989): Murder of five Southeast Asian schoolchildren and wounding of thirty students and one teacher at Cleveland Elementary School in Stockton, California, on January 17. Patrick Edward Purdy, a twenty-four-year-old drifter and loner from an unstable family, fired 105 rounds from an AK-47 semiautomatic assault rifle into children playing at recess in the school yard of the elementary school that he had once attended. Five children were killed, and thirty more students and one teacher were wounded before Purdy opened fire upon himself with a 9-millimeter pistol, committing suicide. Four of the dead children were the children of Cambodian immigrant parents, and one was Vietnamese. Four were girls: eight-year-olds Ram Chun and Oeun Lim and six-year-olds Sokhim An and Thuy Tran. The one boy was nine-year-old Rathanan Or.

Three Buddhist priests lead a prayer service in Stockton for Sokhim Ang, slain several days earlier in the shooting. A table at the left holds a framed photograph of the young victim. (AP/Wide World Photos)

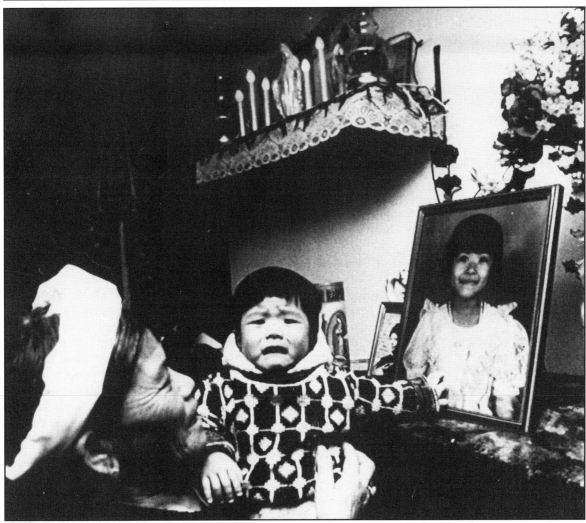

At their Stockton apartment, family members Thu Tran and grandmother Nam Tran lament the killing of Thuy Tran (framed photograph) several days earlier. Nam Tran wears a traditional Vietnamese grieving wrap around her head. (AP/Wide World Photos)

A report from the Office of the California Attorney General concluded that the Stockton school massacre was a hate crime. Purdy acted alone and harbored strong hostilities toward racial and ethnic minorities. He particularly resented Southeast Asians and the fact that they received governmental aid.

Stockton, the county seat of San Joaquin County, is California's leading inland seaport and a major agricultural area. Located forty-five miles south of Sacramento, it has a population of 210,943 (1990 census). Southeast Asian refugees, particularly Cambodians, began coming to the Stockton area during the 1980's, drawn by its low cost of living and rural setting. A January, 1990, report from the California Department of Finance found San Joaquin County to have the highest per capita concentration of Southeast Asian refugees, with seventy refugees for every one thousand residents. The majority reside in Stockton, where they represent about 18 percent of the city's population. At the time of the massacre, 70 percent of the student body at Cleveland Elementary School was Southeast Asian.

The tragedy brought national attention to Stockton's Southeast Asian community. Twelve days after the killings, more than three thousand people attended a public memorial service, which included a speech by the governor of California. Mental health professionals came from all over the state to provide counseling and therapy for the victims and their families. Efforts were made to provide improved social services and educational opportunities for Stockton's Southeast Asians.

Renewed interest in gun control brought about by the killings resulted in precedent-setting legislation against assault weapons. Enacted were a federal import ban on semiautomatic assault weapons, the first statewide ban on such weapons in California, and similar restrictions in many cities and counties, including Stockton.

Student uprisings of 1929-1930: Student strikes and demonstrations held all over the Korean peninsula in opposition to Japanese colonial rule in Korea. These began in Kwangju, Korea, and are therefore sometimes collectively referred to as the "Kwangju student movement of 1929." The uprisings were triggered by an incident in which Japanese male students insulted a group of Korean girl students awaiting a train. Japanese and Korean students then clashed; as the violence escalated, Japanese police arrested some four hundred Koreans, setting off vociferous cries of protest. By the next year the strikes had spread to other parts of the country, eventually involving almost two hundred schools and about fifty-four thousand students. In all more than sixteen hundred people were arrested.

Subba Row, Yellapragada (July, 1896, Madras State, India—Aug. 9, 1948, Pearl River, N.Y.): Physician and researcher. Although not widely known in the United States or India, Subba Row led research to develop cures for many diseases common to both countries. His family lived in Madras, where his father worked as a government clerk. When Subba Row was twenty-two, his brother fell ill. The physician attributed the diarrhea, swollen tongue, and blood-drained skin to sprue—a fatal disease. The family watched as he weakened and died, and Subba Row, struck by the doctor's helplessness, vowed to find a cure for tropical sprue.

Subba Row's first step was to go to Madras Medical School, where he declared to the registrar his intention of conquering sprue. After completing medical school, he took another step toward his goal. He decided to leave his family and India and go to England to study at the School of Tropical Medicine at London University.

At London University Subba Row met Richard Strong, professor of tropical medicine at Harvard Medical School. Strong was awed by Subba Row's determination to conquer tropical diseases and invited him to come to Harvard. With well under fifty dollars in his pocket the young researcher arrived in Boston in 1924. By tending furnaces, working as a hospital orderly and as a night librarian, and rounding up stray

cats for medical research, he was able to provide himself with a dark basement room, tuition, books, and other living expenses.

Subba Row spent a year in Strong's laboratory before undertaking graduate studies in biochemistry. His work with biochemistry professor Cyrus Fiske on phosphorus compounds in muscle tissue required a method for determining small amounts of phosphorus. The pair developed the classic Fiske-Subba Row Method, which was used for more than twenty years. Their work led to the discoveries of phosphocreatine and adenosinetriphosphate, two compounds essential to the process of releasing energy during muscular contraction.

After earning a Ph.D. degree in biochemistry in 1930, Subba Row began research, that would contribute to the cures of pellagra and pernicious anemia. This work won for him a faculty appointment at Harvard in 1938. Preferring research to teaching, Subba Row often spent eighteen hours a day in the laboratory. In 1933 G. W. Clark, who was doing similar research, invited Subba Row to come to the Lederle Laboratories Division of the American Cyanamid Company. For the next seven years, Subba Row spent four days at Harvard and Fridays, Saturdays, and Sundays at Lederle. His early work there contributed to the development of the first vitamins in the B complex group. Studies directed by Subba Row, beginning with experiments using liver extract to treat pernicious anemia, led eventually to the isolation of critical substances in animal and bacterial nutrition. This research formed the basis of the studies leading to the synthesis of folic acid. With the synthesis of folic acid, one of Subba Row's lifelong goals had been achieved—sprue had been conquered. A cure for macrocytic anemia was also on the way.

Subba Row left Harvard and began working as the associate research director at Lederle in 1940, becoming the research director two years later. Among the drugs developed under his direction were teropterin, used in the treatment of cancer and said to have lengthened the life of Babe Ruth, the legendary American baseball player, and relieved his pain; aminopterin used in the treatment of leukemia; and hetrazan, a specific in filariasis—a parasitic disease that afflicts millions of people. Along with an amazing capacity for analyzing data and an astonishing memory, Subba Row also brought an inquisitive, penetrating mind to the problems he researched.

Subba Row considered the United States his home, but restrictive U.S. immigration legislation prevented him from becoming a citizen until after passage of the

LUCE-CELLER BILL OF 1946. He received his first citizenship papers at the time of his death. Throughout his life his good humor, generosity, and spirituality made an indelible impression on colleagues and associates.

Suburbs: For years Asian American communities have been moving away from traditional urban centers into middle-class suburban settings. The result of two decades of large-scale immigration from Asia has seen the emergence of new "Chinatowns," "Manilatowns," "Koreatowns," and "Little Saigons" in suburban areas across the country, according to the 1990 U.S. census. Together they serve an Asian Pacific population numbering more than 7.2 million nationwide.

The Asian American population has increased rapidly since the passage of the IMMIGRATION AND NATIONALITY ACT OF 1965, which eliminated the quota system that previously favored European countries. Several million Asians have immigrated to the United States since 1968, and more than a million refugees have entered since 1975. This rapid influx of new Asian immigrants has resulted in the development of new Asian American communities.

Into the 1990's, the seemingly rapid rise in the number of Vietnamese-owned restaurants, markets, and other stores in suburban communities of the United States is evidence of the greater concentration of Vietnamese settling in these areas. (Ben Klaffke)

The best examples of the suburbanization of Asian Americans can be seen in the areas surrounding Los Angeles and San Francisco. Both cities have historically been the ports of entry for most Asian immigrants and the places where these immigrants initially settled. Yet this pattern has been altered as relatively affluent and well-educated immigrants began bypassing the urban core and moving directly into outlying communities.

During the 1980's the San Gabriel Valley, a region east of downtown Los Angeles, was the scene of demographic shifts so dramatic that they surprised even experienced demographers. The Asian American population more than doubled in well-to-do communities such as San Marino, Hacienda Heights, and Diamond Bar, cities that were once the domain of white homeowners. Easily the most notable location in the area is Monterey Park, which has a population of about sixty thousand and is 57 percent Asian, according to the 1990 census. Monterey Park's population is largely immigrant Chinese and has earned the title of "America's First Suburban Chinatown."

In Orange County, known mostly as the bastion of highly affluent and conservative Caucasians, Asians constitute more than 10 percent of the population. Asians by far outnumber other racial minority groups in Orange County, home to one of the largest concentrations of Vietnamese Americans in the country. The city of Westminster, with a population of about fifty-three thousand, has a bustling Vietnamese commercial district and signs on the freeway directing visitors to its "Little Saigon."

Similar changes characterize the San Francisco Bay area. According to the 1990 census, nearby San Mateo and Santa Clara counties both have Asian populations of roughly 17 percent. In these two counties commercial thoroughfares show a strong Asian presence that was once found only in the inner precincts of major cities. Chinese-owned shops, supermarkets, and restaurants abound, hundreds of Filipino-run stores can be seen, and the number of Korean and Asian Indian businesses have increased by the score.

What makes these demographic changes even more phenomenal to social scientists is the fact that most of these suburban regions have grown wealthier as they have grown more Asian.

Sudden unexpected nocturnal death syndrome (SUNDS): Unexplained death during night or early morning sleep of seemingly healthy adult Asian males from Southeast Asian countries. SUNDS is also known as "sudden unexplained death syndrome" (SUDS) and is closely related to *lai tai* (nightmare death) in Thailand, *bangungut* (to rise and moan in sleep) in the Philippines, and *pokkuri* (sudden and unexpectedly ceased phenomenon) in Japan. The victims are sleeping males, usually between age twenty-five and forty-five, with the majority in their thirties. Sometimes their demise is preceded by severe groans, incoherent speech, and convulsions. Since there are no previously existing symptoms, and since their autopsies reveal no explanation, the cause of death is a mystery.

Incidents of this type of sudden death have occurred in a number of Asian countries, including Thailand, the Philippines, and Japan. It especially has been prevalent among male Southeast Asians employed as guest construction workers, with reports of deaths of Thai workers in Singapore, Brunei, Kuwait, and Saudi Arabia, as well as among Hmong males in Thailand refugee camps.

The first SUNDS case among Southeast Asian refugees and immigrants in the United States was reported in 1977. The U.S. Centers for Disease Control has verified 122 cases of SUNDS between February, 1981, and June, 1990. The highest number occurred in 1981, with twenty-six deaths reported. SUNDS is particularly common among Hmong adult males from Laos, but other Southeast Asian refugee groups have been afflicted, including Cambodians, Khmu, Mien, and Vietnamese. All the victims except one have been males. Since the early 1980's, the number of deaths has declined, along with the number of refugee admissions.

There are various theories as to the cause of SUNDS. The most prevalent is that it is a stress-related condition brought about by severe anxiety and depression resulting from pressure to adjust to a strange new cultural and socioeconomic situation. These factors have a greater impact on many Southeast Asian refugees because of the severe psychological and physical trauma they have suffered in their homeland. Another theory emphasizes the role of traditional religious beliefs, in which nocturnal visits of an evil spirit or nightmare bring about intense fear and paralysis and ultimately heart failure. Physiological factors being investigated as contributing to SUNDS include thiamine deficiency, abnormal potassium level, and structural abnormality of the cardiac conduction system.

Sue, Stanley (b. Feb. 13, 1944, Portland, Oreg.): Scholar. Sue attended the University of Oregon (B.S., 1966) and the University of California, Los Angeles (Ph.D., 1971), where he is professor of psychology and direc-

tor of the National Research Center on Asian American Mental Health. Considered one of the United States' foremost experts on Asian American mental health issues, he has consulted with and advised many agencies and institutions across the nation.

Sugahara, Keiichi "Kay" (1909, Seattle, Wash.—1988): Businessperson. Orphaned at age thirteen, Sugahara rose to a position of wealth and influence in the world of commerce. After being graduated from the University of California, Los Angeles, in 1932, he founded the Universal Exchange Customs Brokerage House. The first Japanese American customs broker in the continental United States, Sugahara, a Nisei, also took an active part in the formation and development of the Los Angeles chapter of the JAPANESE AMERICAN CITIZENS LEAGUE (JACL) and the earliest Nisei Week festivals.

Sugahara had amassed a fortune by his twenty-ninth birthday but lost most of it during World War II, when he was forcibly evacuated to the GRANADA relocation center in southeastern Colorado. The government released him after he volunteered to serve with the Office of Strategic Services (OSS). His term of service took him to India and Japan, where during the U.S. military occupation he was able to influence the United States' formulation of its Japanese policy.

Shortly thereafter the enterprising Sugahara returned to the business world and was restored to wealth, becoming board chair of the Fairfield Maxwell shipping and oil empire. He also chaired the nonprofit United States-Asia Institute, an organization that works to promote the image of Asian Americans. In 1983 he proposed a $10 billion plan to encourage Japanese investment in the United States. Sugahara is interred in Arlington National Cemetery.

Sugar strike of 1909: Walkout by Japanese sugar workers in Hawaii demanding better pay and housing. Also called "The Great Japanese Strike," it began on May 9 when Japanese sugar workers, supported by the Japanese Higher Wage Association, struck at Aiea Plantation, near Honolulu, on Oahu. Strikes followed on the other sugar plantations on the island.

The objective of the strike was to eliminate the difference in pay between Japanese and Portuguese workers and gain equal living quarters for the Japanese. The Japanese received $18.50 per month for twenty-six days of work and were quartered in what they described as "pigsty" dwellings. For the same labor, the Portuguese received $22.50 and respectable quarters.

The four men in charge of organizing the strike were Yasutaro Soga, owner of the Japanese-language *Nippu Jiji* newspaper, Motoyuki Negoro, Yokichi Tasaka, and Fred Kinzaburo Makino. Members of the Hawaiian Sugar Planters' Association (HSPA) controlled the economy of Hawaii, the English-language press, the government, the courts, and the police. After the strike began, the plantation owners evicted the strikers and their families. On June 10, the police, without warrants, arrested many of the strike leaders. When such leaders gained release from jail, the police, in many cases, rearrested them. Probably because the planters considered Soga the greatest menace, they meted out to him the most charges—ten.

The strike leaders were so busy coping with the arrests and trying, often unsuccessfully, to raise bail that they were unable to give appropriate attention to the strike, which ground to a halt.

Hawaii brought the four men to trial on charges of conspiracy to boycott plantation business. After twenty-one days of hearings, the jury found the four guilty in the third degree. The court sentenced each to spend ten months in jail and to pay a fine of three hundred dollars. The Territorial Supreme Court upheld the verdict, and the four were committed to jail on March 10, 1910.

The planters had spent two million dollars to break the strike. When the strike ended, the planters saw more gain in freeing the leaders than keeping them jailed. The lieutenant governor pardoned the four, and they were released on July 4, 1910. The planters began replacing the Japanese quarters with better dwellings. Within three months of the end of the strike, the planters announced that, thereafter, pay would be proportionate to individual ability without regard to nationality.

Sugar strike of 1920: First and only multiethnic strike on the sugar plantations of Hawaii prior to World War II (1939-1945). Filipino and Japanese labor unions led the strike of six plantations on Oahu, which lasted for five and a half months. Some eighty-three hundred Japanese and Filipino workers, representing 77 percent of the Oahu plantation labor force, participated in the strike, along with smaller numbers of Puerto Rican, Spanish, Portuguese, and Chinese workers. Although on strike at the same time, the two unions, the Filipino Federation of Labor (FLU) and the Federated Association of Japanese Labor, did not cooperate closely with each other.

To some extent, the two labor unions were unable to coordinate strike activities because the Filipino union,

led by Pablo MANLAPIT, was not sufficiently organized, even at the plantation level. Consequently, Manlapit had little control over rank-and-file Filipino strikers and had no effective means to communicate with them. Japanese laborers were much better organized for the strike, with local unions on each plantation and federated associations of those units on each of the four major islands.

Both unions made similar but separate demands to the HAWAIIAN SUGAR PLANTERS' ASSOCIATION (HSPA), which represented the plantations. These demands included an increase in wages from $0.77 to $1.25 per day, an eight-hour workday for both field and mill workers, and paid maternity leave for women.

The HSPA rejected the demands of both unions and refused to negotiate with them throughout the strike. The planters' response was to evict striking laborers from plantation housing. Some twelve thousand persons, including more than forty-one hundred children, were therefore expelled. The Honolulu press waged a racist propaganda campaign against the Japanese strikers by arguing that the strike was a plot by them to seize control of the sugar industry and even Hawaii. Given these forces against them, the workers formally conceded defeat on July 1 without having gained their major demand for a wage increase. The strike was the first significant multiethnic working-class struggle in Hawaii, although it did not provide the basis for other such movements in the immediate future.

Sugar strike of 1924: Eight-month strike of Hawaiian sugar plantations led by the Higher Wages Association, a Filipino labor union headed by Pablo MANLAPIT. Referred to as the "Filipino piecemeal strike" because of its slow and sporadic movement through the sugar plantations in Hawaii, the strike impacted twenty-three of the state's forty-two plantations. Four years earlier Manlapit had led Filipino workers in another strike against the HAWAIIAN SUGAR PLANTERS' ASSOCIATION (HSPA). As in the 1920 strike the Filipino union was not sufficiently organized, lacked a strike fund, and had no viable means of communication, but the workers' resolve sustained the strike activities.

The Higher Wages Association presented to the HSPA demands similar to those of 1920: increased wages ($2 a day), an eight-hour work day, and better plantation housing. Other significant demands were for equal pay for men and women and for recognition of their union. More than two thousand Filipino workers participated in the strike, although not all at the same time. Unlike 1920 Japanese laborers did not join the strike; their support was limited to expressions of sympathy in Japanese-language newspapers and some monetary contributions.

The strike is especially remembered for the HANAPEPE MASSACRE, a violent confrontation that occurred between strikers and police on the island of Kauai on September 9, 1924. In a short burst of gunfire sixteen Filipinos and four policemen were killed. Seventy-six strikers were later charged with rioting, and fifty-seven others pleaded guilty to assault and battery charges. Such violence was, however, very uncommon in the labor history of Hawaii.

To eliminate Manlapit from leading the strike, the HSPA had him arrested, its favorite tactic to remove strike leaders. Manlapit was charged with subornation of perjury in an incident involving the death of a striker's child. He was convicted based on perjured and dubious testimony and received a two-to-ten-year prison sentence.

Despite Manlapit's absence the strike continued, although it was essentially over by the end of the year. Nevertheless, striking Filipinos did not all return to work until the following year, indicative of their strong dissatisfaction with plantation working conditions.

Sugar strike of 1946: First industry- and territory-wide strike of the sugar plantations in Hawaii. The four-month-long strike was led by the International Longshoremen's and Warehousemen's Union (ILWU), which had successfully organized plantation workers into "one big union." The ILWU had organized dock-workers in Hawaii prior to the outbreak of World War II (1939-1945). Unlike previous labor disputes in Hawaii, the strike included workers of all ethnic groups, a strategy, together with the comprehensive organizational structure of the union, that contributed to its ultimate victory.

The union's demands in contract negotiations with the sugar industry were for a wage increase of 16.5 cents per hour, a forty-hour workweek, a closed shop with compulsory union membership, a ban on discrimination on the basis of race, creed, or political activity, and an end to plantation-provided perquisites, particularly housing and medical care. The paternalistic perquisite system had been used by plantation owners as a means of labor control, for example, evicting striking workers from housing. With negotiations stalled, union members voted overwhelmingly for a strike, which began on September 1 with a walkout by about twenty-one thousand workers on thirty-three plantations.

The ILWU was much better prepared and organized for the strike than previous plantation unions. Prior to the strike, it had enlisted more than 80 percent of the roughly twenty-four thousand sugar workers. A strike strategy committee was organized by every local unit to direct its activities. A host of other committees was formed, including ones for picketing, finance, food collection, the organizing of nonunion members, and morale.

The strike was settled in mid-November, although an agreement with workers in Lahaina, Maui, was not reached until the end of the year. With most of its demands met, the ILWU won a major victory, particularly in having perquisites converted into cash. More significant, the strike demonstrated to workers the importance of organization and class unity in attaining their goals. As a direct result of the strike, ethnic or "blood" unionism was no longer advocated in Hawaii, and a new era in industrial relations had begun.

Sugimoto, Etsu (1874, Echigo, Japan—June 20, 1950, Tokyo, Japan): Writer. Originally from Nagaoka, she was an unusual Japanese immigrant because her father had been a highly placed vassal in the feudal system before the MEIJI RESTORATION, and because she traveled alone to the United States to marry a merchant husband. One of the few Japanese immigrants to write in English, her books are a record of life during the early Meiji era and tell of the early immigrant experience in the United States. She wrote *A Daughter of the Narakin* (1932) and a memoir, *Daughter of the Samurai* (1934).

Sugimoto, Henry (b. 1901, Wakayama, Japan): Artist. Sugimoto, whose grandfather encouraged his drawing as a child, arrived in the United States in 1919 to join his parents. The latter were operating a Japanese-language school in Hanford, central California. After high school, he enrolled at the University of California, Berkeley, but later transferred to the California College of Arts and Crafts, graduating with a B.F.A. degree in 1928. The following year he traveled to Paris to continue his art studies. Returning to the United States, Sugimoto married and continued to paint, exhibiting his work in numerous galleries and museums.

During World War II, Sugimoto and his family were evacuated to the Jerome and Rohwer relocation centers in southeastern Arkansas, where he produced paintings and drawings depicting camp conditions; lacking canvas, he used bedsheets, pillow cases, and mattress covers. After their release the Sugimotos settled in New York. There Henry illustrated books, including *Toshio and Tama* and *Children of New Japan*, both published in 1949, translated film captions into Japanese, designed fabrics, and exhibited his work at galleries and museums.

By 1962, Sugimoto had saved enough money to leave his job at the fabric company and become a full-time artist. Meanwhile he published a picture book in Japan based on his camp experiences and accepted several medals from both the emperor and the government of Japan for his contributions to Japanese culture in America. In 1984 the Smithsonian National Museum of American History received into its permanent collection internment camp artwork donated by Sugimoto.

Sui, Anna (b. 1955?, Dearborn Heights, Mich.): Fashion designer. Sui is the daughter of Chinese immigrants. Her father is an engineer, while her mother studied painting in Paris. Anna displayed an interest in fashion while in her childhood, when she would array toy soldiers in little tissue-paper dresses. An unconventional dresser even at an early age, she was voted Best Dressed in her ninth-grade class. As a teen she began to clip advertisements and spreads from the pages of fashion magazines, saving them in what she has come to refer to as her "Genius Files." For Sui their contents were a fertile source of ideas and inspiration once she began to create her own designs.

Following her high school graduation, Sui attended the Parsons School of Design in Manhattan. There she formed a creative collaboration with Steven Meisel, who would later achieve fame as a fashion photographer. Throughout the remainder of the decade, Sui worked for a succession of clothing companies but also created her own designs. After selling six original pieces to Macy's department store in 1980, she started her own business, operating out of her own apartment.

Besides her Genius Files, Sui's sources of inspiration have ranged from rock stars to television shows of the past. Past collections have featured the looks of the 1950's, 1960's, and 1970's and have been called eclectic, eccentric, whimsical, and offbeat. Sui was well on the way to greater worldwide prominence following her first runway showing in 1991. An article in *The New York Times* of April 12 of that year described her collection as looking "as if Sly and the Family Stone crashed into Coco Chanel and then got rear-ended by Christian Lacroix." Her spring, 1992, collection featured 1970's-era bell bottoms and hip huggers. Sui opened her own boutique in Manhattan's SoHo district the following fall, attaching further cachet to her $1.75 million business.

Sui Sin Far (Edith Maud Eaton; 1865, England—Apr. 7, 1914, Montreal, Quebec, Canada): Fiction writer. During the period of the Chinese Exclusion Act (1882), and as the first Chinese American fiction writer, Far embraced her heritage by writing truthful depictions of the Chinese community. At a time when most writing described the Chinese as economic threats, unassimilable, and immoral, she portrayed them with empathy and dignity.

Sui Sin Far was born Edith Maud Eaton. Her father was British and her mother, although reared by an English family, was of Chinese ancestry. In order to escape prejudice and ridicule, Far's parents left a comfortable life in England and with their children immigrated to the United States in 1871; they lived at various times in New York, New Jersey, and Montreal. As a child, Far was harassed by both adults and children because of her half-Chinese status. The suffering she felt in her early life eventually prompted her to write.

Although Far was not reared as a Chinese, she found her identity and sense of worth in the Chinese community. She wrote news articles about the troubles of the Chinese and also taught English to Chinese immigrants at a Baptist mission.

Far supported herself throughout her adult life and never married. She earned a living as a stenographer and journalist, but fiction was her passion. Although Far did not speak Chinese, she assumed the pen name "Sui Sin Far," which literally translated means "Narcissus." (In Chinese names, the family name or surname precedes the given name. Thus her adopted surname should have been Sui. However—perhaps because she was unaware of the Chinese practice—she referred to herself in autobiographical writings as "Miss Far.") From 1900 to 1908, many of her stories appeared in such periodicals as *Good Housekeeping*, *The New York Evening Post*, and *Sunset*. In 1912, a collection of thirty-seven of her works was published in the book *Mrs. Spring Fragrance*.

Far's stories explore the conflicts of assimilation and intermarriage, the torment of being Eurasian, and the autonomy of women. Although her tales are short, simple, and sentimental, her portrayal of these themes is realistic.

Far was a pioneer writer who was never fully accepted by either culture. As a Eurasian attempting to reconcile two polar societies, she claimed that "individuality is more than nationality." As a Chinese feminist writer in the early 1900's, she had no peers or literary genres to use as models. Although her work was popular during her lifetime, she did not receive critical attention until the 1970's and the birth of the ethnic awareness movement. She is now recognized as the first writer to define an Asian American sensibility.

Sumida, Stephen H.: Scholar. An associate professor in the department of English at the University of Michigan, Ann Arbor, Sumida has done pioneering work on the literature of Hawaii. With Arnold T. Hiura, he is the author of *Asian American Literature in Hawaii: An Annotated Bibliography* (1979). With Hiura and Martha Webb, he edited *Talk Story: Big Island Anthology* (1979). His book *And the View from the Shore: Literary Traditions of Hawaii* (1991) has received wide acclaim. See also Sumida's essays "Asian/Pacific Literature in the Classroom," *American Literature* 65 (June, 1993): 348-353, a contribution to a symposium ("What Do We Need To Teach?"), and "Sense of Place, History, and the Concept of 'Local' in Hawaii's Asian Pacific American Literatures," in *Reading the Literatures of Asian America* (1992), edited by Shirley Geok-lin Lim and Amy Ling.

Sumitomo Bank: First commercial banking institution in California to offer "Telestatus," an automated customer information service in English, Japanese,

Sumitomo Bank in Japantown district of San Francisco, California. (Robert Fried)

Mandarin, or Cantonese in 1988. This innovation was designed to meet the growing banking needs of the state's diverse Asian American community, which increased by 127 percent from 1980 to 1990.

Sun Fo (Sun K'o; Oct. 20, 1891, Xiangshan, Guangdong Province, China—Sept. 13, 1973, Taipei, Republic of China): Politician. Sun was the only son of SUN YAT-SEN, father of the Republic of China. Sun Fo moved to Honolulu in 1896 with his family, where he received his primary and secondary education. He graduated from the University of California in 1916 and received an M.A. degree in economics from Columbia University in 1917. He then returned to China.

Sun Fo's entire career was linked with the GUOMINDANG (GMD), or Nationalist Party of China, also founded by his father. Sun Fo was mayor of Canton from 1921 to 1925, when the Guomindang's power was limited to Guangdong Province with Canton as its capital city. He worked to introduce the first public utilities and roads to that city, improvements that helped initiate the city's transformation to a modern metropolis.

Beginning in 1923 Sun Fo served on the Central Executive Committee, one of two top governing bodies of the Guomindang. In a period when the Guomindang, the Chinese Communist Party (CCP) and Comintern advisers from the Soviet Union worked in uneasy alliance, Sun Fo was regarded as a rightist by the Communists and as left-leaning by the right wing of the Guomindang.

After CHIANG KAI-SHEK's successful Northern Expeditionary forces purged the Chinese Communists and expelled the Soviet advisers in 1927, Sun Fo and Chiang began two decades of sometimes strained relations in the Guomindang government. Sun Fo held important posts as minister of railways, vice president of the Examination Yuan (akin to a civil service qualifying board), president of the China National Aviation Corporation, and above all as president of the Legislative Yuan between 1932 and 1948.

Under Sun Yat-sen's blueprint, the Legislative Yuan had the task of drafting a provisional constitution for the period of political tutelage that China entered under Guomindang rule beginning in 1928. That draft was completed in 1936; a permanent constitution, which the Japanese invasion of China in 1937 and World War II (1939-1945) postponed, was finished in 1946. The Yuan also supervised the writing of new modern legal codes during the 1930's.

The National Assembly adopted the new constitution in 1947. Sun Fo ran for the vice presidency of the republic in 1948 and lost to general Li Tsung-jen (Chiang Kai-shek was elected president), but Sun was elected president of the Legislative Yuan under the constitution. When the Chinese Communists swept to victory on the mainland in 1949 and Chiang retreated to Taiwan, Sun Fo went to France and then moved to the United States. He returned to Taiwan in 1965 and served as senior adviser to the president and as president of the Examination Yuan.

Sun Yat-sen (Sun Wen; Nov. 12, 1866, Xiangshan, Guangdong Province, China—Mar. 12, 1925, Beijing, China): Military and political leader. Sun was the most prominent leader of China's republican revolution. After leaving his agricultural roots in southern China, he trained as a medical doctor and developed revolutionary ideas opposing Manchu oppression and Western imperialism. His goal was to establish a republican form of government combining traditional Chinese institutions with Western democracy and social ideals. After the 1911 revolution, he relinquished power to Yuan Shikai, whose despotic rule and subsequent period of warlordism prevented Sun from accomplishing his objectives.

Youthful Rebel. Born in a farm village in Guangdong Province, Sun Yat-sen received some classical training. In 1879 he joined his brother, Sun Mei, in Hawaii and began his Western education at Iolani College, where he studied English, science, and Christianity. After returning to China in 1883, Sun revealed growing iconoclastic beliefs by desecrating three statues in the local temple and was expelled from the area. Furthering his education in Hong Kong, Sun attended the Church of England diocesan school in 1883 and Queen's College in 1885. After converting to Christianity, he returned home briefly and accepted an arranged marriage to a village girl, Lu Muzhen. (He later married Song Qingling on October 25, 1914.) Leaving his wife behind, Sun studied medicine in Canton and Hong Kong.

Sun Yat-sen's medical career was short-lived. In the early 1890's Sun engaged in revolutionary activities, organizing his friends into groups opposing the Qing government. In 1894 Sun attempted to join the national stage by writing to the influential official, Li Hongzhang, proposing that China create new technologies, expand education, increase employment, and develop natural resources and agriculture. When ignored by Li, Sun went to Hawaii in November, 1894, and organized the XINGZHONGHUI (Revive China Society) while seeking funds for further revolutionary activity.

March Toward Revolution. After the Sino-Japanese War (1894-1895) Sun expanded his revolutionary work and concentrated on establishing organizations, publishing journals, and forming military units. In addition Sun traveled frequently to Hong Kong, Hawaii, the United States, England, and Southeast Asia seeking supporters and financial contributions. After an aborted uprising at Canton in October, 1895, Sun's life was in danger. While in London on October 11, 1896, Sun was kidnapped by Qing agents and taken to their legation. He was saved by James Cantlie, his mentor at the medical college in Hong Kong. After the kidnapping incident Sun Yat-sen received international fame as a revolutionary leader.

A major base of Sun's operations outside China was in Japan, where he became friends with Miyazaki Torazo and several Japanese leaders. These contacts enabled Sun to use Japan as a safe haven and to obtain military supplies for uprisings in China. After 1900 Sun intensified his travels, particularly to Southeast Asia, where he established branches of the Revive China Society among overseas Chinese, and to the United States and Europe seeking supporters and funds. On July 30, 1905, in Tokyo, Sun and enthusiastic Chinese students formed the Tongmenghui (Chinese United League). This new organization issued a manifesto that focused on overthrowing the Qing Dynasty and in November began to publish the *Min pao* (people's journal), expressing revolutionary ideas.

As the dynasty weakened, Sun's followers participated in a series of uprisings to establish a revolutionary base in China. The incident that began the revolution occurred on October 10, 1911, at Wuchang. An explosion in the Russian concession area led the police to a list of local revolutionaries. When this was revealed to Chinese United League members, most of whom were in the army, they called upon Lt. Col. Li Yuanhong to revolt and seize the area. By the end of the year, south China was in revolutionary hands. When this uprising began, Sun Yat-sen was in Denver, Colorado, and learned about these events from a newspaper on a train to Kansas City. Rather than return, Sun continued to travel eastward and ultimately to Europe seeking recognition and support.

Upon Sun's return to China on December 25, 1911, he was elected president of the provisional republican government already established at Nanjing and took office on January 1, 1912. The imperial government, controlling the northern half of China, called upon Yuan Shikai to handle relations with the south. Sun and the provisional government at Nanjing negotiated

Sun Yat-sen outside his home in the French Concession of Shanghai, China, 1922. (Library of Congress)

Sun Yat-sen (center) addresses an audience at his house in Kweilin, Kwangsi Province, to explain the purposes behind his ongoing military campaign to wrest control of China from the republican government. (Library of Congress)

with Yuan for abdication by the Qing emperor (February 12, 1912). Part of the settlement included Sun Yat-sen's resignation (February 13), followed by the election of Yuan (February 14) as president of the Republic of China. Sun relinquished his duties as president on April 1, 1912.

The Republic and the Second Revolution. Sun's former supporters now created the GUOMINDANG (Nationalist Party) and expected to participate in a democratic government, while Sun agreed to serve as national director of railroad development in the new republic. The assassination of Sun's close associate, Song Jiaoren, and Yuan's abuse of power led Sun to denounce the president. Yuan then dismissed Sun on July 23, 1913. In retaliation seven provinces declared their independence, beginning the "second revolution." To counteract Yuan, Sun encouraged a "constitutional protection movement" and restoration of the 1912 constitution and the old parliament. On August

31, 1917, Sun established a military government and convened a rump parliament at Canton. For the next five years Sun attempted to work with local military leaders, such as Chen Jiongming, but broke with them over policy objectives. Several times Sun was driven out of Canton and took sanctuary in Shanghai, where he wrote his most significant works. Sun's program for China is described in his most significant treatise, the *Three Principles of the People* (Sanminzhuyi).

Nationalists and Communists. Sun's final efforts were devoted to the revitalization of the Nationalist Party at Canton while accepting political guidance from the Comintern and cooperating with the newly established Chinese Communist Party. After extensive discussions, Sun Yat-sen and Adolf Joffe, a Soviet diplomat, issued a joint communique on January 26, 1923, establishing cooperation between the Nationalists and Communists but agreeing that the Soviet system was not suitable for China.

In October, 1923, Sun turned his attention to reorganizing the Nationalist Party. Working closely with Michael Borodin, Comintern representative, on political organization, Sun convened the First National Congress on January 20, 1924, adopting a new constitution and restructuring the Nationalist Party. Having agreed to a northern expedition to unite China, the Nationalist Party established the Whampoa Military Academy in May, 1924, with Chiang Kai-shek as commandant. By mid-February Sun was in Canton leading a new military government but preoccupied with military operations and warlord alliances.

In a final effort to unify China by peaceful means, Sun Yat-sen left Canton in November, 1924, to discuss a solution with Duan Qirui, provisional head of the government in Beijing. En route, Sun stopped in Kobe, Japan, where he spoke on Pan-Asianism, calling for Asian unity against imperialism. He reached Tianjin on December 4, 1924, but he was very ill with cancer of the liver spreading through his frail body. Negotiations by correspondence suggested the meeting with Duan would be futile. Sun wanted labor, peasant, and merchant groups represented while Duan planned to ignore the Nationalist Party. Critically ill by January 26, 1925, Sun was taken to the Peking Union Medical College and was later moved to the home of his friend, Wellington Koo, where he died March 12, 1925. He left a "will" calling upon his followers to carry on the revolution.—*Leonard H. D. Gordon*

SUGGESTED READINGS: • Chang, Sidney H., and Leonard H. D. Gordon. *All Under Heaven: Sun Yat-sen and His Revolutionary Thought.* Stanford, Calif.: Hoover Institution Press, 1991. • Cheng, Chu-yuan, ed. *Sun Yat-sen's Doctrine in the Modern World.* Boulder, Colo.: Westview Press, 1989. • Jansen, Marius B. *The Japanese and Sun Yat-sen.* Cambridge; Mass.: Harvard University Press, 1954. • Scalapino, Robert A., and George T. Yu. *Modern China and Its Revolutionary Process: Recurrent Challenges to the Traditional Order, 1859-1920.* Berkeley: University of California Press, 1985. • Schiffrin, Harold Z. *Sun Yat-sen: Reluctant Revolutionary.* Boston: Little, Brown, 1980. • Wilbur, C. Martin. *Sun Yat-sen: Frustrated Patriot.* New York: Columbia University Press, 1976.

Sun Yat-sen, Madame (Song Qingling; Jan. 27, 1893, Shanghai, China—May 29, 1981, Beijing, People's Republic of China): Political figure. In 1914 she married SUN YAT-SEN, father of the Chinese republican revolution of 1911 and leader of the GUOMINDANG, or Nationalist Party. She served as her husband's secretary and chief confidant until his death in 1925. Later she became a staunch opponent of CHIANG KAI-SHEK, her sister's husband and the eventual successor to Sun Yat-sen as leader of the Guomindang. When Chiang's Nationalist forces fled to Taiwan following the Communist takeover in 1949, Madame Sun remained in China. Thereafter she held several positions in the Chinese government.

Sung, Betty Lee (b. Oct. 3, 1924, Baltimore, Md.): Scholar. Sung has pioneered the field of Asian American studies at the university level. She attended the University of Illinois and the Graduate Center of the City University of New York (CUNY), from which she earned a Ph.D. degree in sociology in 1983. During the last three years of World War II, she was a Chinese transliterator for the U.S. Army in Washington, D.C. That was followed by a job writing radio scripts for the Voice of America (VOA) from 1949 until 1954. After holding several posts as an editor and librarian through the 1960's, Sung became an instructor in the Asian studies department at the City College of New York (CCNY) in 1970. She retired in 1992 as a full professor and former department chair.

Sung authored the prize-winning books *Mountain of Gold* (1967) and *Survey of Chinese American Manpower and Employment* (1976); *The Chinese in America* (1973), a children's book; and *Chinese American Intermarriage* (1990). Her articles have appeared in *East/West*, the *Journal of Comparative Family Studies*, *Chinese American Forum*, and *Kaleidoscope*. The recipient of a number of honors and awards, Sung is listed with such biographical references as *Contemporary Authors*, *International Who's Who of Professional and Business Women*, and *Asian American Almanac*. Through the early 1990's she was busy compiling a study of the early history of New York's Chinatown. Married to Charles C. M. Chung, she is the mother of eight children.

Sunoo, Brenda Paik (b. Feb. 13, 1948, Los Angeles, Calif.): Journalist. Former news editor of the *Korea Times* English edition in Los Angeles, she is a frequent speaker on the role of the ethnic press and race relations. A former reporter for the *Modesto Bee* and the *Orange County Register*, both in California, she was also a features editor at *Rice* magazine, an Asian American monthly. A recipient of a John Swett Award for excellent news coverage of education, she is a member of the Community Media Advisory Board for

Amerasia Journal and is affiliated with the ASIAN AMERICAN JOURNALISTS ASSOCIATION (AAJA).

Survivor's guilt: Guilt felt by persons who go through a traumatic experience in which other people die. For Asian Americans, survivor's guilt is particularly relevant to the populations that have escaped from Indochina after 1975. Vietnamese, Cambodians, and Laotians all suffered during years of war. Those who fled often made dangerous escapes in small boats or across land. Casualties during such trips were sometimes high, with those who took the biggest risks for the benefit of the group often being killed.

People who suffer from survivor's guilt hold themselves morally responsible for the death of the other person. Survivors may feel this way even though they are the only ones holding themselves responsible for the death of the person. Survivor's guilt is likely to be found in refugee populations, military units that have suffered casualties, and areas that have experienced a natural disaster. Survivor's guilt is often correlated with mental health problems. People suffering from survivor's guilt often describe those who have died as having unusually high moral qualities.

Stories about the people who died and the sacrifices they made for the group's benefit are often told and retold by survivors. Such memories may also be recounted to outsiders, and such storytelling is one way that some refugees deal with the extremely painful memories of those who have died. Sometimes, this recounting takes the form of artwork; the Hmong needlework *paj ntaub*, featuring pictures of battles and escapes, may be one example of how art has been used by survivors to tell the story of those who perished. Cambodian refugees who experienced years of suffering in refugee camps, as well as persecution under the POL POT regime (1975-1978), are also likely to have had close friends and relatives die and to suffer from survivor's guilt.

Sutter, John Augustus (Johann August Suter; Feb. 15, 1803, Kandern, Germany—June 18, 1880, Washington, D.C.): Pioneer settler and colonizer. Sutter, a Swiss German, arrived in California in 1839 and, with help from the Mexican government, there established the colony of Nueva Helvetia (New Switzerland), which would later become Sacramento. He also built "Sutter's Fort" in 1841, founded frontier industries, and brought Hawaiians over to cultivate farms on his estate. In 1848, while a sawmill was being erected on Sutter's land, gold was discovered, triggering the California gold rush of 1849—and prompting thousands of Chinese immigrants to seek their fortune in California. This was the first significant flow of immigration from Asia to the United States.

Sutter's Mill: Site of the first discovery of gold in California and a major attraction for the first wave of Chinese immigration. Named after the German-born pioneer and entrepreneur John Augustus Sutter, the mill, located in Coloma, California, was constructed after James W. Marshall, a carpenter and gold miner who worked with Sutter, had discovered gold there on January 24, 1848, during excavations for the sawmill.

Suzuki, Bob H. (b. Portland, Oreg.): Educator and university administrator. Suzuki, a Nisei, is the first native Japanese American to be made president of a major university—California State Polytechnic University, Pomona—in the continental United States. He attended the University of California, Berkeley, and the California Institute of Technology, from which he earned a Ph.D. degree in aeronautics. After more than four years

Bob Suzuki. (Asian Week)

of university teaching, he went back to school, enrolling at the University of Massachusetts, Amherst, where he pursued an interest in Asian American studies. In 1977 he published a pioneering paper criticizing the application of the MODEL MINORITY label to Asian Americans. Suzuki was an administrator with the California State University system for ten years before taking office as president at Pomona in 1991.

Suzuki, Chiyoko "Pat" (b. 1931, Cressy, Calif.): Actor and singer. A Nisei who, along with her family, was held in an internment camp in Granada, Colorado, during World War II, Pat Suzuki was born in Cressy, California, a farming colony founded by Kyutaro Abiko. In 1948, she entered Mills College, and later she attended San Jose State College. While still a student, Suzuki began to sing in nightclubs on weekends. Later, she joined the road company of *Teahouse of the August Moon*, and she also worked for three years at The Colony, a club located in the Seattle, Washington, area.

In 1957, Suzuki won the role of Linda Low in the Rodgers and Hammerstein musical *Flower Drum Song*. As part of her role, she sang the song "I Enjoy Being a Girl," which became a hit. In December of 1958, as a

Pat Suzuki, 1958. (AP/Wide World Photos)

result of her popularity in *Flower Drum Song,* Suzuki was featured, along with Miyoshi Umeki, on the cover of *Time* magazine. Suzuki also appeared in the film version of the musical, although the role of Linda Low was played in the film by Nancy Kwan. She had major roles in the 1969 Burt Reynolds movie *Skullduggery* and in the television series *Mr. T and Tina*. Suzuki continues to appear in films and on television.

Suzuki, Peter T. (b. Nov. 22, 1928, Seattle, Wash.): Scholar. Incarcerated at the Puyallup assembly center (Washington) and in Minidoka (Idaho) during World War II, he later attended Columbia, Yale, and Leiden (Holland) universities. A faculty member at the University of Nebraska, Omaha, since 1973, he has been published in numerous journals, including *Anthropological Linguistics, Dialectical Anthropology, International Third World Studies Journal & Review, Literature East & West: Journal of Comparative World Literature,* and *Sociologus.*

Sze Yup (Siyi): Collective term meaning "four counties" or "four districts," referring to Xinhui (Sunwui), Taishan (Toishan), Kaiping (Hoiping), and Enping (Yanping) counties along China's Tan (Tam) River valley. Before 1912 Taishan was called Xinning (Sunning). Sometimes a fifth adjoining county, Heshan (Hokshan) County, is added, and the group is called collectively Wuyi (Ng yup). The Cantonese subdialects spoken in this region are closely related to one another but are so different from Cantonese as spoken in the Canton region that people from the two areas have difficulty understanding one another.

There was some shifting of county boundaries after 1949. Two major changes are that Jiangmen (Kongmoon) became administratively separate from Xinhui, and a part of Taishan along the Tan River, including Dihai (Dikhoi) and Xinchang (Suncheung), was transferred to Kaiping.

These are counties with heavy emigration. Following are the estimated populations abroad during the 1980's with ancestry from each county: Xinhui and Jiangmen, 570,000; Taishan, 1,105,000; Kaiping, 770,000; Enping, 231,000; Heshan, 228,000. In both Taishan and Kaiping the numbers abroad exceed the populations in the counties.

Sze Yup is a hilly region with limited arable land. During the 1850's and 1860's the area was also the scene for a bitter and bloody conflict between Cantonese and Hakkas during which the former finally prevailed. The destructive effects of the fighting were a contributing factor to an exodus from the region, especially from Taishan.

Up to 1965 Sze Yup people constituted the majority of Chinese in the continental United States. Many of them were unskilled laborers during the nineteenth century. Others were in the cigar-making industry. Still others were connected with laundries and restaurants or were domestic workers. Sze Yup merchants entered the export-import business in great numbers after they broke the monopoly of Sam Yup merchants by means of a long boycott during the 1890's. By the twentieth century, Sze Yup businesses increasingly dominated Chinatowns on the American mainland. Many of the younger American-born generation, however, chose to become clerical workers and professionals.

At their highest point in the nineteenth century, Sze Yup people in the United States numbered about 126,000, with Xinning contributing more than half. The population decreased during the exclusion era, but people of Sze Yup origin still remained the majority among the Chinese population. After 1965 the population increased because of immigration from the People's Republic of China, Hong Kong, and Vietnam. However, there has been no accurate count of the Sze Yup population in the United States during the twentieth century.

T

Tacoma incident (1885): Race riot in which a mob of white citizens of Tacoma, Washington, encouraged by Mayor J. Robert Weisbach, forcibly drove some seven hundred Chinese residents from the city on November 3. As the Chinese were being expelled, the mob set their houses on fire. After the governor of Washington asked for U.S. government intervention, President Grover Cleveland sent federal troops to Tacoma and Seattle, and the riots were ended by November 8. This was the first use of federal militia to protect the lives of Chinese settlers in America. Although ten men were indicted for the incident, the jury refused to convict them, and Judge John P. Hoyt discharged the accused.

Taedon Silop Jusik Hoesa (Great Eastern Business Corporation): Korean American business created in 1910 under the leadership of the KOREAN NATIONAL ASSOCIATION (KNA) to finance the Korean Independence Army.

Taehan Tongnip Manse: Prominent Korean slogan during the MARCH FIRST MOVEMENT (1919), meaning literally, "Long live Korean independence."

Taewon-gun (Yi Ha-ung; 1821—1898): Korean ruler. Regent Taewon-gun, the father of King KOJONG, ruled CHOSON Korea from 1864 to 1873. He categorically rejected the West's diplomatic overtures, wasting a critical period for Korea's national development.

Born as a distant relative of the royal family, Yi Ha-ung spent his young days without a government position. When King Cholchong Chuljong died in 1863, leaving no suitable heir to the throne, the royal family picked Yi's minor son as the successor, providing Yi with an opportunity to rule the country as regent for the minor king.

Taewon-gun (grand prince), Yi's honorary title, was convinced that national rejuvenation would be possible only when it adhered to its traditional Confucian values. As a man of strong will, he strove to restore the order in the court with steely determination, even temporarily quieting the nation's notorious and destructive political infighting. In spite of good intentions, his tenure was full of contradictions, ranging from recharged nationalism and fresh enthusiasm exhibited in extensive national rebuilding programs to anachronistic anti-Western campaigns. As a result, his old-fashioned politics invited growing opposition.

The lasting legacy of Taewon-gun's rule was not its effective and far-sighted administrative undertakings but its disastrous anti-Western campaigns. His anti-West stand was voluminously demonstrated by his regime's steadfast rejection of Western overtures for dialogue and diplomatic relations. He successfully mobilized the nation against the small but better-equipped naval detachments sent by France and the United States. Taewon-gun's extreme isolationism was a stark contrast to Japan's open-door policy during this period. He was one of the Choson Dynasty's most nationalistic leaders. Yet his archaic policy toward the West was highly destructive and hastened the demise of the regime. His enemies, led by his daughter-in-law, Queen Min, ousted him from power, using the legitimate excuse of the king's reaching adulthood in 1873.

Taft-Katsura Agreement (1905): Secret memorandum exchanged by U.S. secretary of war William Howard Taft and Japan's prime minister Katsura Taro endorsing Japanese domination in Korea and U.S. hegemony in the Philippines. Following the July agreement, Japan forced the Korean government to accept status as a protectorate, under the PROTECTORATE TREATY of November, 1905. Korea later became a Japanese colony, from 1910 until 1945 (the end of World War II).

Tagalog: Second-largest cultural-linguistic group in the Philippines. It is also the dialect of the Tagalog, the

Filipino family makes a living by fishing. (Philippine National Tourist Office)

dominant people group of Manila and south Luzon. Tagalog, an Austronesian language like the other Philippine languages, is one of the estimated 70 to 150 different languages and dialects spoken in the Philippine Islands. Pilipino, a version of Tagalog, is the national language and is taught in the public school system. English, however, remains the most widely read and spoken language, and Cebuano is the most widely spoken native tongue.

Tagore, Rabindranath (May 7, 1861, Calcutta, West Bengal, India—Aug. 7, 1941, Calcutta, West Bengal, India): Writer. Tagore is best known as the first Asian to win the Nobel Prize in Literature (1913). He is also famous for his educational philosophy, which became the basis of the university he founded in 1921 in northeastern India, Visva-Bharati University (meaning a "university viewing the world from India"). The significance of Tagore's theory of education is his strong emphasis on individual creativity, an appreciation of the natural world, and a return to more traditional Indian systems. He believed that true education can only be had in one's own language and with subject material pertinent to the student's life and culture. Through Visva-Bharati he also started the Rural Reconstruction movement, a pioneering effort in rural community development in India and Asia.

Tagore was born into an aristocratic family of artists and social reformers. In 1878 he published *Kavi-Kahini*, his first book of poems. During this time he was in India studying English with his brother. Later that same year Tagore went to England to attend private school. He did not complete his studies and returned to India in 1880.

Another volume of verse, *Bana-phul*, appeared in 1880. Tagore continued to compose, in his native language of Bengali, poetry, essays, plays, novels, and songs for the next sixty years, culminating in some sixty volumes of work. His book of poems *Gitanjali* (1910; *Gitanjali [Song Offerings]*, 1912) won for him the 1913 Nobel Prize. He was knighted by the British (who were then the colonial rulers of India) in 1915 but relinquished the honor in 1919 as a form of political protest against British oppression, specifically the AMRITSAR massacre of 1919.

Throughout the second half of his life, Tagore traveled extensively through North America, South America, Europe, and Asia, winning many friends and admirers.

Tagore composed some twenty-five hundred songs, and they are fondly sung in India and in Bangladesh.

Rabindranath Tagore was the first Asian writer to win the Nobel Prize in Literature (1913). (AP/Wide World Photos)

These songs reflect the full range of human experience: loving, longing, suffering, worshiping, and wondering about the relevance of life. These songs form a new musical tradition in South Asia, known as "Rabindra-Sangeet" (music of Tagore). Both India and Bangladesh adopted songs by Tagore as their national anthems. Several of his short stories have been the basis of films by the late Bengali film director Satyajit Ray.

Tai Dam: Ethnic group who originally lived along the Red and Black rivers in the northwestern provinces of Vietnam; also known as "Tai Noir" or "Black Tai." As allies of the French, the Tai Dam were forced to leave their homeland when the Communist VIET MINH government of Ho Chi Minh took control of North Vietnam in the wake of the Geneva treaty of 1954. Most of the Tai Dam fled to neighboring Laos or to South Vietnam. After the fall of Saigon in 1975 and the Communist invasions of Laos and Cambodia, the Tai Dam were displaced a second time. Many sought safety in the refugee camps of Thailand.

When Iowa governor Robert Ray became aware of the desperate needs of the Tai Dam and other Southeast Asian refugees, he established a special task force on Indo-Chinese resettlement in 1975. Once the Tai Dam began to arrive in the United States, they were assigned to American volunteer sponsors who helped them locate homes, find employment, learn English, and master other skills necessary for their survival. As families were reunited and relatives and friends settled near one another, the population of Tai Dam immigrants in Iowa had grown to some twenty-six hundred by the late 1980's. This figure represented approximately 90 percent of the total Tai Dam population in the United States. As the needs of these refugees grew, the state of Iowa established special organizations, such as the Iowa Refugee Service Center in Des Moines and Iowa Sends Help to Aid Refugees and End Starvation (Iowa SHARES), that helped coordinate the sponsorship, job training, literacy training, and other relief efforts of churches, charitable agencies, and individual volunteers.

While many of the younger, American-educated Tai Dam and their American-born offspring have become readily assimilated, older members of Tai Dam society have maintained traditional styles of dress, food, and social behavior and have worked to preserve their native language through books and oral history.

Tai languages: Family of languages spoken in most of Thailand, in parts of southern China, and in the northern areas of Laos, Myanmar, and Vietnam. A few Tai languages such as Khamti are also spoken in the province of Assam in northeast India. Since the term "Thai" is generally used to refer to the official language of Thailand, when discussing the linguistic group as a whole the spelling "Tai" is generally used by most linguists.

Approximately forty different Tai languages exist, and scholars usually divide them into three linguistic groups: Northern Tai, Central Tai, and Southwestern Tai. Major languages include Thai proper (or Siamese), Laotian (the national language of Laos), Shan

Marble temple, Bangkok, Thailand. (John Penisten, Pacific Pictures)

(in Myanmar), and Yuan (in Thailand). Each of these languages is spoken by millions of people, with more than sixty million speakers of Thai alone. Standard Thai itself is one of the major languages of the world, being among the top twenty or twenty-five languages in terms of number of speakers. There are more speakers of Thai than speakers of Greek, Polish, Swahili, Serbo-Croatian, Ukranian, or all the Scandinavian languages combined.

The relationship of the Tai languages to other families is the subject of much debate and speculation among linguists. Because these languages are also tonal languages (where differences in pitch when pronouncing a word can make a difference in meaning), the Tai languages have been thought to be related to the SINO-TIBETAN LANGUAGES of China and Tibet. The exact connections, however, remain to be positively demonstrated. Some linguists claim a connection between the Tai languages and the Kadai languages of Hainan and southern China—arguing for a "Tai-Kadai" language family—while suggesting the possibilities of relating them to the AUSTRONESIAN (Malayo-Polynesian) LANGUAGES of Indonesia, the Philippines, and the Pacific (making an "Austro-Tai" superfamily). Tai languages do seem to be distantly related to the Kam-Sui languages in Guangxi and Guizhou in southern China.

Many structural similarities exist between Tai and SINITIC (Chinese) LANGUAGES. Both have subject-verb-object word order, both have words that consist largely of a single syllable, and both are tonal (with most Tai languages having five tones). Furthermore, adjectives and modifiers precede the noun that is modified in both Tai and Sinitic languages, and, in both languages, grammar for the most part is determined by word order (as it is in English) as opposed to being determined by inflectional endings on words (as in Latin). Tai and Sinitic languages also all require the use of numeral classifiers (such as "two pairs of glasses" or "a flock of geese") to be used with the noun being counted. The Tai and Sinitic languages, however, vary rather substantially in terms of phonology and vocabulary.

Some of the Tai languages have no writing system, but major languages such as Thai and Lao do, using an alphabet derived from India and borrowed in the thirteenth and fourteenth centuries. Like other Indian scripts, symbols for consonant letters already contain an inherent vowel, and other signs are added to this symbol to write other vowels.

Taiko: Form of massed drumming that originated simultaneously in Japan and the United States in the late

Japanese American taiko drum performers, New Otani Hotel, Los Angeles. (Diane C. Lyell)

1960's. The term itself is a Japanese word meaning "drum." In Japan, drums were widely used as musical instruments in festivals and theatrical performances, but they never exceeded three or four at a time. Massed drumming arose as a form of entertainment at hot springs and other tourist centers in northern Japan. The drums were frequently associated with SHINTO and MARTIAL-ARTS traditions, and were limited primarily to male performers.

In the United States, *taiko* groups are more closely connected to Buddhist temples, having developed as a form of Buddhist performing arts called *horaku* (dharmic entertainment). Perhaps the first Japanese American *taiko* group was the Kinnara Taiko, founded in 1969 at the Senshin Buddhist Temple in Los Angeles. The term "Kinnara" comes from the Sanskrit word for celestial musicians in Buddhist cosmology. Developed from the BON ODORI outdoor dance music of Buddhist temples, Kinnara Taiko offers a unique manifestation of Japanese American Buddhist music. Distinct from the Japanese form of *taiko*, the group is a product of American culture. It consists of twelve to fifteen performers (both men and women), and, besides drums of

Taiko drum performers, Bon Odori Japanese Dance Festival, Seattle, Washington. (Unicorn Stock Photos)

various sizes, it uses flutes, shell horns, bells, and percussion instruments. Pieces include dances such as the lion dance, based on *bugaku* (ancient court music), and comic interludes. The Kinnara Taiko has performed annually at the Senshin Obon Festival and has conducted innumerable workshops for temples forming their own *taiko* groups in California, Utah, Hawaii, Colorado, and other states. It has also performed at public schools, universities, folk festivals, and Japanese American gatherings.

Taipei: Capital of TAIWAN. In 1949, when the defeated Chinese Nationalist forces fled from the mainland to Taiwan, Taipei became the capital of their government-in-exile. Today it is a major industrial and financial center, with strong links to segments of the Chinese American community. The city's population in 1991 was 2,724,829.

Taiping Rebellion (1850-1864): Massive uprising against the Manchu Qing government by the God Worshipers Society. The Taiping Rebellion erupted in the southern provinces of GUANGDONG and Guangxi and spread through sixteen provinces, reaching within seventy miles of Beijing, the capital. This was the most destructive rebellion in China's history in terms of territory wasted and lives lost.

Initially the movement aroused support from disadvantaged segments of society such as HAKKAS, unemployed transit workers, landless peasants, secret society members, and pirates. Late QING economic and administrative crises, aggravated by foreign imperialism, burdened such groups with overtaxation, high rent, a shortage of farm land, banditry, local feuds, and government corruption and inefficiency.

HONG XIUQUAN (1814-1864), leader of the movement, attacked MANCHU rule and CONFUCIANISM. Declaring himself Heavenly King of the Taiping Tianguo (Heavenly Kingdom of Great Peace), Hong and his associate kings created a government in Nanjing that blended Christian elements with radical proposals for a tightly regulated society. Laws segregated and equalized the sexes; distributed land to all families; held money in a common treasury; prohibited prostitution, opium, and alcohol; and instituted examinations based on the Bible for men and women.

Hong's revolutionary ideas were inspired by Christian missionary tracts and personal misfortune. After failing the civil service examination three times, the young scholar from a poor Hakka family suffered a breakdown and, in a delirium, experienced a vision in which he met his older brother, Jesus, and God, his heavenly father. After a fourth failure he interpreted the vision as God's instructions to destroy demonic forces, represented by the Manchus.

The general populace opposed the destructiveness and radical nature of the Taipings, and Western powers supported the Qing. Murderous rivalry among the leaders, and their abuse of power, destroyed the faith of followers. The Qing relied on new gentry-led armies to suppress the Taipings. The Xiang army, recruited and trained by Hunan provincial official Zeng Guofan, recaptured Nanjing and crushed the rebels in 1864.

In the aftermath local conflicts between PUNTI and Hakka in south China and impoverishment of the population spurred Chinese overseas migration in the late nineteenth century.

Taira, Linda (b. Tokyo, Japan): Broadcast journalist. In 1985 she became the Cable News Network's congressional correspondent and won the National Headliner Award for her coverage of the U.S. Senate's Iran-Contra hearings in 1987. She hails from Kaneohe, Hawaii, and received her bachelor's degree from the University of Hawaii.

Taiwan: The history of this island has included several phases of foreign conquest. As a result, the country's population is somewhat varied and Taiwanese culture, religion, and language have had numerous influences.

Geography and Climate. Taiwan is not one island but many, consisting of fifteen from the Taiwan group and sixty-four from the Pescadores Archipelago. The main island is bounded on the south by the Bashi Channel, which separates Taiwan from the Philippines; to the east by the Pacific Ocean; to the north by the East China Sea; and to the west by the Formosa Strait, which separates it from mainland China. The western coast of Taiwan is straight and bordered by lagoons and sand dunes. To the east is the Chung-yang Shan-mo mountain range, while the west has fertile plains. Taiwan's rivers are largely unnavigable because of their extreme fluctuations—flooded in the monsoon season and shallow or dried up in the dry season. Because of this geography, most of the popula-

tion lives in western Taiwan and few towns are located alongside rivers.

The climate of Taiwan, partly tropical and partly subtropical, is influenced greatly by the warm Kuroshio Current of the Pacific. There are basically two seasons: Summer is wet, warm, and long, stretching from April to November, while winter is mild and relatively dry. Typhoons occur mostly in July, August, and September. The rainfall in Taiwan is quite heavy, especially in the summer.

Early Immigration and Conquest. For many centuries, Taiwan was known to the West as Formosa, a Portuguese word meaning "beautiful." Many nations, admiring that beauty, have taken the island for themselves. The aborigines of Taiwan, the original inhabitants of the island, were of Indonesian origin. Today they make up only 1 to 2 percent of the population and are divided into nine families: the Atayal, the Saisat, the Paiwan, the Rutkai, the Bunun, the Tsou, the Yami, the Ami, and the Puyuma; of these, the Atayal, Paiwan, and Bunun are the most numerous. There are several aboriginal dialects, and these groups still practice many kinds of tribal worship.

Some of the first immigrants to Taiwan were European. Portuguese explorers landed in the sixteenth century, and the early seventeenth century brought the establishment of Dutch and Spanish settlements. The Dutch immigrants introduced Protestantism to Taiwan,

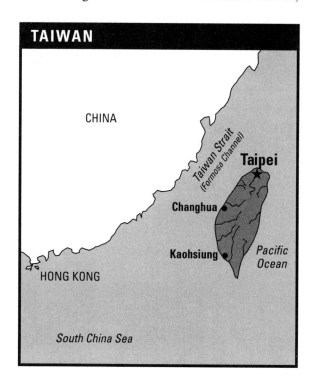

while the Spanish settlers brought Roman Catholicism. Such faraway countries could not compete, however, with Taiwan's powerful neighbor, mainland China.

Chinese immigrants from the provinces of FUJIAN and GUANGDONG poured onto the island, and by the end of the seventeenth century, China had incorporated Taiwan into its vast empire, using it as a resource and an outpost. By the nineteenth century, the city of Taipei had become a center for overseas trade. Today approximately 80 percent of the people on the island trace their heritage to these early Chinese immigrants. They brought the religions TAOISM, BUDDHISM, and CONFUCIANISM and the Chinese dialects of the Fujian Province. (Later the Nationalists, who make up almost 20 percent of the population, would declare Mandarin the island's official language.) Chinese painting, music, dance, and opera are the predominant cultural influences in Taiwan.

In 1895, however, Taiwan fell under Japanese influence when China ceded the island after being defeated in the SINO-JAPANESE WAR OF 1894-1895. The Japanese immigrants introduced the high-grade *pon-lai* rice to Taiwan, which now makes up two-thirds of the rice crop grown there, as well as the religion Shintoism. Japan also made TAIPEI the capital of the island and began programs for industrialization and agricultural modernization. In 1945, when Japan surrendered and brought an end to World War II, Taiwan reverted to China.

Chiang Kai-shek Arrives. The postwar China that Taiwan rejoined was not a stable one: The GUOMINDANG (the Nationalists), under Chinese president CHIANG KAI-SHEK, were at war with the People's Liberation Army (the Communists), under MAO ZEDONG. Moreover, many Taiwanese had cooperated with the Japanese and were not eager to become a part of China again; the Chinese government reacted harshly to such sentiments.

Therefore, in 1949, the people of Taiwan felt invaded once again when the defeated Chiang, 2 million of his troops, and their families fled the Communist forces on the mainland and established a government-in-exile in Taipei, dubbing the island the Republic of CHINA (ROC). To complicate matters, the Nationalists de-

Taiwanese tourists visit the Midwest. (Unicorn Stock Photos)

Mao Zedong reviews Chinese Communist troops, 1949, the year Chiang Kai-shek and his Nationalist government fled to exile in Taiwan. (AP/Wide World Photos)

First Lady Eleanor Roosevelt visits with Madame Chiang Kai-shek at the White House, 1943. (Library of Congress)

Contemporary Taipei, Taiwan. (Taiwan Coordination Council)

clared their administration to be the legitimate government of all China. The Communist government in Beijing, now officially heading the People's Republic of CHINA (PRC), also claimed that title. Both sides agreed, however, that Taiwan was a part of mainland China.

It was fortunate for the arriving Nationalists that the People's Liberation Army concentrated on crushing resistance on the mainland and on conquering Tibet, because this strategy allowed Chiang and his troops to survive until the start of the KOREAN WAR in 1950. That civil war soon became a struggle between the United States and the PRC. Thus, Taiwan now held a strategic position for the West as part of a Pacific system of defense; the United States sent the 7th Fleet to guard the island and offered economic and military aid. In 1953, a more confident Chiang began a series of four-year economic plans for industrial and military development. On December 2, 1954, the United States signed a treaty with Taiwan promising to come to its defense for the indefinite future.

Taiwan Under the Nationalists. Despite heavy bombing in the late 1950's, especially of the islands Matsu and Chinmen (Quemoy) near the coast of mainland China, the Republic of China flourished economically. The agricultural industry now produces rice, sugarcane, tea, wheat, pineapple, and many other fruits and vegetables, some for export. Taiwan has become best known for its manufacturing, which was begun under the Japanese and expanded by the Nationalists. The government manufactures such commodities as coal, paper, sugar, machinery, cement, and aluminum, while textile production is privately owned. Other major industries include electrical appliances, food processing, chemicals, leather goods, glass, tobacco processing, and rubber goods. By the 1990's, Taiwan also had a vital underground economy; many businesses, such as cable television, hotels, and bus services, were being operated illegally by entrepreneurs who could not obtain licenses.

Taiwan has not thrived as a democracy, however, as martial law was in effect from 1949 to 1987 and the

Former Secretary of State Henry Kissinger (left) and former President Richard Nixon. (Library of Congress)

Nationalists continued to have power disproportionate to their numbers. The president of the country is elected by the National Assembly, which is composed of delegates from the counties. The constitution of the ROC gives its citizens the powers of election, referendum, recall, and initiative, but the last two have been suspended; they are exercised by the National Assembly on behalf of the people. Nevertheless, the country is becoming more democratic, as Taiwanese-born politicians such as President Lee Teng-hui emerge to replace the old guard from the mainland. In addition, while the main political party remains the GUOMIN-DANG, the opposition Democratic Progressive Party is growing in influence. Discussion of Taiwanese self-rule is no longer viewed as sedition.

An Uncertain Future. Taiwan's comfortable position under the protection of the United States was shaken in the 1970's when the Nixon Administration began to normalize relations with the People's Republic of China. In 1979, President Jimmy Carter ended defense ties with Taiwan and affirmed mainland China's position that there is only one China and Taiwan is a part of it, thus withdrawing support for Taiwanese self-rule. All ties were not broken, however, as the United States passed the Taiwan Relations Act and continued to sell defensive weapons to the Nationalists.

The ideology of counterattack developed by Chiang Kai-shek, which stated that the Nationalists would one day reconquer the mainland, survived his death in 1975. In 1979, the Communist government undermined this resolve, however, by promising special status to the island if it returned peacefully, such as political autonomy, separate economic systems, and its own armed forces. Taiwan rejected these overtures. Yet by the 1990's, talks between the two longtime enemies were under way. In 1993, four agreements were signed, calling for the delivery of registered letters, the exchange of official documents, a schedule for contact between the two governments, and a plan to deal with crime, illegal immigration, fisheries disputes, legal cooperation, and the protection of intellectual property. Agreements could not be made, how-

Taiwanese Immigration to the U.S., 1982-1991

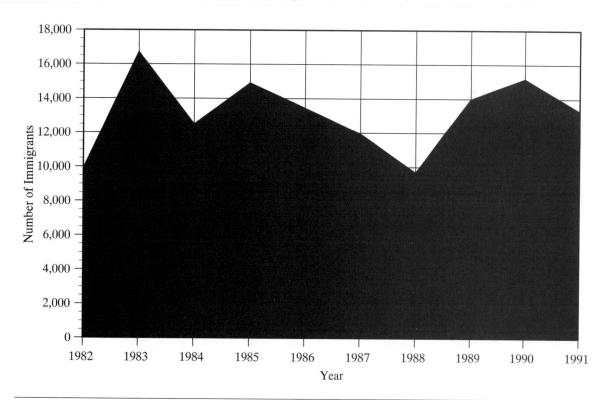

Source: Susan B. Gall and Timothy L. Gall, eds., *Statistical Record of Asian Americans.* Detroit: Gale Research, Inc., 1993.
Note: Taiwanese immigrants were not counted separately by the Immigration and Naturalization Service until 1982.

ever, concerning economic issues.

The import of these talks was unclear. Were they intended to help normalize relations between separate nations, leading to an independent Taiwan, or were they paving the way for peaceful reunification of the "two Chinas"? The only certainties are that both governments continue to consider Taiwan and mainland China to be one country and that an increasingly vocal opposition continues to demand Taiwanese self-rule.—*Tracy Irons*

SUGGESTED READINGS: • Cohen, Marc J. *Taiwan at the Crossroads: Human Rights, Political Development, and Social Change on the Beautiful Island*. Washington, D.C.: Asia Resource Center, 1988. • Fu, Jen-kun. *Taiwan and the Geopolitics of the Asian-American Dilemma*. New York: Praeger, 1992. • Hsieh, Chiao-min. *Taiwan—Ilha Formosa: A Geography in Perspective*. Washington, D.C.: Butterworths, 1964. • Hsiung, James C., et al., eds. *The Taiwan Experience, 1950-1980: Contemporary Republic of China*. New York: American Association of Chinese Studies, 1981. • Kerr, George H. *Formosa: Licensed Revolution and the Home Rule Movement, 1895-1945*. Honolulu: University Press of Hawaii, 1974.

Taiwan independence movement: Effort to establish a sovereign and independent Taiwan that is separate from the Chinese mainland. Such an entity would be autonomous from both the Communist regime of the People's Republic of CHINA on the mainland as well as the Nationalist regime of the Republic of CHINA (ROC) on Taiwan. (See GUOMINDANG.)

The movement developed out of the circumstances that followed the restoration of Taiwan, after fifty years of Japanese colonial rule, to the sovereign jurisdiction of the ROC in 1945. Resentment by the native Taiwanese against mainland rule erupted in an uprising on February 28, 1947, which was violently suppressed by government forces. Native resentment was exacerbated by the resettlement in 1949 of the ROC regime onto Taiwan, in the wake of the Nationalists' defeat by the Communists.

Banned by the ROC government, movement advocates created organizations outside Taiwan—in Japan,

Lantern festival, Chiang Kai-shek Memorial Hall. (Taiwan Coordination Council)

the United States, Canada, and Western Europe. The movement included both moderates and radicals. The moderates, such as the Formosan Association for Public Affairs (FAPA), sought independence through peaceful political means, by lobbying the U.S. Congress, for example. The radicals—the Taiwan Independence League, for example—advocated the employment of violent methods, including terrorism and the revolutionary overthrow of the ROC government. Between 1970 and 1984 movement extremists undertook twenty-six incidents of terrorism in Taiwan and the United States, including the attempted assassination in 1970 of then-ROC vice premier Chiang Ching-Kuo in New York.

In 1987 the ROC government began a series of liberalizing reforms that, among other effects, empowered the TAIWAN independence movement and made it more mainstream. In July, 1987, martial law was lifted, as well as the decades-old ban on new political parties. In this manner the Democratic Progressive Party (DPP), already in existence for a year, was legitimated and quickly established itself as the leading opposition party. In the December, 1992, elections to the national legislature, the DPP won 31 percent of the popular vote, against the ruling Guomindang's 53 percent. With a membership of more than forty-five thousand, composed mainly of native Taiwanese, the DPP became the vehicle by which movement activists became mainstream. On October 13, 1991, the DPP amended its party platform to call for the creation, through a national plebiscite, of a "Republic of Taiwan" separate from mainland China, with its own membership in the United Nations.

Tajima, Renee (b. Sept. 11, 1958, New York, N.Y.): Filmmaker and writer. Renee Tajima, a documentary filmmaker, is best known for *Who Killed Vincent Chin?* (1989), which she made with Christine CHOY. The film, which was originally intended to be a five-minute video supporting the mother of Vincent CHIN, who was beaten to death by two men who were merely placed on probation and fined for their actions, eventually became a full-length documentary and was nominated for an Oscar. Tajima and Choy have also made a television documentary about poverty and *Fortune Cookie: The Myth of the Model Minority*, an examina-

Film director Renee Tajima (left) and producer Christine Choy discuss reactions to their documentary film "Who Killed Vincent Chin?" (AP/Wide World Photos)

tion of "the Asian American success story." Tajima has also written articles and critical pieces for the *Village Voice* and has written for National Public Radio.

Tajiri, Larry (1914, Los Angeles, Calif.—1961): Journalist. A Nisei born in Los Angeles, Tajiri attended Los Angeles Polytechnic High School, where he worked on the school's newspaper. Under his direction as editor, the *Poly Optimist* won an award in 1931 as the best school paper in Southern California. After a single year in college, Tajiri left school to take a post as editor of the *Kashu Mainichi*'s English-language section. In 1934, he moved to San Francisco in order to join the staff of the prestigious NICHIBEI SHIMBUN. Working alongside veteran journalist Kay Nishida as editor, Tajiri continued his own column, "Village Vagaries," originally published in the *Kashu Mainichi*. Known for his interest in labor issues, he supported unionization among Nisei laborers. He helped organize Young Democrat groups among the Japanese American community in the Bay Area. In addition to his journalism, Tajiri produced short stories that were published in several Japanese American literary journals. He left San Francisco for New York City to take a post as staff writer for the Japanese-owned Tokyo and Osaka *Asahi* in 1940. With the declaration of war against Japan in 1941, Tajiri lost his job on the *Asahi* and returned to Los Angeles. He and his wife were invited to edit the PACIFIC CITIZEN, the official newspaper of the JAPANESE AMERICAN CITIZENS LEAGUE (JACL). They continued to edit the paper from Salt Lake City beginning in 1942 and continuing through the early 1950's. In 1952, Larry Tajiri left the *Pacific Citizen* to join the staff of the *Denver Post* as an art and literary critic and wrote for the paper until his death in 1961.

Takaezu, Toshiko (b. June 17, 1922, Pepeeko, Territory of Hawaii): Ceramist, sculptor, and weaver. Takaezu attended the Honolulu School of Art in 1948 to learn sculpture and, subsequently, ceramics. She continued her art studies at an academy in Michigan before teaching briefly at the University of Wisconsin, after which she traveled to Japan to learn Japanese pottery and explore Zen philosophy. She has taught at Princeton University since 1967.

In the United States, Takaezu's works are found in museum collections in such major cities as Boston, New York, and Baltimore. She has in addition staged solo exhibitions at galleries across the country. In 1982 she won the prestigious Dickson College Award. Be-

sides ceramics, she has woven textiles, sculpted bronze bells, and produced paintings.

Takagi, Paul (b. May 3, 1923, Auburn, Calif.): Scholar. Graduated with a Ph.D. degree from Stanford University in 1967, he was professor of education and criminology at the University of California, Berkeley, until his retirement in 1989. He was the first Asian American Ph.D. recipient in sociology from Stanford, the first Asian American tenured professor in the social sciences at Berkeley, and the first in criminology to advance the theory that racism played an important role in police brutality.

Takahashi, Sakae (b. Dec. 8, 1919, Makaweli, Kauai, Territory of Hawaii): State senator. Takahashi, a highly respected officer in the famed 100TH INFANTRY BATTALION of World War II, came home to participate in the Democratic Party "revolution" that changed Hawaii.

Takahashi was born in a Kauai plantation community, where his father owned a country store. Takahashi served as a first lieutenant, then a captain, in World War II. While he was hospitalized for battle wounds, he and Daniel K. INOUYE, a fellow patient who later became a U.S. senator from Hawaii, held long discussions on their frustrations of being unequal citizens of that state.

After using the GI Bill to earn a degree from Rutgers University Law School, Takahashi returned home to become one of the first Japanese American veterans to make a mark in politics. He became part of a group that met regularly with John BURNS, acknowledged Democratic leader of the "revolution" that broke the Republican dominance of the islands. In quick succession Takahashi won a seat on the Board of Supervisors in 1950, appointment as treasurer of the Territory in 1951, and a Senate seat in 1954. His appointment as treasurer was seen as a breakthrough because it was the first time that a Japanese American had served in a cabinet position in the territorial government.

As a senator, Takahashi provided the Democrats with progressive leadership as they worked to implement their goal of a "New Hawaii," with such proposals as a graduated income tax and laws opening up the housing market.

From about 1967 a breach between the Burns faction and Takahashi developed. The latter's disenchantment was based partly on what he saw as an undesirable property developer orientation of the Burns Administration. During the 1969 legislative session,

Takahashi fought against the Burns-backed Magic Island development plan to turn the state-owned parcel of land in Honolulu into hotel and tourist facilities run by private entrepreneurs. Today Magic Island is a public park because, although Takahashi lost, the next legislature was forced to reverse the decision on Magic Island because of public pressure. Years later Takahashi stated simply, "People in the legislature who do not take a stand when they feel that something is wrong have no business being a legislator."

Takahashi v. Fish and Game Commission (1948): U.S. Supreme Court case challenging the California Fish and Game Commission law that prohibited persons ineligible for U.S. citizenship from receiving commercial fishing licenses to fish off the California coast. The Court ruled in favor of Torao Takahashi and dismissed the argument by the state of California that the law under question was passed to conserve fish.

Ronald Takaki, University of California professor of ethnic studies. (Asian Week)

Takaki, Ronald (b. Apr. 12, 1939, Honolulu, Territory of Hawaii): Scholar. One of the most influential figures in the field of ASIAN AMERICAN STUDIES, and a leading scholar of racism and race relations, Takaki is the grandson of immigrant plantation laborers from Japan. He holds a B.A. degree from the College of Wooster (Ohio) and a Ph.D. degree in American history from the University of California, Berkeley. A professor of ethnic studies at Berkeley, Takaki helped to found the university's doctoral program in that field. He has authored several books, including *A Pro-Slavery Crusade: The Agitation to Reopen the African Slave Trade* (1971), *Violence in the Black Imagination: Essays and Documents* (1972), *Iron Cages: Race and Culture in Nineteenth-Century America* (1979), *Pau Hana: Plantation Life and Labor in Hawaii*

(1983), *From Different Shores: Perspectives on Race and Ethnicity in America* (1987), *Strangers from a Different Shore: A History of Asian Americans* (1989), which was nominated for a Pulitzer Prize, and *A Different Mirror: The Making of a Multicultural America* (1993).

Takamine, Jokichi (Nov. 3, 1854, Takaoka, Japan—July 22, 1922, New York, N.Y.): Chemist. He first visited the United States in 1884, settling there in 1890. In 1901, he isolated adrenalin from the adrenal gland, becoming the first to obtain a glandular hormone in pure form. This breakthrough led to widespread medical applications. He discovered Takadiastase, an amylase enzyme from daikon that changes starch to sugar, and also discovered that adrenalin stopped bleeding. He cofounded the Japanese Association of New York and sought to foster cultural exchange between the United States and Japan. He received the third class of Sacred Treasure from the Japanese government in 1922.

Takei, George (b. Apr. 20, 1939, Los Angeles, Calif.): Actor. He was graduated from the University of California, Los Angeles (UCLA), and studied drama in Hollywood. His career has included roles in television, films such as *Walk, Don't Run* (1966) and *The Green Berets* (1968), and theater. He is best known for his role as Sulu in the original *Star Trek* (1966-1969)

Actor George Takei. (Twentieth Century Artists)

television series on NBC. Takei also appeared in each of the six Star Trek motion pictures released between 1979 and 1991. In addition he has spoken out against racial stereotypes in the media and held various governmental appointments. He contributes a regular column to *Transpacific* magazine.

Talk Story Conference: Abbreviated name for the June 19-24, 1978, watershed literary event held in Honolulu, formally entitled, "Talk Story, Our Voices in Literature and Song: Hawaii's Ethnic American Writers' Conference." Organized by the Hawaii Ethnic Resources Center: Talk Story, Inc., under the leadership of Marie M. Hara, Arnold T. Hiura, and Stephen H. SUMIDA, the conference wore the motto, "Words bind, and words set free," which neatly described its goals: to consolidate, celebrate, and encourage the creation of literature by and about Hawaii's peoples, the distinct ethnic groups that compose Hawaii's cultural pluralism.

As demonstrated by the research of Hiura and Sumida published subsequently as *Asian American Literature in Hawaii: An Annotated Bibliography* (1979), individual Asian Americans have been writing poetry, prose, and drama in English in Hawaii since the 1920's. Yet even into the late 1970's, Hawaii's literature was still dominated, plantation-like, by the singular aesthetic of *haole* arbiters in the University of Hawaii's Department of English. The breakthrough significance of Talk Story was in providing an alternate forum for an emerging critical mass of ethnic writers to explore areas of common ground, where the creative matrices of individual writers might overlap—in the vernacular, to "talk story."

In the years following Talk Story, additional conferences, related anthologies, and Hiura and Sumida's bibliography all followed. *Bamboo Ridge: The Hawaii Writers' Quarterly*, which had started publication also in 1978 in that same literary groundswell, came to full flower, encouraging primarily creative writing. Those affiliated with Talk Story and *Bamboo Ridge* further extended their activities to the Hawaii Literary Arts Council and, importantly, into Hawaii's public schools. Later still, Sumida published his pioneering work of literary criticism *And the View from the Shore: Literary Traditions in Hawaii* (1991), using Talk Story as a base for research. In hindsight, a great many of the critical issues that Hawaii writers today face were in some way raised during Talk Story: for example, probably the first public critique of Maxine Hong KINGSTON by Frank CHIN (in absentia); the love/hate relationship

between mainland and local Asian Americans (notably, on whether locals were too apolitical); similar conflicts among the distant yet interconnected local writing communities (Asian American, Native Hawaiian, *haole*); the debate regarding assimilation versus acculturation; the question of Pidgin English's legitimacy; and the differences as a result of gender or generations. That these issues were first articulated during Talk Story is the true mark of its lasting influence.

Tamamoto, T. [Tsunetaro] (b. Japan?): Actor. A well-known veteran of theater and film, he was touted as the first English-speaking Japanese actor in America. Described by critics of his day as a superbly refined actor, he planned to pursue directing and theater management. Between 1909 and 1923, however, he was relegated to playing "stage Orientals" in Broadway comedies and melodramatic potboilers. His silent films include *Paid in Full* (1914) and *The Innocence of Ruth* (1916).

Tamayo, William R. (b. Sept. 4, 1953, San Francisco, Calif.): Attorney. Managing attorney of the ASIAN LAW CAUCUS, a San Francisco-based public interest law office, he has written extensively on the practice of immigration and nationality law, proposed redistrict-

Attorney William Tamayo. (Asian Week)

ing efforts aimed at giving Asian Americans a greater voice in government, and fought against housing discrimination. He chairs the National Network for Immigrant and Refugee Rights and sits on the board of directors of the American Civil Liberties Union (ACLU) of California.

Tambiah, S. J. [Stanley Jeyaraja] (b. Jan. 16, 1929, Ceylon, now Sri Lanka): Scholar. A professor at Harvard University, he is best known for his volumes on Thai Buddhism: *Buddhism and the Spirit Cults in Northeast Thailand* (1970), *World Conqueror and World Renouncer: A Study of Buddhism and Polity in Thailand Against a Historical Background* (1976), and *The Buddhist Saints of the Forest and the Cult of Amulets: A Study in Charisma, Hagiography, Sectarianism, and Millennial Buddhism* (1984). He is also an expert on the political and social economy of Sri Lanka. Tambiah attended Cornell University, earning his Ph.D. degree in 1954.

Tamil: Official language of the state of Tamil Nadu in South India. It belongs to the South Dravidian branch of the Dravidian language family. Along with English, Tamil is recognized as one of the national languages of India. It is spoken in South Asian countries (India, Sri Lanka) and beyond South Asia (Burma, Malaysia, Singapore, Madagascar, Martinique, Mauritius, Trinidad, Fiji, Surinam, Guyana, South Africa, and other countries) by approximately fifty million people, either as a first or second language.

Tamil is written in a syllabic script that is derived from the Brahmi script. It is written from left to right and has twelve basic symbols for the vowels and eighteen for the consonants. Modern Tamil is a descendant of the Old Tamil language. There are three distinct stages of Tamil: Old Tamil (200 B.C.E. to 700 C.E.), Medieval Tamil (700 C.E. to 1500), and Modern Tamil (1500 to the present).

During these three stages of development, Tamil dialects evolved along three dimensions: geography, caste, and diglossia. The last two dimensions are particularly noteworthy. There are two main caste-based dialects: Brahmin and non-Brahmin, which sharply differ from each other in terms of grammar and vocabulary. At the turn of the twentieth century, it appeared that the Brahmin dialect of Madras was destined to become the standard dialect of Modern Tamil. The Pure Tamil movement of the 1900's, however, changed this. It is the high non-Brahmin central dialect, spoken in the cities of Madurai, Tanjore, and Tiruchchirappalli, that is emerging as the standard dialect. The Pure Tamil movement aimed at freeing the language from its foreign elements, particularly its SANSKRIT vocabulary.

Tamil dialects are well known for their diglossic variation, in which the "high" formal variety (*centamiz*) sharply differs from the "low" informal variety (*kotuntamiz*). The high variety is used in writing, radio, television, and political and other formal settings such as literary endeavors, whereas the low variety is used in casual informal communication. The high variety differs significantly from the low variety in terms of vocabulary and grammar.

Tan, Amy (b. Feb. 19, 1952, Oakland, Calif.): Novelist. Tan was born three years after her parents emigrated to the United States. Both Tan's father and brother died within months of each other when she was fifteen. Tan's mother then took her and her younger brother to Montreux, Switzerland, where she completed her high school education. The family later returned to the United States, where Tan completed her college education.

After a career as a technical writer, which left her exhausted, Tan turned to therapy as a way of dealing with unresolved issues in her life. Therapy provided no solutions, so she turned to writing fiction.

In 1985, she enrolled in a writer's workshop. The result was a short story entitled "Endgame." It was first published locally, and later in *Seventeen*. "Endgame" attracted the attention of a literary agent for G. P. Putnam's Sons, who requested that Tan submit a proposal based on stories about her mother's Chinese family and friends. With a $50,000 advance from Putnam's, Tan devoted her time to what eventually would become *The Joy Luck Club*. The book was completed in four months. Published in 1989, it immediately became a popular success. Vintage Books subsequently bought paperback rights for *The Joy Luck Club* for $1.2 million. In 1993, a film version appeared; Tan collaborated on the screenplay. *The Joy Luck Club* consists of interwoven stories of four Chinese women who are members of a MAH-JONGG club. Each story links their past lives in China with those of their American-born daughters.

Tan's second novel, *The Kitchen God's Wife*, was published in 1991. Like *The Joy Luck Club*, it deals with Chinese American mother-daughter relationships and the secrets that women of different generations hold from one another.

Inevitably, Tan invites comparison with Maxine

Hong KINGSTON. Beyond the fact that both writers have Chinese Americans as their subjects, however, there are few similarities in their techniques or narrative styles. Tan's works have a straightforward novelistic approach. She strives for a realism in the depiction of her Chinese characters, and in this sense her works are more unidimensional than the complex overlays of personas, chronologies, and multivocalities found in Kingston's works.

Tanaka, Seiichi (b. June 18, 1943, Tokyo, Japan): Musician. Responsible for introducing *taiko* (Japanese word for "drum") as an art form into the United States, he was the first TAIKO grand master in that country. Since immigrating to the United States in 1968, he has conducted more than one thousand performances throughout the United States, Europe, Japan, Canada, and Mexico. He has also appeared or been featured in films such as *The Right Stuff* (1983), *Apocalypse Now* (1979), and *Rising Sun* (1993).

Tanaka, Togo William (b. Jan. 7, 1916, Portland, Oreg.): Financial executive. He was the English-language editor of the *Kashu Mainichi* newspaper from 1936 to 1941, after which he was hired by the WAR RELOCATION AUTHORITY (WRA) to be the historian at the MANZANAR relocation center, located in California. Prominent in the finance industry, he has served on many boards, most notably those of the Los Angeles Wholesale Produce Market Development Corporation, and the Federal Reserve Bank in San Francisco, both from 1979 to 1989.

Tang, Julie M. (b. Oct. 22, 1949, Hong Kong): State court justice. Elected in 1990 as a San Francisco municipal court judge, she has also served three terms as the president of the San Francisco Community College Board, in 1980, 1984, and 1988, each time receiving the highest number of votes. An advocate of BILINGUAL EDUCATION, she cofounded in 1973 the Wah Mei Bilingual Pre-School in San Francisco.

Municipal court judge Julie Tang. (International Daily News)

Tang, Thomas (b. Jan. 11, 1922, Phoenix, Ariz.): U.S. federal appeals court justice. He received his B.S. degree from the University of Santa Clara in 1947 and his LL.B. from the University of Arizona in 1950. After becoming a member of the Arizona state bar in 1950, he embarked on a career in public service. His first appointment to the bench was with the Arizona Superior Court (1963-1970). He was in private practice from 1971 until 1977, when he was named a judge of the U.S. Ninth Circuit Court of Appeals—the first Asian American ever appointed to a federal appellate court.

Tang Tun v. Edsell (1912): U.S. Supreme Court ruling that refused to let an American-born Chinese back into the United States after he had left the country to travel to China. American citizen Tang Tun visited China in 1884 and returned to the United States thirteen years later, reentering without any problem. He went to China again in 1905 to get married, but when he tried to return with his wife the following year, they were both denied readmission by U.S. customs official Harry Edsell. When questioned, Tang presented papers identifying him and testifying to his U.S. birth and official signed affidavits endorsing his two earlier trips abroad. Moreover, the white customs inspectors who had signed the affidavits testified on Tang's behalf. Edsell rejected their testimony, however, and in the face of further alleged discrepancies refused to let the Tangs into the country.

A round of executive and judicial appeals followed. After the U.S. secretary of commerce and labor affirmed Edsell's action in late 1906, a federal district court upheld Tang's right to enter based on his denial of a proper hearing and his proof of citizenship. Reviewing the facts of the case, a federal appeals court found that the administrative hearing officers had indeed obeyed all aspects of the law in resolving the conflict. Reminding both sides that under established law the decisions of immigration inspectors are final unless reversed by the secretary of commerce and labor or in the absence of unlawful activity by the inspectors, the court overturned the earlier ruling.

Appearing before the Supreme Court, Tang then accused the hearing officers of unlawful behavior and abuse of discretion. Still, the justices voted unanimously to stay the opinion of the appellate panel.

Tanomoshi: Japanese term referring to a group formed to pool money to lend to its members. The *tanomoshi* was an economic practice utilized by Japanese immi-

grants to the United States. It is a form of a ROTATING CREDIT ASSOCIATION. A number of people form a *tanomoshi* when they need access to capital. The members agree to pool money, and the member who wishes to borrow the sum of money can bid to pay interest on the amount borrowed. Each member takes a turn in borrowing the pool of money. Unlike banks, which require collateral to guarantee a loan, the *tanomoshi* relies on the trust between its members.

The members usually drew upon strong relationships such as membership to the same KENJINKAI, or prefectural association. Those immigrants who came from the same prefecture of Japan shared a common culture, dialect, and history. These prefectural relationships resembled kinship ties as they provided a strong common identity and shared values. The viability of the *tanomoshi* was based on the sense of moral obligation or duty among all its members that the loan be paid. A possible penalty for nonpayment of a debt stemming from a *tanomoshi* was ostracism from the group. It was critical for the members of a *tanomoshi* to trust one another to repay completely the loan since there was no other recourse. Although the *tanomoshi* provided small amounts of money among the Issei, Japanese immigrants to America, it was a source of capital for the Issei, who could not acquire loans easily from banks, particularly because of discriminatory treatment before World War II.

The *tanomoshi*, then, was a source of capital when access to loans was unlikely because of discrimination and ostracism. The *tanomoshi* therefore helped Japanese immigrants to begin small enterprises such as stores in the cities and farms in rural areas.

Tanxiangshan (Sandalwood Mountains): Early Chinese name for the Hawaiian Islands, so named for the abundance of sandalwood there. The earliest Chinese arrival in Hawaii is dated to 1789, eleven years after English explorer James Cook first landed there. Merchants engaged in the China trade soon began sailing into Hawaiian harbors and taking sandalwood to sell back in China.

Taoism: Major belief system practiced in China for more than two thousand years, founded by sixth century B.C.E. Chinese sage Lao-tzu. There are two traditions in the development of Taoism in China. One is religious and the other is philosophical. Whereas all Taoists focus on seeking the Tao (literally the "way"), neither the substance of the Tao nor the means of realizing it are commonly agreed upon. A wide variety

God of Wealth in Taoist temple, China. (Library of Congress)

of religious practice occurred, and a wide variety of philosophical speculation exists. (Please note that in this article, in contrast to the general rule in this encyclopedia, the Wade-Giles system of transliteration is used because of the wide familiarity of the term "Taoism" and related terms among Western readers. In *pinyin*, Tao is Dao; Lao-tzu is Laozi.)

What Is the Tao? Generally speaking the Tao is why things happen rather than merely an account of what happened. The *Tao Te Ching*, a text attributed to Lao-tzu, is the locus classicus of Taoism. Literally the "Way and its Virtue," this text takes for granted that there is a connection between truth and virtue, between the way things happen and the way people ought to behave.

The Tao is viewed first as an abstract noumenal force. It is then associated with a deified Lao-tzu. Later this focus shifts from the deified Lao-tzu to various cosmological deities. A later syncretistic phase occurs during the Song Dynasty (960-1279), when the Tao is

incorporated into Neo-Confucianism and Chan Buddhism. It also continues as an independent aspect of Chinese religion and philosophy.

The Author and the Text. The Chinese historian Ssu-ma Chien, in his *Shih Chi* (historical records), attempted to sort out the details of who Lao-tzu was. That attempt continues to the present with two points of general agreement: Lao-tzu (old child) is not a mythic character, and the content of the *Tao Te Ching* is properly attributed to him.

The text opens with an affirmation of the paradoxical. Chapter 1 reads: "The Tao that can be told is not the eternal Tao, the name that can be named is not the eternal name. The nameless is the origin of Heaven and Earth; the Named is the mother of all things." This denial of discursive reasoning does not, for the Taoist, preclude cognition. It does preclude the vanity of intellectual constructs. Taoism focuses on intuition, and that intuition focuses on the Tao. As chapter 25 reads: "Humanity models itself after Earth. Earth models itself after Heaven. Heaven models itself after Tao. And Tao models itself after itself." This model in turn facilitates both religious and philosophical approaches.

Religious and Philosophical Traditions. The religious tradition is represented most voluminously in the *Tao Tsang*, a compendium spanning fifteen centuries and more than a thousand volumes. It is not only massive but also difficult. Filled with esoteric language, accounts of divine revelations received in trances, and undated works with no identified authors, the *Tao Tsang* represents a massive challenge to scholarship. Until that challenge is met, understanding of the *Tao Tsang* and the history of religious Taoism will remain tentative.

The philosophical trend is represented initially by the writings of (or attributed to) Lao-tzu, Chuang-tzu, and Leih-tzu. It is the text attributed to Lao-tzu, the *Tao Te Ching,* that particularly inspired a wide variety of commentaries.

The variety of interpretation of the Tao persists to the present in modern translators of and commentaries on the *Tao Te Ching.* Indeed that phenomenon is wisely anticipated by the *Tao Te Ching,* as in chapter 1: "The Tao that can be told of is not the eternal Tao," and in chapter 56, which cautions that "Those who know do not speak; those who speak do not know." This, however, lends itself to neither skepticism nor nihilism. Indeed, the *Tao Te Ching,* chapter 41, admonishes that: "When the most foolish type of people hear of the Tao, they laugh heartily at it. If they did not laugh at it, it would not be the Tao."

A variety of glimpses of the Tao are possible, and those glimpses that seekers of the Tao find most persuasive correspond with how they perceive reality. There exists, then, a correspondence between one's view of the Tao and one's view of reality.

Historical Development. The historical development of Taoism reveals that the religious and the philosophical traditions alternate from syncretistic to symbiotic association and then yet again pursue their

Taoist temple, Beijing, China. (Library of Congress)

separate paths. So, too, is the case of Taoism vis-à-vis BUDDHISM and CONFUCIANISM.

During the third and second centuries B.C.E., a reconciliation was attempted of the notion of the Tao as articulated in the *Tao Te Ching* with a wide variety of deities and cosmologies. The next major development was the appearance of a divine Lao-tzu. The earliest record of the transformation of Lao-tzu from mortal to deity is found in an inscription from 165 C.E. The interaction of Taoist and Buddhist thought during this period and later is complex and suggestive of mutual influence. The deification of Lao-tzu resonates with the transformation of Buddhism's Sakyamuni in the *Lotus Sutra*, just as later the cosmological deity Yuan Shih Tien Tsun resonates with the Buddhist Vairocana.

During the Sui (581-618) and Tang (618-907) dynasties, the deified Lao-tzu was increasingly replaced by the less personal cosmological deity Yuan Shih Tien Tsun (honored celestial of the original beginning). The debut of that deity is elaborated upon in the Taoist section of the *Sui Shu* (Sui dynastic history).

Both Buddhism and Confucianism enjoyed a symbiotic relationship with Taoism, but to a significant degree, symbiosis became syncretism after the Tang Dynasty. It was then that Chan Buddhism and Neo-Confucianism blossomed.

Within the tradition of Chinese Buddhism, the *Avatamsaka Sutras* lead to Chan Buddhism. It is there that Buddhist and Taoist intuitions merge; it is there that an intuitive approach to nature and life occurs. The goal of those intuitions is sudden enlightenment, where one obtains a vision of the Tao. Within the tradition of Confucianism, the great Song Dynasty philosopher Chu Hsi sums up that syncretism by observing that nature is the concrete embodiment of the Tao. Nature is in fact an exposition of the Tao, a Tao that is naturalistic, rational, indeed, cognizable.

The Taoist tradition continues in many forms, serving well the human predilection to rise from the prosaic to the profound, from the realm of what to the realm of why.—*Arthur Pontynen*

SUGGESTED READINGS: • Lao-tzu. *The Way of Lao Tzu*. Translated by Wing-tsit Chan. Indianapolis, Ind.: Bobbs-Merrill, 1963. • Pontynen, Arthur. "The Deification of Laozi in Chinese History and Art." *Oriental Art* 26 (Spring, 1980): 192-202. • Seidel, Anna. *La Divinisation de Lao tseu dans le Taoisme des Han*. Paris. Ecole Francaise d'Extreme-Orient, 1969. • Welch, Holmes. *The Parting of the Way: Lao Tzu and the Taoist Movement*. Boston: Beacon Press, 1957. • Welch, Holmes, and Anna Seidel, eds. *Facets of Taoism: Essays in Chinese Religion*. New Haven, Conn.: Yale University Press, 1979.

Tape v. Hurley (1885): California Supreme Court ruling that invalidated the decision of the San Francisco school board to exclude Chinese children from attending public school. Mamie Tape was expelled from Spring Valley School by Principal Jennie Hurley, who was acting on orders from the city's superintendent of schools. In October, 1884, the school board ratified the superintendent's order. When the case came up for trial in municipal court, the judge ruled that since public schools are open to all children, the board had acted unlawfully in dismissing Mamie. Moreover, he concluded, to be born Chinese is not a crime in California. On appeal, the state's supreme court affirmed this decision. Subsequently, however, the school board established the Oriental Public School, a separate institution specifically for Asian children, and enrolled Mamie in it.

Tchen, John Kuo Wei (b. 1951, Madison, Wis.): Scholar. He is director of the Asian/American Center and professor of the Department of Urban Studies at Queens College, City University of New York. He has authored many studies of Asian American communities, including the text for *Genthe's Photographs of San Francisco's Old Chinatown* (1984), and has edited *The Chinese Laundryman* (1987), written by Paul C. P. Siu. Tchen is a cofounder of the New York Chinatown History Project, later renamed the CHINATOWN HISTORY MUSEUM.

Tea: A drink made from the processed leaves of *Camellia sinensis* has been known to the Chinese for at least two thousand years. Legends claim even greater antiquity for tea, attributing its discovery to Shen Nong, a mythical emperor who supposedly lived in the third millennium B.C.E. Unlike the South Asian black teas commonly drunk in the West, the teas of East Asia come in an astonishing variety of colors, flavors, aromas, and textures, depending on the climate and cultivation and on the techniques of picking and processing. From the Tang Dynasty to the present day, tea has played an enormous role in the aesthetic, religious, cultural, and economic life of China and the rest of Asia, to which its consumption, cultivation, and export has spread.

History. The first occurrence of the modern Chinese word for tea, *cha* is found in Han Dynasty (206 B.C.E.-220 C.E.) texts; however, an earlier, very similar word, *tu*, may also have meant tea. If so, then tea may have been used in the time of Confucius, by at least some Chinese. Historical accounts indicate that tea was readily available in most of China by the beginning of the Tang Dynasty (618-907) and soon became immensely popular.

According to the *Cha Jing* (c. 770; *The Classic of Tea*, 1974), written by Lu Yu, early Chinese tea preparation differed greatly from modern methods. Lu Yu disapprovingly notes that many people in his day added onions, peppermint, dogwood berries, ginger, or orange peel to the salted boiling water used to make tea. The tea leaves themselves were usually dried over a charcoal fire and pounded until they were "as soft as a baby's arm." Although loose-leaf and powdered teas were available, pressed cakes of tea were most popular. *The Classic of Tea* records a great number of rules governing the ritual preparation and consumption of tea; the detailed descriptions of methods for obtaining the perfect water and selecting the ideal utensil for each stage of preparation show that tea was already assuming a role of great importance for the intelligentsia.

Over the next several centuries tea fashion evolved further, with new areas of tea cultivation and new methods of picking and preparation being discovered. Tea was introduced in Japan by Japanese Buddhist monks returning from study trips to China.

In the Ming Dynasty (1368-1644) tea drinking reached its current form, with loose-leaf teas and modern brewing methods gaining overwhelming popularity. Tea exports were now big business for the Chinese, with small shipments going as far as Europe, where it was initially viewed with suspicion. Like the Chinese, Europeans originally favored oolong teas over the

Chinese Americans enjoy a cup of tea to mark the New Year, New York Chinatown, 1912. (Library of Congress)

black teas now most commonly consumed in the West.

In modern times tea has continued to be the drink of choice for most Chinese, who consider it to be a very healthful beverage; select varieties of tea are believed to alleviate medical conditions ranging from psoriasis to high blood pressure. Demand for quality teas is still high, though the disruptions of the Cultural Revolution in the People's Republic of China and modern advertising in Taiwan have produced younger generations who view tea drinking as old-fashioned.

Cultivation and Preparation. The great range of teas found in the world is produced from a limited number of different subspecies of tea; most of the differences in flavor are the products of varying soil types, climates, and techniques of harvesting and processing. Left in the wild, tea grows into towering trees. Some of the most expensive teas come from these "wild" trees, though the vast majority of the world's teas come from small bushes carefully raised in hillside plantations.

Ideally tea leaves are harvested by hand in the early morning and processed within hours. The treatment the leaves receive determines which of the three general categories of tea—green, oolong, or black—will be produced. Leaves destined to become green tea are immediately steamed or fired in pans to prevent oxidation and fermentation. Oolongs and black teas are allowed to ferment in the sun before being fired. Most teas are then hand-rolled and subjected to numerous other firings and manipulations, all of which contribute to creating distinctive flavors. The human labor involved is generally very great. Complicating an already intricate and delicate process is the fact that the season of picking and grade of leaf also affect flavor. The highest-grade teas are picked before the growth spurt that follows the spring rains; lesser teas are picked throughout the growing year.

Cultural Significance. The tea ritual gradually grew simpler and less formal in China, while thriving and evolving further in Japan. Though the ceremonial significance of tea drinking may have declined, tea-

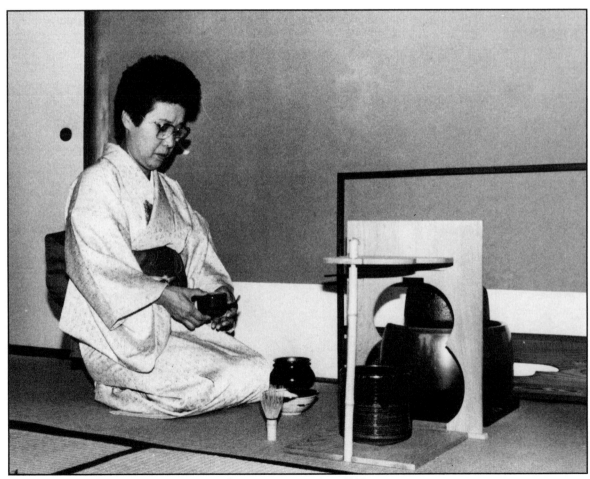

Japanese tea ceremony, 1990.

Proprietor of an Oregon Chinese restaurant serves tea. (Gail Denham)

houses and tea shops still serve important social functions in China, Taiwan, and Chinese immigrant communities, providing attractive settings where tea is brewed and drunk with great enthusiasm and discrimination. In the early morning one can still see old men gather with their newspapers to share tiny pots of strong *lao ren cha* (old people's tea), while airing their pet birds and chatting.

Chinese, Japanese, and Korean scholars have written numerous learned monographs analyzing the influence of tea on literature, religion, and the arts; whole books of poems about tea drinking have been published. Unfortunately few of these works have been translated, but the traveler can easily see the continuing living influence of tea drinking on Chinese culture.

International Importance. From the 1600's, when tea became popular in Europe, the demand for ever greater quantities of tea had enormous worldwide economic impact. The crippling outflow of British silver used to pay for Chinese tea led the BRITISH EAST INDIA COMPANY to experiment with tea production in its colonial possessions: India, Assam, and Sri Lanka—all

big tea producers today. Through a series of unequal treaties, the European powers forced China to allow the importation of opium, grown in British India, as a way of recapturing the European silver spent on tea. It is ironic that the British craving for tea was largely responsible for the misery of China's large-scale opium addiction in the 1800's. Nowadays tea is grown in many countries and consumed everywhere. Besides Europe and Asia the Middle Eastern nations are especially noted for their love of tea.—*Scott Lowe*

SUGGESTED READINGS: • Blofeld, John. *The Chinese Art of Tea.* Boston: Shambhala, 1985. • Harler, Campbell R. *The Culture and Marketing of Tea.* 3d ed. London: Oxford University Press, 1964. • Lu Yu. *The Classic of Tea.* Translated by Francis Ross Carpenter. Boston: Little, Brown, 1974. • Pratt, James Norwood. *The Tea Lover's Treasury.* San Francisco: 101 Productions, 1982. • Varley, Paul, and Kumakura Isao. *Tea in Japan.* Honolulu: University of Hawaii Press, 1989.

Tea ceremony: Formal Japanese ritual involving the preparation and drinking of a bitter green tea. The ceremony is called *chado* (way of tea). Tea had been brought from China as early as the Nara period (710-784) and had been brewed for centuries. The true roots of the modern Japanese tea ceremony, however, began during the last half of the fifteenth century. Tea parties at that time often took the form of competitions in which the major purpose was the ostentatious display of Chinese ceramics and other objets d'art. By the early sixteenth century, a reaction had set in. Under the priest Murata Shuko, great emphasis was placed on the spiritual aspect of the tea ceremony, which now became deeply permeated with Zen concepts.

Shuko created the classic tearoom called Dojinsai. Said to have been derived from the cell of a Buddhist teacher in India, the standard dimensions of the classic tearoom are four and a half mats, or about nine square feet.

An essential tenet of Zen is simplification. As such, Zen is the antithesis of ostentation. The architecture of the Tea Pavilion, as well as the ceremony itself, is therefore designed to emphasize humility, tranquillity, and harmony. Guests must enter by a low doorway deliberately designed to oblige them to crawl on their hands and knees, an act intended to symbolize their humility and common humanity.

In keeping with Zen, the room itself is starkly elegant. All is designed to focus on the beauty of the ceremony itself. During the ceremony, there is no conversation. The guests are expected to savor each deliberate movement in silence. The movements are highly stylized. Even the angle and deliberation with which the implements are held convey a wealth of meaning.

Tenri-kyo (Teaching of the Divine Principle): One of the oldest of the Japanese new religions, Tenri-kyo was founded in 1838 by Nakayama Miki, a Japanese woman who was born in Nara Prefecture in 1798, the first daughter of the Maekawa family. Her birthplace has come to be called the city of "Tenri," the spiritual homeland (*jiba*) for Tenri-kyo adherents worldwide.

Miki acquired the Nakayama name when she married, at age thirteen, a landowner in a neighboring village. She gave birth to one son and five daughters. Always interested in religion, she was given a religious certificate by PURE LAND Buddhists at age nineteen. In 1837 Nakayama received a revelation while serving as a spirit medium for a healer who tried to cure her son. During the healing ritual Nakayama was possessed by a number of deities. Speaking through her, the deities informed those present of her divine calling. She began to practice charity by giving her family heirlooms, furniture, and food to the poor. After the death of her husband in 1853, she began to perform rituals and do faith healing for peasants in the area. Her followers grew in number and founded some of the thousands of Tenri-kyo churches in existence.

Canonical writings of Tenri-kyo include the Ofudesaki, which literally means "at the top of the pen," a set of 1,711 *waka* poems composed by Nakayama. When she died in 1887 at age ninety, there were already twenty-one churches and more than fifteen thousand followers.

Tenri-kyo churches are organized into a distinctive lineage system. The members of a church are all those who were converted by its founder. All are expected to do missionary activity. When a member has converted a sufficient number of followers, he or she may add a new church to the lineage.

There are nearly two million Tenri-kyo adherents in seventeen thousand churches under the leadership of a male descendant of Nakayama, Nakayama Zene. There are Tenri-kyo churches in most large communities of Japanese overseas, including those of Hawaii and the mainland United States. In Brazil there are more than fifty Tenri-kyo churches and hundreds of mission posts.

Tensho-kotai-jingu-kyo (teachings of the heavenly goddess): One of the Japanese new religions, founded by Kitamura Sayo, a peasant woman from Yamaguchi Prefecture, in the mid-twentieth century. In 1945 Kitamura received a revelation that she was possessed by a SHINTO deity, Tensho-kotai-jingu. Rhythmic singing and dancing movements characterized Kitamura's preaching, such that this cult also became known as Odoru Shukyo (dancing religion). In 1970 its membership was estimated at more than 300,000 followers.

Teraoka, Masami (b. Jan. 13, 1936, Onomichi, Japan): Painter and sculptor. Teraoka, who has achieved international recognition as a painter, is best known for his outrageously anachronistic works in which contemporary subjects are rendered in the style of classical Japanese painting; many of these paintings combine the comic and the erotic in a way that intensifies their calculated incongruity. Teraoka received a B.A. degree in aesthetics (1959) from Kwansei Gakuin University in Kobe, Japan, and an M.F.A. (1968) from the Otis Art Institute. His work has been widely exhibited.

Terminal Island: Island located south of Los Angeles, California, near the harbor port of San Pedro. Beginning around 1906, the island village of Fish Harbor was established by Japanese immigrants, many of whom had come to the United States from coastal fishing villages in Japan's Wakayama Prefecture. Fishing boats and canneries provided the main sources of employment for the community's residents, and eventually some 3,000 Japanese Americans were established there. Settled primarily in company-owned housing, the residents of Fish Harbor had access to their own public school, a Japanese school, a Buddhist temple, a Shinto shrine, several Christian churches, and a community center. Community organizations included a fisherman's union, a JAPANESE ASSOCIATION, and a *KENJINKAI* for residents from WAKAYAMA Prefecture; youngsters enjoyed playing baseball, competing in sumo tournaments, watching Japanese films, and joining scouting organizations.

After the Japanese attack on PEARL HARBOR in 1941, the Federal Bureau of Investigation arrested many of Fish Harbor's prominent leaders; the rest of the population was forced to evacuate the village within forty-eight hours on February 25 and 26, 1942. The residents of Fish Harbor constituted the first Japanese American community to be removed in its totality during World War II. Many inhabitants spent the war in the relocation center at MANZANAR in the California desert near the Owens Valley, where they came into contact with many of the more assimilated Japanese Americans from all over California. After the war, many Terminal Island residents relocated to cities in the Midwest and on the East Coast in search of employment. Nevertheless, most residents eventually returned to Los Angeles. Although many expected to return to their homes, they found that their village had been demolished to make way for a massive naval installation and for wartime defense plants and other industrial developments. Despite the physical disappearance of their community, many Terminal Island residents continued to maintain their contact with one another; in 1970, a number of Nisei who had grown up on the island formed the Terminal Islanders Club to host a reunion. The overwhelming response to this initial reunion led the group to sponsor an annual event that continued into the 1990's. In addition to sponsoring such social gatherings, members of the Terminal Islanders Club have also worked to gather artifacts and preserve the oral history of their former community.

Terrace v. Thompson (1923): U.S. Supreme Court ruling that affirmed the constitutionality of the state of Washington's Alien Land Law of 1921, under which aliens not intending to become naturalized American citizens were barred from leasing land. As in the case of *PORTERFIELD V. WEBB* (1923), handed down the same day, the Court upheld the power of the states to regulate matters pertaining to agricultural land. It also announced that the land laws did not conflict with the U.S.-JAPAN TREATY OF COMMERCE AND NAVIGATION (1911), under which Japanese aliens received certain rights while living in the United States.

The Terraces, Washington residents, wanted to lease land to N. Nakatsuka, a farmer born in Japan. Since the state's Alien Land Law prohibited this, however, the Terraces filed suit in federal district court. The Supreme Court, on appeal, declared the law violative of neither the due process nor the equal protection clauses of the federal constitution.

Terrace was one of six major cases heard at this level challenging the constitutionality of the ALIEN LAND LAWS, the other five being *COCKRILL V. PEOPLE OF STATE OF CALIFORNIA* (1925), *FRICK V. WEBB* (1923), *Morrison v. People of the State of California* (1934), *Porterfield*, and *WEBB V. O'BRIEN* (1923). All were decided in favor of the state.

Teruya, Albert (b. 1913, Hakalau, Territory of Hawaii) and **Wallace Teruya** (b. 1915, Hakalau, Territory of Hawaii): Entrepreneurs. The Nisei brothers own the Times Super Market Chain, which, with fourteen locations on Oahu, is one of the largest supermarket chains in Hawaii. They began their business career after leaving the family plantation. After several years of working in restaurants, the two brothers started a small lunchroom in downtown Honolulu. The opened their first supermarket in 1949.

Tet: Vietnamese lunar New Year. Occurring during the first seven days of the first lunar month (usually early February), this holiday celebrates the new year and springtime and is the most important festival of the year. Special foods are prepared, families come together, debts are paid, and new clothes are worn as a symbolic way of bringing in and celebrating the new year to ensure good luck in the months ahead. On this occasion special foods are also offered in homage to deceased relatives and firecrackers illuminate the night at midnight on the eve of the holiday.

Tet Festival, Garden Grove, California, 1991. (David Fowler)

Thai Americans: Before the 1970's, there was very little immigration from Thailand to the United States. Since that time, however, there has been a steady flow of new immigrants from Thailand, creating a substantial Thai American community.

Between 1980 and 1990, the Thai population in the United States doubled, from 45,279 to 91,275. (These are U.S. census figures. Some scholars believe that the Thai American population, including undocumented immigrants, is much larger than the census indicates.) Many of the Thai immigrants in the late 1970's and the 1980's were young professionals, particularly doctors, nurses, and white-collar workers; students and spouses of U.S. military personnel also contributed to the growth of the Thai American community. In the 1990's

TOP 5 METROPOLITAN AREAS AND STATES OF THAI AMERICAN RESIDENCE, 1990

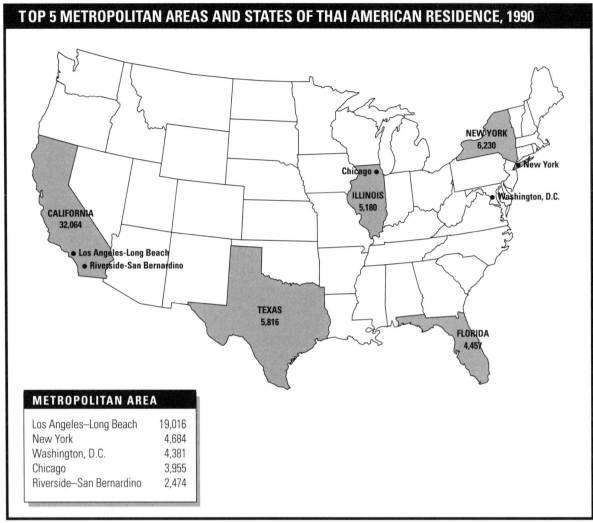

NEW YORK
6,230

New York

Chicago •

Washington, D.C.

ILLINOIS
5,180

CALIFORNIA
32,064

• Los Angeles-Long Beach
• Riverside-San Bernardino

TEXAS
5,816

FLORIDA
4,457

METROPOLITAN AREA	
Los Angeles–Long Beach	19,016
New York	4,684
Washington, D.C.	4,381
Chicago	3,955
Riverside–San Bernardino	2,474

Source: Susan B. Gall and Timothy L. Gall, eds., *Statistical Record of Asian Americans.* Detroit: Gale Research, 1993.

Thai restaurant, Columbus, Ohio. (Chuck Doyle)

a higher proportion of new Thai immigrants have been unskilled workers; many are women who are employed in garment factories with low pay and substandard working conditions.

Nearly half of the Thais living in the United States in 1990 (46.8 percent) had settled in the West, followed by the South (26 percent), the Midwest (14.2 percent), and the Northeast (12.9 percent). In 1990 more than a third of all Thai Americans lived in a single state: California, where the Thai population was about 32,000.

Thai restaurants are the most visible sign of the rapidly growing Thai American community. Ranging from the elegant to the economical, Thai restaurants are increasingly popular in Los Angeles and other urban centers throughout the United States.

Thailand, Kingdom of: Tropical mainland Southeast Asian country, flanked from west to northeast by Myanmar, the People's Republic of China, and Laos and on the southeast by Cambodia. The southern part of Thailand extends in a long finger down part of the Malay Peninsula. The nation has an area of 198,115 square miles and was formerly called "Siam."

Almost 70 percent of Thailand's approximately 58 million people live in rural villages; the other 30 percent dwell in the country's rapidly growing urban centers. The capital city of Bangkok, with a population of 7.5 million people, is by far the largest and most important city in the country. According to the 1990 U.S. census, as many as 150,000 Thai people have come to live in the United States.

Land and People. The heartland of Thailand's four main geographical regions lies in the Central Plains, a flat, fertile rice-growing region through which the country's major river, the Chao Phraya, flows out below Bangkok into the Gulf of Thailand.

Much of the northern and western part of the country is mountainous. Thailand's highest mountain, Doi (mount) Inthanon, 8,514 feet high, is located in this zone. Chiang Mai, the northern capital, is one of the largest cities in the nation.

A broad plateau covers much of the northeastern part of the country. Alternating droughts and flooding make life hard for northeastern farmers, and the standard of living in Isan (northeast) is the lowest in Thailand.

The interior of Thailand's southern peninsula is mountainous and covered in dense jungle. Rainfall is extremely heavy, and parts of the region receive a double monsoon. Primary occupations include fishing, tin mining, and rubber production.

More than 80 percent of the Thai people speak languages that belong to the TAI LANGUAGE family and are found among a variety of peoples in southern China and mainland Southeast Asia. Approximately 14 percent of Thailand's population is Chinese, concentrated in Bangkok and other urban centers. Smaller population groups include the Thai-Malay of southern Thailand, groups speaking Cambodian languages, and hill tribes from Thailand's mountainous north and west.

History and Government. The Thai are descended from Tai peoples who migrated into mainland Southeast Asia from northern Vietnam and southern China beginning in the eleventh century. There they mixed with the Mon and KHMER, who had long inhabited the area and who had been strongly influenced by Hindu and Buddhist beliefs brought in by Indian traders in the early years of the first millennium C.E. The Tai adopted BUDDHISM and ideas about kingship from the Mon and Khmer.

The Thai people date their history from the founding of the Tai kingdom of Sukhothai (c. 1240-1438). Its greatest ruler, King Ramkhamhaeng, is famous for his stone inscription describing his kingdom and written in the earliest recorded example of Thai writing.

Ayudhya (1351-1767), Sukhothai's successor kingdom, lasted for more than four hundred years. European traders, who began penetrating Southeast Asia during this period, set up trading settlements at Ayudhya. The kingdom was known to foreigners as "Siam" until 1939. Ayudhya was abandoned in 1767 following its destruction by Burma (now MYANMAR), its age-old enemy.

Order was restored under the early rulers of the Chakri Dynasty (1782-   ). They moved the capital of the country to Bangkok and encouraged numerous Chinese traders and craftsmen to settle in Siam and help restore the economy.

From the 1820's onward Siam was threatened by the expanding Western presence in Southeast Asia. Although it was never colonized, under King Mongkut

Thai dancers, Bangkok, Thailand. (John Penisten, Pacific Pictures)

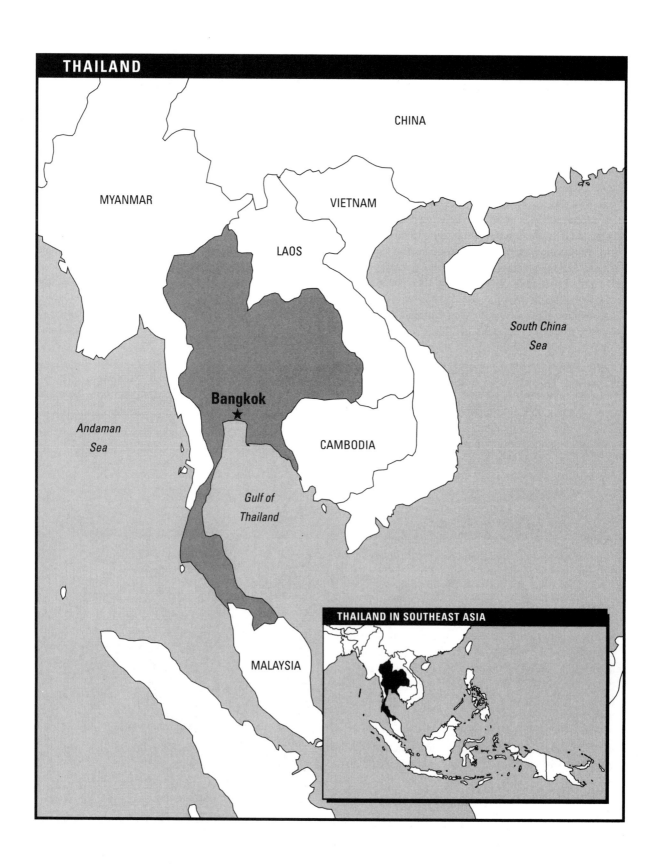

THAILAND

CHINA

MYANMAR

VIETNAM

LAOS

Bangkok

Andaman
Sea

CAMBODIA

South China
Sea

Gulf of
Thailand

MALAYSIA

THAILAND IN SOUTHEAST ASIA

the country was forced to grant certain legal and financial rights to Western nations. Mongkut was the first Siamese monarch to study Western languages and modern science and to permit the establishment of missionary schools and Western-style medical facilities in his kingdom.

During the reign of his son, King Chulalongkorn, the government bureaucracy was reorganized, rail and telegraph networks linking the kingdom together were established, a modern school system was introduced, and slavery was abolished.

By the 1920's a middle class had begun to emerge in Thailand. Many resented their exclusion from governmental power under an absolute monarchy. In 1932 a group of Thai led by Pridi Phanomyong, a lawyer, and Luang Phibunsongkhram, a military officer, conducted a coup that changed Thailand from an absolute to a constitutional monarchy and established a National Assembly.

World War II and the Early Postwar Period. During World War II Thailand joined with Japan against the Allies. Many Thai did not accept their government's decision and joined the anti-Japanese Free Thai underground movement.

Wat Po Temple, Thailand. (John Penisten, Pacific Pictures)

After 1949 Thailand became increasingly anti-Communist and pro-American, sending troops to fight with the United States in the Korean and Vietnam wars. In turn from 1957 onward the United States provided Thailand with large amounts of aid.

Although the 1932 coup was supposed to make Thailand a democracy, most governments since then have been controlled by the military. In 1973 and 1992 there were serious public protests against military rule. In 1992 an elected government made up of a coalition of civilian parties took office; the future of democracy in Thailand, however, remains uncertain.

The Economy. Thailand is in the midst of an economic boom that began in the 1960's. Now one of the wealthiest nations in Southeast Asia, it is close to becoming a newly industrialized country (NIC) like South Korea or Singapore.

Thailand is currently expanding its trade with Asian nations, especially Japan. Although 70 percent of its labor force is engaged in agricultural occupations, most Thai exports consist of manufactured goods such as food products, textiles, and plastics, although rice, rubber, tin, precious stones, and silk continue to play

Boys pray at Buddhist temple. (John Penisten, Pacific Pictures)

an important part in the nation's export as well as its domestic economy. Tourism has become the nation's chief source of foreign exchange.

Religion. Approximately 95 percent of Thai are Buddhists belonging to the Theravada (doctrine of the elders) tradition. Community life in traditional Thailand centered around the local *wat*, or Buddhist temple-monastery. There is also a small Christian community in Thailand, accounting for less than 1 percent of the population. The second most important religion in the country, followed by most Thai-Malays of Thailand's southern peninsula, is ISLAM, while the majority of Chinese practice ANCESTOR WORSHIP.

The Changing Social Fabric. The rapidity of social and economic change in Thailand has caused strains in the nation's social fabric, among them a growing gap between rich and poor, urban overcrowding, pollution, environmental degradation, and a prostitution rate that has contributed to a serious acquired immune deficiency syndrome (AIDS) epidemic. The challenge facing the nation is how to maintain traditional cultural ways while at the same time dealing with the problems as well as the benefits that have come from the dramatic growth of the Thai economy.—*E. Jane Keyes*

SUGGESTED READINGS: • Bunge, Frederica M., ed. *Thailand: A Country Study.* Washington, D.C.: U.S. Government Printing Office, 1981. • Girling, John L. S. *Thailand: Society and Politics.* Ithaca, N.Y.: Cornell University Press, 1981. • Keyes, Charles F. *Thailand: Buddhist Kingdom as Modern Nation-State.* Boulder, Colo.: Westview Press, 1987. • Wyatt, David K. *Thailand: A Short History.* New Haven, Conn.: Yale University Press, 1984.

Theatre of Yugen: San Francisco-based theater company that works with traditional Japanese forms of No (tragedy) and *kyogen* (comedy), founded in 1978. The company, the only one of its kind in the United States (in 1993), produces translations of contemporary Japanese plays and adaptations of Western classics and contemporary plays to Japanese styles. Their performances, mostly in Japanese and English, have been featured in Canada, Japan, and the United States.

Theosophy: Religious philosophy having mystical concerns. The term "theosophy" is derived from Greek and means "divine wisdom." Among the characteristics of theosophy are an emphasis on mystical experience, an interest in esoteric doctrine, a fascination with the occult, a preference for monism, and an affinity for Asian thought.

Theosophy is identified with the Theosophical Soci-

Spiritual leader Krishnamurti with his hosts, The Logans, near Bristol, Pennsylvania, 1932. (Library of Congress)

ety, which was founded in 1875 by Helena Petrovna Blavatsky, an American of Russian descent, and Henry Steel Olcott, an American. Both were interested in spiritualism and met in 1874 in Vermont at a meeting of spiritualists. In 1882, they established the society's headquarters at Adyar, in the state of Madras, India, and within two years they had founded one hundred branches in India as well as several in Europe and the United States. In 1886, the society opened a school.

The main ideas of the theosophists were expounded in Blavatsky's *Isis Unveiled* (1877) and *The Secret Doctrine* (1888) and were propagated in the journal *The Theosophist*. Theosophists developed an idea of rebirth and spiritual progress in which each person descended from the ego of the universal soul down to the world of matter. Each person was composed of a physical body, an astral body, and a divine soul that passed from rebirth to rebirth. Thus, the theosophists merged the Western spiritualist tradition with Hindu-Buddhist ideas.

The three goals of the Theosophical Society are establishing a nucleus of the universal alliance of human beings; encouraging the study of comparative religion, philosophy, and science; and studying the unexplained laws of nature and the powers latent in human beings. After the death of Blavatsky in 1891, the society continued operating under the leadership of Olcott and was joined in 1893 by Annie Besant, who took over as president after Olcott's death in 1907. Besant founded the Central Hindu College at Benares (Varanasi) in 1898.

The movement attracted a wide range of followers in India, reaching a peak of popularity in the 1920's, with around forty-five thousand members. This popularity was in part a result of the cult that surrounded the spiritual leader and philosopher Jiddu Krishnamurti, who was proclaimed the world teacher, but it declined when he resigned from the Theosophical Society in 1930. There have been various splinter groups of the Theosophical Society from its earliest days, but the society has remained active in India, the United States, and Europe, even with sharply reduced numbers of followers.

Theravada Buddhism: Major form of Buddhism. It adheres to the "Doctrine of the Elders" (that is, Theravada) and is primarily found and practiced in Cambodia, Laos, Myanmar (formerly Burma), Thailand, and Sri Lanka (formerly Ceylon).

The oldest existing form of BUDDHISM, Theravada preserves and follows the teaching of the Buddha,

which is contained in the canon of scriptures written in the PALI language. The Buddha's teaching was transmitted orally by disciples from the fifth century B.C.E. until it was committed to writing in the first century B.C.E. in Ceylon. These Pali texts became the authoritative guide for Theravada doctrine and practice.

The fundamental beliefs of Theravada include the Buddha's declaration of the Four Noble Truths, which are suffering, the cause of suffering, the cessation of suffering, and the path to deliverance from suffering, and his teaching regarding the Eightfold Path, which consists of the right view, the right thought, the right speech, the right action, the right livelihood, the right effort, the right mindfulness, and the right concentration.

Theravada views existence in this life as one of unsatisfactoriness (*dukkha*), impermanence (*anicca*), and no eternal selfhood (*anatta*). The ultimate goal of the Theravada Buddhist is attainment of Nirvana, the extinction of cravings and desires. Upon attainment of NIRVANA, the Theravada practitioner becomes an *arahant*, one who, in meditation and moral conduct, has conquered the passions and desires of this life and is freed from the cycle of existence.

Theravada Buddhism spread from northeastern India southward until it was introduced to Ceylon in the third century B.C.E., where it was preserved. Theravada missionaries also reached southern Burma by the fifth century C.E., but the country did not embrace their teachings fully until the eleventh century. In the thirteenth century, the rulers of Thailand sent for Theravada monks in Ceylon to come and establish their teaching there. By the fourteenth century, Cambodia had been influenced by the Theravada cultures of Thailand, Burma, and Ceylon. Laos became a Theravada country sometime during the fourteenth and fifteenth centuries C.E. after being introduced to Theravada teachings from Cambodia.

Although an ancient religion, Theravada Buddhism still plays a vital role in the societies of Southeast Asia. Its teachings form the religious and cultural roots of the majority of Southeast Asians as they endeavor to follow the example of the Buddha in their daily lives.

Thirty-eighth parallel: Artificial line of demarcation, also known as the "demilitarized zone" (DMZ), that separates North and South Korea. It was first established in July, 1945, at the Potsdam Conference as a temporary division, following escalating tensions between the democratic nationalists and the Communists in Korea. The Soviet Union occupied the northern part

President Clinton visits a guard post in Camp Oulette in the demilitarized zone between North and South Korea, 1993. (AP/Wide World Photos)

of Korea (which became the Democratic People's Republic of KOREA, or North Korea) and the United States occupied the southern part (which became the Republic of KOREA, or South Korea).

Three Principles of the People. *See* **Sanminzhuyi**

Tiana (Thi Thanh Nga; b. Saigon, now Ho Chi Minh City, Republic of Vietnam): Filmmaker and actor. Among American audiences, Tiana is known best for her autobiographical documentary *From Hollywood to Hanoi*, which premiered in 1993. As a child she spent much time traveling between Saigon and Washington, D.C., where her father, then South Vietnam's minister of information, was stationed during the early 1960's. The family left South Vietnam in 1966, however, and settled permanently in Washington, where Tiana's father later worked for the Voice of America (VOA) and

where she led a privileged life as the daughter of a diplomat. The family eventually moved to San Jose, California.

Following her high school graduation, Tiana ran off to Hollywood dreaming of an acting career. She was cast in small roles in the film *The Killer Elite* (1975), the television miniseries *Pearl*, and a few low-budget martial arts features. In Hollywood she was also the sole female student of gung-fu master Bruce LEE.

In 1987, after attending a showcasing of Vietnamese films at the University of California, Los Angeles, Tiana returned to Vietnam with little more in mind than an unscripted plan to record her experiences there on film. She visited the country a dozen times over the next three years, interviewing government officials, war survivors, and doctors treating patients felled by Agent Orange (a toxic defoliant used by the U.S. military against Communist troops during the Vietnam

War). She shot footage in numerous locations, including nightclubs, private homes, and hospital wards. On one level, *From Hollywood to Hanoi* is about life in Vietnam since the war. On another level, it is a journey of self-discovery—the filmmaker's attempt to reconcile her ethnic Vietnamese heritage with her identity as an American.

Tiananmen Square incident (1989): Violent crackdown by the Chinese government-backed People's Liberation Army (PLA) against prodemocracy demonstrators who had gathered in Beijing's Tiananmen Square to protest official corruption and the suppression of freedoms. During the June 4 incident hundreds, possibly thousands, of students and civilian workers were killed by automatic gunfire or military vehicles. The demonstrators had been in Tiananmen almost continuously since the April 15 death of Chinese leader Hu Yaobang, former general secretary of the Chinese Communist Party (CCP). He was highly regarded by student reformers for having been removed from power for supporting the students during the 1986 demonstrations.

Hu's unexpected death triggered large demonstrations, which continued from his death and funeral, through the traditional May 4 holiday, through Soviet President Mikhail Gorbachev's mid-May visit, through the May 20 declaration of martial law, until June 4. These frequent demonstrations drew progressively larger crowds, to the embarrassment of Chinese leaders. The latter were particularly offended when the student-led Democracy movement attracted Western media attention during Gorbachev's visit, which had been billed as a major Chinese diplomatic victory since no top Soviet leader had visited the People's Republic of China in thirty years.

After Gorbachev left party hard-liners attempted to crack down by removing Party Secretary Zhao Ziyang and declaring martial law, but they were initially stymied by huge crowds of civilians that blocked the streets as the army tried to enter Beijing. The army refrained from using force initially, vainly hoping that the demonstrations would diminish by themselves. Party leaders were further provoked by the erection of the "Goddess of Democracy," a plaster statue resembling the American Statue of Liberty, in the square on May 30, and they determined to clear the square using lethal force if necessary.

As the PLA marched on Tiananmen Square, the statue was smashed to pieces and an undetermined number of people were killed. The next day another

two hundred civilians were massacred. Some PLA troops, however, began to turn against one another on June 6, reflecting dissension within the army over the actions being taken against the protestors. Some army officers publicly sided with the students.

In the wake of the crackdown, at least twenty-seven demonstrators were publicly executed. Many others remained imprisoned until 1990. The following year the party tried and convicted some of the most well-known dissident leaders, dealing a further blow to the right of free expression in China.

Tibet: Autonomous region located in southwestern China. It is 471,700 square miles in size and contained a 1990 population of almost 2.2 million. The first mention of Tibet is found in the records of the Shang Dynasty (c. 1766-1122 B.C.E.). Because of its strategic location along ancient trade routes, Tibet was mentioned in the geographies of ancient Greek authors. By 608 C.E., the Tibetans sent their first tribute mission to China. Although viewed as primitive and secluded, the Tibetans built a powerful empire that finally collapsed in 840.

Twelfth century Indian refugees made a big impact on Tibet. Tibetan Buddhism developed unique customs and dogmas, which included extensive shamanistic practices at the popular level. Buddhist monasteries

The Dalai Lama rules Tibet, now an autonomous region of China. (The Nobel Foundation)

dominated Tibet economically and politically until 1959.

The twentieth century history of Tibet is in some ways unique and also similar to many small nations drawn into international conflict because of their strategic location. Tibet struggled hard to minimize Chinese influence until 1950, but relied on unsteady British support to achieve that goal. Complex diplomacy combined with monastic factions to leave Tibet vulnerable to a determined neighbor willing to use force to dominate. The Chinese Communists chose to assume that role in 1950, when China reasserted its suzerainty over Tibet.

MAO ZEDONG and the Communists held the traditional view of Chinese leaders that Tibet was an integral part of China. Even before Chinese control was completely consolidated, the Communists launched a propaganda assault followed by a military invasion of Tibet in October, 1950. Distracted by the KOREAN WAR (1950-1953), the Free World offered Tibet no significant help. Faced by military defeats and traitorous factions, the Dalai Lama ruling Tibet signed a treaty with the Communists in 1951. After the compromises were violated by the Chinese, and following an anti-Chinese revolt, the Dalai Lama and eighty thousand Tibetans fled to India in 1959. Tibet was assimilated by China as an autonomous region in 1965.

Officially, Tibet has received generous treatment from Beijing. Immigration and antimonastic campaigns, however, led to skirmishes between the Tibetans and Chinese troops in the 1980's.

Too weak to defend itself, too strategic to be left alone, and unable to develop lasting alliances with powerful allies, Tibet met the fate of many small nations in the twentieth century. The onset of the Cold War meant the end of Tibetan independence.

Tibetans: A people originating in the Tibetan plateau of Inner Asia. While the people are culturally and racially related to the Mongols, the Tibetan language is of the TIBETO-BURMAN group and uses an alphabet derived from SANSKRIT. Tibetans live in a broad section of Central Asia, from the southern foothills of the Himalayan range in India, Nepal, and Bhutan, across the Tibetan plateau of the Tibet and Xinjiang autonomous regions, and Gansu, Qinghai, and Sichuan provinces of the People's Republic of China. Tibetans exhibit a wide variation in physical type. Primarily Mongoloid, some Tibetans have large bony frames and aquiline noses, resembling North American Plains Indians. Others are gracile and of delicate physiognomy,

Tibetan youth wears traditional clothing, New York City. (Richard B. Levine)

similar to many Burmese. There is a marked lack of sexual dimorphism.

Tibetan subsistence technologies include nomadic animal husbandry (yak, sheep, goats), farming (barley, orchards), mercantilism, and itinerant trading. A small percentage of this primarily patrilineal society practice fraternal polyandry, with several brothers sharing a single wife. Traditional Tibetan society also had a high percentage of celibate Buddhist monks and nuns.

Tibetans are representatives of an ancient civilization—a unique culture influenced by Indian, Chinese, and Turko-Mongol elements. The greatest influence on the development of Tibetan culture was the introduction of BUDDHISM from India and China beginning in the seventh century. While Buddhist monasticism disappeared in the land of its birth, it flourished in Tibet—especially the tantric schools of Buddhism, which were the last to develop in India. Popular religion among the Tibetans was a mixture of pre-Buddhist shamanism, exoteric Mahayana Buddhism with its redeeming saints and *bodhisattvas*, and the rituals of the esoteric tantric schools. Under Mongol patronage in the thirteenth and fourteenth centuries, a theocracy developed. This form of government was renewed in the seventeenth century under Mongol and Manchu patronage with the institution of the Dalai Lama, a spiritual leader who ruled from the Potala palace in Lhasa. Tibetan independence ended in the 1960's, when Tibet became part of the People's Republic of China. Nearly one hundred thousand Tibetans became refugees in India, Nepal, and the West.

Tibeto-Burman languages: Family of languages of Asia. They are spoken in the Himalayan countries (Nepal, Bhutan, Tibet), western China, eastern India, and parts of Southeast Asia, particularly Burma and Thailand.

Probably more than forty-five million or fifty million people speak a Tibeto-Burman language. Investigations of Tibeto-Burman languages are still relatively incomplete, and even their exact number is not precisely known. There are at least fifty, and maybe as many as one hundred, Tibeto-Burman languages still spoken today. Their location in areas both geographically remote and politically sensitive has hindered their thorough study.

Most scholars agree that the SINO-TIBETAN LANGUAGES (the family of related languages found in China and Tibet) can be divided into two separate branches. "Sinic" includes most of the Chinese languages, such as Cantonese, Hakka, and Mandarin (the national language of china and Taiwan). The second group—Tibeto-Burman—is more problematic. Some scholars divide these Tibeto-Burman languages into four general groups: Tibetan-Bodic, spoken in most of the Tibetan Autonomous Region of the People's Republic of China; Baric, spoken in India; and Burmic and Karen, spoken in Burma.

By far the most influential languages of this family are Tibetan and Burmese. Not only are they the dominant languages—socially and politically—in their regions but also they have a long literary tradition dating back to the seventh century and eleventh century, respectively. They both have an extensive body of Buddhist texts. Both Tibetan and Burmese writing are derived from Indian scripts.

The phonology of the Tibeto-Burman languages includes two or three series of "stop" sounds (that is, pairs of sounds such as *p* and *b*, *t* and *d*, and *k* and *g*). There are also nasal sounds such as *m*, *n*, or *ng* and fricatives (such as *s* and *z*). Vowels are also relatively few, usually less than a dozen different sounds. Many times, however, they are pronounced with a special rounding of the lips (as is sometimes the case in

French or German) or are laryngealized (pronounced with a constricted "creaky" sound in the back of the throat). Also, most of the Tibeto-Burman languages are tonal, where a difference in pitch intonation determines a difference in meaning. For example, in Lahu, the word *ca*, if said with a rising intonation, means "join," but if said with a falling intonation, it means "feed." Most of the Tibeto-Burman languages use a half-dozen or so different tones.

The Tibeto-Burman languages, except those of the Karen branch, are so-called verb-final languages, that is, they have a word order of subject-object-verb (as opposed to the subject-verb-object word order found in English). As is usually the case with verb-final languages, directional words such as "to" or "from" come after the noun they modify rather than before. For example, in Akha, the phrase, "I am going to town," would be *Meu-ah i ma* (literally "[I] town to go").

Tien, Chang-lin (b. July 24, 1935, Wuhan, Hubei Province, China): Scientist and educator. Chang-lin Tien calls himself a member of "America's global population." Before coming to the United States in 1956, Tien lived in Shanghai, as well as Taiwan, where his family fled after World War II.

Tien completed his undergraduate education in mechanical engineering at National Taiwan University. From 1956 to 1957 he attended the University of Louisville. He earned a master's degree at Louisville in 1957 and then a second master's and a Ph.D. degree at Princeton University in 1959. In the same year, Tien joined the faculty at the University of California, Berkeley.

Tien taught mechanical engineering at Berkeley. In 1962 Tien, at the age of twenty-six, became the youngest professor to win the school's prestigious Distinguished Teaching Award.

After serving as the chair of the Department of Mechanical Engineering from 1974 to 1981, Tien was appointed Berkeley's vice chancellor in charge of research (1983-1985). Tien left Berkeley in 1988 and served for two years as executive vice chancellor and Distinguished Professor at the University of California, Irvine.

Tien took office in July, 1990, as Berkeley's seventh chancellor—the first Asian American to head a major research university in the United States.

Chancellor Tien has achieved a remarkably distinguished record as a scientist and educator. He is internationally recognized for his research in the field of heat-transfer technology. He has published books, review

Scientist and educator Chang-lin Tien. (San Francisco Chronicle)

and monograph articles, and more than 250 refereed research papers in heat transfer, infrared radiation, and other related energy and environmental subjects.

Tien has also received many honors, including a Guggenheim Fellowship and the Max Jakob Memorial Award, the highest honor in the field of heat transfer. He has been a member of the National Academy of Engineering since 1976 and was elected in 1991 as a Fellow of the American Academy of Arts and Sciences.

As the chancellor of one of the most prestigious research institutions in the United States, Tien made clear his commitment to building Berkeley into a culturally diverse and academically open and supportive campus.

Tiger Brigade (Manghokun): World War II Korean American brigade. It was incorporated into the California National Guard and was established on December 29, 1941. At a time when the Los Angeles Korean American population was about five hundred, the brigade began training with 50 Korean American women and men, ages eighteen to sixty-five, and then increased to 109. Despite its pledge of patriotism, the brigade was relocated to the civilian militia because the law prohibited inclusion of a "foreign" unit in the U.S. armed forces. A similar unit was established in San Francisco.

Ting, Samuel (Samuel Chao Chung Ting; b. Jan. 27, 1936, Ann Arbor, Mich.): Physicist. Ting was born in the United States, where his parents, both University of Michigan graduates, were temporary visitors. The two-month-old infant was taken back to the Tings' native area in Rizhao, Shandong Province. Because of chaotic political conditions in China during his childhood, Ting did not receive much formal schooling before he was twelve, although his parents were always connected with institutions of higher learning.

In 1948 the family settled in Taichung, Taiwan. He was graduated from Chien-kuo Middle School in Taipei and then entered Cheng Kung University. One year later, in 1956, the twenty-year-old student returned to the land of his birth to enroll in the college of engineering of the University of Michigan, Ann Arbor. By the second year his interest had turned, however, to mathematics and physics, and in 1962 he received his doctorate in those two sciences.

In 1963 Ting became a Ford Foundation Fellow at the Centre Européen de la Recherche Nucléaire (CERN) at Geneva. He also began teaching physics at Columbia University from 1964 to 1967. By 1965, at the age of twenty-nine, he was promoted to associate professor. In 1966 he also led a research group at Deutsches Elektronen-Synchrotron in Hamburg, West Germany. In 1967 he became associate professor in physics at the Massachusetts Institute of Technology and in 1969 was promoted to full professor. Ting became program consultant of the Division of Particles and Fields of the American Physics Society in 1970.

It was during one of the experiments he conducted at the Brookhaven National Laboratory synchrotron that he discovered a new long-lived product particle, the J/psi particle, which was also discovered independently by Burton Richter at Stanford. In 1975 Ting became a fellow of the American Academy of Arts and Sciences and in 1976 received the Ernest Orlando Lawrence award from the U.S. government and also shared with Richter the Nobel Prize in Physics. In 1977 Ting was elected a member of the National Academy of Sciences. In the 1980's Ting continued to make new discoveries in experiments on particle physics conducted in West Germany.

Tingley Bill: Proposed legislation introduced to address the problem of a labor shortage that plagued California during the boom years of the early 1850's. State representative George B. Tingley authored the bill, which was designed to provide the state with a means of facilitating the hiring of CHINESE CONTRACT

LABORERS by signing them to ten-year contracts at fixed wages. Anti-Chinese feeling was running high in California, however, and those opposed to Tingley's plan lobbied the state's governor to propose legislation that would allow the state to levy taxes in order to limit Chinese immigration and to exclude Chinese laborers altogether. Ultimately, the bill was defeated.

Tinikling: Traditional Filipino dance from Leyte Province representing the flight of herons. It involves the use of long, clashing bamboo poles over which dancers step. As with this dance, many traditional Filipino dances represent different aspects of nature.

Togasaki, George Kiyoshi (b. 1895, San Francisco, Calif.): Civic and business leader. As a child, he was one the Japanese students affected by the San Francisco Board of Education's school segregation directive announced in 1906. After serving in the U.S. Army during World War I, he returned home and in

Traditional Filipino dance represents the flight of herons. (Filipino American National Historical Society)

George Togasaki was one of the founders of the Japanese American Citizens League. (Pacific Citizen)

collaboration with other Nisei organized the AMERICAN LOYALTY LEAGUE (ALL), a precursor of the JAPANESE AMERICAN CITIZENS LEAGUE (JACL). Relocating to Tokyo, he served as president of the English-language newspaper *Japan Times* and the 600,000-member Rotary International and as the first board chair of International Christian University.

Tokioka, Masayuki (b. May 22, 1897, Okayama, Japan): Businessperson. An investor based in Honolulu, Hawaii, he helped finance half of the Japan Center complex in San Francisco but later sold his interest in the center. He was president of National Braemer and became owner of the National Mortgage and Finance Company.

Tokuda, Kip (b. October 8, 1946, Seattle, Wash.): Activist. A social worker by training, he was appointed in 1986 by Washington governor Booth Gardner as executive director of the Washington Council on Child Abuse Prevention. He received his B.A. degree and his M.S.W. degree (1973) from the University of Washington and has served on the boards of several community-based agencies.

Tokuda, Wendy (b. 1950, Seattle, Wash.): Broadcast journalist. An Emmy Award-winning news anchor, Tokuda is a third-generation Japanese American. Her mother and father met at MINIDOKA, the camp in Idaho where both were interned during World War II. Tokuda grew up in Seattle. She attended Whitman College and the University of Washington; a political science major, she was graduated with honors.

Tokuda entered broadcast journalism in Seattle, moving to San Francisco's KPIX in 1978. In 1980, she became the station's lead anchor for the 6 o'clock and 11 o'clock news. After more than ten years at KPIX, Tokuda moved to Los Angeles, where she became a coanchor at KNBC in December, 1991.

Wendy Tokuda. (Asian Week)

In 1979, Tokuda married Richard Hall, an assignment editor and producer at KPIX who has since become an independent producer of news specials and documentaries. They have two daughters, whom they are raising as Jewish. Tokuda and Hall have collaborated on two children's books, *Humphrey the Humpback Whale* (1987) and *Shiro in Love* (1989).

Tokugawa era (1600-1867): Third and final phase of feudalism in premodern Japanese history. It began with the reunification of Japan by Tokugawa Ieyasu after his victory over rival samuari chieftains in the Battle of Sekigahara in 1600. After his victory Ieyasu requested from Emperor Go-Yozei the title of *sei-i tai shogun* (barbarian-subduing generalissimo), commonly known as "SHOGUN" in its abbreviated form, to rule Japan. As founder of the Tokugawa *bakufu* (shogunate or government), Ieyasu built Japan into a highly centralized feudal state that lasted until 1867. The Tokugawa era is generally regarded by historians as a precursor to modern Japan.

Tokugawa Bakufu. In 1605 Ieyasu stepped down from his post in favor of his son Hidetada, who became the second shogun, so that he could devote his energies to building the framework of his administration. Ieyasu proceeded to establish a feudal bureaucracy in Edo (present-day Tokyo), which consisted of such administrative offices as *tairo* (great elders), *roju* (elders), *wakadoshiyori* (junior elders), *soba-yonin* (chamberlains), *metsuke* (inspectors), and *bugyo* (commissioners).

For the rest of the country Ieyasu distributed the *han* (fiefs) among the *daimyos* (feudal lords). In doing so Ieyasu carefully divided the DAIMYOS into three types: *shimpan* (collateral), *fudai* (hereditary), and *tozama* (outer). While *shimpans* consisted of those who were collateral members of the Tokugawa family, *fudais* were defined as those feudal lords who had been the allies of Ieyasu before the reunification in 1600. By contrast, the *tozamas* included those feudal lords who had been the enemies of Ieyasu until 1600 but thereafter swore allegiance to him. They were considered untrustworthy and were under the watchful eyes of Tokugawa inspectors.

The system of control established by Ieyasu and the succeeding shoguns was so effective that the Tokugawa shogunate was able to hold the country in check for more than two and a half centuries. This Tokugawa rule was further reinforced by the pronouncement of Buke Shohatto (ordinances for the military houses), which first appeared in 1615 and was amended time after time by later shoguns. These ordinances spelled out such virtues as loyalty, obedience, sobriety, and frugality. In time these virtues were codified into so-called BUSHIDO (way of the warrior). As the Tokugawa rule became firmly established, so was the feudal social order in the precedence of warrior, farmer, artisan, and merchant.

Sakoku (Seclusion Policy). The early decades of the

Five-story Toshogu Shrine was built in 1817. (Japan Air Lines)

Tokugawa era saw a rapid expansion of Japanese activity abroad and a significant rise in the volume of Japan's foreign trade. As Ieyasu recognized the potential profits attainable from trading, he was eager to establish trade relations, especially with Europeans. Yet what worried him and, later, his successors was the close connection between trade and Christianity insofar as Europeans were concerned. As an increasing number of peasants and even members of the high-ranking warrior class were converted to Christianity following the arrival of Jesuit missionaries, Ieyasu began to see Christianity as a threat to social stability that would undermine the foundation of Tokugawa rule.

The issuance of seclusion orders actually took place after the death of Ieyasu, during the administration of the third shogun, Iemitsu, who ruled from 1623-1651. Orders issued in 1633, 1635, and 1639 had the effects of closing Japan's doors to the outside world, with the exceptions of the Chinese, who were allowed to trade in Nagasaki, and the Dutch, who were eventually confined to Deshima, an islet in the Nagasaki harbor. In addition all Japanese were forbidden from leaving the country or from returning to Japan if they had gone abroad more than five years. Violation of any of these seclusion orders would constitute an offense punishable by death.

The Tokugawa seclusion policy, though far from perfect, enabled the government to keep out foreigners and disturbing foreign ideas, restore the social order, and turn the nation's attention to its internal cultural development. Yet these achievements came at a tremendous cost, for Japan lagged far behind the technologically advanced West during more than two centuries of self-imposed isolation. When the doors were finally opened in the mid-nineteenth century, the Japanese experienced a sobering realization that they had to catch up with the West in order to survive—a major theme in modern Japanese history.

The Opening of Japan and the Collapse of the Tokugawa Shogunate. By the middle of the nineteenth century, the end of Tokugawa isolation was apparent. The newly industrialized European nations had steadily made their presence felt in East Asia. It was the United States, however, that became the first country to open the doors of Japan and to put an end to Japan's self-imposed isolation.

American interest in Japan had been fast rising by the middle of the nineteenth century. There was a growing desire to open Japan for trade and to establish coaling stations for American steamers bound for China. Moreover many Americans were concerned about the cruel treatment of American castaways who accidentally entered the Japanese waters, thereby violating Tokugawa seclusion policy.

In July, 1853, Commodore Matthew C. PERRY arrived in Edo Bay with his squadron of four vessels. Having overcome a few days of obstructions by the Tokugawa officials, Perry succeeded in delivering a letter from U.S. president Millard Fillmore to the Tokugawa authorities, spelling out American demands. Perry then left the bay for the Ryukyu Islands, indicating that he would return for a formal reply the following spring with a much larger force.

Perry's "gunboat diplomacy" paid off. When he returned to Japan in February, 1854, with eight vessels, the Tokugawa authorities were in no position to resist. After a short period of negotiation the TREATY OF KANAGAWA was signed on March 31, 1854. By this treaty Japan agreed to open her two ports, Shimoda and Hakodate, as coaling and supply stations, to treat American castaways humanely, and to exchange consuls with the United States. Within a year the Tokugawa shogunate had signed similar treaties with the British, the Russians, and the Dutch.

Japanese commissioners dine aboard the USS Powhatan *in Japanese waters, 1856.* (Library of Congress)

Commodore Perry's delegation lands in Japan in 1853. (Library of Congress)

The collapse of the Tokugawa shogunate came with relatively little bloodshed. Seeing the vulnerability of the shogunate under the Western pressure, a group of young, able, and ambitious lower-rank warriors from the southwestern fiefs of Satsuma, Choshu, Tosa, and Hizen took the lead in opposition. They challenged the Tokugawa rule by effectively utilizing the proemperor slogan *SONNO JOI* (revere the emperor and throw out the barbarians). After having lost a series of battles to the combined forces of the southwestern warriors in 1866, the fifteenth and last Tokugawa shogun, Keiki, agreed to step down from his post in 1867.—*B. Winston Kahn*

SUGGESTED READINGS: • Boxer, Charles R. *The Christian Century in Japan, 1549-1650*. Berkeley: University of California Press, 1951. • Boxer, Charles R. *Jan Compagnie in Japan, 1600-1850*. 2d rev. ed. The Hague: Martinus Nijhoff, 1950. • Cooper, Michael. *They Came to Japan*. Berkeley: University of California Press, 1965. • Sansom, George. *A History of Japan, 1615-1867*. Stanford, Calif.: Stanford University Press, 1963. • Totman, Conrad D. *Politics in the Tokugawa Bakufu, 1600-1843*. Cambridge, Mass.: Harvard University Press, 1967. • Webb, Herschel. *The Japanese Imperial Institution in the Tokugawa Period*. New York: Columbia University Press, 1968.

Tokyo: Capital and largest city of Japan, located in the southeastern part of the island of Honshu. The city's 1991 population was almost 8.2 million people. It is part of Tokyo Metropolis, a region of 836 square miles. Founded c. 1456, Tokyo has become the administrative, cultural, financial, commercial, and educational center of Japan—as well as a major world financial center. It is also the site of an extensive complex of industrial suburbs that produce metals, machinery, transportation and electronic equipment, and chemicals. One of the nation's principal tourist centers, the city, known as "Edo" until 1868, hosted the 1964 Summer Olympic Games.

Tokyo Rose (Iva Toguri d'Aquino; b. July 4, 1916, Los Angeles, Calif.): Popular name used by American military personnel in the Pacific theater of World War II to apply to a number of female announcers broadcasting music and propaganda from the overseas bureau of the Japan Broadcasting Corporation. Iva Toguri d'Aquino came, by a series of accidents, to be the only one bearing that nickname and the stigma attached to it.

Toguri, a Nisei, was graduated from the University of California, Los Angeles, in 1941. She traveled to Japan to help a sick relative and was caught by the outbreak of the war. Unable to return when the U.S. consulate delayed verification of her citizenship status, she ran out of money and took a job as a part-time typist at the Japan Broadcasting Corporation. She married Felipe d'Aquino, a part-Japanese citizen of Portugal, in 1945. Although she never renounced her U.S. citizenship, as a native English speaker she was recruited as a broadcaster for a program called "Zero Hour" organized by three Allied prisoners of war.

Calling herself "Orphan Annie," she, along with other Nisei females, played popular music interspersed with light banter that frequently addressed the fears and loneliness of American armed forces members. The appeal was subtle rather than blatant, and the music was appreciated by most of the serving forces. The single radio personality of Tokyo Rose, however, composite or not, became symbolic of the "sneaky" side of Japanese propaganda efforts, made worse by the fact that it was delivered in vernacular American English. Therefore, after the war, American newspapermen Clark Lee and Harry Brundidge made great efforts to ferret out Tokyo Rose. Iva Toguri d'Aquino, partly out of naïveté and partly because she was offered two thousand dollars for "her" story, offered herself as the "one and only Tokyo Rose."

D'Aquino was arrested by American military occupation authorities in October, 1945, on suspicion of treason but was released in 1946 after thorough investigation of her wartime activities. In 1948, pressure from the American press led to her prosecution for treason in San Francisco. A biased judge and false testimony led the jury to convict her, and she served more than six years. In 1977, she was formally pardoned by President Gerald R. Ford.

Tolan, John H. (Jan. 15, 1877, St. Peter, Minn.— June 30, 1947, Oakland, Calif.): U.S. representative. He practiced law in Oakland, California, before being elected to the House of Representatives in 1935. A Democrat from the seventh district of California, he was head of the World War II TOLAN COMMITTEE, which held hearings in an attempt to solicit public opinion concerning Japanese Americans on the West Coast. The committee ultimately recommended the evacuation of all persons of Japanese ancestry away from the coast.

Tolan Committee (also, House Select Committee Investigating National Defense Migration): Appointed on April 22, 1940, by the Speaker of the House, at least partly in response to John Steinbeck's novel (1939) and the subsequent film version (1940) of *The Grapes of Wrath*. At the end of 1941 the committee consisted of the following five members of the U.S. House of Representatives: California Democrat John TOLAN (committee chair), Alabama Democrat John Sparkman, Illinois Democrat Laurence Arnold, Nebraska Republican Carl Curtis, Ohio Republican George Bender, and research staff director Robert Lamb.

The committee was originally charged with studying the common American agricultural practice of hiring migratory farm laborers. During World War II, however, because approximately half the people of Japanese ancestry (including both U.S. citizens and resident aliens) living in California were agricultural workers, the Tolan Committee interrupted its hearings in Washington, D.C., to become the first governmental body to address the implications of EXECUTIVE ORDER 9066. (That order, issued on February 18, 1942, authorized the forced wartime evacuation of Japanese Americans and aliens from the West Coast.)

The committee convened hearings on the evacuation order in San Francisco (twice), Portland, Seattle, and Los Angeles during February and March of 1942. Approximately 150 witnesses were heard. The committee's findings and recommendations were then printed on March 19, 1942, and released to the 77th Congress as House Report 1911. In it, despite noting the risk of violating constitutional rights, the committee concluded that there was "no alternative" to the proposed evacuation plans.

The committee's next report, released in May, 1942, as House Report 2124, expressed similar views. This latter report dealt not only with the Japanese on the West Coast, but also with proposals to evacuate German and Italian residents from all U.S. coastal areas; in it, the committee recommended that all individuals being considered for evacuation receive hearings—a recommendation that was never acted upon.

The committee's final report, filed on January 8, 1943, made only a brief reference to the evacuation order and reflected a steadfast belief, both within the committee and throughout the United States, that the extreme danger of invasion warranted extreme measures. The prevailing attitude was that any temporary injustices—no matter how serious—could be rectified later by the courts. The United States has since witnessed the limited extent to which reparations may be made to victims of wartime hysteria.

Toler, Sidney (Apr. 28, 1874, Warrensburg, Mo.— 1947): Actor. In 1938, Toler was chosen to succeed the late Warner OLAND as Chinese sleuth Charlie CHAN in the popular series of detective films. The films featuring Toler were not as successful, commercially or critically, as those with Oland, but some received respect: *Charlie Chan in Honolulu* (1938), *Charlie Chan in Reno* (1939), *Murder over New York* (1940), *Charlie Chan in Panama* (1940), and *The Scarlet Clue* (1945). After Toler's death, Roland Winters took over the role.

Tom, Maeley L. (b. Dec. 10, 1941, San Francisco, Calif.): Administrator. She was the first minority and woman to serve not only as chief administrative officer in the California Assembly but also as chief of staff to the California Senate president pro tempore. She assisted in the formation of the first Asian Pacific Affairs Office in the California Legislature, organized the first

Maeley Tom served as administrator for the California Assembly. (Asian Week)

national Conference of Asian Pacific Democrats, and was the only Asian American executive committee member of the 1989 Democratic National Committee.

Tomita, Teiko (Teiko Matsui; Yukari; Dec. 1, 1896, Osaka Prefecture, Japan—1990): Poet. An Issei, Tomita composed *tanka* that describe her experiences in America and provide a glimpse of pioneer life in the rugged Pacific Northwest of the 1920's. The second of nine children born to the Matsui family, she began writing poetry in high school and there acquired the pen name "Yukari." After teaching elementary school, she married Issei farmer Masakazu Tomita in 1920 and went to live on his farm on the Yakima Indian Reservation in southern Washington State. There Teiko was one of a number of pioneer Japanese women who constituted the largest group of nonwhite ethnic women in the state for most of the first half of the twentieth century.

Pioneer life in the rural Yakima Valley was primitive. The change of seasons brought unbearable temperature extremes—days and nights that were either extremely cold or extremely hot. The two-room makeshift cabin in which the Tomitas lived had no electricity and no running water. Tomita's *tanka* from this period describe her yearning for reunion with her family and her former life back home in Japan, the isolation and loneliness of living in an alien environment, and the severity of nature.

Shortly after arriving in Washington, the Tomitas were forced to abandon their tract, having lost the lease to their farm by operation of the state's anti-Issei Alien Land Laws. By 1929 they were living in Sunnydale, near Seattle, and operating their own nursery. Tomita once again began to compose *tanka* and to publish some of them. She joined a Seattle *tanka* club in 1939. During this period of her life she also converted to Christianity, a change reflected in many of her later poems.

After the United States declared war on Japan in 1941, Japanese living on the West Coast came under a cloud of suspicion by the U.S. government. Tomita, concerned that her and her husband's safety not be compromised by the appearance of incriminating "ties" to Japan, destroyed her work. Yet she continued her writing during their internment at the Tule Lake relocation center in Northern California and the Heart Mountain relocation center in northwestern Wyoming, even retranscribing many of the poems previously lost. After World War II ended, they returned to Seattle, after living for a short time in Minnesota under the conditions of a work release from the camp. Her poems appear in *Renia no yuki* (snow of Rainier), an Issei poetry anthology published in 1956.

Tomita's life and work were brought to the attention of a wider audience by Gail M. Nomura's article "Tsugiki, a Grafting: A History of a Japanese Pioneer Woman in Washington State," *Women's Studies* 14 (1987): 15-37. Nomura, who interviewed Tomita for the article, also includes translations of a number of Tomita's poems.

Tong K. Achik (Tong A-chick; Tang Tingzhi; Tong Mow-chee; 1827, Tangjia village, Xiangshan, Guangdong Province, China—1897, Shanghai, China): Interpreter, merchant, community leader, and comprador. Tong was among five students enrolled in the first class of the Morrison Education Society school when it opened in Macao in 1839. In 1843 he became one of two students sent to Shanghai as an interpreter for the first British consulate in the city. Returning after a year and a half, he returned to the school, which had moved to Hong Kong. When it closed in 1849 Tong studied in the Church of England Anglo-Chinese School of Hong Kong.

In 1847 Tong was appointed interpreter for the Magistrate's Court. In 1851 he was charged with being in league with pirates and was replaced a few months later. In the meantime he was baptized; he also became embroiled in a controversy involving a prostitute.

In January, 1852, Tong left for California with his uncle, bringing with him letters of introduction to San Francisco church people. Soon after his arrival he joined the first Bible class for Chinese organized by the Presbyterian church. He was also elected head of the YEONG WO COMPANY, succeeding Norman ASSING. This involvement may have been the reason why the Reverend William Speer failed to enlist Tong as a charter member when the first Chinese Christian congregation formed in San Francisco in 1853. Tong, however, helped raise money among the Chinese for a mission building.

When California governor John Bigler made a speech in 1852 against the entry of CHINESE CONTRACT LABOR, Tong was cosigner of two open letters in the press explaining the Chinese position. He also visited the governor as representative of the Chinese community. In 1853, when the legislature's Committee on Mines and Mining Interests held hearings on a FOREIGN MINERS' TAX bill, Tong was interpreter for the companies' presentations of the Chinese position. When the legislature passed the law in 1853, the state commissioned Tong to translate it into Chinese. In 1854 he interpreted for the police paraphernalia and documents seized in a police raid of a Triad Society (Chinese secret brotherhood).

After visiting Hong Kong briefly around 1853-1854, Tong returned to China permanently around 1857 to join the staff of the Chinese customs service. In 1871 he became comprador for Jardine, Matheson and Company in Tianjin. In 1873 he succeeded his brother Tong King-sing as the company's Shanghai comprador and held this position until dying in 1897.

Tong wars: Internecine feuds among American Chinatown subgroups. *Tong* means "hall" or "parlor"; the term refers to an indigenous Chinese social organization that Chinese immigrants used to maintain their culture in a hostile new land.

Soon after they reached the United States, the Chinese organized various benevolent societies, clan/family groups, trade and craft guilds, and SECRET SOCIETIES for mutual help and protection. Most of these organizations were called *tongs*. Because of the proliferation of *tongs*, there was much confusion about the use of the word. The American public often identified a *tong* as a group of criminals who lived off opium smuggling, gambling, and prostitution. Yet the clandestine organizations of the so-called highbinders or hatchet men actually constituted only a small percentage of the *tongs*. Among the many *tongs* a large number remained free from intersociety feuds and unlawful activities. These were often referred to as the "nonfighting" *tongs*. Even so, it was difficult for outsiders to distinguish a militant *tong* from a pacific one. This problem was compounded by overlapping membership, since many Chinese belonged to more than one *tong*.

The most influential secret society, which also carried negative connotations, was called the Hong League, also known as the Triad Society. The American Hong League was, however, never a united body, as it developed into several separate societies, each claiming membership in the Triad family and acting independently of the others. Lodges were established in Boston, Baltimore, St. Louis, New York City, and even in the Rocky Mountain region. In general they confined their interests exclusively to the Chinese population and rarely terrorized non-Chinese residents.

Historians are uncertain as to when the true *tong* wars began, but by the late 1880's the *tong* wars had started escalating and were viewed with alarm by outsiders. The problems drew the attention of both public officials and popular writers, several of whom published unsubstantiated, sensational stories about this group of Chinese gangsters. Measures were later taken by both the Chinese and the American authorities to combat the *tong* wars, and by 1900 violence in U.S. Chinatowns had declined dramatically. Furthermore, by the start of the twentieth century, there were more native Chinese Americans, and they were less easily intimidated by criminal elements. Since 1921 *tong* wars have been practically nonexistent in American Chinese communities.

Tongans: Polynesians who live in the Kingdom of Tonga, an archipelago, or who originate therefrom. Their ancestors arrived in the islands about 500 B.C.E., possibly by way of Samoa. They probably formed part of the first group of migrating Polynesians. Archaeologically it is possible to say that the earliest human settlement of Tonga took place about 1200 B.C.E. Tongan traditions offer no tales of migration to account for the peopling of Tonga. Their official language is Tongan, but English is taught in the schools and is widely spoken in the main towns.

Tonga is an island kingdom protected but never ruled by a Western power. It became a fully independent nation in June, 1970, after seventy years as a British protectorate. The kingdom, composed of about 150 islands, is situated in the Pacific Ocean southeast of the Fiji Islands and southwest of Samoa. It has a total land area of only about 289 square miles.

The 1993 population of Tonga is estimated at 104,000. Approximately 98 percent of the inhabitants are pure Polynesians, closely akin to the SAMOANS in physical appearance, language, and culture. The number of Tongan immigrants is increasing. For example the 1990 U.S. census indicates 17,606 Tongans living in the United States, the majority of them living in only three states. About forty-five percent live in California, 22 percent are in Utah, and 18 percent live in Hawaii. Compared to the 1980 census, which counted 6,226 Tongans in the United States, the 1990 census represents an almost threefold increase over ten years. A conservative estimate of the number of Tongans settling in foreign countries, including New Zealand, Australia, Samoa, and Fiji, for example, exceeds thirty thousand. This fast-increasing Tongan population outside the Kingdom of Tonga is considered both an advantage and a loss.

European Contact. The first Europeans to visit Tonga were Dutch navigators Willem Corneliszoon Schouten and Jakob LeMaire on May 9, 1616, but they did not land. They named Niuatoputapu "Traitors' Island" and called Niuafoou "Good Hope." Dutchman Abel Tasman visited next and was the first European to set foot in Tonga, on January 19, 1643. He named Ata Island "Pylstaart" and called Eua and Tongatapu "Middleburgh" and "Amsterdam," respectively. In August, 1767, British explorer Captain Samuel Wallis visited Niuatoputapu but was unaware that Schouten and LeMaire had visited there more than one hundred years earlier.

Then came a visitor who was more inquisitive. This was British captain James COOK, who visited Tonga on three separate occasions. In October, 1773, Cook anchored off the northwestern corner of Eua, which he recognized as Tasman's Middleburgh. Cook's third visit to Tonga took place on May 1, 1777, when he reached Nomuka, Haapai. This time he remained in Tonga for two and a half months, moving from island to island. These stops gave Cook opportunities to learn about Tongan life. He witnessed boxing and wrestling exhibitions and displays of music and dancing. Cook also presented the chiefs with some cattle, sheep, horses, goats, and turkeys and planted melons, pineapples, and pumpkins.

Spaniard Francisco Mourelle visited Tonga when he chanced to anchor at Vavau in February, 1781. Observ-

Tonga today. (Tonga Consulate General)

ing the Tongans' zeal for agriculture, Mourelle gave them some beans, maize, pimento, and rice. On December 27, 1787, French navigator Jean-Françoise de Galaup reached Vavau. Because of threatening weather, however, he sailed on without anchoring at Vavau, stopping for about thirty-six hours off Tongatapu's southern coast for astronomical observations.

The crew of HMS *Bounty*, under William Bligh, who had visited Tonga with Cook in 1777, landed in Nomuka for water and provisions in April, 1789. Thirty-six hours after the *Bounty*'s departure from Nomuka, mutiny broke out in which Bligh and eighteen others were cast adrift in an open seven-meter boat while the mutineers set sail for Tahiti. Captain Edward Edwards was sent from England to search for the mutineers. Having anchored at Nomuka, his officers planted orange trees ashore, leaving there a legacy of a new food plant.

Finally Alejandro Malaspina, on an exploratory voyage for the Spanish crown, reached Vavau on May 20, 1793, intending to annex the Vavau archipelago to Spain. Before the expedition's departure, a cere-

mony was held in Vavau in which a document was buried in a bottle at the observatory site proclaiming the annexation of the Vavau archipelago to Spain. Malaspina was the last European to visit Tonga before the first permanent European settlers arrived there.

These European settlers were six deserters from the American merchant ship *Otter*, which visited Tonga in March, 1796. One deserter stayed in Haapai, while the other five men remained at Eua. These individuals preceded the arrival of the first European missionaries, sent by the London Missionary Society, who landed in Tonga in 1797.

Education. Primary education has been compulsory since 1846. The 1974 Education Act requires that every child between the ages of six and fourteen attend school. In 1990 there were 115 primary schools in Tonga, with government operating 104 and churches operating 11. The total enrollment for primary education in 1990 was 16,522, with a teacher-pupil ratio of 1:24.

There were 40 secondary schools in Tonga in 1990. Only 7 of these were operated by the government; 32 were operated by churches and 1 by a private organi-

Tongan dancers preserve traditional Polynesian customs. (Tonga Consulate General)

Tongans leave church after Sunday services. (Tonga Consulate General)

zation. The total enrollment in these schools was 13,890. The teacher-pupil ratio was 1:17.

Opportunity for postsecondary or university education is very limited and must be sought overseas.

Culture. The bedrock of the Tongan social structure is the traditional way of life—*anga faka tonga*—and the extended family. Tonga's special quality comes not from the islands but from the people themselves. They are hard working, respectful of authority, and passionate in their attachment to the church. Christian values and practices have profoundly affected Tongan life. Stores are closed on Sunday. The Sabbath is observed with great strictness. According to Tonga's constitution it is not lawful to work, play sports, or trade on Sunday.

For the Tongans, hope for the future, in this small island kingdom or elsewhere, rests upon the successful blending of traditional Polynesian customs and institutions with those of the Western world. Education plays a very important role in making this blending work.—*Inoke F. Funaki*

SUGGESTED READINGS: • Goodwin, Bill. *Frommer's South Pacific '92-'93*. Englewood Cliffs, N.J.: Prentice-Hall, 1992. • Minister of Education. *Report of the Ministry of Education for the Year 1990*. Nukualofa: Government of Tonga, 1991. • Rutherford,

Noel. *Friendly Islands: A History of Tonga*. Melbourne: Oxford University Press, 1977. • Tremblay, Edward A. *When You Go to Tonga*. Derby, N.Y.: Daughters of St. Paul, Apostolate of the Press, 1954. • U.S. Bureau of the Census. *We, the Asian and Pacific Islander Americans*. Washington, D.C.: Government Printing Office, 1980.

Tongg, Ruddy F. (Tang Qinghua; 1905, Territory of Hawaii—Aug., 1988): Businessperson. Tongg's father came to Hawaii in 1890 as a contract laborer for a sugarcane plantation, and Tongg's childhood was spent in poverty. After he graduated from public high school he continued his education at the University of Hawaii, supporting himself by jobs in hotels and pineapple canneries, and was graduated with a bachelor's degree in engineering in 1925. In 1926 he started the bilingual weekly *Hawaii Chinese News*, the first such publication in the islands' Chinese community, and a small printing firm with a $500 bank loan.

After the Japanese attack on PEARL HARBOR on December 7, 1941, Tongg seized the opportunity to purchase properties put on the market by islanders seeking a safe haven on the mainland. His acquisitions included a glass bottle factory, a small travel business in a tourist area, an insurance company, and a ranch. As a result he became a wealthy man.

In 1946, Tongg together with other Asian American investors founded Trans-Pacific Airlines to compete with the existing Hawaiian Airlines, which at that time was discriminatory against Asians. However, due to successful delaying tactics by the rival airline, the Civil Aeronautics Board did not grant permanent certification for the new airline until 1954, by which time it had nearly used up its $1 million in capital. In 1958 the almost bankrupt group invited entrepreneur Hung Wo Ching to take over the presidency of the board. The airline was reorganized as Aloha Airlines and raised additional capital of $2 million. Gradually business developed and the airline attained a competitive position with its rival.

Tongg was also a leading land developer in Oahu. He was at various times board chairman of Honolulu Trust, American Finance, Tongg Publishing, and an officer or director of numerous other local firms. Tongg owned the Honolulu Hunting Preserve, the only such facility in the islands. His favorite sport was polo, and he was the owner of the Santa Barbara Polo Club as well.

Tonghak movement: Indigenous Korean religion that combines elements of CONFUCIANISM, BUDDHISM,

TAOISM, SHAMANISM, and Roman Catholicism. Tonghak (Eastern learning) was founded in 1860 by Choe Cheu. The ultimate goal of the Tonghak movement is the establishment of peace and righteousness in the world. Its underlying sacred belief is that all individuals are one with God. All individuals are therefore equal; each one is significant to the overall vision of an egalitarian world in which social freedom and harmony prevail. In 1905 Tonghak acquired a new name, "Chondogyo" (religion of the heavenly way).

Choe's philosophy of societal change made him an enemy of the civil authorities, who executed him in 1864. Members of Tonghak staged the TONGHAK REBELLION in 1894 against the ruling YI DYNASTY (1392-1910). They also took part in the independence movement during the Japanese occupation of Korea from 1910 to 1945.

Tonghak rebellion (1894): Large-scale peasant uprising, led by the Tonghak (Eastern learning) religious movement, against the *yangban* (scholar-official ruling class) of the ruling YI DYNASTY (1392-1910). Ever since the Korean government outlawed Tonghak in 1892, movement leaders had waged a largely unsuccessful campaign to restore their right to practice their religion and end discrimination, persecution, and economic exploitation by the oppressive *yangban*. The rebellion that broke out in 1894 in Cholla Province employed military operations on an expansive, and briefly successful, scale. The rebels were, however, decisively defeated by Korean government forces, assisted by Japanese troops.

The Tonghak rebellion is considered to be the first such revolution in Korea whose goal was the restructuring of society based on equality, It is also viewed as leading directly to the SINO-JAPANESE WAR OF 1894-1895.

Tong-hoe. *See* **Dong-hoe**

Tong-jang. *See* **Dong-jang**

Tongji-hoe (Comrade Society): Organization founded in Hawaii in July of 1921 by Syngman RHEE to support his activities and goals for the Korean nationalist movement.

In 1921 Rhee returned to Honolulu from Shanghai under fire after serving six months as the president of the newly created Korean provisional government. Wanting to have an organization that would give him unreserved support, Rhee established the Comrade So-

ciety in Hawaii. The society's bylaws declared that its objective was to defend the provisional government in Shanghai (whose president was Rhee until his dismissal in 1925) and that its mission was "to assist the grand policy of the President and to obey his instructions absolutely." In 1924 the society's convention decided to make Rhee the president of the society for life, and Rhee in turn outlined his Three Great Principles for the society, namely self-sacrifice, concerted efforts, and self-sufficiency.

In order to realize the goal of self-sufficiency, in 1925 the Comrade Society established an investment company, with $70,000 in capital, and purchased forest land on the island of Hawaii to develop it into a Comrade Society community. Because of mismanagement and a lack of capital and adequate equipment, however, this venture ended in failure in 1929. The Comrade Society also supported other projects of Rhee, such as the publication of *The Pacific Weekly*, which carried columns by Rhee himself. The society also sponsored the Korean Christian Institute, a boarding school for Korean youths in Hawaii founded in 1918 and run by Rhee until 1953, when it was dissolved and a part of the funds obtained from the sale of its property donated to the establishment of Inha University in Inchon, South Korea. Society members also were the backbone of the Korean Christian Church that Rhee founded in Honolulu in 1918.

The Comrade Society existed to promote the nationalistic struggle for Korean independence in the United States. Because of Rhee's uncompromising personality, however, the society also became a source of disunity in the Korean American community.

Tongmenghui (Chinese United League): Revolutionary organization founded by SUN YAT-SEN in Tokyo in 1905. Its formation was critical in the development of the revolutionary movement that culminated in the overthrow of the QING DYNASTY in 1911. Until then, the movement had been splintered into several groups. The Tongmenghui mobilized large numbers of Chinese students studying abroad into the ranks of the revolution and was the first organization to call explicitly for a revolution.

The first branches of the Tongmenghui were actually created in Brussels, Berlin, and Paris in the spring of 1905, when Sun was invited to visit Europe by Chinese students studying there. Altogether, the three branches' membership came to about seventy students. It was in Brussels that Sun spoke on the Three Principles of the People and the "five-power constitution," which became the formal ideology of the Tongmenghui as well as its successor, the GUOMINDANG (Chinese Nationalist Party).

In July, 1905, Sun arrived in Tokyo. At that time, Japan was a center of Chinese students and political exiles. On August 20, the Tongmenghui was founded in Tokyo by more than three hundred students, with Sun and Huang Xing as their leaders. The new organization combined at least three prior groups: Sun's XINGZHONGHUI (Revive China Society); Huaxinghui (China Revival Society), and Guangfuhui (Recovery Society). Upon joining the Tongmenghui, members took an oath to "banish the Manchus, restore China, establish a republic, and equalize land rights." On November 26, 1905, the first issue of *Minbao*, the Tongmenghui's official newspaper, was published.

The Tongmenghui expanded rapidly after 1905 both in and outside China and attempted at least eight uprisings between 1907 and 1911. Those uprisings were aided by members of Chinese SECRET SOCIETIES and the dynasty's New Army, which had been converted to the revolutionary cause.

In 1911, when revolution broke out in Wuchang and rapidly expanded across all China, the Tongmenghui played a major role both in providing ideological leadership and in guiding the course of the revolution. The fact, however, that the Tongmenghui did not have an army of its own also meant that it was not completely in control of the revolution or of the subsequent efforts to construct a new government.

Tongnip Sinmun (*Independence News*): Principal publication of the Korean provisional government in exile (1919-1945). This newspaper served to heighten the world's awareness of the Korean independence movement and preserve the concept of liberation in the minds of the Korean general public.

Tongnip Sinmun (*The Independent*): Daily newspaper founded in 1896 by So Chae-pil (later known as Philip JAISOHN). *The Independent* served to spread the ideas and opinions of the Tongnip Hyophoe (Independence Club; 1896-1898), a Korean political organization devoted to securing national independence and modernization and preserving popular rights.

Topaz: One of ten U.S. government camps under the administration of the WAR RELOCATION AUTHORITY (WRA) used to house Japanese American evacuees during World War II. The camps were officially designated as "RELOCATION CENTERS." Located in central Utah, Topaz was prone to extremes of temperature and a shortage of water. Its landscape was quite a shock to the internees, the great majority of whom came from urban areas, primarily from Alameda and San Francisco counties in California.

Topaz opened on September 11, 1942, and closed on October 31, 1945; it was one of the last among the ten relocation centers to be opened. Its maximum population was slightly more than 8,100. Topaz internees sought to duplicate the achievements of the Mormons in Utah and tried to construct the type of community that would earn the respect of other Americans. Cover crops and flower gardens were planted, giving birth to the internees' nickname for the camp, "the Jewel of the Desert."

The camp consisted of army-style barracks divided into family living quarters. Because some internees were granted short-term leaves for agricultural work in labor-depleted Western states and others were permitted to reestablish themselves in the Midwest (commonly in Chicago), by late 1943, as the population began to decline, the average living space for individual family members was about 114 square feet.

By the spring of 1943, an informal system of camp management by internees had been established at Topaz. Although different from the formal organization that characterized some other camps, such as TULE LAKE in California and POSTON and GILA RIVER in Arizona, the community management at Topaz was similar in many ways. Nisei councils and Issei managers represented camp blocks, and the two worked together to serve as a liaison with the camp's administrative staff.

The inmates at Topaz established a school system, with some three thousand internees studying a variety of subjects from English and American studies to the Japanese art of flower arranging and technical/mechanical classes such as auto mechanics. Other evacuees published a newspaper, the *Topaz Times*.

A different form of camp organization at Topaz took place in 1943 during the period of registration. The registration program was formulated by the War Department to offer an opportunity for internees to demonstrate their loyalty to the United States by volunteering for service in the Army. The program raised questions and doubts in the minds of internees. Block meetings were immediately held, and each block elected two representatives, one Nisei and one Issei. Committees were also established to examine all aspects of registration and to express the community's majority sentiment to camp administrators. This type of activity occurred in other relocation centers and generally disappeared once the crisis had passed.

Like other relocation centers, Topaz was troubled by tensions and intergroup difficulties. In one 1943 incident, for example, an elderly male internee, who apparently had no intention of escaping, was shot by a guard because he stepped beyond the barbed wire that marked the camp's boundary. A large demonstration was held at his funeral to protest the killing, and the camp population was shaken for weeks following the incident.

In general, more Americanized internees were less critical of the camp and the policies of the United States. Conversely, those with the greatest experience in and exposure to Japan mounted protests and sent petitions to the War Department regarding their treatment at Topaz. The closure of the camp, in 1945, did not completely eliminate the tensions that had developed at Topaz.

Toyama Kyuzo (1868—1910): Emigration advocate and organizer. The Okinawans were the last of the large prefectural groups from Japan to emigrate to Hawaii. Toyama Kyuzo is considered to be the father of Okinawan emigration, for it was he who fought for the right of Okinawans to emigrate. Toyama, though raised in poverty in Kin village in northern Okinawa, became one of the first educators in Okinawa after it became a prefecture of Japan in 1879. Because of internal politics, however, he left education to become a civil rights leader to oppose the autocratic policies of the governor of Okinawa, a non-Okinawan appointed by the central government.

After the civil rights movement failed, Toyama stayed briefly in Tokyo, where he came to realize that emigration would help solve the twin problems of overpopulation and food shortage in Okinawa; he therefore returned to his island to organize overseas emigration. Initially the governor refused approval, arguing that Okinawans, who did not speak standard Japanese and who had customs different from the Japanese of the main island, would make poor representatives of Japan. Eventually, however, the governor relented. Okinawans were fortunate that Toyama was persistent in gaining approval because eight years after emigration had begun, the GENTLEMEN'S AGREEMENT of 1907 restricted emigration from Japan to the United States.

The first group of Okinawan immigrants reached Hawaii on January 8, 1900. To their disappointment, they found life on the sugar plantation much more difficult than anticipated. Meanwhile, in Okinawa there was consternation because there was no news of the pioneers. When, however, six settlers returned to Japan only a few years later and, despite their tales of hardships, began to buy good rice fields and build houses with tile roofs, both signs of wealth, there was renewed enthusiasm for emigration.

For the second group, Toyama selected farmers more adaptable to the working conditions of Hawaii and accompanied them there. Toyama exhorted the men to work hard and save money, explaining that this would both help their families in Okinawa and promote the cause of emigration. The pioneers' struggle was made into a patriotic cause. After six months in Hawaii, Toyama returned to Okinawa and continued to promote emigration.

Toyo Theater: Former state and national historical site in Honolulu, Hawaii, a Japanese movie house modeled after the Tosho-gu Shrine in Nikko, Japan. Completed in 1938, the theater attracted many Japanese patrons. It thrived until the early 1970's, when local interest in Japanese films waned and plans for urban renewal were developed. Despite attempts to preserve it, the theater was destroyed in 1988.

Toyota, Tritia (b. Oreg.): Broadcast journalist. Toyota has been one of the most high-profile news anchors in

Television broadcast journalist Tritia Toyota. (Asian Week)

Los Angeles through the 1980's and 1990's and is one of only a handful of Asian American on-air newscasters working in the continental United States. She attended Oregon State University and the University of California, Los Angeles, from which she earned a master's degree in journalism in 1970. At KNX 1070 Newsradio she worked her way up from copyperson to on-air reporter before becoming a weekend anchor at KNBC-TV Channel 4 in 1972. She also hosted public affairs programs for the station. In 1985 she jumped to KCBS-TV Channel 2 to coanchor one of the station's weekday newscasts. A cofounder of the ASIAN AMERICAN JOURNALISTS ASSOCIATION (AAJA), she received the group's Lifetime Achievement award—one of many awards that she has been given by various sources.

Toyota v. United States (1925): U.S. Supreme Court ruling that denied American citizenship to a Japanese alien who had served in the U.S. armed forces during World War I. In electing to refuse citizenship, the Court saw no reason to enlarge the categories of aliens eligible for naturalization under federal statutes and noted that recent laws allowing naturalization to aliens applied to Filipinos rather than Japanese. Toyota Hidemitsu, an Issei, joined the U.S. Coast Guard in 1913, served during the war, and was honorably discharged in 1923. Several years earlier, in U.S. district court he had successfully petitioned for naturalization based on a 1918 act, under which alien war veterans honorably discharged were eligible to become citizens. The government subsequently filed for revocation of Toyota's naturalization in the U.S. First Circuit Court of Appeals, which cancelled his naturalization certificate based on a finding that it had been unlawfully obtained. This decision was upheld by the Supreme Court.

Transcendental meditation (TM): Indian meditation technique. Though imitators have borrowed the name, TM properly refers to a simple meditation technique brought to the West in 1959 by Maharishi Mahesh Yogi and subsequently taught to several million meditators worldwide. Part of TM's popularity comes from Maharishi's insistence that the practice is not religious and requires no changes in beliefs or lifestyle. Celebrity endorsements and scientific studies demonstrating TM's beneficial physiological effects also enhance its appeal. It is unlikely that any meditation technique in history has been more popular or widespread than TM; certainly, none has been more influential in the West.

Maharishi attributes TM to his guru, Swami Brahmananda Saraswati, but it appears that the specifics of the practice were created by Maharishi himself. What distinguishes TM from other forms of meditation is Maharishi's emphasis on effortlessness, in contrast to the concentration and mental discipline usually taught. Maharishi contends that the mind naturally tends to seek deeper, more enjoyable states of consciousness; all it needs is to learn to turn within, instead of looking outwardly. TM is believed to provide the proper initial impetus; once the practice starts, nature does the rest.

Instruction in TM is done by authorized initiators who first perform a short SANSKRIT ceremony (*puja*) adapted from traditional Indian sources. Beginners are then given a one or two syllable sound (mantra) and taught the method of effortless mental repetition. The preceding, plus the fact that the goal of TM is a state where the meditators realize their essential oneness with the universe, has led critics to accuse Maharishi of teaching HINDUISM in a secular guise.

TM enjoyed its greatest growth in the early 1970's. As new initiations declined late in the decade, Maharishi introduced the TM Sidhi program, in which advanced meditators are taught to develop Yogic powers such as clairvoyance and levitation. Despite skeptical media coverage, tens of thousands of meditators have paid substantial sums to learn the techniques.

In the 1980's, Maharishi began teaching his interpretations of Indian astrology, architecture, music, and medicine to his followers. As time passes, the TM movement is developing an increasingly "Indian" look, feel, and vocabulary.

Transcendentalism: Philosophical and literary movement. It emerged in the Boston area in the 1830's among New England intellectuals, foremost among whom were the well-known writers Ralph Waldo Emerson and Henry David Thoreau. Reacting against the rationalism and empiricism of their eighteenth century forebears and the materialism and competitiveness of their nineteenth century contemporaries, the New England transcendentalists wanted to awaken the perception of the infinite that they believed most truly characterized the human mind.

The Bhagavadgita, available in the 1785 translation of Charles Wilkins, confirmed, as traditional Western religious orthodoxy could not, the transcendentalists' intimations of an immanent cosmic awareness accessible to the individual. Along with translations from the *Upanisads*, it also provided a model of poetic, visionary spirituality. For Emerson, the Bhagavadgita was simply "the first book." Thus a profound affinity drew the transcendentalists to Indian works; these works in turn exerted a powerful influence upon those who were drawn to them. It is never possible, of course, to say where such affinity ends and influence begins. Thoreau in *Walden* (1854) sees the ice cut from Walden Pond and shipped by New England merchants to India as emblematic of his own immersion in "the stupendous and cosmogonal philosophy of the Bhagvat Geeta," as he believed that the "pure Walden water is mingled with the sacred water of the Ganges."

Such a mingling for these authors, and for the poet Walt Whitman, who praises the "primal thought" of India, includes some of the most central concerns of HINDUISM, especially as they are expressed in the Bhagavadgita. Among these are the desire for the intensification of life through simplification; the appreciation for the inaction inherent in right action; the insistence upon the unreality of the material world, and the refusal to be dominated by the senses; the feeling for the identity of opposites, of knower and known, subject and object; the call for work done sacramentally, without attachment to results; the discovery of individual destiny or duty as cosmic law; and, finally, the celebration of the identity of the self with God.

Transpacific: Magazine that debuted in December, 1986, as *AsiAm*, a glossy national monthly aimed at young, upwardly mobile Asian Americans. Renamed *Transpacific* in the fall of 1989, it celebrated its seventh anniversary in December, 1993. The magazine combines substantial personality profiles and features on business, entertainment, and fashion with photos of scantily clad women. George TAKEI contributes a regular column.

Trask, Haunani-Kay: Scholar, writer, and activist. Director of the Center for Hawaiian Studies at the University of Hawaii, Trask is a leading figure in the movement for HAWAIIAN SOVEREIGNTY. She is a member of Ka Lahui Hawaii, one of several groups seeking self-government for Native Hawaiians. Trask, who received a Ph.D. degree in political science from the University of Wisconsin, Madison, is the author of *Eros and Power: The Promise of Feminist Theory* (1986) and *From a Native Daughter: Colonialism and Sovereignty in Hawaii* (1993). *Her first volume of poems, Light in the Crevice Never Seen*, was published in 1994.

Treaty of Annexation (1910): Treaty concluded between Japan and Korea in which the Korean peninsula became a Japanese territory. The Treaty of Annexation was a formality that signaled the conclusion of Japan's total usurpation of Korea's sovereign power. With the treaty, the YI DYNASTY (1392-1910) was officially disbanded. The treaty was coerced by the Japanese military and was widely protested in and outside Korea.

Japan's actual takeover of Korea goes back to 1905, when it forced the Choson court (the name CHOSON of the ancient state was revived by the Yi Dynasty) to sign the treaty of five articles, placing in Japanese hands all Korea's diplomatic functions. Japan openly demanded that foreign legations stationed in Seoul withdraw. The treaty provisions also included the creation of the post of Japanese resident-general, who was to reside in Seoul and to have the right to consult the Korean emperor whenever necessary. Once this de facto regency was established for political control, Japan systematically expropriated most commercial interests. Japan's preparation for long colonial control of Korea was extensive and deliberate.

In 1910, Japan secured a few Korean collaborators to sign the Korean-Japanese annexation draft, which effectively ended the existence of independent Korea. The ceremony was guarded by large numbers of soldiers and police officers. Koreans everywhere waged violent protests to no avail. By then, the West, the only power that might have had some influence to curb Japanese aggression in Korea, had given up on Korea. Both China and Russia, Japan's early competition in Korea, were effectively eliminated when they lost wars to the Japanese. The West, including the United States, had never shown sufficient interest in Korea to challenge the rising power of Japan.

Some Korean court officials were led to support the treaty, believing erroneously that Japan's short-duration annexation would help Korea develop and reform its antiquated systems along the Japanese line. On the contrary, Japan had strategic goals in the region: to acquire physical footholds in mainland Asia. The treaty was the result of Japanese territorial ambition and the Korean court's absolute lack of geopolitical instincts.

Treaty of Chemulpo (1882): Treaty between the United States and Korea. It was initiated and negotiated by China's Li Hongzhang and U.S. commodore Robert W. Shufeldt, and it was Korea's first treaty with the West. Also known as the "Korean-American Treaty," it stipulated mutual support between Korea and the United States. Its provisions included foreign-settlement and trade arrangements, rights protecting U.S.

citizens in or near Korea, a most-favored-nation clause, real-property purchase rights for citizens of both countries, bans on the opium trade and on the Korean export of grain and red ginseng, and protection and assistance for students.

Treaty of Kanagawa (1854): Treaty between Japan and the United States that opened the Japanese ports of Shimoda and Hakodate to American ships. It was signed following Commodore Matthew C. PERRY's efforts to "open up" Japan through "gunboat" diplomacy. Japan had previously been closed to foreign trade, with few exceptions. Perry, anxious to establish lucrative trading routes for American business and the U.S. government, sailed to Japan with an armed fleet of ships prior to the signing.

Treaty of Kanghwa (1876): Treaty concluded between Japan and Korea. It was modeled on Western treaties imposed on China and ended Korea's 250 years of self-imposed isolation. According to the terms of the treaty, Korea was declared a free and independent state, equal to Japan. Japan's aim in this statement, however, was to end Korea's relationship with China in order to exploit Korea without China's interference, until the day Japan annexed Korea, in the TREATY OF ANNEXATION (1910). The treaty also provided for the exchange of diplomatic missions between Korea and Japan and the opening of Korean ports to Japanese trade.

Treaty of Nanjing (1842): Agreement ending the first Opium War between Great Britain and China (1839-1842). The Treaty of Nanjing, followed shortly by the Anglo-Chinese Treaty of the Bogue (1843) and the Sino-American Treaty of Wanghia (1844), represents the first of the "unequal treaties" concluded between China and the West in the nineteenth century. The treaties provided the basis for the treaty port system and the principles of nontariff autonomy and extraterritoriality.

Opium smoking had long been banned in China, but by the early nineteenth century, Anglo-Indian merchants, anxious to find desirable articles for trade, began rapidly increasing traffic in Indian opium near the city of Canton. The trade further spread in South China following the dissolution of the BRITISH EAST INDIA COMPANY's monopoly in China in the early 1830's.

By the end of the decade, reports of widespread use of opium in the southern maritime provinces had alarmed the Chinese government sufficiently for the emperor to send an imperial commissioner, Lin Zexu, to stop the traffic. Arriving in the spring of 1839, Lin promptly burned the foreign opium stocks and blockaded the ships of suspected opium merchants in port. British traders appealed to London for help, and the Foreign Office used the issue to press the Chinese on several long-standing problems of law and diplomatic usage, such as Chinese insistence on group responsibility and refusal to allow resident foreign ambassadors in Beijing.

From the commencement of hostilities in late 1839, the British navy ranged along the China coast and, with few exceptions, Anglo-Indian army units occupied Chinese coastal cities almost at will. Fighting briefly halted in 1841 but resumed with the failure of either government to ratify the resulting Chuenpi Convention. By the summer of 1842, with the British driving on the walled city of Nanjing, the Chinese came to terms.

The treaty, concluded by Sir Henry Pottinger and two Chinese commissioners on August 29, provided for the cession of Hong Kong to Great Britain, the opening of the ports of Fuzhou, Ningbo, Xiamen, and Shanghai to British trade, the right of British consular officials to reside in the ports, a large indemnity payment, and British approval of Chinese tariff rates.

As the result of the first clash between the industrializing West and imperial China, the Treaty of Nanjing is considered by most historians of China to mark the beginning of the modern period in Chinese history.

Treaty of Paris (1898): Peace treaty signed by the United States and Spain at the conclusion of the Spanish-American War in 1898. Terms of the treaty included the provision that the Philippine Islands would become a territory of the United States. Filipinos were to be considered U.S. nationals, but the rights of U.S. citizenship were not extended to them. In addition to providing the United States with the controversial trappings of an overseas empire, the treaty contained provisions that were to become significant for Filipino immigrants to the United States, since—as U.S. nationals—they were not affected by the restrictive IMMIGRATION ACT OF 1924, which, in conjunction with earlier legislation, virtually excluded immigrants from Asia. Filipinos lost the right to unrestricted immigration with the passage of the TYDINGS-MCDUFFIE ACT OF 1934.

Treaty of Portsmouth (1905): Peace settlement between Japan and Russia that concluded the RUSSO-JAPANESE WAR (1904-1905). It was mediated by President Theodore Roosevelt and was signed at Kittery, Maine. In this treaty, the defeated Russians recognized Japan's growing interests in Korea and gave their regional leases, including Sakhalin Island and Port Arthur, to Japan. The United States thus succeeded in curbing Russian expansion in East Asia by endorsing Japan's domination of Korea.

Treaty of Shimonoseki (1895): Arrangement that ended the SINO-JAPANESE WAR (1894-1895) and that allowed Japan to establish its hegemony over Korea. China was forced to make several concessions, including ceding Taiwan, the Liaotung Peninsula, and the Pescadores Islands to Japan, recognizing Korea's independence from China, and opening several Chinese ports to Japanese trade.

Treaty of Tientsin (1885): Agreement signed between China's Li Hongzhang and Japan's Ito Hirobumi. It stipulated the withdrawal of Chinese and Japanese forces from Korea, the formation of an all-Korean army, and prior communication between Japan and China if either government were to send troops to Korea to mediate any disturbances or revolts. The treaty also ended the Sino-French War (1883-1885) and ceded Vietnam to France.

Triads. *See* **Chee Kung Tong**

Tsai, Gerald, Jr. (b. Mar. 10, 1929, Shanghai, China): Financier. Arriving in the United States in 1947, Tsai became a naturalized American citizen in 1954. He earned an M.A. degree in economics from Boston University in 1949, then chose a job as a securities analyst with Bache Securities in New York over pursuing an M.B.A. degree. From 1952 until 1965 he worked for Fidelity Management and Research Company of Boston and rose to become one of the firm's star stock analysts in the mutual funds department. Tsai eventually established his own mutual fund, which he later sold for millions of dollars in profit. Using that money to form his own company, G. Tsai & Company, in 1965, he began buying up other businesses in an effort to enlarge his portfolio. As a result he was appointed a director of American Can Company in 1982; he helped build the company into a prosperous financial investment house, Primerica, serving as chairman and chief executive officer from 1987 until 1988.

Tsai, Shih-shan Henry: Scholar. A professor of history who has served as chair of the Asian Studies program at the University of Arkansas, Tsai has contributed significantly to the study of the CHINESE DIASPORA. Among his books are *China and the Overseas Chinese in the United States, 1868-1911* (1983) and *The Chinese Experience in America* (1986).

Tsuji, Kenryu Takashi (b. Mar. 14, 1919, Mission City, British Columbia, Canada): Buddhist clergyman. The son of Kamejiro and Suye Minaguro Tsuji, he married Sakaye Kawabata in 1946. Arriving in the United States in 1959, he became a naturalized American citizen in 1964. He attended several universities in Canada and Japan. After receiving ordination as a minister of the Buddhist church in 1941, he served in various temples in both Canada and the United States, including a term as bishop of the Buddhist Church of America from 1968 until 1981. Tsuji was also involved in the making of several documentary films on Buddhism-related topics.

Tsukiyama, Wilfred Chomatsu (1897—Jan., 1965, Honolulu, Hawaii): Lawyer and state court chief justice. One of the earliest Japanese American lawyers in Hawaii, Tsukiyama became the first chief justice of the Hawaii Supreme Court. He began to forge a career in public service not long after his graduation from the University of Chicago Law School, winning appointment in 1929 as deputy attorney for the City and County of Honolulu. Four years later he was made chief attorney. During World War II, with the United States and Japan at war with each other, he resigned his appointment to go into private practice. He held a Hawaii state legislative seat from 1946 until 1959, when he became chief justice. The government of Japan honored Tsukiyama in 1963 for his efforts in promoting good relations between the United States and Japan.

Tsutakawa, George (b. Feb. 22, 1910, Seattle, Wash.): Artist and teacher. Tsutakawa has enjoyed a lengthy career as a painter, sculptor, and art professor at the University of Washington. A long-time resident of Seattle, he has long been considered one of the world's leading water fountain sculptors.

Tsutakawa was born in the United States but attended public school in Japan from 1917 until 1927, when he returned to Seattle. Until enrolling at the University of Washington School of Art in 1932, he had for many years been producing different kinds of art. During World War II his family was interned at the TULE LAKE relocation center in Northern California.

Tsutakawa himself had been inducted into the army soon after the PEARL HARBOR attack; visiting the family on furloughs, he met Ayame Iwasa, later to become his wife. After the war he went back to Seattle and continued to paint and sculpt, taught art at the university, and married Ayame. He was made a full professor of art in 1955, achieving emeritus status in 1976.

On a visit to Japan in 1956, Tsutakawa acquired a new appreciation for his Japanese heritage and particularly for the traditional artistic forms and materials of Japan. Also that year, inspired by the stacked rock piles called *Obos*, he began fashioning similar vertical structures out of wood and, later, metal. These forms later became the basis for his water fountain designs.

Tsutakawa executed his first public fountain in 1960 at the Seattle Public Library and for the next thirty years went on to sculpt sixty more in the United States, Canada, and Japan. He described his work as an attempt to express the oneness of humanity and nature; his fountain sculptures, he explained, are an effort to unify water, symbolic of life, fertility, and regeneration, with "immutable metal."

In 1987, Tsutakawa was awarded the Order of the Rising Sun, Fourth Class, by the emperor of Japan. Tsutakawa also holds several honorary doctorates. In addition to his fountains, paintings, prints, and other sculptures, he has designed and built furniture. The Bellevue Art Museum staged a sixty-year retrospective exhibition of his work in 1990.

Tuan, Yi-Fu (b. December 5, 1930, Tianjin, China): Scholar. A professor of geography at the University of Wisconsin, Madison, Tuan is best known for his innovative interdisciplinary studies. The son of a Chinese diplomat, Tuan came to the United States in 1951 after receiving a B.A. degree from the University of Oxford. He received an M.A. from Oxford in 1955 and a Ph.D. from the University of California, Berkeley, in 1957. Among his many books are *Space and Place: The Perspective of Experience* (1977), *Landscapes of Fear* (1980), *Dominance and Affection: The Making of Pets* (1984), *The Good Life* (1986), and *Morality and Imagination: Paradoxes of Progress* (1989).

Tule Lake: One of ten U.S. government camps under the administration of the WAR RELOCATION AUTHORITY (WRA) used to house Japanese American evacuees during World War II. Initially designated as a "RELOCATION CENTER," the offical term for the ten WRA camps, Tule Lake also became a special "segregation center" in 1943 when the WRA and the War Department sought to segregate in a single camp internees who were suspected of disloyalty to the United States or of giving primary allegiance to Japan.

Located in Northern California, the Tule Lake camp was opened on May 27, 1942. It reached its maximum population of almost nineteen thousand late in 1944. As a relocation center it received internees from Washington and Oregon as well as from California.

Tule Lake camp, 1943. (National Archives)

Japanese American males of draft age who pledged allegiance to the U.S. government were eligible to join the U.S. armed forces. U.S. Army battalion, Italy, 1942. (National Archives)

Loyalty Oath. In February, 1943, the WRA and the War Department launched a program to determine the loyalty of internees over the age of seventeen. Questionnaires were distributed in all the relocation camps; among the questions asked were numbers 27 and 28, and these created the most serious problem for the Japanese American respondents. Both were confusing and alarming. Question 27 tested the internee's willingness to serve in the armed forces of the United States. Question 28 asked the internee (whether an American citizen or a Japanese alien) to swear allegiance to the United States and to denounce "allegiance or obedience to the Japanese emperor."

A total of 75,000 internees filled out the questionnaire. Many of the 6,700 Japanese Americans and Japanese aliens who responded to question 28 in the negative did so for reasons that had nothing to do with loyalty. Some resented the abrogation of their rights as American citizens; others, Japanese aliens, who could not become American citizens, were fearful that if they answered in the positive, they would become stateless. Of the more than 2,000 who qualified their answers, some demanded the return of their citizenship rights as

a condition precedent to an affirmative response, and a few hundred left the question blank. Yet whether they answered in the negative, qualified their response, or refused to answer made no difference to the officials of the WRA. All those who failed to answer yes were to be sent to Tule Lake. In addition, several other categories of internees categorized as "disloyal" or "troublemakers" were transferred to Tule Lake, including persons who had requested repatriation or expatriation to Japan.

The population of Tule Lake after the segregants were shipped there in 1943 rose to approximately 18,000. About a third were family members of those who were considered disloyal; another third were original internees, "Old Tuleans" who for one reason or another had refused to move.

Factionalism and Protest. The mix of the camp's population was calculated to cause factionalism and dissension. Conditions at Tule Lake, as well as at the other relocation camps, were primitive. There was overcrowding, no privacy for families, a shortage of milk, and deplorable sanitation. The project director, Raymond R. Best, a former marine, was a poor administrator who had little understanding of and less sympathy for Japanese customs.

By the fall of 1943 the camp was ripe for civil disobedience. In October, 1943, a truck carrying 28 internees overturned; five were seriously injured, and one was killed. Best refused permission for a public funeral, but the ceremony, attended by thousands of internees, was held against the project director's orders. On October 26, after a ten-day work stoppage on the Tule Lake farm, a fourteen-member negotiating committee met with Best, but there was no redress of grievances.

When the national director of the WRA, Dillon S. MYER, visited the camp at the beginning of November, the internees staged a massive and largely peaceful demonstration. A confrontation occurred, however, during which a WRA internal security officer was clubbed by protesters. Best then called in the army. A 7 P.M. to 6 A.M. curfew was declared; there were mass arrests of internees; and martial law was instituted. Army tanks patrolled the camp; tear gas was used to disperse unruly crowds. The schools were closed, recreational activities were stopped, and work crews were curtailed. Among the internees there were threats against those suspected of collaborating with the army, several beatings, and one murder. Some of the dissidents and later the members of the negotiating committee were incarcerated in a stockade. On New Year's Day, 1944, 200 inmates in the stockade began a series of hunger strikes. As the unrest at Tule Lake threatened to become an international scandal, the Japanese government retaliated by suspending negotiations for the exchange of Americans in Japanese prison camps.

By April, 1944, when the Japanese government's protest against the treatment of the Tule Lake internees had been received by the American state department, the relocation center had been returned to civilian jurisdiction. Many of the internees had gone back to work on the farm, collecting their paltry sixteen dollars a month. A total of 276 detainees were freed from the stockade; only the fourteen members of the former negotiating committee remained and were held incommunicado. In August, 1944, a representative of the Northern California branch of the American Civil Liberties Union (ACLU), Wayne COLLINS, threatened that, unless the imprisoned Japanese Americans were released from the stockade, he would petition the federal district court for a writ of *habeas corpus* on their behalf. Confronted with Collins' ultimatum, the WRA officials capitulated; the fourteen men were released, and the stockade was finally abandoned.

Renunciation and Repatriation. On July 1, 1944, U.S. president Franklin D. Roosevelt signed Public Law 405, an amendment to the Nationality Act of 1940 that allowed American citizens, with the permission of the U.S. attorney general, to renounce their citizenship during time of war. From the Tule Lake relocation center and to a much lesser degree from the other centers, 7,222 applied for repatriation or expatriation to Japan after World War II; of these, 65 percent were American-born and thus American citizens. Many had been pressured by more militant Japanese internees to take the drastic step of renunciation; others were fearful of being expelled from Tule Lake and forced to return to their homes without funds and means of support amid the hostility of a wartime atmosphere in America. (See DENATIONALIZATION ACT OF 1944.) In part as a result of the renunciation issue, Tule Lake was the last of the WRA camps to be closed, shutting down on March 28, 1946.—*David L. Sterling*

SUGGESTED READINGS: • Daniels, Roger. *Concentration Camps, North America: Japanese in the United States and Canada During World War II.* Malabar, Fla.: R. E. Krieger, 1981. • Irons, Peter H. *Justice at War.* New York: Oxford University Press, 1983. • Thomas, Dorothy Swaine, and Richard S. Nishimoto. *The Spoilage.* Berkeley: University of California Press, 1946. • Weglyn, Michi. *Years of Infamy: The Untold Story of America's Concentration Camps.* New York: Morrow, 1976.

TVB, Hong Kong: One of the oldest television stations in Hong Kong, broadcasting, via cable, Chinese-language programs watched by many overseas Chinese. Programming includes situation comedies (sitcoms) and soap operas.

Ty-Casper, Linda (b. Sept. 17, 1931, Manila, Philippines): Writer. Although known as an award-winning novelist and short-story writer, Ty-Casper was educated as a lawyer. She earned an LL.B. degree at the University of the Philippines in 1955; a master's (LL.M.) degree from Harvard followed in 1957. Her shorter works have appeared in such well-known anthologies as *Best American Short Stories.* Among her many books are *The Peninsulars* (1964), *The Secret Runner and Other Stories* (1974), *The Three-Cornered Sun* (1979), *Wings of Stone* (1986), *Ten Thousand Seeds* (1987), *A Small Party in a Garden* (1988), and *Common Continent: Selected Stories* (1991). She has contributed articles and stories to such publications as *Nantucket Review, Prairie Schooner,* and *Solidarity.*

Tydings-McDuffie Act of 1934: Also known as the "Philippine Independence Act," passed by Congress to grant commonwealth status to the Philippines, with independence to follow in a decade. The act set up the conditions for the adoption of a constitution and the formation of a Philippine government. The Tydings-McDuffie Act also limited Filipino immigration to the United States to fifty persons annually.

Status of Filipinos. The Philippines was a Spanish colony from the sixteenth to the nineteenth centuries. The Philippines was an American colony from 1901 to 1946. Under U.S. rule Filipinos were given the status of "American nationals" and were able to immigrate freely to the United States. In the early 1930's the Filipino population in the United States was estimated at more than forty-five thousand, two-thirds of whom resided in California. This predominantly bachelor society was the new target of a loose coalition of anti-Asian exclusionists who had successfully supported the restriction of immigration from China, Japan, Korea, and India. Advocating on behalf of Filipinos in the United States were large-scale farmers, educators, and church leaders.

The Exclusionist Perspective. The exclusionists painted the Filipinos as unfair competition to Caucasian labor already hurt by the Depression. Filipinos, who openly sought the company of Caucasian women, were deemed a sexual threat. Filipinos were also branded a public health and sanitation menace. C. M. Goethe, an exclusionist, wrote an essay in 1931 that described Filipinos as a danger to the American standard of living: "These men are jungle folk. . . . The Filipino tends to interbreed with near-moron white

girls. The resulting hybrid is . . . undesirable. . . . Immediate exclusion is tragically necessary to protect our American seed stock." In 1929 the California Assembly passed a resolution asking Congress to restrict Filipino immigration. Since the Philippines was still an American colony, however, exclusion of the "American NATIONALS" was a complicated matter. The exclusionists adopted another tactic. They echoed Filipino groups and anti-imperialist groups in calling for Philippine independence.

Filipino Nationalism. Widespread Filipino rebellion against the Spanish colonizers began in the late nineteenth century. The Spanish were replaced by Americans following the Spanish-American War (1898) and the PHILIPPINE-AMERICAN WAR (1899-1902). During the American colonial period, Filipinos never stopped the fight for independence. Members of nationalist groups, such as the Partido Nacionalista, were the majority in the first Philippine assembly, elected in 1907. The Partido Nacionalista platform included the cry for "complete, absolute, and immediate independence." The acknowledged political leaders of the day were Sergio Osmeña and Manuel QUEZON y Molina. Both men championed the cause of Philippine independence.

Congressional Bills for Philippine Independence. There were numerous bills brought before Congress that addressed the issue of independence for the Philippines. The Jones Bill, presented to the House in 1912, proposed sovereignty for the Philippines in eight years, with American presence maintained as a safeguard against foreign aggression for twenty years. This bill was unsuccessful. Support for Philippine independence was tempered by the fear that Japan would

Sixth Filipino Intercommunity Conference, Fresno, California, 1944. (Filipino American National Historical Society)

Filipino Women's Club of Seattle, 1934. In 1934, Filipino women were vastly outnumbered by Filipino men who had emigrated in search of employment opportunities. (Filipino American National Historical Society)

welcome American withdrawal from the Philippines as an opportunity to gain influence in the islands. A revised Jones Bill was passed by the House in 1914. This revision called for American recognition of Philippine independence when the Filipinos had formed a stable government. The Jones Bill became law in 1916. The momentum for Philippine independence suffered setbacks whenever Republicans were in power in the presidency or in either of the chambers of Congress. This was the case in 1920, when Republican Warren G. Harding was elected president. In 1930 Senators Harry B. Hawes and Bronson M. Cutting drafted a bill to grant independence to the Philippines in five years. This bill passed the House in 1932. A revised bill passed both the House and the Senate in 1933. (See HARE-HAWES-CUTTING ACT OF 1933.) This revision gave the Philippines commonwealth status, to be followed by independence in ten years. Although President Herbert Hoover vetoed the bill, his veto was overridden. In the Philippines, however, the act was rejected by the Philippine Assembly, which focused on unequal trade terms and the continued maintenance of American military bases in the Philippines. Quezon y Molina, who now presided over the upper chamber of the Philippine Assembly, went to the United States to advocate on behalf of a better independence act. The result was the Tydings-McDuffie Act.

Provisions of the Act. The Tydings-McDuffie Act was signed by President Franklin D. Roosevelt on March 24, 1934. The act was to "provide for the complete independence of the Philippine Islands, to provide for the adoption of a constitution and a form of government for the Philippine Islands." It gave the

Philippines commonwealth status, with independence following in ten years. The Philippine Assembly was given directions to hold a convention for the purpose of drafting a constitution. Mandatory provisions of the constitution were also listed, including religious toler-

The Mancao family demonstrates the strong family values of many Filipino Americans (1929). (Filipino American National Historical Society)

Filipino American medical technicians at Glendale Adventist Hospital. (Martin A. Hutner)

ance and the maintenance of a public school system, with English as the preferred language of instruction. The drafted constitution was to be submitted for approval to the president of the United States and then, after his certification, submitted to the Filipino people for ratification. Once the constitution was approved, the election of government officials of the commonwealth could proceed. The Tydings-McDuffie Act explicitly described the nature of trade relations with the United States, specifying the types of duties to be applied to Philippine products.

The Tydings-McDuffie Act limited Filipino immigration to the United States to a fifty-person annual quota. This quota was, at the time, the lowest assigned for any nation. One exemption from the quota allowed Filipinos to be brought to Hawaii as labor demands necessitated. Filipinos in Hawaii were restricted from moving to the mainland. The status of Filipinos in the United States changed overnight from that of "American nationals" to "aliens." As "aliens," Filipinos were ineligible for New Deal programs and federal relief.

According to historian Carey McWilliams, "[W]e forced the Filipinos to accept exclusion only by making exclusion the price with which they had to pay for independence." McWilliams' analysis of the Tydings-McDuffie Act details that Americans in the Philippines enjoyed the same rights and privileges as Filipino citizens and held $258 million worth of investments, including sixty-three million acres of land. In contrast Filipinos in the United States were limited to a token quota, were relegated to the lowest-paying jobs, and were routinely discriminated against in all aspects of their lives. While the Philippines was granted political control, the United States still maintained economic control.

The Tydings-McDuffie Act was approved by the Philippine Legislature in May, 1934. A few months later a constitutional convention was convened. Quezon y Molina was elected the first president of the Commonwealth of the Philippines, with Osmeña elected as his vice president. Independence for the Filipinos was delayed by World War II. The Philippines was formally declared an independent nation on July 4, 1946.—*Linda A. Revilla*

Suggested Readings: • Cordova, Fred. *Filipinos: Forgotten Asian Americans.* Dubuque, Iowa: Kendall/Hunt, 1983. • Karnow, Stanley. *In Our Image: America's Empire in the Philippines.* New York: Random House, 1989. • McWilliams, Carey. *Brothers Under the Skin.* Rev. ed. Boston: Little, Brown, 1964. • Melendy, H. Brett. *Asians in America: Filipinos, Koreans, and East Indians.* Boston: Twayne, 1977. • Quinsaat, Jesse. *Letters in Exile.* Los Angeles: UCLA Asian American Studies Center, 1976.

U

Uchida, Yoshiko (Nov. 24, 1921, Alameda, Calif.—June 21, 1992, Berkeley, Calif.): Writer. Uchida is among the most widely loved of Asian American storytellers. She wrote more than thirty books, most of them for young readers. She won numerous awards, including the American Library Association's Notable Book citation and the Commonwealth Club of California Medal, twice each.

Uchida grew up in Berkeley. Her father was a manager for Mitsui, a large Japanese corporation, her mother a housewife with strong literary and artistic interests. Both parents were Christians and graduates of Doshisha University. Yoshiko Uchida entered the University of California at age sixteen and studied English, philosophy, and history, earning her B.A. in 1942. Almost immediately after the bombing of Pearl Harbor, Honolulu, by Japan, Uchida's father, as a successful Japanese American businessman, was seized and detained by the Federal Bureau of Investigation (FBI). In April of 1942, the family (except for the father, who would be held in a prisoner-of-war camp in Montana) was evacuated to the TANFORAN assembly center not far from San Francisco.

That September Uchida and her family were moved to the TOPAZ relocation center in central Utah. While at Topaz, Uchida served as a voluntary elementary schoolteacher until the spring of 1943. At that time, with the help of the National Japanese American Student Relocation Council, she secured her release from camp in order to attend Smith College in Northampton, Massachusetts, on a graduate fellowship. She earned her M.Ed. degree from Smith in 1944.

After working in New York and Philadelphia for a period of years, Uchida returned to the Bay Area and began to pursue a career writing children's literature. Her books reflect her childhood in the tree-lined, sunlit streets of Berkeley as much as they do the more dramatic events of World War II. Her first published work, *The Dancing Kettle and Other Japanese Folk Tales* (1949), was a collection of Japanese stories she had heard as a child. In 1952 she went to Japan on a Ford Foundation fellowship to collect more folktales, which appeared in *The Magic Listening Cap—More Folk Tales from Japan* (1955) and *The Sea of Gold, and Other Tales from Japan* (1965). The trip reawakened in her the gentle pull of what she called the "invisible thread" tying her to her parents' homeland, to other Japanese people, and to Japanese culture and values. She determined to give the Sansei generation a sense of ethnic pride by writing for them the kind of books about Japanese and Japanese Americans that she had never had as a child.

Most of Uchida's books speak to the joys and dilemmas of young girls growing up. These girls include central characters Keiko in *The Promised Year* (1959) and Sumi in *Sumi's Prize* (1964), *Sumi's Special Happening* (1966), and *Sumi and the Goat and the Tokyo Express* (1969). The most celebrated is Rinko, a Nisei girl and the main character in *A Jar of Dreams* (1981), *The Best Bad Thing* (1983), and *The Happiest Ending* (1985).

Nisei writer Yoshiko Uchida. (National Japanese American Historical Society)

As the years passed, Uchida took on more political themes, and she also began to write for older audiences as well as the young girls who constituted the main part of her readership. She wrote about the concentration camp episode in the widely acclaimed works of fiction *Journey to Topaz: A Story of the Japanese-American Evacuation* (1971) and *Journey Home* (1978), as well as in a family autobiography, Desert Exile: The Uprooting of a Japanese-American Family (1982). Her purpose was simple: that America should remember and never let it happen again. Her novel *Picture Bride* (1987), describes the difficult life of an Issei woman. *The Invisible Thread* (1991) is Uchida's autobiography.

Uchida never lost sight of the fact that the novelist's gift lies in telling the story of a life individually lived. She took on the human pain of discrimination and imprisonment with a gentle spirit, free of bitterness. Her prose was clear, simple, and direct, yet always rich with feeling. She brought joy and insight to hundreds of thousands of readers and served as a model for younger writers.

Uchinanchu: Term used by Okinawan immigrants and their descendants, especially in Hawaii, to identify themselves as an ethnic group distinct from the Yamatunchu or Naichi of Japan's four main islands. Though Japanese, linguistic and cultural differences as well as their late arrival in the islands had made the Uchinanchu targets of Naichi prejudice.

Umeki, Miyoshi (b. 1929, Otaru, Hokkaido, Japan): Singer and actor. Daughter of a Japanese iron factory owner, Umeki developed a talent for singing at a young age. After the conclusion of World War II, she was befriended by soldiers of the American occupation forces who invited her to sing with them. She learned to sing in English by listening to popular singers on U.S. Army radio broadcasts and began to earn a living by singing at G.I. service clubs and later on Japanese radio and television. After traveling to the United States in the 1950's to work as a nightclub singer, Umeki appeared on the Arthur Godfrey television show and was discovered by a Hollywood casting director. She was hired to play the role of Katsumi opposite Marlon Brando in the Warner Bros. production of *Sayonara* (1957), based on the novel by James Michener. Her performance earned for her an Academy Award nomination as best supporting actress; on March 26, 1958, she became the first person of Japanese descent to win an Oscar. Umeki went on to appear

Miyoshi Umeki in 1958. (AP/Wide World Photos)

on Broadway in the Rodgers and Hammerstein musical *Flower Drum Song* (1958) and reprised her role as Mei Li in the film adaptation in 1961. Her other films included *Cry for Happy* (1961), *The Horizontal Lieutenant* (1961), and *A Girl Named Tamiko* (1963). Umeki went on to launch a successful career in television, appearing as housekeeper Mrs. Livingston opposite Bill Bixby on the series *The Courtship of Eddie's Father* from 1969 to 1972.

Unification Church: Founded by the Reverend Sun Myung Moon in South Korea in 1954 as the Holy Spirit Association for the Unification of World Christianity. Born of the chaos that followed World War II, the church began as a small collection of followers of a charismatic pentecostal preacher. It has grown into a worldwide institution with a universalistic mission, a presence in at least a hundred non-Asian countries, and a membership reported to be about one million.

Moon's teachings, collected in a volume entitled the *Divine Principle* (1973) comprise the church's doctrinal beliefs—a syncretic combination of Western Christianity and Eastern thought and religious practices. The doctrines turn on an interpretation of Judeo-

Christian scriptures in which God's plan is conceived to have been deflected from its purpose by Satan's seduction of Eve and the subsequent corruption of Adam. In this manner, what God had intended to be the Perfect Family, the vehicle of human fulfillment, became compromised.

The Unification Church teaches that only through redemptive action and sacrifices can God's plan once again shape humanity's destiny. In particular, "central persons" are required to "indemnify" the human race—and the church believes that Moon is the central person in the present time. Through the perfection of family life, humankind will achieve physical salvation, supplementing the spiritual salvation that was achieved by the sacrifice of Jesus of Nazareth. The church serves as a surrogate family for its members, inspiring their loyalty and extracting their labor and sacrifice in order to provide itself with a material base of support in commercial and industrial enterprises.

The Unification Church shares some traits with other new religions, such as the Mormon and the Christian Science churches. Like them, the Unification Church has survived charges of sexual exploitation and of recruitment through deception and mind control; its leaders have also been criticized for living in material comfort and engaging in extensive commercial and industrial enterprises. Where the Unification Church differs from the other established religions is in the degree of institutionalization. The continuity of the church will hinge on whether it survives the death of its founder.

Union Bank: Largest Japanese-owned commercial banking institution in California, with $17.2 billion in assets (1992 figures). Headquartered in San Francisco, this bank has more than two hundred branches in the state and five overseas facilities in Tokyo, the Cayman Islands, Saipan, and Guam.

The Reverend Sun Myung Moon, founder of the Unification Church. (AP/Wide World Photos)

Union Pacific Railroad: Transportation company that, along with the Central Pacific Railroad, in 1862 received a U.S. government contract to build the western half of the transcontinental railroad linking the United States' Pacific and Atlantic coasts. The Union Pacific would build westward from Omaha, Nebraska, on the Missouri River. The Central Pacific would push eastward from Sacramento, California. The Central Pacific used Chinese laborers to construct the railroad and to break strikes; the Union Pacific also employed immigrant laborers, such as the Irish. The transcontinental railway was completed in 1869.

United Cannery, Agricultural, Packing and Allied Workers of America (UCAPAWA): Labor union chartered in 1937 by the Congress of Industrial Organizations (CIO). The union sought to organize seasonal workers in the agricultural and cannery industries and recruited heavily among Filipino and Mexican laborers. Filipino writer and union activist Carlos BULOSAN helped to found the UCAPAWA. It later changed its name to the Food, Tobacco and Agricultural Workers International before being expelled from CIO membership because of Communist infiltration.

United Chinese Society: Organization established in 1882 by a group of Chinese merchants in Hawaii in order to improve conditions for the Chinese immigrant community in the islands. The merchants were encouraged by Chinese government officials to form a centralized organization to address issues in Hawaii, thus adopting the approach taken by the Chinese Six Companies in San Francisco, California. Chinese ethnic minorities, such as the Puntis and the Hakkas, who had previously worked closely within their own social hierarchies, were persuaded to set aside their differences in order to work collectively to combat anti-Chinese prejudice in Hawaii. The organization continued to serve the Chinese community in Hawaii into the 1930's.

United Farm Workers Organizing Committee: Labor organization founded in 1966 as a part of the American Federation of Labor-Congress of Industrial Organizations (AFL-CIO). This union of Filipino and Mexican farm laborers fought for higher wages and better working conditions in the agricultural industry. It was formed through the merger of the Agricultural Workers Organizing Committee, a predominantly Filipino organization, and the National Farm Workers Association, led by César Chavez.

United Japanese Society of Hawaii: Organization founded in 1958 to promote the welfare of the Japanese and their descendants living in Hawaii through religious, charitable, educational, literary, or other benevolent means and to foster understanding and friendship between the United States and Japan.

A precursor to the society was the similarly organized and intentioned Honolulu United Japanese Society, founded in 1932 and disbanded when war between the United States and Japan began in 1941. The Honolulu Japanese Chamber of Commerce also fulfilled a similar role following the war, until the United Japanese Society of Hawaii was created.

Thereafter, the newly renamed organization became the preeminent voice of the Japanese Hawaiian community and a frequent representative of Hawaii for visiting members of both the United States and the Japanese governments. The society has also been active in organizing relief campaigns for victims of natural disasters.

The society initially welcomed members from any Hawaiian organization having more than fifteen members, with a maximum of five representatives from any organization having more than three hundred members. The society grew quickly, to seventy-seven member organizations by 1970; membership grew more slowly in the 1970's and by the 1990's had stabilized at ninety-two organizations. In addition, forty-eight memberships were held by individuals. Operating expenses for the society have been met by a combination of member dues, donations, and ticket sales to events sponsored by the society.

Because of the many Americans of Japanese ancestry living in Hawaii and their desire to maintain Japanese cultural values, the United Japanese Society has been more successful and enduring than most ethnically based organizations in the United States. Nevertheless, it is not clear that this society or others like it can survive indefinitely; despite the advantages of ethnic identification, as the apparently inevitable process of Americanization continues, this and other ethnic societies may face declining membership and, ultimately, their demise.

United Nations High Commissioner for Refugees, Office of the (UNHCR): Agency established in 1950 to provide legal representation to refugees remaining in Europe after World War II (1939-1945). It later played a central role in the protection of refugees from Laos and Vietnam who fled to Thailand, Malaysia, Hong Kong, and other Asian countries starting in

Illegal aliens detained by U.S. border patrol officers in San Francisco, California, in 1993. (Louis DeMatteis)

1975. It played a lesser role in the reception of Cambodians who fled to Thailand beginning in 1979.

The UNHCR played a critical role in negotiating agreements between countries of first asylum, such as Thailand and Malaysia, and countries of final asylum, such as the United States, France, Canada, and Australia. It also carried out negotiations with the governments of Laos, Cambodia, and Vietnam in connection with both an Orderly Departure Program and a voluntary return program. Of the approximately two million refugees who fled Vietnam, Laos, and Cambodia between 1975 and 1990, about half have been resettled abroad, mostly through agreements negotiated by the UNHCR.

The UNHCR has provided legal protection services and has delivered humanitarian aid to refugee groups on every continent. In each country, camps to accommodate the refugees were established with money that the UNHCR solicited from American, Japanese, and other governments. This money was spent to provide food, shelter, and legal services to arriving refugees. Central to the role of the UNHCR were the negotiations it conducted for the safe reception of arriving refugees. In most countries of asylum, these negotiations were a difficult task. The refugees were often perceived as being a threat to the national security, and in every country there were domestic political pressures urging the governments to declare the refugees to be "illegal immigrants" who should be sent back to their home countries.

The UNHCR's high commissioner is elected to a five-year term by the General Assembly upon the recommendation of the secretary general. The headquarters of the high commissioner is in Geneva, Switzerland, but there are also approximately sixty field offices around the world. During the 1980's, the budget of the UNHCR tended to be between $400 million and $500 million annually. The office of the UNHCR received the Nobel Peace Prize in 1954 and 1981. The 1981 award was, in large part, awarded for the agency's role in Southeast Asia.

United Okinawan Association (UOA): Pro-Okinawan umbrella organization established in 1951 in Hawaii.

The main purposes of the UOA are to promote Okinawan culture, conduct cultural programs, forums, and lectures, and sponsor written materials on Okinawan and Okinawan American culture and history. Its members are Okinawan organizations from all the major islands of Hawaii. As of 1992 it has forty-eight member clubs.

World War II spurred the establishment of the UOA. When the war ended the Okinawans in Hawaii organized relief groups to aid devastated Okinawa and sent clothing, medical and school supplies, and farm animals. From this experience some individuals saw the need for an organization to unite the Okinawans in Hawaii. Thus, despite some opposition, the UOA began with fourteen charter clubs.

In the early years of the UOA, activities were directed to assist the people of Okinawa in the rebuilding of their homeland. The Hawaii-Okinawan Friendship Mission helped foster better relations between the Americans governing Okinawa and the people of Okinawa. The Hawaii-Okinawa Farm Youth Training Program helped strengthen Okinawa's agriculture.

As Okinawa was rebuilt the focus of the UOA shifted to the promotion of Okinawan culture in Hawaii. The major activities include the Okinawan Festival, anniversary celebrations of the coming of Okinawans to Hawaii every ten years, study tours to Okinawa, and cultural programs. The Okinawan Festival is a two-day affair open to the general public. Cultural activities include song, dance, martial arts, and food booths. The 1990 ninetieth anniversary celebration of the coming of Okinawan immigrants to Hawaii was a year-long series of activities. Special activities such as a *hari* (Okinawan boat) race in Hilo, Hawaii, were held.

Through donations from the government of Okinawa and from families and businesses in Hawaii and Okinawa, the UOA built the Hawaii Okinawa Center in 1990. It is adorned with an Okinawan tile roof donated by the people of Okinawa.

U.S.-China People's Friendship Association (USCPFA): Nonprofit educational organization in the United States for promoting better understanding between U.S. citizens and the People's Republic of CHINA.

From 1950 to 1972 U.S. citizens were forbidden to travel to the People's Republic of China. Thus diplomatic contact during these Cold War years was carried

Nixon at the Great Wall of China, 1972. (National Archives)

out largely through third-party nations. Events of the late 1960's, however, signaled a dramatic change on the part of both countries that by the early 1970's had begun to occur. These events included a growing opposition to U.S. involvement in Vietnam, burgeoning programs in Chinese and East Asian studies, and an increased American interest in Maoism, the Cultural Revolution, and socialism in China. The opening of diplomatic exchanges by U.S. national security adviser Henry A. Kissinger in 1971, the visit to China by President Richard M. Nixon in 1972, the SHANGHAI COMMUNIQUÉ (1972), and the accompanying rounds of "Ping-Pong diplomacy" all served to heighten American awareness of China and to spark interest over the wide range of possible educational and commercial exchanges.

It was against this backdrop that the first committees of the USCPFA were founded in New York and San Francisco in 1971. Branches were quickly organized in other major metropolitan areas, with a national committee formed during a meeting in Los Angeles in 1974. From its national headquarters in New York, the association works as a clearinghouse for informational and educational exchanges between Americans and Chinese, issues a catalog of programs for academic and business contact, maintains a collection of low-cost elementary and high school educational materials available through its Center for Teaching About China, and publishes the quarterly *U.S.-China Review*. Individual chapters also periodically sponsor programs for teaching English in China and sponsoring Chinese scholars and students in the United States.

U.S.-China relations: U.S. relations with China began with trade soon after the former became an independent nation. Missionaries followed. Later, when the United States became a Pacific nation, China became a security concern inasmuch as it was thought that a European power controlling China could threaten the United States. From China's point of view the United States was simply another foreign power that the isolationist Middle Kingdom sought to keep at arm's length. In subsequent years, however, Chinese rulers perceived the United States as different from the European nations and eventually came to see it as a key to China adjusting to a Western dominated world. Relations between the two nations were generally good throughout the years but were often characterized by misunderstanding and by overestimating each other. In 1949 Mao Zedong and his Chinese

Communist Party won political control of China, and the two countries became arch-enemies and twice, indirectly, went to war. After 1969 relations improved to the point that some viewed the two countries as allies (against the former Soviet Union). This lasted until 1989, when China's human rights abuses and other issues damaged its image internationally. Moreover the close of the Cold War ended the strategic imperative upon which better relations had been built.

Early Relations to the First Opium War. With independence the United States sought to build commercial relations with other nations. Not finding much success in Europe, it looked elsewhere, including China. In 1784 the *Empress of China* sailed for Canton. It brought back tea and other products that sold in America for a healthy profit. By 1801 more than thirty U.S. vessels had sailed to China. Missionaries also went in search of Chinese souls to convert. Both endeavors stimulated interest in China.

The lure of the China market increased over the years notwithstanding the fact that trade did not increase by large amounts—in fact never exceeding 2 percent of America's foreign commerce. In the 1830's the clipper ships that engaged in the China trade helped make the United States an expansionist power. The Chinese government, meanwhile, regarded China as an autarchy not in need of trade. In fact China sought neither commercial nor diplomatic relations with foreign countries. China's knowledge of the United States was thus limited to information provided by a few Americans in China and Chinese laborers who came to the United States for awhile and returned home.

In 1832 Edmund Roberts led a diplomatic mission to the Far East and signed treaties with Siam (now Thailand) and Cochin China (now Vietnam) and later Japan, but he did not attempt such with China for fear of angering the Chinese government and disturbing the trade relationship. American trade at the time fared a bit better than most European countries in terms of the imbalance of exports and imports. American traders found a market for furs, ginseng, sandalwood, and silver. Americans, who had to operate without relying on U.S. naval power, which was weak in those days, also earned a reputation among the Chinese as being a bit less arrogant than the other Westerners.

The Opium Wars Through the Open Door Policy. The First Opium War (1839-1842), a turning point in Chinese history, marked the beginning of humiliation by the West. When Chinese officials cast British opium into the sea and shut London out of the China trade, Great Britain went to war with China—defeating Chinese forces with superior naval power. Britain acquired Hong Kong and forced open five ports to trade. Meanwhile, American merchants stepped in temporarily and took over the opium trade.

With England having a commercial advantage—being protected from discriminatory tariffs and having its own port—the U.S. government looked for a way to ensure that trade remained open and fair. Lawrence Kearney, in 1842, signed an agreement with Chinese officials giving the United States most-favored-nation status. Two years later, in 1844, Caleb Cushing, in the Treaty of Wangxia, formalized this distinction and added extraterritoriality. Thus, without going to war, the U.S. government won concessions given to the United Kingdom. The Chinese government willingly extended these privileges without reciprocity, seeking to "play the barbarians off against each other." Nevertheless these actions eventually caused considerable harm to China.

The Opium War, and more so the TAIPING REBELLION—a civil war that decimated China from 1850 to 1864—revealed China's decay and its need to end its isolation and come to terms with the world that was dominated by the West. Anson Burlingame, who went to China in 1858 as the U.S. representative and who became leader of the foreign diplomatic corps, sought to help China. In 1867, after he retired, he was made an envoy to represent China abroad, which he did with skill. In 1868 he negotiated the BURLINGAME TREATY—starting China on the road to diplomatic ties with nations of the world.

Toward the end of the nineteenth century, U.S.-China relations became influenced by America's growing security concern about China: China, it was thought, might become the colonial possession of a European power that could by virtue of its advantage in ruling China threaten the United States from the Pacific side. This view became even stronger after the U.S. government acquired the Philippines in 1898, becoming an Asian colonial power.

The Open Door Policy to World War I. By 1899 it appeared to most observers that China was on the verge of being divided into a collection of Western colonies. Its unwillingness to accept international rules of diplomacy, its defeat in war by Japan in 1895, and its inability to manage its own affairs were the causes. The United States, being the second-largest trader with China but not having any sphere of influence to turn into a colony, and not wanting to anyway, was in an unfavorable position. Thus, in 1899 U.S. secretary of state John Hay sent notes to the foreign powers suggesting that China be allowed to maintain its territorial integrity and that measures be worked out to keep commerce open and stable. He called this the "Open Door" policy.

At this juncture rebellion broke out, and the Chinese government foolishly sided with the Boxers, experts in the martial arts and religious fanatics, thinking they might be able to rid China of foreign influence. China looked not only weak but also incompetent to rule itself and appeared to be certain prey for the foreign colonial powers. Except for Britain, which favored Hay's plan because British interests were better off than if China were colonized, the other powers were not supportive of Hay's idea. Yet they did not know what the others thought. Thus Hay bluffed, saying that there was agreement. This allowed China a brief respite. The Open Door policy henceforth came to represent the view that the United States had a stake, in terms of both commercial relations and national security, in keeping China free, meaning not colonized or controlled by another power, and open, to both trade and missionary work, and that America was a friend of China.

The United States made a gesture of goodwill toward China following the Boxer indemnity settlement, in which China was forced to pay a huge sum of money to the other powers for inciting the rebellion. America took payment but returned it to China in the form of grants for Chinese students to study in the United States.

A few years later the U.S. government had an opportunity to establish even closer relations with China in the person of SUN YAT-SEN, who, while born in China, grew up in the United States and came to admire that country and its people and political system. In 1911 the Manchu Dynasty was overthrown by Sun's followers, who planned to establish a republican government in China. Sun, however, was a southerner, while the government was in the north, and the foreign powers, including the United States, reacted as was customary: dealing with whoever was in control of Beijing.

World War I to World II. It was America's responsibility to preserve Western interests in China against Japan during World War I. Posted in the form of the Open Door policy, this effort almost brought the United States to war with Japan. China appreciated the U.S. help, but much less so President Woodrow Wilson's idealistic efforts to build a postwar democratic peace, which Japan exploited. Tokyo grabbed German concessions in China and much more, causing China to refuse to sign the peace treaty.

Washington subsequently sought to contain Japanese predatory designs through diplomacy. In 1921 the United States signed the Four Power Pacific Treaty with the United Kingdom, France, and Japan to cancel the Anglo-Japanese Alliance treaty of 1902. The next year the U.S. government took the initiative to work out the Nine Power Pact, which formally affirmed the Open Door policy—though without foreseeing the need for force to back it up. The treaty protected China's territorial integrity only as long as Japan cooperated.

Washington still refused to grant Sun Yat-sen the support many thought he deserved and instead dealt with whichever warlord sat in Beijing. When CHIANG KAI-SHEK, however, assumed Sun's mantle of power after his death and led a military expedition north to capture Beijing and consolidate control over all of China in 1928, the United States was the first to conclude a commercial treaty with the new regime. This gave the Chinese government tariff autonomy for the first time in years. China was pleased with the result and looked forward to better relations between both countries.

China, however, was disappointed with U.S. inaction when, in 1931, Japan invaded northeast China, or Manchuria, and made it a part of the Japanese Empire. Washington, afraid of isolationist sentiment at home and not having membership in the League of Nations, instituted a policy that consisted of trying to use international law and nonrecognition of Japan's territorial claim in order to pressure Tokyo to withdraw. This effort failed.

In 1937, when Japan invaded China proper, U.S. president Franklin D. Roosevelt condemned Japan but did not go much further. Chiang Kai-shek, perceiving that the United States would go to war with Japan, threw his best troops into combat against Japanese forces to give the war added publicity in the United States and Europe. Roosevelt sent loans and supplies to China, though this policy forced him to continue to sell gasoline, scrap iron, and other needed war supplies to Japan. In the name of the Open Door policy, the U.S. government took other steps to help China, which gradually helped bring the American and the Japanese closer to war.

World War II. After December, 1941, America came to China's rescue with more help: military and economic aid. Although America's "Hitler first" policy was not favored by China, and although some other issues remained unresolved, relations between the two countries improved as a result of the wartime cooperation.

In 1942 the United States ended it extraterritorial "privileges" in China. The next year, in 1943, the Americans terminated the Chinese Exclusion Act. At the Cairo Conference that same year, Roosevelt gave China big power status—even though U.S. allies did not think this was justified given China's lack of military power. Roosevelt wanted China to stay in the war to occupy a million or so Japanese troops that might otherwise be deployed to fight American forces elsewhere in Asia.

Madame Chiang Kai-shek addressed a joint session of the U.S. Congress during the war, presenting the Nationalist Chinese cause to the American people, who were sympathetic. There was, however, disappointment among some American military leaders, particularly General Joseph Stilwell, that Chiang was not doing enough to win the war against Japan and was diverting resources to fight the Communists. Chiang espoused the view that America would defeat Japan and that the Communist threat was ultimately more serious than that posed by Japan.

At Yalta U.S. officials made concessions to Joseph Stalin that hurt China. Mongolia, claimed by China, was allowed to remain a Soviet satellite, and the Soviet Union was given special privileges in China. Chiang Kai-shek, in return, got Soviet diplomatic recognition and aid (though Soviet aid also went to the Chinese Communists). The Yalta agreement was criticized in both the United States and China as a betrayal and an action that opened up China to communism.

The U.S. government compensated for this to some degree after the war by giving China global power status: permanent membership on the United Nations Security Council and a voice in other international organizations. At Potsdam the Allies confirmed that territory taken by Japan would be returned. Thus, Taiwan and the Pescadores, which had been in Japanese hands since 1895, were restored to China.

1945-1949. After World War II the United States hoped for a free and democratic China that would ensure peace in Asia and support American interests there, thinking that Japan would never again be a power in the region. This hope, however, was dampened by the fighting between the Nationalists and the Communists.

General George Marshall went to China in late 1945 to persuade the two sides to come to peace, but he was unsuccessful. Marshall finally gave up and returned to Washington. The U.S. government continued to send aid to Chiang Kai-shek, but it was frequently not what he needed and was overpriced. Moscow sent aid to Mao, though in much smaller amounts. A combination of things, including the Nationalists' inability to win the support of the peasants, inflation, corruption, and

Mao's effective propaganda machine and tough guerrilla fighters, weakened the Nationalist government and its military.

In 1948 the United States tried to help Chiang prevent Manchuria from falling into Soviet hands. (The Soviets were in Manchuria as a result of the Yalta accords.) Nationalist troops were airlifted to that northeast region of China, only to experience defeat at the hands of Mao's forces, with massive losses of weapons and soldiers. This defeat led to others and finally to the end of Nationalist rule over the Chinese mainland. Chiang, his government, and remnants of his military fled to Taiwan in 1949.

Following Mao's victory the United States looked for a scapegoat for the defeat and the "loss of China." A "White Paper" issued in August, 1949, put the blame on Chiang and the Nationalist government for corruption, misrule, and failure to win the support of the masses. Others pointed to Communist infiltrators in the U.S. State Department. In any case, America's Open Door policy was defunct and a period of mutual hostility was to follow.

1949-1969. The Chinese Communists' treatment of American diplomats in China in 1949, the Sino-Soviet Alliance in February, 1950, and the KOREAN WAR, which started in June, 1950, all made China an enemy of the United States during the Cold War era. In fact Americans came to view China as the worst of the

Responding to a call by Mao Zedong, millions of Chinese youth revolted against the Communist Party's bureaucracy and restored Mao's influence in China. Here youths at a rally in Beijing, 1966, raise a banner of Karl Marx and wave copies of The Thoughts of Mao Zedong. *(AP/Wide World Photos)*

President Nixon and Chairman Mao negotiated an agreement in 1972 that paved the way to better relations between the United States and China. (National Archives)

Communist Bloc countries—more radical, more desperate, and more antistatus quo than the Soviet Union. China likewise perceived the United States as its archenemy: the leader of the "capitalist bloc," the superpower that sought to surround China with its military bases and contain Chinese influence in the area, and the country that protected the Chiang Kai-shek regime and prevented the unification of Taiwan with mainland China.

Tensions between China and the United States heightened in 1954-1955 and again in 1958 when Mao attacked the Nationalist-held Islands of Quemoy and

Matsu, causing the American government to come to Chiang's rescue. U.S. interests also collided with Chinese foreign policy objectives throughout the world during the 1950's and 1960's, but most notably in Africa and Asia. U.S. containment policy as a result came to apply to China more than the Soviet Union.

Some observers thought that after 1960, in view of growing differences and tension between China and the Soviet Union, better U.S. relations were possible. U.S. president John F. Kennedy spoke of this, but nothing happened. The Vietnam War, which became an American war following the Gulf of Tonkin inci-

Through the 1980-1981 trial and conviction of the Mao-loyalist "Gang of Four," the Chinese government, behind the modernist policies of Deng Xiaoping, indicated its intention to abandon the repressive leftist policies of Mao. Jiang Qing (far right), Mao's widow, committed suicide in 1991. (AP/Wide World Photos)

dent in 1964, and the Great Proletarian Cultural Revolution, which was launched by Mao in 1966 and which pushed China further to the Left politically and isolated Beijing, precluded a U.S.-China rapprochement during the late 1960's.

A breakthrough in relations came after Richard M. Nixon became president. He had a mandate to get out of the Vietnam War and perceived that to do this the country needed a new and different relationship with China. Helping to make this possible, China's relations with the Soviet Union had deteriorated to the point that the two engaged in "war" on their border over an uninhabited river island in the spring of 1969. With the strategic perspectives of the Chinese and the Soviets changing dramatically, relations took a new course.

Relations 1969 to 1989. After an American "tilt" toward China during its 1969 border conflict with the Soviet Union and moves by China that were thought to show a willingness to help the U.S. government get out of the Vietnam War and support the Nixon Doctrine, U.S.-China relations began to change markedly. The Soviet Union's rapid military buildup, considered a threat to both Washington and Beijing, served as a motive for the Americans and the Chinese to continue to improve relations and use each other as a "card" to play in the triangular diplomacy game with the Kremlin.

Ping-Pong diplomacy followed. In 1971 it was an-nounced that Nixon would visit China. There, in 1972, Nixon toasted Chinese leaders and signed a joint agreement, the SHANGHAI COMMUNIQUÉ, paving the way for better relations in the next few years.

Although closer political ties were impeded by the Watergate scandal, the U.S. defeat in Vietnam (which was supposed to have been avoided by better relations with China), and Mao's death in 1976, trade and cultural relations improved steadily. Military cooperation also advanced, and at times the United States and China thought of each other, as reflected in their leaders' statements, as partners and even allies.

In December, 1978, President Jimmy Carter an-nounced that the United States would establish formal diplomatic ties with the People's Republic of China, effective January 1, 1979, and at the same time break relations with the Nationalist government in Taiwan. This was made formal in the Normalization Agreement signed between the two countries, in which the U.S. government announced a one-China policy and declared, in compliance with Chinese wishes, that Taiwan was a part of China. A few months later, however, Congress passed the Taiwan Relations Act (1979), which in essence treated Taiwan as a sovereign nation-state and restored economic and security guarantees to Taipei. This created two different China policies and restored the ambiguity necessary (according to many observers) to America's relationship with China. Beijing ignored the act and proceeded to improve relations with the United States—continuing to regard it as an ally against the hegemonist Soviet Union and as the key to the capitalist economic reforms started by Deng Xiaoping in 1978.

Relations with the United States, however, created some problems for the rightist, reformist Deng Xiaoping. By 1982, with his modernization problems becoming identified as capitalism and his hard-line opponents making an issue of Taiwan, he pressured the American government into an arrangement, encapsulated in the August Communiqué, whereby Washington promised to decrease and ultimately end arms sales to Taiwan. At the same time, China adopted what Western observers called an "equidistance policy" with respect to the United States and the Soviet Union. Deng sought improved relations with the Kremlin but continued to view the U.S. relationship as more important.

Relations After 1989. In June, 1989, political reform in China under Deng Xiaoping suffered a serious blow when leftist hard-liners forced Deng to purge party secretary Zhao Ziyang and accept a brutal military solution to students demonstrating for democratic change. This happened at a crucial juncture: when the Soviet bloc was on the verge of collapse and a new world order, no longer characterized by a polarization of the world into capitalist and communist camps or by nuclear deterrence between the United States and the Soviet Union, was evolving.

As a result the Soviet Union ceased being America's enemy, and its reforms, not China's, became more admired in the West. Moreover, with democracy succeeding in Taiwan and failing in China, Taipei passed its pariah state image to Beijing. China to some degree became once again the U.S. enemy.

In the ensuing years, three issues dampened Sino-American relations: China's human rights abuses, America's unfavorable balance of trade with China, and Beijing's arms sales and alleged transfer of nuclear technology. China, its hard-line leaders at least, perceived that the United States was trying to overthrow the government in China through what it called "peaceful evolution."

China's human rights record, while not as bad as

Prodemocracy protesters in Beijing, 1989, link arms during a demonstration against the government's brutal military suppression earlier at Tiananmen Square. (AP/Wide World Photos)

during the Mao era, when millions were persecuted as class enemies and were put in labor camps, remained bad by global standards, and the American public and media would not allow Washington to discard the issue. China's continuing efforts to export and earn foreign exchange, resulting in an increasing trade imbalance with the United States, also became a contentious issue. The Americans criticized the Chinese for cheating on trade. The United States as a rule had disregarded such practices by developing countries, but American economic difficulties had turned trade issues into political ones. Finally American critics expressed concern about China's increasing arms sales abroad, particularly to nations that the U.S. government labeled terrorist states or for some reason believed should not have weapons. More disturbing yet was China's alleged transfer of nuclear capability (and perhaps more) to Pakistan, North Korea, Iran, Iraq, and Libya.

There was also general apprehension in the United States that China was becoming a military superpower as a result of increased defense spending after 1989 and massive purchases of sophisticated weapons at bargain prices from the former Soviet Union. Some speculated this would lead to a regression back to bipolarity, with the United States pitted against China, or a regional arms race between China and Japan that would involve the United States. American arms sales to Taiwan, which increased markedly in 1992, seemed to reflect this kind of thinking.

China's reformists tried to play down these issues and keep economic ties on track. Hard-liners, however, regarded U.S. criticism of China and some of its policies as interference in its domestic affairs. China's economic development and political change, the latter proceeding more slowly than the former, seemed auspicious for the reformists and for U.S.-China relations. Moreover, support for trade and a favorable view of China in the U.S. business community, plus the realization that the United States must maintain at least amicable relations with China, seemed to ensure that relations would not seriously deteriorate.—*John F. Copper*

SUGGESTED READINGS:

• Barnett, A. Doak. *Communist China and Asia: A Challenge to American Policy*. New York: Vintage Books, 1960. Very comprehensive book on China, covering the rise of Mao, Chinese Communist ideology, domestic Chinese politics, and foreign policy in an effort to indicate how the United States should respond to the China threat in Asia and elsewhere. It focuses on the post-World War II period, when both

countries were arch-enemies.

• Copper, John F. *China Diplomacy: The Washington-Taipei-Beijing Triangle*. Boulder, Colo.: Westview Press, 1992. In this book the author examines the four documents that are said to constitute the formal basis for U.S. China policy and Sino-American relations: the Shanghai Communiqué (1972), the Normalization Agreement (1978), the Taiwan Relations Act (1979), and the August Communiqué (1982). He looks at both Beijing's and Taipei's reaction to the documents and argues that the documents have created two China policies but also useful ambiguity.

• Fairbank, John K. *The United States and China*. 4th ed. Cambridge, Mass.: Harvard University Press, 1983. A popular book on Chinese history in which the author seeks to make China understandable to Americans. U.S.-China historical ties are given special emphasis. This book provides good background material to understanding current U.S.-China relations, issues, and problems.

• Harding, Harry. *Fragile Relationship: The United States and China Since 1972*. Washington, D.C.: Brookings Institution, 1992. A comprehensive study of U.S.-China relations from the Nixon visit in 1972 to 1991. The author notes that the U.S.-China rapprochement was built upon strategic common interests relating to the Soviet threat. After 1989, following the massacre of students in Tiananmen Square and the end of the Soviet-American confrontation, this changed. The change makes U.S.-China relations now fragile but, as Harding argues, still important.

• Mosher, Steven W. *China Misperceived: American Illusions and Chinese Reality*. New York: Basic Books, 1990. The author assesses the mistakes in perception that Americans have had of China, the reasons for errors in understanding Chinese strategies and goals, and the consequences. Mosher focuses on historical misperceptions and the writings of some noted scholars, plus Chinese efforts to confuse and deceive Americans, in explaining recent and current U.S. China policy.

• Sutter, Robert G. *The China Quandary: Domestic Determinants of U.S. China Policy, 1972-1982*. Boulder, Colo.: Westview Press, 1983. In this book the author looks at the domestic scenes in America and China, especially in the United States, to elucidate the course of U.S.-China relations in recent years. Sutter analyzes U.S. China policy in the context of U.S. foreign affairs, relations with the Soviet Union, the foreign policy process, and factors that influence American policy-making.